THREE STUDIES IN
EUROPEAN CONSERVATISM

PUBLISHED BY

Constable & Company Limited
London W.C. 2
.

BOMBAY
CALCUTTA   MADRAS
LEIPZIG

Oxford University
Press
.

TORONTO

The Macmillan Company
of Canada, Limited

THREE STUDIES IN EUROPEAN CONSERVATISM

METTERNICH : GUIZOT : THE CATHOLIC
CHURCH IN THE NINETEENTH CENTURY

BY

E. L. WOODWARD

FELLOW OF ALL SOULS COLLEGE AND
LECTURER AT NEW COLLEGE, OXFORD

LONDON
CONSTABLE & CO LTD
1929

Printed in Great Britain by T. and A. CONSTABLE LTD.
at the University Press, Edinburgh

PREFACE

In writing these studies I have attempted a commentary rather than a narrative, and I have had in mind those discussions which are part of the routine of teaching in the older universities of England. A tutor in such a case expects from his pupils an outline knowledge of events, a certain " choice of the actions that are most profitable to be known." In return, he will make clear any doubtful points of fact, or correct any failure of method ; but his main business is to suggest or uphold a point of view, a theory, a judgment ; to explain motives which may have escaped notice in the text-books ; to set a group of actions or happenings in a wider historical context ; in short, to encourage, and, if possible, to answer, the questions of a pupil who has awakened " to the care of knowing causes."

The authorities which I have been able to use have differed in character and in value, and have contained within themselves exercises in the discipline and technique of historical criticism. The unreliability of Metternich as an historian of his own time, and the caprice of his editors, have been the subject-matter of more than one critical study. Guizot was less careless, and had less to conceal. In his *Mémoires pour servir à l'histoire de mon temps*, and in most of his speeches, the events and ideas of the time are set against a background of universal history. Rarely has a philosopher of the state carried more of his own work into the conduct of public affairs. For this reason few of those who come within the orbit of Guizot's luminous and powerful mind can fail in some measure to submit to its attraction ; nor is it always easy to remember that resistance to any single interpretation of an age is the first duty of an historian.

Many of the documentary sources of the history of the Catholic Church in the nineteenth century are locked in the archives of the congregations, or other storehouses of historical material to which the non-catholic layman cannot easily obtain access. The diplomatic correspondence between the curia and the catholic courts of Europe, and the published acts of the Holy See, do not always touch the springs of policy, and often leave unanswered the only questions which a later generation cares to ask. The writings and correspondence—published and unpublished—of liberal catholics in France, Germany, and England are useful within certain limits. Much detail remains obscure ; but it is possible to reconstruct clearly enough in outline the attitude of the leaders of the Catholic Church to the political and intellectual movements of a century ago.

I have found much of the material upon which my judgments are based in the publications of French, German, Italian, and Austrian historians. I hope that I have mentioned by name in the proper context all those from whom I have learned. Here I can only acknowledge in general terms how much I owe to those scholars whose work has helped me to form some idea of the unity of European life and culture. Nor is it easy for any one whose time is given to the study of history to know which are the happier hours—the hours of reading, or those hours of sustained excitement when the fragments of knowledge gained from many quarters seem of themselves to take the shape and image of the past.

CONTENTS

THREE STUDIES IN EUROPEAN CONSERVATISM

INTRODUCTION

THE three essays in this book are an attempt to understand three types of conservative thought and action in the period between Waterloo and Sedan, and thereby to show the attitude of some of the men who were the political governors of Europe towards the new and turbulent ideas of their age. Two of the essays are studies of the political ideas of statesmen ; the third essay approaches a subject wherein no one man's thought or action stands out with sufficient clearness to be taken as a pattern or a type. It is of itself significant that in these fifty years of European change the history of the Catholic Church is, paradoxically, the history of an institution without a leader.

Neither Metternich nor Guizot, the two statesmen whose ideas I have studied, was without a theory of government. The theory consisted, in each case, of a diagnosis of the conditions of European society ; a forecast, based upon experience, of the practical consequences of the spread of certain ideas, notably the ideas of the French Revolution ; an attempt to keep these ideas within certain bounds, and to restore to Europe a stability which had existed, or appeared to have existed, before the revolutionary storm had broken upon the world. It follows that Metternich and even Guizot, during the latter years of his political life, were " reactionaries." The word is unpleasing to a modern ear. There is indeed a type of unthinking resistance to change, common to sluggish minds, and the counterpart of undue restlessness or unthinking discontent. Thoughtful men have long spoken of these opposite defects as an exaggeration of human instincts, tendencies, dispositions, or what not, each of which possesses, or has possessed, a high biological value for human survival. Once their existence is assumed, and reckoned with, these extremes

A

take to themselves historical importance only when circumstances have left them in a rare setting, or surrounded them with such power that their commonplaceness becomes the instrument of tragedy.

This tragic element might be studied in the lives of certain monarchs of the nineteenth century. The emperors Francis I. and Francis Joseph of Austria (Ferdinand is a case only for the pathologist) might be chosen to show the havoc wrought upon a state in modern times by the short-sightedness of its rulers.[1]   Above all, there is Nicholas I. of Russia. This man of violent activity, with a dark sense of duty, and a darker strain of fear, cruelty, and irresolution, is a figure for the Latin of Tacitus or the English of Gibbon. His power of self-delusion was too great, and his " conservatism " was too ignorant, too obvious, and too local, to form the subject-matter of a study of modern political interest, or to throw light upon the development of political ideas. His actions are of immense importance for the history of Europe ; but they are without intellectual sequence, and often reveal little more than the panic of a haunted mind. What could be expected of a tsar who thought that the burning of the English parliament house in 1834 was a sign of God's displeasure at the passing of the Reform Act of 1832 ?

None of the other " conservative monarchs " of the middle years of the nineteenth century has more than a passing significance. Frederick William IV. of Prussia might be saved from forgetfulness, as a man as well as a king, because

[1] One instance, taken from a critical time in Austrian history, is enough to put Francis Joseph in his place. At the outbreak of the Austro-Prussian war in 1866 Francis Joseph appointed General Benedek to be commander-in-chief of the Austrian armies in Bohemia. Benedek was a rough soldier whose fighting had been done in Italy, and who " knew every tree on the road to Milan." The Archduke Albert, who was a trained strategist, and familiar with the military geography of Bohemia, was sent to command the army of Italy. After Moltke had won the victory of Königgratz, Francis Joseph not only dismissed Benedek with ignominy, but made him promise never to attempt a public justification of his actions. As soon as this promise had been given, an attack was made upon Benedek in the most important official newspaper. Francis Joseph had made this extraordinary choice because he was afraid of the political effect of a defeat of a general belonging to the imperial house. The same motive accounts for the silencing of Benedek.

he had a certain openness of mind, and in spite of his appearance was more of a romantic *littérateur* than the drill-sergeant proper to his line. But his reflections upon the place of kings in a modern Europe, for all their mediæval colouring, were nothing but the threadbare theme of Prussian sovereigns. History will remember him, not for any new way of thought, but for his refusal of a written constitution to his subjects because he could not allow " a piece of paper with writing upon it to come between Our Lord God in Heaven and this land, like a second Providence, to rule us with its paragraphs, and supplant the old sacred loyalty." Of the kings and princes who were Stockmar's pupils another story might be told ; but this would belong to a different range of ideas.

Therefore it is not among the monarchs, but among the statesmen, or, as their enemies call them, the politicians, that the more interesting phases of conservative thought and action are to be found. Within this group of men Talleyrand and Bismarck are in many ways more remarkable than Metternich and Guizot. Bismarck has had a better historical press in his own country ; he enlisted professors where Metternich only silenced them. Talleyrand and Bismarck were among the best company in the world ; while Metternich was a little tiresome, and Guizot too remote. For a generation Bismarck seemed the successful man of his age, and Talleyrand never failed for long. But unless an extreme cynicism be counted wisdom nothing remains of Talleyrand's political insight. . . . " Il y a quelqu'un qui a plus d'esprit que M. de Talleyrand : c'est tout le monde." Nor can his display of conservatism after he had left Napoleon—or, as he would have said, after Napoleon had deserted his own principle of order—count for more than another graceful change of style. Even in his own time men of better European judgment thought he had done poorly for his country in his defence of the principle of " legitimacy " at the congress of Vienna. Bismarck was incontestably a nobler man than Talleyrand ; Nature had built his mind and body on a more titanic scale. He was more masterful towards the kings he served ; much of his work is splendid and lasting, and for all the

STUDIES IN EUROPEAN CONSERVATISM

evil which came after him he cannot be held responsible.
In his talk, as in his writing, there is an insight into the
ways of men, and much truth of a kind. In his choice of
means, his moderation, and his courage he was a greater
statesman than Metternich. He had little of Metternich's
vanity, and none of his conceit ; he worked harder, and
with a violence of concentration and a fire of conviction
which Metternich never knew. Yet Metternich and Guizot
were quicker to understand the drift of their age. Bismarck's
earlier view of society was crudely provincial ; the rule of
soldiers and squires ; a world modelled on the isolated
monotony of east Prussia. Years of experience and action
polished the surface of his mind ; but from a modern
European point of view Bismarck remained provincial to
the last. His bold manœuvres covered the whole field of
the tradition of *raison d'état* ; but a world of new ideas left
him almost untouched.

There is little speculative interest in the outlook of English
conservative statesmen during these years. Neither Castlereagh, with his care for the peace of Europe, nor Peel,
with his practical wisdom and honesty, cared to look much
beyond the business of the moment. Canning was a mocker ;
astute, tolerant, brilliant. Disraeli moved on a byway
from the high road of western thought, and his early
political ventures were those of a nomad in the settled life
of western civilisation.[1] The Toryism of Gladstone was as
insular as the Oxford Movement.

Whatever their place in the general order of talent,
Metternich and Guizot give more opportunity for the study
of conservative ideas than any other of the statesmen of
the early and middle years of the nineteenth century.
These two men belonged to an age which was occupied
with the after-effects of the French Revolution, as we are
occupied with the consequences of the Great War. They
were forced, as we are forced, to take up an attitude towards
a problem of European magnitude and of world-wide

[1] Disraeli was, in a sense, nearer to the mystical way of thinking of the
pan-Slav party in Russia than to the conservatism of England or France
or Germany.

interest. Their analysis of society was dominated, as ours must be dominated, by a fear of the return of great calamities, and by an uncertainty about the value of great political experiments. They were sure that the process of change was taking place too rapidly, though the nature, methods, and limits of their opposition to change were very different. The antecedents, the history, and the character of the two men might seem to make a comparison between them almost idle. In public and private life Metternich had the loose standards of behaviour common to the upper class of his time ; from a boy he knew the corruption of the great European world which Guizot only entered as a middle-aged and successful man. Metternich was a catholic nobleman from the Rhineland ; Guizot a protestant French bourgeois. Guizot had been a professor under Napoleon ; Metternich helped to cause Napoleon's fall. Guizot rose to political distinction in opposition to the Bourbons, and directed a government born of the revolution of 1830 ; Metternich was a minister of the Habsburgs. The France of Louis Philippe was a compact, or seemingly compact, state, with free institutions, freedom of discussion, and a turbulent political life. The Habsburg empire was a collection of kingdoms and principalities, divided by differences of nationality, tradition, and economic interest ; an empire without the means of political self-expression, Byzantine in its court ceremonial, its uncertain militarism, its graded aristocracy, and its secular religion.

The difference in age between Metternich and Guizot was not great ; yet it was enough to give the elder man a direct knowledge of the old régime, and to make the younger a child of the revolution. The two men never met before they were both exiles in England. It is curious that a few months before the revolutions which were to mark the end of their political domination they exchanged letters of the utmost cordiality. Guizot wrote to Metternich : " Je ne connais pas de plus grand plaisir que l'intimité avec un grand esprit. Nous sommes placés à des points bien différents de l'horizon, mais nous vivons dans le même horizon. Au fond et au-dessus de toutes les questions, vous voyez la question sociale. J'en suis aussi préoccupé que vous. Nos sociétés modernes ne sont pas en état de décadence ; mais, par une coïncidence qui ne s'était pas encore rencontrée dans l'histoire du monde, elles sont à la fois en état de développement et de désorganisation, pleines de vitalité et en proie à un mal qui devient mortel s'il dure, l'esprit d'anarchie. Avec des points de départ et des moyens d'action fort divers, nous luttons, vous et moi . . . pour les préserver ou les guérir de ce mal. C'est là notre alliance."

Metternich answered that the character of the age was, and would long remain, one of transition. " The game of politics has seemed to me inadequate to the needs of the time. I call myself a socialist-conservative. The principles of conservatism apply to the most diverse situations ; their application is not confined within narrow limits ; these principles are the enemies of anarchy, moral and material." [1]

Metternich was the less hopeful of the two men. He served not an older, but a more antique state. The Habsburg monarchy could hardly survive into a new time ; the empire could not survive the ruling house. Metternich guessed that the end was not far away. He was too idle and too frivolous in his leisure to dream of the future. He was content to think of a period of transition and great trouble before a new order could be established ; but he had set himself to stave off an immediate calamity. Whatever might be the ultimate result, there was some consolation for a vain man in the thought that he alone stood between Austria and the inevitable dissolution.

Guizot was more instructed in history ; his mind was open to loftier speculation ; his character was stronger ; unlike Metternich he did not scatter the substance of his inner life in small change. Nor could his environment allow him Metternich's uncritical self-esteem. Guizot had continually to justify himself before a brilliant parliamentary opposition ; Metternich could be content with the reiteration of his own ideas before subordinates whom he directed

---

[1] Metternich, *Mémoires*, vii. 400-3. Guizot had the advantage of Metternich in the elegance of his style. A few weeks later he wrote : " J'ai appris avec grand plaisir que la santé de Votre Altesse était excellente. J'en fais mon compliment à l'Europe." (*Ibid.*, p. 405.)

or monarchs whom he despised. The France of Louis
Philippe was a whole stage further than the Austria of
Metternich along the road taken by the peoples of western
Europe. Guizot's countrymen gave him every reason for
hope ; they had lived through a long crisis which would
have broken the Austrian empire to pieces ; there was no
need to despair of a distant future.

Therein lay the fundamental difference between the outlook of the two men. Both fought hard for the maintenance
of order in an unquiet time ; both worked to bring about
a recognition of certain fundamental political realities which
had been denied—with terrible consequences—by an excited
generation. The end which Guizot foresaw was a rule of
liberty which Metternich could not imagine.

Once, in a talk about the great men of thought and action
of the nineteenth century, Morley and Acton put Guizot
in the first place. This judgment of two politicians who
were historians upon the pre-eminence of an historian in
politics may seem too kindly ; yet no one has ever set
Metternich in so high a place. His countrymen must long
be divided about him, since his policy may well be called
decisive for their own fate. But his sensitiveness to the
existence of general European interests beyond the interests
of particular states raises him above the category of statesmen of purely nationalist aim, and makes it worth while
to rescue his ideas from a purely formal condemnation.

.   .   .   .

Resistance to the idea of the sovereignty of numbers is
the question which is continually before the reader of
Metternich's despatches and Guizot's speeches. At one
point or another, but definitely, and with more than words,
a barrier must be set to revolution. This " revolution "
was one of the mental pictures which men make up out of
a whole complex of circumstances and events. It is not
easy to reconstruct the fixed ideas even of a hundred years
ago ; nor are the impersonal methods of modern history
always a help in this reconstruction. The causes of the
French Revolution are pushed back in time, and analysed
into a multitude of economic particles. Where once there
was a spectacular battle of personality, there is now a

series of minute happenings, with a thousand and one causes, a thousand and one divagations, cross currents, contrary results. If this study of particulars is not to lead merely to scepticism, the details must be brought together, and seen as a contemporary sees them, in a stream of life. The expert needs a certain philistine courage to acknowledge that there was a French Revolution in the literal catastrophic sense in which it appeared to Burke and to Louis XVI., and in which it was fixed and used to the full by Napoleon. This is the revolution, seen in its violent happenings, and not in its interpretation by heavenly spirits ironic, which set a mark upon the men who were to govern Europe in the next generation. The recognition of a new principle of government, the sovereignty of the people in direct exercise of power, the affranchisement of men from the rule of kings and priests and from a discipline which had become a tyranny, were the central facts of this revolution. The novelty of the discovery, the greatness of the emancipation are clear when we see that the men who achieved the revolution were themselves afraid of it ; afraid lest they had destroyed not only the machinery of government, but the moral authority of any kind of rule, and left a broad and open way for the exercise of military force. The Europeans, freed from the chains of unreason, were not merely the "êtres morales et intelligents" of Rousseau's *Contrat social* ; they were men who had come together to a social life vaguely, through external fear, and chance, and hope of betterment ; men who were kept in society uneasily, by habit, by common need, by authority as imperfect as themselves. Sudden power blinded some, tempted others, and deluded all. Many had plans, but none could build ; in a few years the work of centuries seemed to be falling into ruin.

This time, which appeared to many as the last days of an old civilisation, was the opportunity of Bonaparte. Here is a type of man for whom as yet no artist's imagination has been sufficient. Here is an appearance in human history which in its power is near to the great forces of nature ; the glaciers or the tides. Napoleon restored in France, and maintained for Europe—even for his enemies—

the principle of order, and a sense of the reality of good and evil ; no one has broken more contemptuously through the tyranny of words. No Ozymandias' boast is stronger than Napoleon's resolution to control the political thought of Europe in his own time and dominate with his own ideas the minds of future generations.[1] Napoleon had but two contemporaries, Goethe and Beethoven, and within his own sphere of creation his genius is even lonelier in its magnificence. Yet Napoleon was mortal, and even before time did its work on the living man, the energies and the traditions of Europe asserted themselves again. Napoleon was thrown down by the very forces which he had used in the setting up of his power. He could have no successor. Who, then, was to affirm an order of government—and what order of government—in the states which had been harrowed by war and excitement and political experiment for nearly twenty-five years ?

Here, to me, is the interest of the types of thought and action which I have studied. Guizot wanted to combine order with liberty. He would achieve by reason what Napoleon had attempted by force, and would close the era of revolution, secure the rule of the many without destroying the permanent safeguards of authority. Metternich wanted to restore in men's minds a view of society which had been lost through human presumption, and would return when men took a colder view of their affairs. No truce could be made with false ideas ; the danger to civilisation was continuous and not lessening in intensity, for there was a limit to the material power of resistance and of recovery. No concessions could be made, no weakness shown, until the poison had left the body corporate of Europe.

. . . . .

What place would the Catholic Church take in this changing western world ? Perhaps its leaders might find a chance of reasserting a dignity which the church had been losing before the advance of the secular power during the old régime. Subservience to the princes of the temporal order did not belong to the tradition of the papacy, still less to the essence of Christianity. The eastern and protestant

[1] See p. 239.

churches were a warning against the danger of allowing spiritual authority to depend too closely upon the support of kings and commonwealths. The violence of the revolutionary attack upon the church in France had set a cleavage between catholics and the revolution ; but the despoilment of her goods and the disruption of her hierarchy had been due in no small part to the closeness of association between the church and the old monarchy, while, in Germany, the princes themselves had been most active in the destruction of ecclesiastical privilege. Here, then, was an occasion for the papacy, with all the prestige of its moral resistance to Napoleon, to take a stand between the extremes of left and right ; in other words, to be conservative in the sense of Guizot's conservatism. More than this ; the little kingdom of the popes was now at the mercy of the greater powers, and an encumbrance to freedom of action within the domain of things spiritual. Now, if ever, the papacy could free itself from a government which was an embarrassment in time of peace, and a danger in time of trouble. The occasion might even have been taken for a more difficult work : was it not a time to bring certain doctrines and practices of the church more into harmony with the way of thinking of an age which had definitely broken with mediæval modes and terms of thought ?

In fact, the Catholic Church was bound by its leaders more closely than ever before to the party of extreme resistance to a new order. Temporal power and mediæval doctrine were reaffirmed with abandonment of speech and heedlessness of practical consequences. I have tried to show the reason for this. The maintenance of a temporal kingdom had become part of the routine of the papacy. Force of habit, the interest of those employed in secular administration, upheld the existing order ; the process of selection within the hierarchy made it unlikely that a pope would bring to his office any originality of idea or great power of execution. Once the papal curia had determined to keep its Italian lands, force of historical events would drive the church into the support of the Bourbons, the Habsburgs, and all the débris of the past. North of the Alps there were many who saw whither this policy

would lead ; but against the vested interests long established in Rome they could never make headway. It followed that no attempt would be made to understand the
new learning which itself seemed to come from the pit of
revolution. In any case it is easier now to see that no
attempt at a restatement would have been successful. The
doctrines of the church had been affirmed too often and with
too great assurance in the plenitude of mediævalism for men
trained in mediæval logic to use another language. The
very nobility of mediæval hope : " Ave crux, spes unica,"
could not be translated into a modern tongue. Scholastic
philosophy was to the papacy what the manifold races and
geographical necessities of the Habsburg empire were to
Metternich. As in the state, so in the church, there could
be no compromise, no progress, only a return to the past.
Therefore the churchmen continued within their antique
walls to draw the last consequences of their syllogisms ;
while their enemies wrote essays with the title : *Comment les
dogmes finissent.*

. . . . . .

There is no need to develop here the modern interest of
these reactions to inevitable change. While they were
taking their course, an even greater transformation was
coming over society, and leaving as historical survivals
most of the " progressive " opinions of the first revolutionary age. A hundred years have gone by, and we find
ourselves again in a time when civilisation seems to have
broken its barriers, and to have made more conquests than
it can secure. The work of statesmen of the third and
fourth generation after Metternich and Guizot is not made
easier because the tide of religion has ebbed further from
our world and left us without the old sureness of touch
and unity of design. For this reason alone the history of
the Catholic Church in the nineteenth century has an
interest beyond the history of any secular experiment ;
though it may seem the inevitable history which has befallen
the empires and beliefs, the kings and peoples of an earlier
time.

I
METTERNICH

I

METTERNICH

It is characteristic of Austrian history that the most remarkable minister of the Habsburgs in the nineteenth century should have been a Rhinelander who had never seen Vienna until his twenty-second year.[1] It is significant for the history of Metternich that the occasion of his coming should have been an advance of the armies of the French revolution. In the ecclesiastical principalities where he had spent his boyhood (his family were counts of the empire, and his father was, from 1774, in the imperial service), Metternich had learned the easy, debonair way of life of an upper class whose standards were high only in matters of elegance and taste. As a young man he had watched the disruption of an old order of government, and had occasion to judge both the moral weakness of the conquered and the moral confusion of the conquerors. None of these impressions left him. To the last he cared for the pleasure and grace of living, and fostered intellectual interests remote indeed from the thought and talk of the magnates of Austria or Hungary. To the last he judged revolution by its excesses, by the delusion upon delusion which it brought to the Rhinelanders. He had seen the change from triumph to anger in those who had cheered the news of the revolution, and welcomed the French troops. He had known at first hand the stories of the demagogues, and the coming of the Terror. One of his tutors, J.-F. Simon,[2] became a

[1] 1794. Metternich was born at Coblenz on May 15, 1773. By chance he had come to England a few months earlier, and had seen what he might well call one of the noblest sights of his life : the sailing of the east and west India fleets, under convoy, from Spithead roadstead ; over four hundred ships on a June morning.

[2] Simon had the dexterity to survive the revolution, and ultimately to become tutor in German to the sons of the future king, Louis Philippe. In 1829 he went to Vienna, and asked Metternich for money ! For

15

revolutionary journalist, a supporter of Marat, and com-
missionaire national du pouvoir exécutif at Mainz. Nor
could he forget the fecklessness of the military and civil
opposition. He met the French émigrés at their headquarters in Mainz and Brussels ; he saw a little of the
methods of diplomacy and of the armies while acting as
secretary to his father. He might have found material
enough for criticism in his own home. Count Metternich
was a good example of the men who could not believe
that times were changed. He had been promoted in 1791
to the position of imperial minister in the Austrian Netherlands. Six years later he was sent as plenipotentiary to
Rastadt. At an hour when his world was crumbling about
him, Count Metternich was occupied in regulating the
etiquette for the reception of Bonaparte's envoys, and
counting the number of steps to be taken on entering and
leaving the audience chamber ! Yet already in 1794 the
advance of the French armies had compelled him to bring
his family away from Brussels, and to go to Vienna in
search of a new diplomatic post.

The high Viennese society was not too ready to receive
immigrants from the Rhineland, and only after a marriage
with the granddaughter of Kaunitz [1] was the way open for
Metternich's abilities. Even so, Metternich's father-in-law
was unwilling for him to take any active part in the service
of the state ; such was the curious indifference of the
Austrian aristocracy to the fate of their own country.
Metternich's own excuse, in later years, was that he had
disagreed with the policy of those in power, but was too
modest and too diffident to show this disagreement ! Only
in 1801 did his official career begin. He was minister
plenipotentiary at Dresden from 1801 to 1803, ambassador
at Berlin from 1803 to 1806, and at the court of Napoleon
from 1806 to 1809. In 1809, after the battle of Wagram,
he became minister of foreign affairs. This rapid pro-

J.-F. Simon's career see *Mélanges publiés pour le cinquantenaire de l'École
pratique des Hautes Études.* (Paris, 1921.)
    Another of those who welcomed the revolution on German soil was
the dramatist Kotzebue. He too lived through all its phases—to be
assassinated in 1819 as a reactionary journalist in Russian pay.
    [1] This marriage was celebrated in 1795—at Austerlitz !

motion was due in part to the absence of men of ability and high birth whose policy had not been entirely discredited by the successive defeats of Austrian diplomacy and Austrian arms. By force of circumstance Metternich had come into direct contact with Napoleon. No man could meet Napoleon in the day-to-day business of diplomacy and remain unchanged. The years between Austerlitz and Wagram, between Wagram and the last coalition, left Metternich with no illusions about the way in which a man of action could deal with men of words. In a sense he was more practical than Napoleon himself. Napoleon worked for his dynasty, and took no account of his own mortality ; Metternich built up his plans upon the one certain fact of the time—the fact that Napoleon was mortal, and would grow old and die like other men. Therefore Metternich taught Austria to bow her head in the evil days. He manœuvred his country through the wars of liberation ; he secured not only the fall of Napoleon but the restoration of Austria, and defeated Talleyrand and Alexander as well as Bonaparte.[1]

Little wonder then that he should regard the world after 1815 as full of small men ; that he should have seen what the " little kings " never understood. He realised that Europe had defeated Napoleon, but that Napoleon alone had defeated the revolution. The master had fallen ; the principles of the revolution remained ; and those who had fought Napoleon now had to fight the revolution. Metternich might well think that he had no one else to fear. In his own country—if Austria can be so called—no general, no statesman came near to the immense distinction of his service. No new issue could take the place of the unfinished

[1] He summed up his policy in a note written to the emperor on August 10, 1809 : " from the day we make peace " (Austria had been defeated at Wagram on July 5-6) " we must confine our system entirely to manœuvre, evasion, and compliance. In this way alone can we hope possibly to maintain our existence until the day of general deliverance. We have only one expedient ; we must reserve our power for better times." (*Mémoires*, ii. 305.)

Two years earlier Metternich had commented upon the instability of Napoleon's work : " It is curious that Napoleon, while tormenting and modifying incessantly the relations of all the European states, has not yet taken a single step which will tend to assure the permanence of his successes." (*Ibid.*, ii. 120.)

battle between the " idealogues " and the man of order.
No crisis could upset the nerves of the man who had come
into power after Wagram ; no situation could be so full of
foreboding as the year before Leipzig. Metternich could
be afraid of no one after he had stood out against the flattery
and the anger of Napoleon.

Thus the thirty-three years of Metternich's political career
after 1815 were almost an epilogue, an anticlimax. He was
quick to realise that he had passed the epic period of his
life. As early as 1819, in speaking of the notes he had left
to serve as an autobiography, he explained that he had not
gone beyond the year 1815. " Tout ce qui vient après
rentre dans le domaine de l'histoire ordinaire. . . . L'époque
postérieure " (as we talk of the post-war age) " . . . est re-
devenue une ' simple story.' " [1] Hence Metternich's un-
bounded confidence in his own powers, in his prescience, in
his infallible diagnosis of every ill in Europe. Hence his
contempt for the men whom Napoleon's example had taught
him to despise, his hatred of the verbiage which had led to
the slaughter of a generation of Europeans. For this reason
he idealised the years before 1789, and insisted upon the
need for the lasting co-operation of the powers against the
revolution. He had seen the early victories of the French ;
victories won only because their enemies were selfish, preoccupied, and blind. As early as 1794 he had published
an attack upon what he called the old diplomacy, and demanded the arming of the peoples against the revolution.[2]
After 1815 he said to Wellington : " Depuis longtemps
l'Europe a pris pour moi la valeur d'une patrie." Metternich, like Napoleon, had adopted a country ; he could
practise diplomacy, as Napoleon pursued power, in the
abstract and as an art ; the country of his adoption was
his point of departure and not the end of his activity.[3]
Finally, he had seen enough of the passivity, the fickleness,

---

[1] *Mémoires*, iii. 312.

[2] A pamphlet with the title : *Ueber die Nothwendigkeit einer allgemeinen
Bewaffnung des Volkes an den Grenzen Frankreichs : von einem Freunde der
allgemeinen Ruhe.*

[3] This attitude of Metternich was recognised by Anton Springer
(*Geschichte Oesterreichs*, i. 129). To Springer, writing in the 1860's, it is
Metternich's condemnation.

the delusions, the simple loyalty of the common people ; he would put little store by popularity. Napoleon had shown that it could be bought, and that it was not worth the price.

Metternich cannot be judged merely by the magisterial certainty, the immovable self-confidence, the false clearness of his later years. Still less can he be judged by the circumstances attending his own fall. He foresaw this fall as few men have foreseen their own destruction. He knew the weakness of the Austrian government and the civil service, the reigning house and the army. He understood the dangers of a situation which he judged beyond his powers of control. Stronger men would not have been content with this fatalism. Metternich, for all his belief in his own realism, was always ready to mistake a diagnosis for a remedy. Yet it is difficult to refute his claim that if he had not been willing to take most things as he found them, the catastrophe would have come sooner. Europe has judged Metternich's actions, and judged also the historians, like Treitschke, who condemned him out of hand.[1] It is possible to discover his intentions from his own voluminous letters and papers. By these he wished to be appraised, and, for this reason, often clouded his intentions and acts in a mist of words—the least sure of all methods of deluding posterity ![2] Another source is available for us which has

[1] Metternich naturally came off poorly at the hands of German liberal and nationalist historians. The earliest attempt at an impartial judgment was made by Adolf Schmidt, *Zeitgenössische Geschichte* (1859). The only biography of Metternich in French is C. de Mazade, *Un Chancelier d'ancien régime* (1889). There is an interesting life of Metternich in English by G. A. C. Sandeman (1911). In 1925 Heinrich Ritter von Srbik published a biography in two volumes : *Metternich : der Staatsman und der Mensch*. (F. Bruckmann, Munich.) Any student of Metternich's life and ideas must be under a deep and continuous obligation to von Srbik for the wide scholarship, thoroughness, and deliberation of his book. Von Srbik's interpretation of Metternich's character and policy seems to me to hold the field, in spite of the violent attacks made upon it by Bibl, *Metternich in neuer Beleuchtung*. (Vienna, 1928.)

[2] Twenty years after Metternich's death his son Prince Richard Metternich published a selection from the letters, papers, and documents in the family archives at Pless. This publication was always in Metternich's mind ; in 1820 he had suggested a delay of fifty years after his death ; but he lived longer than he might have expected. The selection was made by Baron von Klinkowstroem, and appeared simultaneously

an interest of its own because it was an apology made not for posterity but for a contemporary who was one of the cleverest women in Europe. A man does not tell the more obvious lies, nor can he hide the more obvious truths, in such a case.

Metternich and the Princess Lieven met for the first time in October 1818 at the congress of Aix-la-Chapelle. They met again in November for about a fortnight : then for a short time in 1821 at Hanover and Frankfurt, and at the congress of Verona in 1822. Their next meeting was in England after the revolution of 1848.

At the congress of Aix-la-Chapelle Mme de Lieven was in her thirty-fourth year. Thirteen years earlier Sir Thomas Lawrence had painted her portrait. The portrait—now in the National Gallery—shows a wayward, proud woman ; not beautiful (the nose is too pointed, and the ears too large), but wonderfully vivacious and quick-witted ; selfish, and a little matter-of-fact.[1] Her history was curious in itself, and seems curious to us, though it was not uncommon in her own narrow circle. Her mother had been a friend of the empress of Russia, the wife of Paul I. She died a young woman ; after her death the empress saw to the daughter's education. In our sense of the term, the daughter was scarcely educated at all. She was sent for a time to the Couvent des demoiselles nobles at Smolna ; but most of her childhood was spent in the corrupt and somewhat make-shift luxury of the Russian court at the turn of the century.

in French, German, and English. The French and German editions were each of eight volumes ; the English edition was not continued after the fifth volume, nor was this fifth volume complete.

The appearance of these documents did little to raise Metternich's prestige. The editors had taken liberties with the text, and their method of selection was often arbitrary. Metternich himself had shown little care for historical accuracy in his autobiographical chapters, and the self-satisfaction with which he offered himself to the judgment of pos- terity—the judgment of the Germany of the year 1880—was unlikely to increase his reputation, or to destroy the legend of his imperturbable conceit.

The references in this essay are taken from the French edition (*Mé- moires, documents, et écrits divers laissés par le prince de Metternich*). The title of the German edition is : *Aus Metternichs nachgelassenen Papieren.*

[1] There is another portrait at Holland House. This portrait, pre- sented by G. F. Watts in 1856, is reproduced (p. 176) in L. G. Robinson's *Letters of Dorothea, Princess Lieven, during her Residence in London, 1812-1834.*

In 1800 she was married, in her sixteenth year, to Count Lieven, whose family, like her own, came from the Baltic provinces. Only a few months later her husband was called to the Winter Palace in the early hours of the morning. He was told by the messenger that the emperor was ill [Paul 1. had been assassinated] and that " the Grand Duke Alexander, that is to say the emperor," had sent for him. Such was the atmosphere of the court that Lieven had to decide at once whether the summons was genuine, or merely a plot to involve him in a charge of high treason. He guessed right, and went to the palace ; as a result, he and his wife lived for nine years in high imperial favour. In 1810 M. de Lieven was sent as ambassador to Berlin. Here he stayed for the three years of Prussian humiliation and discord with Russia. No one in Berlin seems to have taken special notice of Mme de Lieven. The quickness of her intelligence wanted for its full development a larger experience of the world. She had nervous vitality and grace of breeding rather than beauty ; there was needed the life of a society west of Berlin to give charm and poise and light to her face. She—and others—had long taken the measure of her very ordinary husband. When in 1812 Alexander sent Lieven as ambassador to London, she soon found the place which a young and clever woman could make for herself ; circumstances helped her, for Russia alone among the Great Powers was represented by an ambassador at the English court in 1812. Six years later, when she went with Lieven to Aix-la-Chapelle, she knew to the full the pleasures of the diplomatic game, a game which she found the more pleasant in that she never troubled herself with the terrible realities behind it. " Elle ne dépassa jamais les horizons des ambassades et des salons." [1] Nor was she troubled with many scruples. How could a child of the Russian court, with no natural gift of introspection, see the world as it is for most people, or feel respect for moral laws which few in her decadent environment heeded ? [2]

[1] *Revue d'histoire moderne et contemporaine*, v. 138.
[2] For the most recent account of Princess Lieven see *The Unpublished Diary and Political Sketches of Princess Lieven together with some of her Letters.* Edited by H. W. V. Temperley. (London, 1925.)

Metternich, who knew her world, was attracted by her as in earlier days he had been fascinated by more beautiful and more tempestuous mistresses.   Yet it is clear that both were moved by other motives than passion. Metternich, who could never trust Alexander, and never dominate Castlereagh, might well have found it worth while to charm the woman who knew the secrets of the courts of England and Russia.   Mme de Lieven, who ever favoured the winning side, might find more than a romantic attraction in the man who controlled central Europe and could talk so well about Napoleon.   For these reasons the letters which Metternich wrote to Mme de Lieven [1] have something artificial in them even when they are most self-revealing. Metternich was tired when he wrote them ; he was writing to a woman whom he had only known for a few weeks under circumstances which hardly made him inclined to trust her.   The letters would be disappointing to any one who had the illusion that nobility of thought, fire of passion, and splendid imagery would be found in the love letters of those who directed the affairs of Europe, and incidentally spent most of its wealth.   The tone of the letters is heavy and middle-aged, very sure and very selfish.   There is a wearisome insistence upon certain rather cheap jokes— Mme de Lieven as " la mère des diplomates " in London. Again, Metternich, who knew that the letters of the imperial family were opened in the post, was never certain that the letters would reach their destination, never sure that the secret police would not read them.[2]   Hence there is a self-consciousness which is in itself a sort of self-revelation.

Metternich makes himself out a martyr to his duties, " J'ai

---

[1] The letters of Metternich to Princess Lieven during 1818 and 1819 were published, with an introduction by M. Jean Hanoteau, in Paris in 1909.   The exchange of letters is known to have lasted until 1826.   An examination of the " extracts from private letters " in Metternich's memoirs seems to give reason for believing that some of these extracts are taken from letters written to Mme de Lieven.   None of Mme de Lieven's letters to Metternich have been published.

[2] One at least is known to have been read by them.   With the subtlety of their kind they inferred from the text that Metternich had been the father of an illegitimate child—at a date when he was ten years old !

un fonds de réserve que je dépense en paroles, en actions, en calculs, c'est de ce fonds que je tire des matériaux que je rédige en mémoires et en protocoles ; mais mon véritable capital—celui qui doit fournir à ma vie, celui qui fonde mon bonheur—ne se mêle jamais avec l'autre " ; a neat excuse, incidentally, for not giving away secrets in his letters ! He wrote on his way to the Diet at Frankfurt : " If I had no other source of happiness in the world than that which is provided for me by the Germanic Diet, I would drown myself in the Rhine." [1] Or again : " la vie d'un ministre est une vie affreuse . . . Il existe une seule classe d'individus faits pour ce métier ; c'est celle qui, avec une grande force de tête, n'a aucun besoin de cœur. Je ne suis pas de ces hommes-là. Le monde me croit bon ministre, tandis que je ne vaux rien pour le métier que je fais " ; [2] a judgment which Mme de Lieven gave back with interest ten years later when she quoted to Earl Grey the duke of Wellington's opinion of Metternich : " I never shared the view that he was a great statesman ; he is a society hero, and nothing more." [3] It is easy to see the half-truth in this from Metternich's own words. His hours of work were long indeed ; though how far their length was the result of his own long-windedness is another question. In one of his letters he gives an account of a typical day in Vienna : " Would you like to know how I live ? I get up between eight and nine o'clock. I dress, and take my breakfast with Mme de Metternich. . . . My children are there, and I stay with them until ten o'clock. I go to my study and work or interview people until one o'clock." (The French term " je donne des audiences " would be nearer the mark.) " If the weather is fine, I go out riding. I come back at half-past two. I work until half-past four." (Notice again the pedantic half-hours.) " Then I go to my salon. I always find there eight, ten, or twelve persons who have come to dine with me. At half-past six I am back again in my study. Nearly every day I go to the Emperor.

[1] *Lettres du Prince de Metternich à la Comtesse de Lieven*, p. 47.
[2] *Ibid.*, p. 88.
[3] *Correspondence of Princess Lieven and Earl Grey*, i. 234. Cf. ii. 138 : " As to ' l'homme le plus franc et le plus loyal ' . . . I believe him capable of anything."

I stay there a good while, and then come home to work until half-past ten or eleven ; thence to my salon to meet our own callers or any strangers. I generally spend an hour in talk with your children in Vienna " (" tes enfants de Vienne," that is, the diplomats ; again the poor joke). " I say a word to the ladies, and then I go to bed at one o'clock." There is a significant addition. " If there should be a ball which I cannot escape I go for an hour or two between eleven and one o'clock." [1]

Later letters and the evidence of others show that this was a fair account ; though it was difficult indeed to escape the balls. Only a splendid and balanced physique could bear the strain. Metternich worked quickly, so quickly that when he wrote he was always missing out the nouns and verbs.[2] Napoleon and the men of action set more store upon these most vigorous parts of speech ; Metternich preferred the adjectives ! He found these hours of diffused application a weariness ; the sense of responsibility was an even greater strain. Others, Gentz for example, noticed the effect upon Metternich of the anxious months before and after the Grand Alliance. Metternich himself said that he could not drink tea at night if he wanted to sleep ; " ce sont les événements glorieux de 1814 et 1815 qui m'ont rendu ce service." [3] Anyhow he had to read for an hour before he could get any sleep. Livy was one of his books ; [4] in general he chose books of science or travel—rarely novels, and these only when they were classics : " Le roman ordinaire ne m'intéresse pas ; je le trouve toujours bien au-dessous de ce que j'éprouve." [5] In 1819 he wrote that an intaglio of himself six years earlier showed him as much too young : " j'ai vieilli de vingt ans depuis la Sainte Alliance." [6] Five years later, when he was fifty-one, he did not expect to live to be seventy-four, and so to equal the years of Kaunitz' service.

The strain was greater because he knew himself to be alone, and because he had to deal with such unstable elements. All his later judgments show that he realised

---

[1] *Lettres*, pp. 104-5. [2] *Mémoires*, iii. 381.
[3] *Lettres*, p. 214. [4] *Mémoires*, iii. 547.
[5] *Ibid.*, p. 315. [6] *Lettres*, p. 108.

his isolation in Austria.   His rivals were discredited before
he came to power : he had enemies enough, but there was
none to dispute his authority in his peculiar sphere of
foreign affairs.   Towards the Emperor Francis he always
showed admiration, and even real affection ; but he was
too adroit a man not to hope that for posterity the greatest
proof of the sound judgment of the emperor would lie in
his choice of Metternich, and his unchanging loyalty to his
minister.   Loyalty to their ministers was not a characteristic of the kings of Europe in the early nineteenth century,
and Metternich might well write in 1820 : " Providence
has set me by the side of a man who was, one might almost
say, made for me." [1]   Towards crowned heads in general
Metternich felt as any able man must have felt when he
looked around him.   Many of these high personages would
have been lost in the crowd but for the accident of birth,
and their loss would not have been felt.   " If you knew
what I think about the inhabitants of these lofty regions,
you would take me for an out-and-out Jacobin. . . . I have
seen so many of those who live in this atmosphere that I
know all about them."   How could it be otherwise ?
How few men of ability were there in the world, how few
again of this small company could keep their talent if they
were " set on an altar, and surrounded by the poison of
error, ignorance, servility, and flattery." [2]   The ennui of
courts was distasteful.   " I hate courts and everything
belonging to them : my very nature is foreign to them : I
cannot, for example, remain standing for a long time : I
do not like to be bound to fixed hours ; I cannot endure
to be kept waiting." [3]   Or again : " long and cold corridors :
overheated rooms ; a stilted bearing ; not a thought which
comes from the heart, never a word which is not a set
piece or even a show." [4]   In this atmosphere, with these
relationships, the feeling of responsibility was almost a
consolation ; responsibility both to the emperor and to the
peoples of the empire.   " I find myself in control of immense
interests ; there is not a moment of the day when I can
forget my obligation to a man who trusts me, and to whom

[1] *Mémoires*, iii. 362.   [2] *Lettres*, p. 207.
[3] *Ibid.*, p. 57.   [4] *Ibid.*, p. 81.

I am devoted because I can respect him ; every mistake which I make affects nearly thirty million human beings ; I am afraid only of mistakes, because I can be sure of my intentions." [1]

These were not entirely idle boasts to impress Mme de Lieven. Metternich expected other statesmen, if they were worthy of the name, to show the same consideration for their responsibilities. He spoke contemptuously of the light-mindedness of Capo d'Istria : " this sort of behaviour, with fifty million men in the background, is unworthy of a great man." [2] A certainty about his intentions. This is the famous " infallibility " of Metternich. Whatever his political enemies may have assumed, Metternich was never foolish enough to think himself infallible in act ; but in his diagnosis of society, its evils, its tendencies, its composition, its unchanging elements, the guarantees of its stability, the danger signals of its dissolution, in the metaphysical analysis of the bases of civilisation, in all these things he thought he knew the whole truth, and that nothing more remained to be discovered. So Mill thought he had said almost the last word upon the economic laws governing the production of wealth. In particulars Metternich might be wrong : " I could wager that if I had been a general, I should have won battles, and been badly thrashed in skirmishes." [3] But in the essentials of statesmanship Metternich believed that he had discovered certain truths, and that from these truths his action never consciously deviated. In 1819 he could write from Teplitz : " I am writing from the same room, and at the same table which saw the signing of the quadruple alliance six years ago. The time of year is almost the same. Everything has changed since then, except myself. . . . When I sit at this desk, and review the questions which then occupied my mind, when I see once again all that existed at that time, and is now no more, I cannot but allow myself a slight feeling of vanity, and deep sense of satisfaction and content. . . . There is a wide sweep about my mind. I am always above and beyond the preoccupations of most public men ;

[1] *Lettres*, pp. 172-3. [2] *Mémoires*, iii. 550-1.
[3] *Lettres*, p. 170.

I cover a ground much vaster than they can see, or wish to see. I cannot keep myself from saying about twenty times a day : ' how right I am, and how wrong they are.' " [1] " I would rather die an hundred times than admit the truth of something which I consider to be plainly false." This sounds bombastically vain ; but how often did Bentham, or Mazzini, or Karl Marx, or Mr. Gladstone think that they could be mistaken in their first principles ? " Et combien il est facile de la découvrir, cette raison si claire, si simple, et si naturelle ! " [2] Did the last three say this, or did Metternich ?

This confidence in his grasp of the positive laws governing the life and death of human societies was independent of success or failure in action. " If I am right, seven-eighths of my contemporaries are mad enough to be put under restraint ; if I am mad, then the number of wise men alive to-day is countless." [3] Whatever he might think of its folly, Metternich knew that the world " n'en ira pas moins son pitoyable train." [4] It was in exile, when all his work seemed to have tumbled into ruin, that Metternich said to Guizot : " l'erreur n'a jamais approché de mon esprit." [5] He was more explicit when he wrote to Mme de Lieven : " mon âme est toute positive et par conséquent toute historique, toute à la vérité. Je ne me fais illusion sur rien." [6] The good side of this outrageous certainty was that in Metternich's case it was not accompanied by personal vindictiveness against his opponents. Von Humboldt noticed in Metternich an absence of feeling, an absolute insensibility which was incapable of hate.[7] Metternich himself spoke of his " double nature, a nature which has made many people believe that I have no heart." [8] The dark history of the duc de Reichstadt gives hints of an absence of pity ; [9] but the two cardinal points of Metternich's policy were rigorous action to secure a given end, and clemency wherever the conditions made clemency possible. There was nothing

[1] *Mémoires*, iii. 224-5.　　[2] *Ibid.*　　[3] *Ibid.*, iii. 459.
[4] *Ibid.*, iii. 224-5.　　[5] Guizot, *Mémoires*, iv. 21.
[6] *Lettres*, p. 72.　　[7] See Bibl, *op. cit.*, p. 18.
[8] *Mémoires*, iii. 337.
[9] Srbik (*op. cit.*, i. 784, note 3 to p. 675) decisively rejects the charges made against Metternich by Bibl (*Der Herzog von Reichstadt*).

of the brutality of a General Haynau [1] about him. He
disliked despotism as the sign of incapacity.   In 1824, after
the Piedmontese rebellion of 1821, he had an interview
with Count Confalonieri, the leader of the Lombard
conspirators.   Confalonieri was on his way to the Spielberg
prison.   The character of the interview shows a cold pre-
cision of mind, free from anger or caprice, indifferent to
the fate of individuals in the execution of a policy of state.
There was no question of amnesty or pardon ; nor, on the
other hand, was there a deliberate attempt to take advantage
of the nervous strain which had been put upon a delicate
and gently-nurtured man, and to snatch information which
would lead to the arrest of Confalonieri's fellow-conspirators.
Metternich was concerned with the " European " aspect
of the conspiracy, and wanted to find out the relations of the
secret societies in Italy with the European enemies or
rivals of Austria.   Confalonieri had offered to give this
information.   For Metternich the interview had no more
and no less justification, no other significance.[2]   Metternich
seems to have shared Gentz's hope that the student Sand,
the assassin of Kotzebue, would die of his self-inflicted
wounds.   No good and much harm would come from his
recovery.   No importance could be attached to Sand's
disclosures of a " conspiracy " ; none of the guilty would
be caught, while " the distress into which the complicity
of other young men would plunge more than one decent
family would not be of any use to us." [3]   At the same time
he did not shrink from strong measures of repression.
Sentimentality in politics was an element of weakness,
and the more so because the other side was never sentimental.   " Amnesty or pardon are terms which have no
meaning for them, and therein they are right." [4]

The pity of the world was its unwillingness to see the
truth.   Where were the wise men ?   Of emperors, kings,
princes, grand dukes, and the like he took little account ;

[1] It is interesting that when Metternich went over Barclay's brewery
(one of the sights of early Victorian London) in 1848, at the height of
the Chartist agitation, he met with none of the treatment afterwards
meted out to Haynau.

[2] See Srbik, *op. cit.*, i. 484-8, and notes.

[3] *Mémoires*, iii. 240.

[4] *Ibid.*, vi. 283.

nearly all other statesmen were foolish, or at best mediocre !
After 1815 Napoleon had suffered civil death. " The one
giant whom the eighteenth century produced is no longer
of this world ; all the stir of to-day is made by men of a
pitiable stamp. It is hard indeed to play well with such
poor actors." [1] Even after 1848 Metternich could say that
he had met more fools than knaves. If the governors were
such poor creatures, the governed were good at heart,
but, like children or nervous women, " ils croient aux
fantômes." [2] " The people let themselves be duped easily
enough ; you cannot exaggerate the goodness of the
people, I might even say of all peoples ; but their ignorance
is as great ; therefore they must be led." [3] Little wonder
that men should have commented upon the habitual irony
of Metternich's laughter.

Because of his willingness to face facts in an age of delusion and romanticism, because he was " tout à terre,"
Metternich knew that he was bound in the end to fail.
Hence there is a certain fatalism, a hopelessness about his
own work which is a sure sign that he had nothing of the
unresting, creative mind. " I have had the misfortune to
belong to the revolutionary epoch. This age will pass like
all other human follies. Happy those who will have
learned to keep themselves upright amid the ruin of several
generations. . . . Fate has laid in part upon me the duty
of restraining, as far as my powers will allow, a generation
whose destiny seems to be that of losing itself upon the
slope which will surely lead to its ruin." [4] " Our society
is on the downward slope. Nothing in the moral or physical
world comes to a standstill. Society had reached its zenith ;
under these conditions a further ' advance ' was bound
to mean a ' decline.' Disease also reaches its climax, and
then declines. Evolution of this kind seems exceedingly
slow to contemporaries ; but what are two or three centuries
in the annals of history ? " [5]

In 1830, when the revolution in France seemed to have

---

[1] *Mémoires*, iii. 225.

[2] *Ibid.*, iii. 459. Cf. *ibid.*, p. 482 : " Le peuple est partout bon, mais
enfantin."

[3] *Ibid.*, iii. 357.

[4] *Ibid.*, iii. 307-8.
[5] *Ibid.*, iii. 369.

undone the work of fifteen years, Metternich wrote to Nesselrode : " my most secret conviction is that the old Europe is nearing its end. I have determined to fall with it, and I shall know how to do my duty. On the other side the new Europe is not near to its beginning ; between the end and the beginning there must be a chaos." [1] He wished that he had been born in a different age. " My life has coincided with a most abominable time. I have come into the world too soon or too late ; I know that in these years I can accomplish nothing. Earlier I should have had my share in the happiness of the time " (it might be said that notwithstanding the evils of the age he had his share in " les jouissances qu'offrait l'époque " !), " later, I should have taken part in the work of reconstruction ; as things are, I am spending my life in underpinning buildings which are mouldering into decay. I ought to have been born in 1900, with the twentieth century before me." [2] Austria in the twentieth century, and the end of the Francis Joseph whom Metternich had known as a young man ! On the day before the outbreak of the revolution of 1848 which drove him from Vienna, Metternich wrote to the Austrian minister in Rome : " Dreams pass ; the truth remains ; this will be clear enough to our great-nephews." [3] The thought that the future would justify him was continually before his mind. It was a sign of weakness, perhaps, as much as strength ; a desire for applause, a feeling that he must justify a line of action, a consistency which his contemporaries misunderstood. " It may be that some one in the year 2240 will discover my name, and tell the world that in this distant past there was at least one man less limited than the mass of his contemporaries who had pushed fatuity to the point of believing that they had reached the apogee of civilisation." [4]

On the whole Metternich would have chosen to have lived

[1] *Mémoires*, v. 23. To the end of his life Metternich believed himself to be living in one of the " ages of transition." He wrote in 1858 : " La seule idée juste qu'on puisse se faire du temps actuel est celle qu'il constitue une période de transition. Le dénoûment et la limite extrême de périodes de ce genre, Dieu seul les connaît ! " (*Ibid.*, viii. 426.)
[2] *Ibid.*, iii. 369. [3] *Ibid.*, vii. 605.
[4] *Ibid.*, iii. 451-5.

earlier.[1] Like most men with a sense of the transience of
things, or, indeed, like all who are middle-aged, he disliked
writing the figures of a new year.[2] His intellectual clear-
sightedness, never fired by a sense of intellectual adventure,
or by the excitement of the romantic or the perilous, had an
effect upon his moods. In middle and later life he was
continually depressed. Whatever outsiders might think
of his imperturbability, those who knew him best knew also
that he had little hope of a good future. Treitschke, with
his bourgeois confidence in the merits of his own time and
country, makes easy sarcasm about Metternich's five
metaphors : volcanoes, plagues, floods, fires, and cancerous
growths. He might have added that Metternich found
three other terms useful in describing the state of society :
powder magazines, influenza, and the cholera !
Metternich's third wife, a woman of little political understanding and much impetuousness of speech, was always
noting in her journals the melancholy of her dear, her wise,
her misunderstood husband. He belonged to the age which
was not afraid of tears in the presence of others. On the
other hand the hours of depression at the crookedness of
the world and the unthankfulness of a prophet's duties
revenged themselves in a conceit which finally made him
ridiculous to strangers. He did not underrate the value of
his unerring prescience. He believed himself to be a moral
power in Germany, and perhaps in Europe. He wrote
only half in jest that the Diet of Frankfurt was waiting for
him as for a new Messiah.[3] He uses a phrase about his
own crucifixion which is in bad taste even in a private
letter. He fell into the trap which in his wiser moments
he knew to be set for the highly-placed, and allowed himself to be flattered. When Nicholas I. spoke of him as the
keystone of an arch,[4] he seems to have taken the comparison
seriously, and to have believed in the tsar's sincerity when
he told him in 1833 : " Je viens ici pour me mettre sous
les ordres de mon chef. Je compte sur vous de me faire
signe si je commets des fautes." [5] In a letter from Paris

[1] *Mémoires*, iv. 26.   [2] *Lettres*, p. 99.
[3] *Mémoires*, iii. 112-13.
[4] *Ibid.*, vi. 83.   [5] *Ibid.*, v. 446.

Metternich says that he is regarded as " a lantern in a dark night."

This conceit was the more troublesome to others because it was joined to a long-windedness which became almost intolerable in his old age. There was little temptation to be brief for a man who could dictate to a whole staff of clerks, who had to make his meaning clear on very difficult questions to stupid superiors, and who was aiming rather at delay than at action. Nor was the tradition of the Austrian civil service in favour of an abrupt or a staccato style. In Metternich's old age the habit of writing very long despatches or of reading disquisitions upon first principles became almost second nature ; conversation with him needed a patient listener. Mme de Lieven, who never forgave him his second marriage with a beautiful girl of lower rank than himself (" le chevalier de la sainte alliance a maintenant fini par une mésalliance "), spoke of him a little maliciously in his old age as " plein de sérénité, de satisfaction intérieure, d'interminable bavardage, bien long, bien lent, bien lourd, très métaphysique, ennuyeux quand il parle de lui-même et de son infaillibilité, charmant quand il raconte le passé et surtout l'Empereur Napoléon." [1] His letter-writing was endless. Almost his first act after leaving Vienna in 1848 was to send letters of apology for his fall to the emperors of Austria and Russia and the king of Prussia. To the end of his life, in spite of the pose that he was glad to be free at last from the burden of public affairs, he composed long minutes, more doctrinaire than illuminating, upon every question of the day ; minutes which showed how little he understood of the new Europe which had at last begun to take shape.

A graver consequence of his conceit was that he never knew his own worst failing—a liking for the tortuous and the mystifying for its own sake. The fault ran through his whole character. He lacked the seriousness of the greatest statesmen—he had not their mastery of passion because he had not their intensity of feeling. Little interests and empty victories too often preoccupied him. He wasted time at Vienna over women and dancing ;

[1] Barante, *Souvenirs*, vii. 421.

his enemies called him " le ministre-papillon." He was less dilettante than they believed, but even Gentz, the last man with any right to complain, feared the effects of his flippancy. It shows how little he or the circle in which he moved knew of the deepest of human passions and the simplest of human loyalties that after the death of his first wife he could write of their " vie commune qui n'a été troublé par aucun nuage." Yet he had been continually unfaithful to her, and owed it only to her tact that his intrigue with Mme Junot had not been the ruin of his career.[1]

Because he lacked a final nobility of mind, he came to like clever execution for its own sake and to prefer a neat intrigue to a conflict of wills. Napoleon had seen this fault in him : " il prend l'intrigue pour la politique." There are two curious passages in his letters where he talks about spiders. " I have begun to understand the world, and to perceive that if flies are eaten by spiders it is because they die too young, and therefore have no experience and do not know what is a spider's web. Spiders indeed interest me. I often watch them ; they are the best barometers, and, their ugliness apart, the most charming little creatures, always busy, and arranging their houses with the greatest neatness in the world." [2] Eighteen months later, after Laibach, he wrote again : " I have the feeling that I am in the middle of a web which I am spinning after the manner of my friends the spiders, whom I like because I have so often admired them." He explained how he had caught Alexander. " This is what I mean by my spider's web. A net of this kind is pleasant to behold, woven with art, and strong enough to resist a light attack, even if it cannot stand a gust of wind." [3] Little wonder that the austere Castlereagh, whose household carefully kept the English Sunday at Vienna, and who wanted to get back from Viennese dances to the debates of the English parliament, should speak of Metternich as a " political harlequin."

[1] Hanoteau (quoting F. Masson), *op. cit.*, Introd., p. xxv. Napoleon once risked his soldiers' lives that one of his mistresses might see an attack ; but he never wasted an hour with women when his own career or the interests of France were at stake.

[2] *Mémoires*, iii. 340.   [3] *Ibid.*, iii. 473.

This absence of ruggedness showed itself in all Metternich's tastes. He was "more polish than steel." He disliked solitude, loved large rooms, flowers and light and gardens, wide and sunlit views. " I have something of the palm tree about me. . . ." [1] " Ma nature tient de celle des orangers." [2] He cared much for his garden ; from his exile in 1848 he wrote with one of the sudden touches of the poetry of old age : " give my greeting to the lilac if it is flowering now." [3] His taste was classical, and of the eighteenth century. He found in Rome (which he first saw in his forty-seventh year) the things which he liked best : " grands souvenirs, luxe et bon goût " ; monuments on the grand scale. He took a curious pleasure in the noise of guns : " j'ai une grande faiblesse pour les coups de canon." [4] He liked music ; " elle me fait l'effet du souvenir." [5] Painting and sculpture affected him more directly ; he could speak of them with greater knowledge. In 1819 he took with him to Italy a landscape-painter whom he had sent to South America two years before. Sir Thomas Lawrence was one of his personal friends : it is characteristic of him that he should have chosen an artist who flattered his clients.[6] He was proud of his patronage of art. " I have under me the four academies of Vienna, Milan, Venice, and Rome. I am happy to have the opportunity of helping many artists : artists are worth infinitely more than savants." (He might have added that they gave a great deal less trouble to the censorship !) " They are often a little queer in the head, but their hearts are right : with the savants the opposite is the case." [7]

Even his dislike of professors—a dislike shared by Bismarck, who thought that their way of life was too dim—only applied to those professors of the theoretic subjects whose ideas had led men astray for a century from the path of positive knowledge. For the physical sciences and their teachers he had an interest more real than any other statesman of his time. The social dangers of the new

---

[1] *Mémoires*, iii. 215.   [2] *Ibid.*, iii. 219.   [3] *Ibid.*, viii. 252.
[4] *Lettres*, p. 302.   [5] *Ibid.*, p. 74.
[6] Metternich made Lawrence alter his (Metternich's) portrait because the mouth was too sardonic.
[7] *Lettres*, p. 235.

knowledge seemed negligible in comparison with the
trouble caused by the theories of the new political philosophy.
He liked positive conclusions based upon observation and
cast in an abstract form ; the little " dodges " and intricate
machinery of scientific experiment attracted him.   He
could not forget that from the scientists came practical
suggestions for increasing the wealth of states.   Metternich
had studied medicine with a certain seriousness ; it was not
entirely an exaggeration for him to say that he had passed
" par dessus tous les degoûts," and lived in hospitals and
dissecting rooms.[1]   In his correspondence he gives careful
analyses of the health of himself, his family, and his friends.
He liked to talk with scientists, and to hear about their
discoveries and watch their experiments.   His rooms in the
Ballplatz were full of scientific instruments.   If his own
metaphysical deductions from the science of his time were
somewhat jejune, he was not ignorant of the data of science,
and never underrated the importance of new inventions.
Thiers thought that the locomotive would be a new toy
for the Parisians ;   Wellington feared that railways would
be a danger to the security of England ;   the king of Prussia
believed that no gentleman would ever travel in a steam-
drawn train.   Metternich saw at once that railways were
" one of those innovations which arise suddenly in the course
of years and modify profoundly the existence of society." [2]
In 1838 he was anxious that the Austrian government
should subsidise the Austria Lloyd company in order to
secure the valuable contract for the transport of the Indian
mail.[3]

This interest in scientific discovery and taste for " grands
souvenirs " gave to the intellectual life of Metternich a largeness which is wanting from his moral life and his personality
as a whole.   He must indeed have learned much from
Napoleon, and have seen the truth in Napoleon's splendid
boast :   " j'avais le goût de la fondation, et non celui de la

---

[1] *Lettres*, p. 225.

[2] Princess Mélanie (Metternich's third wife) first saw a locomotive in
1834.   She wrote in her journal :   " I came with strong prejudices
against the invention ; but I was at once enchanted with this admirable English device."   (*Mémoires*, v. 587.)

[3] *Ibid.*, vi. 305-7.

propriété." He had a little of that care for the judgment
of posterity in external things which is one of the signs of
the grand style, if not of greatness.   He intended to build a
mausoleum for his family which should be the most splendid
in Europe : " j'aime tout ce qui défie le temps." [1] He
set up a bridge which passers-by would take to be " as old
as the world " until they read his name on a column by
the side of the public road.[2] He hoped to make a noble
house in which his descendants would live in a princely
leisure denied to himself ; [3] his own achievements had
raised his family to an equality with the great names of
the monarchy. He founded a museum at Königswart
for the most valued of his possessions, and did not forget
to care for it while in exile. He was glad that his name
would be linked with great happenings, and that the state
archives would be full of his work. Metternich once crossed
into Italy by the new Austrian road over the Valtelline.
He noticed that there was no monument to preserve the
name of the Emperor Francis, as the name of Napoleon
would be remembered by those who took his road over the
Simplon. Thereupon he chose a rock side where the name
of the emperor and the year of the building of the road might
be cut in letters twelve feet high.[4] This is not the way of a
man of mean spirit.

[1] *Mémoires*, iii. 355.   There is something of the same spirit in Metternich's remark that there is a kind of " moral property " which is
" under God's will the nobler sort." (Metternich to Wrede, 1833. Bibl,
op. cit., p. 368.)

[2] *Mémoires*, iii. 308.

[3] His enemies said that he had taken care to give his family the
material property necessary for this leisure. Metternich was not
acquisitive in the most unpleasant sense of the term. He may have
accepted money offered him by Russia, but there is not the slightest
evidence that his policy was ever dictated or deflected by considerations
of personal gain, or by gifts and promises of money.

[4] *Mémoires*, v. 183.

II

THE POLITICAL "PRINCIPLES" OF METTERNICH

In face of the revolutionary theories of his political enemies Metternich always claimed to act upon a reasoned view of society. His enemies said that he acted upon a " system." He denied that he had a " system," and took care to distinguish " system " from " principles." [1] His " principles " led him now to this, now to that course of action, as the needs of the day might determine. The view of society, from which the " principles " were drawn, must be true because it took account of the unchanging nature of man— " the French Revolution did not make men nobler " ; [2] because it was based upon history, and could be tested by history. He contrasted his own " principles " with the generalisations of passion or doctrinaire inexperience.

What were these " principles " ? How did Metternich apply them ? Did he really believe in them, or were they only a means of making a hand-to-mouth policy look respectable, and of cloaking local and temporary expedients with an appearance of universality? The " principles " were not original : nor did Metternich develop them ; they remained as little changed by time as his own handwriting. He had little cause to change them. They were based upon the experience of his early life, and the philosophy of history which he had learned from his professors at Strasbourg and Mainz. The events of his youth seemed to justify

---

[1] In a fragment written between 1849 and 1855, and called by Metternich his " testament politique," there is a reference to the " false denomination of the ' system of Metternich,' which is applied to the former attitude of the Empire of Austria." (*Mémoires*, vii. 636.) In 1852 he wrote that " the so-called ' system of Metternich ' was not a ' system ' but the application of the ' laws ' which rule the world." (*Ibid.*, vii. 630.)

[2] Metternich to Wrede, 1833. (Bibl, *op cit.*, p. 364.)

the conclusions of this philosophy ; the events of his long political life only confirmed them ; his views were formed before he came into the service of the Habsburgs ; [1] the conditions of the Austrian empire would have led him to the conclusions which he already held.   Finally, the " principles " opposed to his own seemed to him never to change, in whatever local or temporal form they might manifest themselves.   If the principles of the revolution remained the same, why should the principles of the counter-revolution alter ?

The basis of Metternich's philosophy was the idea of the balance of power as a cosmic principle, for so it seemed to eighteenth-century philosophers who drew their analogies from the mechanistic science of their age.   The idea of a stability, a balance between extremes, was applied to man as to the forces of nature, and was a more scientific statement, or a statement in more modern scientific terms, of the Aristotelian doctrine of the mean.   The political lesson was obvious.   The ineluctable laws of the universe compelled men and things to seek repose as the only way of escape from dissolution ;   a repose which was an equilibrium between conflicting forces.   In the political world stability could only be found in a balance of power between the different states which were the units of the great human society, between the different classes and interests in particular states.   As in the physical, so in the political world the balance could easily be disturbed ;   a disturbance of equilibrium would mean civil war within a state, external war between states, just as it would mean calamities in the physical world or moral anarchy in the nature of man. This doctrine is doubly pessimistic because it leads to a belief in stability rather than progress and finds in history no more than a variation upon a single theme ;   a recurrent

[1] Metternich's most important teachers were Koch and Vogt.   His contemporaries did not regard Metternich as an assiduous student ; but it is impossible to avoid noticing the effect upon him of this early teaching.

There is a long account of the sources, the content, and the application of Metternich's political " principles " in Srbik, *op. cit.*, vol i. bk. 3.

This account is challenged by Bibl ; in my opinion Srbik's main conclusions are right, though he is inclined to take Metternich's reasoning a little too seriously.

cycle of repression and anarchy, with only a few intervals of repose. There seems no lasting alternative between chaos and stagnation. Apply the doctrine to the life of man, and the same melancholy conclusion is inevitable. The balance of opposing forces is maintained rarely, and for a short time ; while death may come at any hour and destroy the balance for ever. None the less death must always win in the end ; nor is a view of human society necessarily false because it is unpleasing to comfortable men.

Under the domination of this conception of the physical laws which govern the world and of the consequent philosophy of history—a philosophy shared by the greatest of Greek historians—Metternich found the balance badly upset in his own time ; the pendulum had swung in the direction of anarchy. Hence it was the duty of statesmen to act upon the defensive ; to counter exuberance by repression and to oppose stability to movement. It must be the continual work of those in power to secure a redress of the balance in the direction of repose ; such action was in accordance with an instructed conception of natural law. This is why Metternich called himself " tout à terre, tout historique," and objected to the claim of his opponents that they alone were " socialist." [1] For this reason he insisted always that the duty of statesmen was to " govern."

If it were the duty of statesmen to lean towards the side of strong government when the unscientific thought of the time was driving European society towards anarchy, it followed that a co-operation between governments was necessary. Experience proved this. The mischievous indifference of Austrian and Prussian statesmen to the common danger of the French Revolution had resulted in the unexpected victories of the French armies, the rise of Napoleon, and long years of war and tyranny. Firm and united

---

[1] In a letter to Guizot written in 1827 (see above, p. 6) Metternich called himself a " socialist-conservative." By " tout historique " he meant that he put events into their proper setting in time, and related the present to the past and the future. " I belong to the class of men who live more in the future than the present. My mind has an historical tendency which makes me pass over a multitude of temporary difficulties. . . . I do not despise the present. . . . I value it at what it is worth, though it is not worth much." (*Mémoires*, iii. 454.)

action at the outset, a coalition based upon common principles, would have prevented untold miseries. Only after bitter lessons did the European powers really act together ; then at last their action, borne on the stream of favouring circumstances, brought about Napoleon's fall. Yet the " principles " of the revolution could not be burnt out of men's minds by victories in the field. The Peace of Paris had brought material, not moral, tranquillity.[1] A generation of repose was needed in which the young might learn the true laws governing the life of man in society. The transition from a period of movement to a period of repose was always difficult.[2] During these years of moral education the incurable revolutionaries of an older time must be held down by force. For this work the co-operation of all the states of Europe was essential. Co-operation implied intervention. The " principle of non-intervention " was purely arbitrary, and was not based upon natural law. It was not recognised by the revolutionaries themselves, however often they might appeal to it in times of distress. " The revolution reckoned upon the separation of states."

Metternich repeated Burke's remark that a man has an interest in putting out the flames when his neighbour's house is on fire. Revolution was a kind of disease, and measures of public health ought to be international. Intervention must be on the side of authority. Therefore support must be given to the monarchical principle as such, however unworthy its representatives. A Neapolitan or a Spanish Bourbon, a Dom Miguel in Portugal, were to be supported not because of their personal merits—they had but few—nor because of any divine right of kings, whatever the Bourbons might think, but because the right of hereditary succession was a guarantee of other rights, and, as a consequence, a guarantee of the whole social order. Metternich never thought that the " principle of legitimacy " belonged of itself to the moral order. Kingship was not the only form of government ; hereditary monarchy

---

[1] Metternich to Kübeck, Feb. 14, 1851. (*Metternich und Kübeck : ein Briefwechsel*, p. 150 (Supplement to Kübeck's *Tagebücher*). Vienna, 1910.)
[2] *Ibid.*

was not the only form of kingship.[1] Napoleon had no predecessor. The monarchical principle was to be upheld because in the Europe of the early nineteenth century it happened to be the constituted source of authority ; the visible sign of the rule of law. In short, it must be defended not because it was inevitable but because it was attacked by those who wished to overthrow more than monarchy.

Popular sovereignty was set over against monarchy. Popular sovereignty as set forth by its supporters must have led ultimately to an attack upon all forms of property. Its fancied justification was the equality of all men. But men are equal only before God and the law ; there is no equality apart from this. Any society which based authority upon the general equality of men was building upon the fallacy, widespread among eighteenth-century philosophers, that man could reach perfection, or upon the simple rule : " ôte-toi, que je m'y mette." It is an indication of the limits of his reading that Metternich never quoted Aristotle's wise analysis of " the universal and chief cause of revolutionary feeling . . . the desire of equality when men think they are equal to others who have more than themselves ; or, again, the desire of inequality and superiority, when conceiving themselves to be superior they think that they have not more but the same or less than their inferiors." In other words equality is of two kinds, numerical and proportional ; and from the confusion between the two arise wars, tumults, and confusions.[2]

If popular sovereignty was a conception likely to destroy the balance of states, and hence to lead to calamity, monarchy based upon popular sovereignty must be a contradiction in terms. For this reason Metternich was bound to regard the monarchy of July as a sham from the beginning.[3] The English monarchy was an apparent exception ; but it was only possible because of an historical tradi-

---

[1] Metternich held that " the monarchical form offered to a large state the advantage of great stability." He believed that history supported the generalisation. (*Mémoires*, vii. 638.)

[2] Aristotle, *Politics*, v. 2, 2.

[3] Princess Mélanie, who followed her husband's opinions without much regard to tact, once answered a compliment from the French ambassador on the beauty of her tiara : " At least it is not stolen " !

tion which did not exist on the continent of Europe. The American constitution was a perpetual *tour de force* ; in any case American conditions were more local even than those of England. As a rule invented constitutions, or *chartes*, as the French liked to call them after 1815, were of no value in themselves, nor was there any universal receipt for their composition. To Metternich a constitution was much more than a written document, as marriage was something more than a marriage contract. He agreed with Burke that a constitution was the sum of the conditions of the life of a state, the product of the national character, not of a moment of excitement. Magna Charta in English history was a beginning, and not an end, and was followed by centuries of bloodshed and civil disturbance. To make a constitution was to give legislative shape to a revolution. In fact the constitutions asked for by revolutionary agitation were "representative constitutions," based upon popular sovereignty. Here was the great distinction ; the form was indifferent, so long as the monarchical principle was maintained. Once the idea of the sovereignty of the people was accepted, the life of the state, the working of its institutions, would be hampered by talk, corruption, disputes. Inefficiency would lead to chaos ; the only escape from anarchy would be despotism. The cycle leading from 1793 to 18 brumaire was of the order of nature. "Like Saturn, revolutions always devour their own children." [1]

These were, in outline, the "principles" of Metternich. Such a philosophy may be superficial ; it was certainly "doctrinaire," and certainly based upon the "half-truths" and the shallow learning which Metternich claimed to despise. Much of it was commonplace enough ; though a reading of the eighteenth-century political writers, whose work made history a generation later, shows that one generation may easily forget the commonplaces of another. The so-called generalisations from experience were out of date when the romantic revival led to a restoration of the belief in the "manifoldness" of history. They ignored—

[1] Metternich to Wrede, 1832. (Bibl, *op cit.*, p. 329.) The remark has been made before and since !

could it have been otherwise?—the psychological basis of
popular sovereignty, the evolutionary value of the instincts,
impulses, dispositions, be the word what it may, to give a
lead, to play a part in the social group. Liberty is more
than the " certitude du lendemain." [1] In the long struggle
of human creatures with an unkind environment, no horde,
no group, no society could live where the members did
not have their say or contribute their ideas to the common
stock. We are the heirs of a hardly-won inheritance, and
we cannot throw away the weapons by which it was won,
for these weapons are part of ourselves. Metternich was
fighting against the dead, the one battle in which the
living must always be the losers.

[1] *Mémoires*, iii. 459.

III

THE GENERAL APPLICATION OF METTERNICH'S
" PRINCIPLES "

How did Metternich apply these " principles " ? How did they determine his policy in general, or affect the settlement of particular questions ? It is both expedient and fair to take an exposition of his policy which belongs to the middle period of his life ; to the years of his greatest mental powers and his greatest external success.

In 1820 Metternich thought himself able to dispose of the last of the liberal views of the Emperor Alexander. He was less successful than he imagined. To the end of his life Alexander could believe that he had postponed but not abandoned the carrying out of a liberal policy in Russia and Poland, and that this postponement was due to a series of accidents which had not very much to do with Metternich's arguments. But Alexander was wise enough to appear to be persuaded. After a long talk he asked for a written statement of Metternich's views. Nothing could have pleased Metternich better. He drew up a " profession de foi politique." The time and the occasion might call for a review of the state of Europe. Five years had passed since the battle of Waterloo. The allied armies of occupation had left France at the end of 1818. Stability seemed within measure of attainment, when in 1820 revolution broke out in Spain, Portugal, and Naples. The condition of Germany was dangerously unquiet. Advantage had been taken of the high words of excited students and of one act of political assassination to force the smaller states of the Germanic confederation to make an end of liberalism. Measures were passed (the so-called " Carlsbad decrees ") to curtail the liberties of the universities, and to strengthen the censorship. Metternich knew that the idea of popular sovereignty would no more be destroyed

44

by the police than by the soldiers of Blücher and Wellington. Moreover, Alexander of Russia had openly favoured
liberalism among the German states, and Russian agents
had done their best to embarrass Austria in Italy. A
mutiny among his own troops had a chilling effect upon
Alexander, while the continued opposition and (from the
tsar's point of view) ingratitude of the Poles made him
less hopeful of all liberal reforms. It was important for
Metternich to hasten Alexander's conversion. During the
congress held at Troppau to secure the suppression of
the Neapolitan revolution, Great Britain had refused to
recognise any unlimited right of interference, and the
French—unwilling to see the extension of Austrian power
in Italy—had only been lukewarm. Metternich therefore
set himself to convince Alexander that the conservative
powers were acting upon principles of universal validity,
and were interpreting the will of Heaven more clearly
than were those other guides to whom the tsar had inclined
himself.

Metternich began his profession of faith [1] by claiming
that statesmen ought to make clear the principles of their
action ; it was their duty not to abandon the " terrain
moral " to the whole crowd of " esprits superficiels pleins
de satisfaction de leur demi-savoir, juges impudents des
premiers intérêts de la société . . . criailleurs sans idées
bien arrêtées, victimes de leurs propres erreurs, et faux
prophètes." The state of Europe could not be described
more accurately than in the terms of an older judgment :
" l'Europe fait aujourd'hui pitié à l'homme d'esprit,
et horreur à l'homme vertueux." The foundations of
society were being attacked : religion, public morality,
laws, customs, rights, duties. The mass of men were only
lookers-on. Some indeed were vaguely favourable to change ;
the great majority wanted a " tranquillity which has ceased
to exist, and of which the first elements seem to have been
lost."

What was the source of these evils ? Could they be
remedied ? Metternich thought that he could give an

---

[1] This curious essay, which Metternich himself called a " pièce peu
diplomatique," is printed in the *Mémoires*, iii. 425-45.

analysis of the deep-set causes of all the trouble. The nature of man was unchanging. The main needs of society are and must remain the same ; apparent differences could be explained by a study of the physical factors operating upon the different races : variations of climate, soil, and position.[1] These variations have effects which reach beyond the domain of the merely physical ; they perpetuate themselves in institutions, and even in religions. But institutions themselves suffer change ; they grow in importance ; they are perfected ; they decay ; they conform to the nature of man, and have their ages of childhood and youth, of force and reason, and, at the last, of senility. Two factors alone remain constant and ineluctable in their influence : the precepts of morality, social and religious, and the necessities of the environment. (Metternich used the language of the eighteenth century : " les besoins créés par les localités.") Sooner or later, if men leave the path made for them by these " sovereign arbiters of their destinies," calamities will follow. (Here we have the idea of a balance.) History is full of the terrible consequences which have resulted from the neglect of these determining conditions ; never were these consequences more sinister than in the years which followed the French Revolution. The reason was not hard to find. History does not go back very far ; it begins, strikingly enough, with the fall of great empires. " Là, où elle semble nous conduire au berceau de la civilisation, elle nous conduit à des ruines." The fall of the great empires was followed by the rise of republics ; these republics quarrelled among themselves, and fell under the rule of the most successful soldier. One of the republics—Rome—

---

[1] G. Monod, in his last work on Michelet (i. 286 *et seq.*), pointed out that the " specific form under which the influence of geography on history appeared in the eighteenth century, that is to say, the theory of climates, was the direct result of the works of those travellers (Cook, Bougainville, Pallas, the Jesuits) who, since the sixteenth and above all in the eighteenth century, had brought to the knowledge of Europe immense areas inhabited either by savages or by peoples whose ideas, morals, and costumes had nothing in common with those of Europe." These differences could only be explained by differences of climate and environment. Hence the theories of Montesquieu, Turgot, and Herder on the subject.

passed through all the phases common to society (the term " evolution " had yet to make its way),[1] conquered all the scattered parts of the civilised world, and became an almost universal monarchy. This universal monarchy in its turn underwent the fate of all political entities. (Metternich cannot avoid the pessimism inherent in the theory of equilibrium.) Its mainspring was weakened and destroyed. Centuries of darkness followed the barbarian invasions, but the rise of Christianity made impossible a complete return to barbarism. New Christian states arose, upon foundations which could stand at all times and in all places ; their formation was followed by the crusades, which Metternich called an " assemblage bizarre de bien et de mal." Then came three discoveries whose influence upon civilisation was decisive : the inventions of printing and of gunpowder, and the discovery of the new world. Upon these discoveries followed the reformation. Metternich did not attempt to show any causal connexion between the earlier discoveries and the reformation ; though he spoke of its incalculable effects upon the " monde moral." Printing meant a more rapid interchange of ideas ; gunpowder an entire revolution in the methods of attack and defence ; the discovery of America, and the consequent influx of gold and silver, caused a sudden reversal of existing values in property, and offered the chance of a splendid career for the adventurous.

Hence, during the last three centuries—Metternich was writing in 1820—there had been a more rapid progress in human enterprise than in human wisdom. Add to this serious threat to the stability and balance of society the mistakes in theory and practice of some of the most dis-

---

[1] Metternich came very near to the idea of natural selection when he contrasted in the life of states and individuals progress of a " regular " kind with " progress by leaps." The normal method of progress is the development of conditions in a logical and natural sequence ; an " irregular " progress breaks the chains which bind these conditions together. Everything in nature follows " the way of development, of the aggregation of things " : such a mode of advance alone makes possible the elimination of those elements which are harmful, and the development of those elements which are good. Brusque transitions imply new creations, but " men can never create anything." (*Mémoires*, vii. 641.)

tinguished monarchs of the later eighteenth century, and
the result was a revolution in France.[1] The revolution
first appeared among the French because they were a
nation quick to understand ideas, though scarcely capable
of calm judgment ; a frivolous people, in spite of their
high civilisation. The cause of this revolution, and of all the
errors which threaten to disinherit society, could be summed
up in one word : presumption. This presumption was
itself a natural consequence of the rapid advance of the
human mind to completeness of achievement in many
spheres. Religion, morality, legislation, economics, public
administration, and even science seemed to have become
common property accessible to all.

Metternich describes the presumptuous man. Experience
has no value for him ; in place of faith he puts a so-called
private judgment. This judgment is made without examination and without study, for such methods of approach seem
unnecessary to the man who can embrace in a *coup d'œil* a
whole agglomeration of facts and problems. Laws have
no meaning for the presumptuous man because he did not
share in their making. It is beneath his dignity to take any
account of the restraints imposed by a brutal and ignorant
past. Authority resides in himself. What need is there
for him to submit to a rule useful only to men devoid of
enlightenment and knowledge ? Authority from without
is unsuitable to the age of reason and the degree of universal
enlightenment which German innovators have called " the
emancipation of the peoples." The presumptuous man
does not dare openly to attack morality, since without
it he would not be safe ; but he gives to morality an interpretation of his own, and allows others to do the same,
provided that they neither rob nor kill him. Thus society
is " individualised " ; every man is judge of his own
beliefs, principles, and actions. In the last resort even
nationality, which is one of the most natural of human
sentiments, is " struck out of the liberal catechism," save
where it is used as a lever to promote disturbance or to
involve governments in disruptive action.

[1] Metternich, like de Maistre, had no hesitation in admitting the
European prestige and authority of French thought.

This account of the presumptuous man is followed by a description of the different circumstances favouring an extension of the evils of the time. Some of these secondary causes are beyond human control, " so closely interwoven with the nature of things that no human prudence could have forestalled them." These causes Metternich took for granted. It is one of the weak points in his argument that he does not discuss them in detail. If these secondary causes are beyond human control, their effects cannot be prevented. It would then seem the wiser part for a states- man who was " tout à terre, tout historique," frankly to accept them, and to build up what he could out of the material at his disposal. This would ask for a power of creation which Metternich did not possess. He accepted the inevitableness, and foresaw the confusion ; but the new Europe which was to rise out of the ruins of the old must be left to come into existence of itself.[1] Certainly he could give no hint of its shape ; he cared only to stave off the calamity of the change, unheeding of the danger that he might be prolonging the travail and birth-pangs of the new creation.

This fatalism would have little effect upon the conver- sion of Alexander. Hence Metternich turned to the causes of unrest within human control.

The weakness and inertia of the governments were the chief reasons for the extension of the dangers threatening society. No eighteenth-century government was entirely unaware of these dangers ; but those in authority were blind to the number of able men conscious of their own power and of the weakness of the existing order. These men, indifferent to the social results, because their only motive was hatred, deliberately set themselves to subvert society. " C'est la France qui a eu le malheur de ren- fermer le plus grand nombre de ces hommes." It was in France that religion, morality, authority, and all that they protected were attacked with the greatest vigour and deter- mination ; it was in France that the arm of ridicule could be used with the greatest effect. " C'est dans les palais des rois, dans les salons et dans les boudoirs de quelques villes que la révolution était déjà achevée, tandis qu'elle

[1] See above, p. 30.

D

ne faisait encore que se préparer dans la masse du peuple."
" Parlez d'un contrat social, et la révolution est faite."
Nor would it be possible to avoid noticing the harmful
effect of parallels drawn from the peculiar conditions
of England, and applied without regard to the fundamental differences between English habits and institutions and the states of the continent. In this dangerous
excitement of public opinion the French government was
imprudent enough to give help to the American revolutionaries. Henceforward any important change in France
must have led to revolution. The French government was
alone in its failure to realise this necessity.

The revolution broke out, and in a short time worked
through the cycle of such happenings. The horrible
atrocities of its earlier phases, and the wars of aggression
which followed, kept the contagion from the neighbours of
France ; but the military despotism of Napoleon broke
through the existing order in every country, and gave
revolution in Germany, Italy, and, later, in Spain, the
chance of hiding its aims under the veil of patriotism. The
return of Napoleon in 1815 had the gravest consequences.
" In a hundred days Bonaparte undid the work of the
fourteen years during which he had been in power. He let
loose the revolution which he had suppressed in France.
He brought men's minds back, not to the 18th of brumaire,
but to the principles which had been adopted by the Constituent Assembly in its deplorable blindness." The encouragement given by Prussia to the secret societies, the
treachery of some of the lesser German princes to their
own order and their own interest, and the weakness of
the French government between 1815 and 1820 only
aggravated the situation.

Was there a remedy ? To every evil there was a remedy,
if the cause were analysed without passion, without prejudice, and without a preconceived idea of what the remedy
must be. An examination of society showed that the middle
class was most affected by the revolutionary contagion.
The great mass of the people remained, and must remain,
unaffected. Most men were occupied with getting a
living, and had no time for vague and ambitious abstrac-

tions. The ordinary man wanted above all things to be sure of the morrow. He wanted security for the fruits of his work, for his family, for his property.[1] Therefore Metternich felt certain that no immediate trouble on a large scale was to be feared in France or Germany, in Italy or Spain. The necessity for peace and tranquillity was felt too strongly by the majority in each of these countries. " Révolutions de palais " or in the upper circles of the governing class were another matter. A few members of the higher classes of society always joined the revolutionaries ; but their career was brief. Either they were " faux ambitieux " or " esprits pervers et perdus." Most of them were the first victims of their own reforms ; the few who survived were wont to become the humble servants of those of a lower class now risen to the great places of the state.

The source of trouble lay in the classes between the people and the aristocracy ; [1] the financiers, the civil servants, the men of letters, the lawyers, the persons in charge of public education. The financiers have a clause to themselves : " véritables cosmopolites, assurant leurs profits aux dépens de tout ordre de choses quelconque." It is curious that an old aristocracy, grudging the power taken from it in the sixteenth and seventeenth centuries, should use almost the very words of the proletarian battle-cry against capital.

The Emperor Alexander knew less of the middle class than Metternich, less indeed than any man in Europe with as much experience of the world. He might well be a good listener to an account of middle-class agitation. This agitation took the form of a demand for constitutions. The demand was not uniform. Under pure monarchies the middle classes wanted national representation ; in countries where a representative system was already known they asked for an extension of guarantees, fundamental laws and a written constitution. In England, where constitutionalism was most advanced, they worked for electoral reform. Everywhere, behind these pretexts, was the middle-class jealousy of power, of place, of fortune. In one

[1] It is interesting to compare the similarity between the views of Metternich and Guizot upon the fundamental political indifference of the lower classes of society, and the divergence between their views upon the educated middle class. (See below, pp. 219-22.)

of the few passages of his politico-philosophical disquisitions which show anger as well as disdain Metternich speaks of these agitators of the " classe intermédiaire de la société," as standing between rulers and their subjects, " breaking the sceptres of the kings, usurping the voices of the peoples," anxious to justify their covetousness by attacking " all the work of the centuries which has achieved a title to the respect and allegiance of human beings." [1]

How could the governments meet these attacks ? In the first place they must not lose confidence in themselves. They must be firm.   They must remember from the lessons of the past the impossibility of carrying out reforms in times of passion.   In such critical hours of history the duty of statesmen must be to maintain authority and conserve the existing order.   The principle of stability should be announced to the world as the device of monarchy. Stability does not imply immobility ; but improvement must come from above, and from constituted authority ; wise reform can be defined as the " progressive development of institutions accomplished by legal methods."   There must be no concessions to factions powerless to use what they have won.   Above all, the monarchs of Europe must be united if they wish to save society from complete ruin ; there must be a league between all the governments against the factions of every state ; in other words, no limit must be set to the principle of intervention.   Moreover, two elements must be distinguished within the enemy camp ; the levellers and the doctrinaires.   The former are more dangerous in action ; the latter never include men of strong will and determination, and are more to be feared during the deceiving calm which precedes thunderstorms in the social order.

From this point the document tails off into a number of practical measures which lack general interest to-day, and were never more than commonplace.

* * * * * *

Ten years after Metternich's exposition of his " principles "

---

[1] The vehicle of these attacks was the press. Metternich doubted whether the existence of a free press, " a scourge unknown to the world before the second half of the seventeenth century, was compatible with the continued existence of society."

to the Emperor Alexander the Bourbons were driven from the government of France. The revolution of July had its effect upon opinion in Germany and Italy. Once again Metternich was given a chance of testing, and of repeating to the world, his belief that the troubles of society came from the middle class. In France the evil had gone deeper. " In Germany the attack still comes from the middle class against the throne and the upper classes ; in France, where these two latter elements have already disappeared, the mob is now rising against the bourgeoisie. This is the logical sequence." [1] . . . A judgment which seemed less wild in 1848 than in 1831 !

In Germany the state of affairs was almost as serious : " weak or narrow-sighted princes ; an utterly corrupted middle class and civil service ; the lower orders sound, and not in need of healing." . . . The first need of every people was to be ruled ; this was understood by the German people, who were " always ready to be ruled well, or, *faute de mieux*, to be ruled badly." [2] " The politically apathetic masses " [3] were never ready to do without authority ; " but many princes have given up ruling altogether, and the middle class has insinuated itself into their place. In this short sketch stands the image of the present world. The first instrument in the hands of the middle class is the modern representative system ; this caricature of the English constitution, because it has none of the fundamental conditions whereby it could attain to its model, is a ' non-ens ' between the English monarchy based upon the aristocratic principle and the democratic free states of America." [4]

The revolution of 1830, once it had ceased to be an immediate danger, seemed to Metternich a good opportunity for awakening the bourgeoisie to the danger of supporting a movement which must lead to their own destruction. " The revolution of July and the English Reform [*sic*] have of necessity divided the liberals into three camps. One section has become wiser and attached itself to the

---

[1] Metternich to Wrede, 1831.   (Bibl, *op. cit.*, p. 284.)
[2] *Ibid.*, pp. 256-7.   [3] *Ibid.*, p. 130.
[4] *Ibid.*, pp. 256-7.

banner of the old practical support of 'right'; others have gone over to the radicals. Only a few wrong-headed and feeble people have remained on the played-out field, and have failed even yet to realise that they have no solid ground under their feet [sic]."[1] Every year, and to every correspondent, the lesson is repeated. "I prefer always to have things out in the open, and not concealed." "No one with eyes, ears, and sense to-day can doubt any longer what liberalism is aiming at, what it is, and whither it is bound to lead states which surrender to it. Before such proofs doctrine must be silent. Popular representation in the modern sense, freedom of the press and political associations must be the ruin of any state, monarchical or republican. Only anarchy is possible; the learned at their desks may protest against this as much as they will."[2] Or again: "Liberalism is but the accomplice of demagogy, and serves, very often unconsciously, to drive a road for it, and often to level it most conveniently. Liberalism shares the fate of all forerunners. Once the true lord appears it is almost impossible to find any traces of the forerunner. Nothing is further from liberalism than demagogy; this latter is categorical, tyrannical, in its ends as in its choice of means. All means are good enough; 'ôte-toi que je m'y mette' is its true symbol, and it knows how to keep true to this end.[3] For thousands of years its motto has been that the end justifies the means; the end is no other than this saying I have quoted."[4]

.   .   .   .   .   .

There was more behind this attack upon the bourgeoisie than the contempt of a grand seigneur for a class which lacked the elegancies of living. Metternich had known the contemptible and corrupt society of the Directory, or at

[1] Metternich to Wrede, 1832. (Bibl, *op. cit.*, p. 356.)

[2] Metternich to Wittgenstein, 1832. (Bibl, *op. cit.*, pp. 170-1.)

[3] There is an inscription on a house at the French spa of Plombières which exactly bears out Metternich's favourite quotation. The house was built for the ladies of the noble order of Remiremont. It passed into the hands, among others, of the princesse de Saxe, the cardinal de Rohan, the princesse de Lamballe (who was torn to pieces by the Paris mob during the revolution). The next occupant was the citizen Reubell, himself one of the Directors! The last name on the inscription is that of Napoleon III.

[4] Metternich to Wrede. (Bibl, *op. cit.*, p. 368.)

any rate those members of this society who had accepted
Napoleon's terms—and Napoleon's titles.   When he thought
of a renegade upper class, there was an " Anacharsis "
Clootz, a Mirabeau, a Talleyrand, or a Barras to prove
his case.   There was some truth in his view that the lower
classes in France, Germany, and Italy were indifferent,
at all events for the time, to revolutionary agitation.   The
political reforms which would give office and importance
to the liberal bourgeoisie had little interest for the agricultural labourer, the small proprietor, or the factory worker.
On the other hand, Metternich did not see that the protection of property could hardly appear the first duty of
government in the eyes of the landless and propertyless
members of society.   Metternich was not without pity for
the workpeople and the peasantry.[1]   It is as much to his
credit as to theirs that the men on his estate offered to
protect him when he was forced to escape from Vienna in
1848.[2]   But he had no particular interest in the "social
question."   He shared the views of the eighteenth century
about hours of labour ; views based upon the habits of
peasants working in their fields.   He once praised in terms
worthy of Defoe the arrangements of a factory where
children could work out of school hours.[3]   The contempt
which Metternich showed for the middle class had an even
slighter basis of truth.   The middle class in the early nineteenth century was narrower in outlook, as it was smaller
in numbers, than the middle class of fifty, a hundred years
later.   It had fewer opportunities for travel or recreation,
less chances—and in the case of its womenfolk practically
no chance — of obtaining a liberal education.   Yet it
would hardly be possible to exaggerate the work done for
Germany by the Prussian civil servants and teachers in
the first half of the nineteenth century.   Their impatience
of the control of the German states by a less honest and less
cultured, if more " finished," upper class was a sign of
health rather than of disease.

There was however a rough truth in Metternich's estimate of the helplessness of the professorial and academic
class in action.   Metternich wrote to Gentz in 1819 that

[1] *Mémoires*, iv. 23.   [2] *Ibid.*, viii. 3.   [3] *Ibid.*, vi. 202.

revolution would never come from the German universities, though a revolutionary generation might be formed in them. The students were only boys ; as for the professors, " there could be no clumsier conspirators than the professors, taken individually or together. A revolution could be successful only if it were directed against things, not against dogmas " (though Metternich was forced to admit that the professors of theology were dangerous). Savants and professors were useless in action, and had little real wish to apply the revolutionary principle : " ôte-toi que je m'y mette." The lawyers were a more serious problem. Scarcely any savant understood the value and importance of property, but lawyers were always dealing with it. Professors were theorists ; lawyers were practical men.[1] Yet when all this has been said, Metternich, like Bismarck, misunderstood the world in which the bourgeoisie lived and moved. The concentration of upper-class statesmen upon the practical management of affairs made it impossible for them to look at the world with the detachment of the middle class. The social canons of their time, accepted by Metternich and Bismarck without question, the outward display and magnificent apparatus of the life of the aristocracy, made it difficult for men accustomed to judge events largely by their external displacement and immediate effect to see that the intellectual leadership of Europe had passed into other hands ; into the hands of a class without the old sureness of touch and easy acceptance of rule, but with a new seriousness, a new knowledge, a new political capacity, and, in the last resort, better manners.[2]

[1] *Mémoires*, iii. 262.

[2] Metternich's third wife probably did her husband a great deal of harm by cutting him off entirely from contact with the highly cultivated upper bourgeoisie of Vienna ; a society with which he had a great deal in common, particularly in his later years. Princess Mélanie refused to entertain any one below her own station. The well-known story of the barricade of card-tables set up by the princess and her friends against the ladies of the upper bourgeoisie at a charity ball throws some light upon the causes of the revolution of 1848 in Vienna. In 1852 the princess noted in her diary that she met (at a ball given by Schwarzenberg) the " second society " of Vienna ; the women of this society were overdressed, and there was no trace of " fusion " with the " first society." (*Mémoires*, viii. 123.)

IV

METTERNICH AND THE AUSTRIAN PROBLEM

METTERNICH as a practical statesman must be judged by his own standard. He assumed that the stability of society was secure only so long as men gave heed to the moral law and to the ineluctable conditions of their physical environment. Histories of diplomacy, and the evidence of his own letters, show how lightly Metternich could treat the moral law in the choice of means to an end, in the skirmishes wherein he confessed himself no good commander. How far did he understand the second factor which should determine the actions of statesmen ? How did he interpret the necessities of the environment, " les besoins créés par les localités," when he was dealing with the " historic " problems of Austria-Hungary, of Germany, of Italy ? The measure of his knowledge of these conditions must be the test of his practical wisdom ; the consistency of his action, based upon such a knowledge, must be the test of his power of will ; the results of his action must be the test of his achievement and provide material for the verdict of posterity to which alone he looked for justice.

Consider first the Austrian empire. Politically, this empire was composed of " different provinces united under one sovereignty by reason of historical fact, legal arrangement, measures of prudence, or the force of things." [1] In other words, it was a geographical unity. Physical geography determined the unity of the empire within its borders ; historical and economic geography determined the political connexion with north Italy and the states of Germany. The empire was formed round the Danube basin ; towards this basin were directed the inward slopes of its frontier mountains. These mountains were as natural a means of defence as Vienna was a natural meeting-place

[1] *Mémoires*, i. 117.

of roads.   The different races deposited within these mountain barriers during the chaos of the barbarian invasions and migrations of the peoples had a certain predetermined political unity ; no one race or nationality had economic or military or political self-sufficiency.   Therefore no one race or nationality would be wise to push to its logical conclusion the idea of the national state.   Those who believed that " nationality " was enough to justify an absolute political independence were fighting against mountains and rivers, against a distribution of corn lands and high pastures, trade routes and minerals.   Such a conflict with " les besoins créés par les localités " could never lead to an equilibrium within this microcosm of Europe.[1]

Nevertheless the racial and national differences could not be ignored ; they too were a part of the environment : the legacy of a Roman empire unable to defend its frontiers against invaders.   Hence the paramount importance of the Habsburgs.   The Habsburgs were more than a reigning house ; their policy was more than dynastic.   They were the embodiment of an historical idea ; one of the necessities of a particular environment.   Their European mission had been to save and extend the eastern frontier of European civilisation (Metternich, like Napoleon, would not regard Russia as a " civilising " state) ; their mission within their own dominions was to protect the rights of the different nationalities, and to safeguard the pre-eminent claims of the most civilised nation, the Germans.   There could be no substitute for the house of Habsburg.   The personality of the emperor might be unequal to the high dignity and burden of his office.   Such was the paradox of the Emperor

---

[1] This belief in the " historical " necessity of a state uniting the inhabitants of the Danubian basin was found in unlikely quarters after the revolution of 1848.   Count Palacky, the Czech nationalist, wrote : " The true life-stream of this necessary union of peoples is the Danube ; its central authority ought not to go far from this river. . . . In fact, if the Austrian imperial state had not been in existence for a long time the interests of Europe and humanity would at once demand its creation." Without this unity, the peoples of different race and language bordering the Russian frontier could not hope to stand against the overwhelming power of Russia.   (See Redlich, *Das Österreichische Staats- und Reichsproblem*, 1. i. 149.)

Ferdinand who succeeded Francis I. in 1835. Ferdinand's mental and physical incapacity could be reckoned among those difficulties which belonged to the nature of things and could not be avoided. In such a case the principle must be safeguarded by finding a way round the present trouble. Count Ficquelmont, in an analysis of the causes of the revolution of 1848, described the consequences of this " interregnum of sovereignty." " An idolatrous cult of the principle of monarchy " might make it possible to fortify the sovereign power, and at the same time dispense with the personal initiative of the sovereign. This power therefore was thought of " as an ark of the covenant, upon which no one dared to lay his hand. If it were necessary to set it in motion, in order to show it to the people, the greatest care was taken that no one should approach it too closely. This sanctuary, this altar upon which was set a principle hallowed by right, was covered with a veil, and every effort was made to make this curtain impenetrable." [1]

Federalism was no real solution of the difficulty of combining local and national interests with the common interest of the empire. If federalism meant nothing more than administrative decentralisation, it was not enough to satisfy the extreme nationalists ; if it meant a real recognition of national independence, it would endanger the cohesion of the whole. The federal solution was made impossible by the existence of racially " mixed " districts and enclaves, by the attraction of racially related peoples outside the empire, by the traditional superiority of Germans and Magyars. No Austrian statesman, least of all Metternich, who claimed the Vienna settlement as his master-work, could be expected to sacrifice the position which Austria had gained in Italy ; to risk a war with Hungary in the interest of the Slavs ; to surrender to Prussia the hardly-won leadership of the Germanic confederation. Yet only on these terms, if at all, could federalism be attained.

The historical and physical conditions which demanded the Habsburgs also limited their action in two ways. They must take account of the differences of race, culture, language,

----
[1] Quoted in Redlich, *op. cit.*, I. i. 71-2.

and tradition within their empire. The unfortunate experiment of Joseph II. must not be repeated. The aim must be unity, not amalgamation. Any process of levelling must be considered in historical rather than logical terms, and must avoid the temptation of haste. The culturally superior race, the Germans who alone understood the meaning of the term " state," must civilise the rest of the empire, but must not attempt directly to " Germanise " it. In 1846 Metternich commented upon the methods of the French who used the term " Polish nationality " when they meant the " political predominance of France " in the east, as in the west, of the European continent. " One knows how the French interpret the respect which should be paid to nationality ; witness the empire of Napoleon, when Rome and Hamburg became ' villes frontières françaises,' and ten or twelve million Germans or Italians were declared to be ' Frenchmen.' Austria has never put forward a claim of this kind. . . . This sort of juggling with words has never been to the taste of the Austrian monarchy ; never has this monarchy given the name of Germans to Hungarians, Italians, or Poles. On the other hand Austria has always concerned herself with the common life of the different races linked together in political union. . . . And it is to Austria that the French venture to preach the doctrine of respect for nationalities ! " [1] There is special pleading here, no less than in the French concern for Poland in general and the republic of Cracow in particular. But Metternich was always careful to define what he meant by the policy of strengthening the German element, " the civilising principle " in the Magyar or Slav regions of the empire.[2] " I do not mean what is generally understood by the term ' Germanise.' The ' transformation ' of a race is a long process, and takes place under the influence of circumstances peculiar in themselves.[3] We must aim at

[1] *Mémoires*, vii. 212.

[2] In 1817 Metternich spoke of the task of " civilising " Hungary. (*Mémoires*, iii. 65. For Metternich's Hungarian policy see Srbik, *op. cit.*, i. 465-71.) In a letter written to Kübeck in 1850 Metternich remarked upon the prominence given by Joseph II. to the Germans as the " civilising " element in the Austrian empire. (*Metternich und Kübeck, op. cit.*, p. 59.)

[3] *Mémoires*, vii. 214.

the development of the Germanic element . . . through the effect of its prestige and its civilisation in the true sense of the term."

On the other hand, the common life of the different races could not find expression in a general constitutional parliament. This form of unity would be artificial and unhistorical. Nor was a parliament of this type necessary to safeguard the interests of the nationalities. The Austrian emperor, wrote Metternich to Wrede in 1831, was not " absolute " ; all parts of his empire had constitutions ; but these constitutions were a legacy of the past, and therefore not " representative, nor based upon popular sovereignty." [1]

Modern political writers are in agreement, or at any rate in sympathy, with Metternich in his refusal to consider the establishment of an imperial parliament. The experience of the latter days of Austrian history showed that the solution for the jealousies and the conflicting interests of the different nationalities within the empire did not lie in bringing representatives of the nationalities into the excited atmosphere of a grand assembly. Since Metternich's time Europe has had another century of parliamentary experience, and has learned, like Chatham in his maturer years, to consider the instruments of government more coolly.

Yet even when right, or common sense, was on his side, Metternich was too doctrinaire. Was he justified in keeping a hard and fast line between the principles of monarchy and of popular sovereignty? Was it certain that any deviation from the principle of monarchy must lead to the other extreme? The representative system could not have been applied to the empire as a whole ; there was much to be said for its application to the parts. The local and national assemblies of magnates might have been afforced by representatives from other classes. Long ago an English king had made the experiment, with the most fruitful and far-reaching results. Metternich's answer would have been that the age of easy political experiment was closed, and that in a society more compactly knit

[1] Bibl, *op. cit.*, p. 249.

together the consequences of failure were more disastrous.
France had taught this lesson to the whole of Europe.   If
the shock had been too great for the European state most
favoured by geographical position and past history, most
advanced in culture, and most disposed to novelty, what
hope was there for the assimilation of a new principle in
the empire of the Habsburgs ?   Partial concessions must
have involved surrender of the entire position.   The magnates would never have been willing to give up their monopoly of power ;   the nationalities would never have been
content with local representation.   Furthermore, the idea
upon which the representative system was based applied
as little to the nationalities as to the empire as a whole.
Behind the idea of representative assemblies was the
liberal theory of society as a mass of individuals, each
possessing equal rights.   The first requirement of
Austrian conditions was the correlation of the claims,
not of individuals, but of nationalities ;   nor could progress come from a theory which regarded popular
representation, in any form, as the safeguard of individual rights ;   the very existence of these rights depended
upon the definition and limitation of the privileges,
rights, and duties of the nationalities ;   an equilibrium
—here we are back again at the foundation of Metternich's political beliefs—which could only be secured by
an extra-national power ;   an authority standing outside
the conflict, and interested pre-eminently in the maintenance of the balance.

For better or for worse, the empire required the personal
sovereignty of the house of Habsburg ;   a policy of
wise administration which would secure unity without
destroying diversity ;   a careful levelling up of the less
civilised nations and classes, and a steady financial and
economic policy.   All these things Metternich saw.   Yet
his long tenure of power brought about no change for
the better in the relations between the races or the
classes within the empire ;   no improvement in the
bureaucracy, or in the administration of the imperial
revenues.   Hungarians, Czechs, Italians tried to break
away in 1848 ;   upper class and bourgeoisie, bourgeoisie

and people never worked together for more than limited or destructive ends.[1]

Were the events of 1848 a condemnation of Metternich's statesmanship ? The settlement of the Austrian problem was a task beyond the powers of any one man ; by definition, it needed favourable European conditions, the direction of an enlightened emperor, and the co-operation of an enlightened upper class. The position in the autumn of 1815 might have seemed extremely favourable. Napoleon was gone ; Austria was at peace, and might reasonably expect that the territorial settlement made at Vienna would last for a generation. Within the newly defined frontiers of the empire there was no effective desire for separation. The emperor had won a certain popularity by his patient endurance of misfortune. The government had the prestige of victory.

The revolutionary and Napoleonic wars had come upon a state already disorganised and disorientated by the excessive centralisation and excessive haste of Joseph II. The Habsburgs could not afford to be without a sense of history. Nearly twenty-five years of war (and only two of victory) had left the country without money, and without any settled policy. The bureaucratic routine had been confused by changes of direction which had followed defeat. The training of civil servants had been interrupted by annexations or sacrifices of territory. The intelligence of the state had been occupied with war and preparation for war. An immense labour lay in front of the government. Yet there was no machinery for carrying out, or even for thinking out, any co-ordinated scheme of reform. Cabinet government, in the western European sense of the term, and ministerial responsibility were unknown in Austria. The person of the emperor was the only connecting link between the different branches of the administration, just as the imperial house was the only bond of union between the different races and nationalities of the empire. Maria

[1] Let an Englishman who finds it hard to be gentle towards Metternich's denials and refusals consider English history from one of two points of view : the Irish question, or the relations between the Dominions and Great Britain in fiscal matters and the control of foreign policy.

Theresa had instituted a council of state ; but owing to pressure of business this body had become subdivided into a number of sections, unco-ordinated with one another and with the regular bureaucratic departments. These departments were organised upon a collegiate system which precluded individual responsibility and destroyed initiative.

The interference of the emperor added to the confusion, the delays, and the arbitrariness of every branch of the service. The fiction of imperial omniscience, when translated into fact, meant that the emperor discussed questions with whatever minister or departmental chief or court officer he might choose to take into his confidence. He could not act with full knowledge ; the reports which he received and the instructions which he gave were one-sided, without sequence, and destructive of any uniform and deliberate policy.

It is to Metternich's credit that he tried to introduce a better system. He had seen the working of Napoleon's *conseil d'état*, and knew the importance of a clear and single direction of public business. He proposed the establishment of a similar institution in Austria. The plan, as might have been expected, met with the strongest opposition when it was first brought forward in 1811. Metternich's criticism of alternative proposals, and the great prestige of his position, at last persuaded the emperor to agree to an advisory council. In 1814 this council came into being. Its purpose, according to Metternich, was to reinforce and give material form to the unity of the empire, and to prevent this unity from becoming merely a dynastic connexion, dependent in the last resort upon the marriage policy of the Habsburgs of an earlier age.[1] The council was

---

[1] The extreme complexity of the Habsburg administrative system can hardly be explained in anything short of a treatise. Not only is the machinery without parallel in England, and therefore scarcely comprehensible to Englishmen without careful study ; the terminology of chancellors and aulic counsellors, of auditors and presidents, is confusing. Metternich's proposals of 1811 and of 1817 are printed in his *Mémoires*, ii. 442-51, and iii. 63-75. References to his intentions are also given in the *Mémoires*, i. 117-18 ; viii. 527-30 ; and (in a long footnote) iii. 75-7. Metternich's attitude towards the administration and his plans for reform are well described in Srbik, *op. cit.*, i. 456-64. Srbik assumes that his readers understand the organisation which Metternich attempted to reform.

to contain all the chief officers of state. Its business was advisory. It had no executive power, and could only deliberate upon matters brought before it by the emperor. Foreign affairs did not come within its province. Metternich felt that the subject-matter of foreign policy did not lend itself to treatment in council ; nor would it be possible to print and circulate the despatches of foreign powers and discuss in general session the relations of these powers with one another and with Austria. The experiment of a conference dealing with foreign affairs had been tried by Kaunitz ; the difficulties had been found insuperable. Metternich might have added that he had no intention of sharing his control of foreign policy with any one ; and least of all with a committee !

A proper use of this council would have made possible the wide consideration of larger schemes, and relieved the emperor and his immediate advisers of the mass of unimportant detail which occupied most of their time.[1] Yet the scheme never worked well. The members of the council were trained in the niggling, hand-to-mouth methods of the bureaucracy. They could not bring themselves to leave enough independence to the heads of departments. They were still overwhelmed with little things, and never considered the greater problems of the empire dispassionately and at leisure. Above all, the emperor would not keep the spirit of the reforms he had sanctioned. He could always annul the decisions or ignore the recommendations of the council ; he continued those audiences in isolation which precluded a proper and regular conduct of business and cut at the root of all responsibility.

Metternich had also asked in 1814 for the creation of ministries of a modern type in place of the departmental and collegiate organisation. By these means he hoped ultimately to reform the antiquated procedure of the administration, and, above all, to bring about an improvement in the management of the imperial finances ; but little was

[1] It is interesting that Metternich suggested as one of the incidental advantages of his council of state the value of such a body in the training and selection of civil servants, and in the political and administrative education of the heir to the throne.

done to carry out this plan. In 1816 Stadion became minister of finance ; while he lived a certain order was established in the business of restoring the coinage and the credit of the empire ; after his death the old confusion reappeared.

In 1817 a step was taken towards a better division of the work of the executive. The letter with which Metternich accompanied his plan of reorganisation shows the difficulty of getting the Emperor Francis to agree to any kind of administrative changes. Metternich appealed to the emperor's knowledge of his minister's character as a guarantee that he had no liking for reforms as such. He insisted that his proposals were simple, and already known to the emperor ; he agreed that the moment was not suitable for reforms on a large scale. His suggestions were in no sense radical ; they did not touch the perilous question of the Hungarian constitution. His one aim was to relieve the congestion of business due to the excessive centralisation of the day-to-day machinery of government. It was essential that some relief should be provided ; for there would come a time when the monarchy and the whole world would have to face a natural calamity. . . . In such delicate language was hidden a reference to the death of Francis and the succession of Ferdinand !

Decentralisation was inevitable, because the only alternative was fusion. The policy of fusion of the different nationalities had been abandoned after the experience of Joseph II. An attempt to revive so hazardous a plan would have an unexpected consequence ; there would be a demand for a central representative body of the united " nation " ! No more need be said—especially to the Emperor Francis.

On the other hand, if the Austrian empire, with a position almost as exposed as that of Prussia, was to develop a strength equal to its needs, care must be taken not to waste any possible source of energy. One cause of a lack of harmony (here again is the theory of an equilibrium), and therefore of friction and loss of power, was the privileged position of Hungary and its " annexed " states. Another reason was the isolation and effacement of the other provinces under the existing system of administration. " From this inequality there results for the Hungarian a privilege which exalts him to a point at which he believes himself independent, while the national sentiment of the other Austrian states—a sentiment which deserves to be taken into consideration—wastes and loses itself in conflicts between the (central) government and the provinces. Moreover, the actual organisation of the superior authority of the German nationality in the governmental organisation represents a positive tendency in the direction of fusion," while the political mechanism of the empire was based, and ought to be based, upon the opposite principles. The result was a paralysis of the machine, " a mania for interference in petty questions, which destroys the real character of the government." [1]

There could be no clearer analysis of the Austrian problem. Yet the remedy which Metternich proposed was curiously inadequate : the establishment of a ministry of the interior under a minister or chancellor-in-chief. This new minister would have four subordinates, " whose sphere of action should be determined by the nationality of the provinces and the local considerations directly arising therefrom." Within the ministry these four officers would defend the interests of the nationalities ; outside the ministry they would educate the nationalities to a large and generous understanding of the unity of the empire. The division of the non-Hungarian lands was easy enough, if no account were taken of enclaves or racial minorities : Austria and the outlying provinces in which German was spoken (Styria, Salzburg, the Innviertel, and the Tyrol) ; Bohemia, Moravia, and Galicia ; Illyria and Dalmatia ; Lombardy and Venetia ; four groups of roughly equal geographical importance, though on different levels of culture and political education. Metternich's plan was put into effect with slight modifications : Galicia was detached from the Czech provinces, and Illyria attached to Austria.

The success of the scheme depended upon a change of attitude on the part of the bureaucracy. The emperor had no wish, and Metternich no power, to work this miracle.

[1] *Mémoires*, iii. 70-1.

The result was that one more complicated piece of machinery was added to an overburdened administrative organisation. For a time there was more confusion and overlapping ; Francis took the line of least resistance, and the " reform " was abandoned. From Metternich's point of view the failure was particularly unfortunate, because it inclined the emperor to listen to the advice of others, and especially of Kolowrat in internal affairs. After Francis' death the opposition of Kolowrat, supported by the archdukes, stood in the way of any plan for the simpler disposal of the administration.

Although Metternich had rejected any idea of a representative national assembly, with its sinister suggestions of popular sovereignty, he had in mind the establishment of a council general of the empire. Some of the members of this body would be nominated by the emperor ; others chosen by and from the provincial assemblies. Its business would be the discussion of the budget and legislation of general interest.

The emperor, according to a note which Metternich left uncompleted among his papers,[1] promised to consider the plan ; but for ten years it was forgotten. After a severe illness in 1827, Francis began to think of the scheme. He delayed for another seven years ; in December 1834 Metternich was told that a decision would be taken before the end of 1835. Two months later the emperor was dead.

A new council of state ; administrative decentralisation ; respect for the interests of the nationalities ; the co-operation of those classes whose loyalty and good sense could be trusted : these seemed to Metternich the essential conditions for the good life, for the very existence of the Habsburg empire. The conditions were not realised. Here then we come to a question not of intelligence but of driving force and will power. What judgment are we to pass upon Metternich's relations with the Emperor Francis ? Was it his duty to take a stronger line, or even to resign if he could not carry through the internal reforms which he held to be necessary ?

[1] *Mémoires*, iii. 75-7, and viii. 527-30. See also *Metternich und Kübeck*, *op. cit.*, pp. 150-1.

The emperor had a certain intelligence, a sense of duty, and a willingness to work. He was shrewd in his judgment of men, and not without humour. He cared for some of the members of his own family, especially for his daughter Marie Louise, the duc de Reichstadt, and the young Francis Joseph. Even in his personal affections he was selfish. The empress complained that her health was endangered by the walks she had to take with the emperor in the heat of the day. The duc de Reichstadt might have lived to manhood if more care had been taken to keep him alive. Francis I. had the more obvious and negative domestic virtues. A Swiss observer at the congress of Vienna compared him to a good *Kleinbürger* of a provincial town. Upon these narrow excellencies industrious pane-gyrists built up the legend of the " good Kaiser Franz." No judgment upon a ruler of thirty millions could be more damning. Francis himself believed the legend ; but he had nothing of the great-heartedness, the passion, the generosity and vitality needed for the government of men. His sense of duty was satisfied by daily routine work. His pedantic legality disliked new ideas or bold resolutions ; the letter of the law meant more to him than any act of human kindness. He interpreted his responsibility to mean that everything should be centred in himself. His supervision took the form of an arbitrary interference which made the work of government a hundred times more difficult for his officers of state. Conversely, if he were necessary to the empire, the whole welfare of his dominions must be subordinate to the interests of the imperial house. " Peoples ? What does that mean ? I only know subjects." In the proclamation to his " subjects " at the most dramatic moment of his reign he struck out the word " Fatherland " [1] and substituted the word " Kaiser."

As he had no sense of wide issues—Metternich compared his method of working at a problem to the narrow penetra-tion of a gimlet—he administered but did not govern. He never trusted capable subordinates, nor supported his own men. He had come to the throne in 1792 as a young man, without much education, and without interest in science

[1] Bibl, *op. cit.*, p. 34.

or art ; he never cared for the spiritual development of his subjects. His one aim was stability, his one fear revolution.

What could Metternich do with a man of this kind entrenched behind half a thousand years of history ? His position might well be compared with that of a man standing at the wheel of a firmly anchored ship ! Nor was it to the good that, in spite of a complete difference of temper, Metternich was in practical agreement with the emperor's aim and policy. Francis and his minister were on common ground in their support of the monarchical principle and their insistence upon the need for the repression of any liberal speech or writing. Metternich cannot therefore escape blame for the " immobility " of Austrian policy.

If he were in general agreement with the emperor, would he not have every opportunity of carrying through those administrative reforms which were necessary even for the maintenance of the existing order ? Metternich was in a strong position. His services were so splendid, his reputation in Europe so outstanding, that the emperor would have found it difficult to keep him out of power, even if there had been a substitute ready to hand. His grace and quickness, his courtesy, his acceptance of the emperor's point of view, gave him the chance of putting forward proposals which would have had no hearing if they had come from other quarters. Francis felt as much affection towards Metternich as he could feel towards any one not connected with his own house ; Metternich, on his side, was attracted by the emperor's patriarchal manners and bourgeois kindness.

But there were limits to his influence over the emperor. Where affairs of state were concerned, where Francis' narrow ideas of duty came into play, none of his ministers could afford to show much independence. There is no doubt that Metternich often found in this imperial obstinacy an excuse for his own inaction ; yet there is also some truth in his words : " j'ai gouverné l'Europe quelquefois, l'Autriche jamais." This was not a chance saying. In 1829 Metternich could tell the Russian general Krasinski : " I know that the Emperor Nicholas has the idea that I can bend to my will the master whom I serve. But this is a wrong judgment upon the Emperor of Austria. His will is strong, and no one can make him do anything which he does not wish to do. He overwhelms me with kindness, and gives me his confidence ; but he does this because I follow the direction which he lays down for me. If I had the misfortune to leave this prescribed path, Prince Metternich would not be minister of foreign affairs for twenty-four hours longer." [1] Metternich was not the man to take any risks on this point. Nor is it necessary to look upon him as clinging to office out of vanity or the mere desire for power. He enjoyed office, and incidentally the enormous salary and dotations which office brought him ; yet it is clear from any reading of his character that he thought himself indispensable not only to Austria but to the peace of Europe, and believed that any minor points of difference in domestic affairs were never enough to outweigh the importance of this first and last consideration. The battle which he was fighting would decide " the future not of a single empire, but of the whole social order." [2] He wrote in 1828 to his son Victor that the world still had need of him, if only because no one else could fill his place. " It is as impossible to replace an old minister as an old tree." [3]

Towards the end of his life, in his "testament politique" he repeated the phrase that he had never " governed " the Austrian empire.[4] He gave as his reason the rigorous definition of authority in all its forms within the empire. The exercise of power was kept within narrow and clearly marked channels by a meticulousness which itself hampered the march of affairs. " One of the greatest obstacles against which I have had to contend throughout the whole course of my ministry has been the lack of energy in the internal administration." Personal rivalries, preconceived ideas had their share in producing effects which were in turn responsible for the partial failure of Metternich's work in the field of diplomacy. The claims of the different nationalities affected the system of promotion within the

---

[1] Srbik, op. cit., i. 453-4.
[2] Mémoires, iv. 545.
[3] Ibid., iv. 423.
[4] Ibid., vii. 642.

imperial service ; it was difficult to find men who were both capable and impartial. " Politically and morally, I was alone. . . . Consider the situation of our empire and of Europe between the years 1809 and 1848, and ask whether one man, one single intelligence, could transform this state of crisis into one of definite cure. I venture to say that I understood the position ; I will admit also my powerlessness to set up a new building in our empire and in Germany. This is why I attempted little more than the preservation of what was already in existence." [1]

Was this admission of the limits of his power merely an apology after the event ? It must be remembered that Metternich's experience and detailed knowledge of the internal conditions of the empire were insufficient to give to his judgment the weight that it carried in matters of European policy. In 1801 he had entered the Austrian service almost as a stranger. For the next eight years he was employed in diplomatic service outside Austria. He made his name as a diplomatist and as foreign minister at a time when he had no leisure to form an independent judgment upon the needs of the different provinces of the empire. The reforms which he suggested did not go beyond the highest posts in the administration ; with these alone was he familiar. Hence he was unable to counter the influence of the high aristocracy and the Josephist bureaucratic tradition. The aristocracy had none of the political capacity of the English peerage.[2] The whole interest of the upper class, looked at from their own short-sighted point of view, was bound up with the existing system of administration. Unless the nobles were willing to give up most of their social, legal, and financial privileges, there could be no real improvement of the agrarian situation. Unless a liberal-minded and strong-willed emperor put an end to aristocratic influence and patronage in the civil service, men of lesser birth and greater capacity could rarely find their way to the important posts.

One man might have accomplished these things. It is true that he would have accomplished them without the

[1] *Mémoires*, vii. 642-4. Cf. *ibid.*, viii. 491.
[2] *Ibid.*, viii. 192.

Emperor Francis. But by 1815 Napoleon was politically not of this world, and the little kings were come into the inheritance he had left for them. Under these conditions no ordinary statesman could have done more, unless it were to resign his post. In whose favour could Metternich have resigned? Therefore the old machinery was never modernised. The old routine continued. Metternich accepted the situation. The emperor was content; his clear-sighted minister could only look with foreboding at a catastrophe which he felt powerless to prevent.

After Francis' death this catastrophe might have come at any time. Here indeed was an occasion for resolute action. The recognition of Ferdinand as emperor contradicted the very principle of Habsburg sovereignty; the axiom that rulers should rule. How could he be set aside? Who would take his place? Could the supporters of stability come to terms with revolution? Was it not better to institute a kind of collective " mayoralty of the palace "? Yet this council of state, presided over by an archduke who would himself take no responsibility, became a battle-ground between Metternich and Kolowrat.[1] Metternich had lost his greatest supporter at court, and was unpopular among the members of the imperial family. Only the absence of any political press and any well-organised opposition, and the momentum of the slowly moving governmental machine, saved Austria from a breakdown in the ten years before 1848. " Our government is that of the Dalai Lhama, and we are his high priests." [2]

The breakdown of government—no milder term would meet the case—in Austria-Hungary was the more serious in that it deprived Metternich of the means of asserting Austrian hegemony in Germany and Italy. This hege-

[1] For an account of Kolowrat (who has left neither memoirs nor diary behind him), and of the unfortunate consequences of the rivalry between Metternich and Kolowrat before and after the death of Francis, see Srbik, *op. cit.*, i. 540-6. See also Kübeck, *Tagebücher*, 1. 2. 768.

[2] Kolowrat to Kübeck. Kübeck, *op. cit.*, 1. 2. 679.

Kolowrat once said to Kübeck that any one who was forced to serve for any length of time in the immediate neighbourhood of the emperor must be either " a philosopher, an intriguer, or a brute beast." Kübeck's answer was that " of those three possibilities most people choose the *juste milieu* ; that is to say, intrigue." (Srbik, *op. cit.*, i. 539.)

mony seemed to partake of the nature of things, and to be an inevitable corollary of the historical geography of central Europe. Austrian pre-eminence was recognised in the treaty settlements after the Napoleonic wars. Metternich saw no other protection against the military despotism of Russia and Prussia, no other guarantee that the principles of international right would continue to govern the relations of the European states, no other safeguard of the peace of the western world.

Yet this European mission of Austria carried heavy obligations. It implied a large army ; an efficient administration ; the development of industry and commerce ; a policy which should meet the needs and satisfy the pride of Germans and Italians. But the resources of Austria could not maintain such an army without starving the administration. Like another empire which had kept the marches of Europe, and had known no national independence within its borders, the cost of defence swallowed up the wealth which might have been employed in productive enterprise. As in the later Roman, so in the Habsburg empire, the administration had lost touch with the needs of the localities ; the interests of the constituent parts were sacrificed to the paramount claims of the centre. Metternich had also to face a peculiar danger which late Roman statesmen never knew. The development of industry in Austria would mean the rise of an active middle class ; a numerous and powerful class which could not be denied an active share in the government. Yet it was precisely in the middle class that Metternich saw the greatest danger to the stability of the existing order. The free activity— too free indeed, and too much uncontrolled by thought for the general interest—which accompanied the industrial revolution elsewhere in Europe was incompatible with the paternal despotism of Austrian theory and the censorship, clericalism, and immobility of the Austrian " police-state."

Nor could there be any lasting care for the particular interests of Germany and Italy. Within the central European provinces of the empire there might be a certain unity of interest, however crudely this interest was expressed or however feebly represented in the personality of the ruler or the Byzantine archdukes who made up the reign-ing house. But Italian interests and German interests were not likely to gain from Metternich's policy of stability and unchanging conservatism. Even if the unquiet spirit of political nationalism were laid, there was no chance of reconciling the simplest economic needs of Italy and Germany with those of Austria until the world had gone many years further (would that we in our time could say how many years) in understanding and enlightenment.

If therefore Austria could only maintain her influence in the outlying spheres of her authority by the force of armies, and if the resources of the empire were not enough to provide these armies in sufficient strength, was Metter-nich justified in attempting a policy which he could not maintain against any serious challenge ?

Herein is the gravest charge against Metternich. There is some excuse for his powerlessness to reform the internal administration of the empire, or to find a substitute for the *roi fainéant* who succeeded Francis I. His persistence in office when he could not carry his plans of reform might be excused under the plea of duty. At the end it was inexpedient for him to leave the control of the empire in the hands of a few archdukes and the unstable, quarrel-some Kolowrat. But if he renounced the Austrian problem as beyond his powers, ought he not to have adapted his foreign policy to the means at his disposal ? However magnificent in conception (and in the dark century which has followed the Vienna treaties there is magnificence about a policy conceived in terms of general European interest), however rich in advantages and prestige for Austria, there could be no political wisdom in a plan which ignored or defied " historical " facts.

Upon an answer to this question, more than upon his failure to remodel the internal administration of Austria, must rest our judgment of Metternich as a statesman " tout à terre, tout historique."

V

METTERNICH AND THE GERMAN QUESTION

METTERNICH claimed that his attitude towards the German problem was based upon a view of the " historical facts." Others might talk of the political unification of Germany, or even of a liberal German republic ; but the " facts " were against them. Germany was unsuited for political unity. Particularism was deeply rooted in the nature and history of the German tribes, states, and regions.[1] " The German people (*das deutsche Volk*) is made up of Teutonic tribes (*aus germanischen Volkstämmen*). It is unhistorical to imagine that any one tribe (*Stamm*) can lay claim to the title of ' German nation.' The name ' Deutscher ' is a general name : the Austrians, Bavarians, Saxons, etc., are Germans, without ceasing to belong to their own tribe. There are Germanic races outside the Confederation, *e.g.* Batavians, Flemings, German Swiss, or the inhabitants of several French provinces." [2] The interests of those different groups of Germans were different, and often mutually conflicting.[3] North Germans and south Germans differed in temperament and character and could not live together in a real political unity. Any form of liberal unification must be a " levelling down," and, as such, neither permanent nor desirable. Neither Europe nor Germany needed this artificial uniformity. A Rhinelander, with the traditions of the imperial service, and the cultural associations of the borderland between France and Germany,

[1] Metternich uses the indefinite German term " Stamm " very loosely, and indeed treats the whole question of racial distinction unscientifically. When he compared the attitude of the Germanic confederation towards the question of German unity with the attitude of the Austrian empire, he spoke of the " races of the same nationality " within the confederation, and the " differences of nationality " within the empire. (*Mémoires*, viii. 482.)

[2] *Metternich und Kübeck, op. cit.*, p. 211.

[3] *Ibid.*, p. 116.

76

might think thus of the Germans whom he knew ; but the
history of France was enough to prove Metternich wrong.
In France historical differences between north and south
had been no less acute than in Germany ; yet Frenchmen,
for all their divisions of party and belief, had outlived all
thoughts of political separation.   Metternich went further
in his analysis.   He divided Prussia, the new Prussia
created by the congress of Vienna, into seven parts—
Brandenburg, Prussia, Posen, Silesia, Saxony, Westphalia,
and the lower Rhine,[1] and regarded these divisions as a
lasting expression of differences of climate, position, tribe,
and language.[2] Geography and race migrations had made
these differences ; history had accentuated them.   The
explanation of Prussia was simple enough.   Prussia was a
state " imprisoned by certain geographical conditions." [3]
Metternich followed Frederick the Great and Talleyrand
in describing the land-hunger of the Prussians as inevitable
for a people, or rather for a government, which had undertaken the obligations, without possessing the resources, of
a power of the first order.[4] Upon this view Metternich
based his opposition to Prussia as an element of disturbance and his support of the lesser sovereignties as the
guarantee of stability within the Germanic confederation.
He thought that the Prussian land-hunger was in permanent contradiction with the reality of German tribal
differences.   From this contrast between north and south
arose the dislike of the south Germans for the militarism
and " Junkerthum " of Prussia.   If Prussia worked for disunion, Austria had no further territorial ambitions within

---

[1] *Mémoires*, iii. 182-3.
[2] *Ibid.*, iii. 181. Metternich even defended the view that, apart
from differences in language and manners, the Austrian empire possessed
more of the conditions of unification than the kingdom of Prussia.   The
territories of which the Austrian " state " was composed were more
favourably situated, and had a sharper geographical delimitation.
Nearly thirty years later Metternich returned to this view.   In 1847 he
criticised the proposals for a united diet in Prussia on the ground that
" a central representation is unsuitable for an agglomeration of units
set on a long line which lacks breadth [*sic*].   Between the needs of
localities as far apart as Memel and Aix-la-Chapelle there are few
material connections."   (*Ibid.*, vii. 372.)   " Prussia needs density."
(*Ibid.*, viii. 502.)
[3] *Ibid.*, vii. 378.   [4] *Ibid.*, v. 538.

the confederation ; her interests, her position, her resources compelled her to maintain the existing order. Austria was a " politically saturated body." [1] Out of self-interest she had come to be a guarantee of the peace of Europe. Here was the strength of the Austrian, here the weakness of the Prussian claim to the moral leadership of Germany. Prussia represented the conquering, the revolutionary and threatening power in the German-speaking world ; Austria stood for the rights of the other German states.

" In German affairs Austria makes no claim which is not in the interest of Germany. . . . Austria looks to the Confederation as the bulwark of the peace of the Empire ; the Confederation seeks from Austria the force which the Empire can provide. Between these two political entities there is a reciprocity based upon their geographical position, a ' do ut des ' in the best sense. . . . If any difference exists between their respective positions, the balance is on the side of Austria. For Austria can exist without Germany, while Germany could not maintain herself without Austria." [2]

This monopoly of righteousness must be used to further the good cause, and to strengthen the German rulers in the performance of their duty towards Europe. This duty was simple enough. As in Austria, so in the smaller states of the confederation, the business of the governors was to govern ; to bear their responsibilities, and not to attempt to share them with the middle class. As in Austria, the false liberalism of the bourgeois must be held in check until the coming of a new generation untainted by revolutionary disease. Education must be controlled in the interest of order ; subversive ideas must not be spread through the press or popular literature imported from other countries. Austria would lend her help in cases of difficulty ; and behind Austrian persuasion lay Austrian force.

[1] *Kübeck und Metternich, Denkschriften und Briefwechsel*, p. 53. (A. Beer in *Denkschriften der Akademie der Wissenschaften.* Vienna, 1897.)

[2] *Metternich und Kübeck, op. cit.*, p. 117. These expressions of Metternich's views made after the revolution of 1848 show his persistence in holding the opinion that geographical and historical reasons would nullify any liberal schemes for German unity, and that Prussian liberals only put forward the plea of " German nationality " to hide the Prussian schemes of conquest in Germany.

There could be no more superficial reading of the position. It was true that the smaller states were jealous of Prussia ; it was true that the south German princes had been willing enough to yield to the temptations held out by Napoleon. Prussia herself had shown little enough care for the sovereigns whose estates she coveted. But the strength and the success of the war of liberation had lit a fire in Germany which no censorship could put out. However much the settlement of 1815 might please the princes—and few of them were satisfied—the German people were disappointed and disillusioned. Some had hoped for a federal state ; others for an empire. A few even thought of the possibility of incorporating Holland, Belgium, Switzerland, and Denmark within a great Germany. These were indeed idle speculations, which took no account of the rivalry between Austria and Prussia ; the vested interests of the princes ; the sovereignty of the King of Denmark in Schleswig and Holstein ; and of the King of Holland in Luxembourg ; the English connexion with Hanover and the Romanoff connexion with Oldenburg. The German committee at the Vienna congress, before the fear of Napoleon had overtaken them, found it difficult enough to get any settlement at all. Their solution was at best a makeshift. They established a confederation of thirty-eight (later thirty-nine) states whose territories had formed part of the old Germanic empire.[1] The executive council of the confederation was little more than a conference of ambassadors. Austria could always count upon a majority of votes belonging to the smaller states against any strengthening of the central body at the expense of the power of the princes. Unanimity was needed for any fundamental change in the constitution.

Such a " shadow-power " was of no use to Germans, and yet was substantial enough to bar the way to further progress. Well might the men who had taken up arms in the war of liberation think that they had been tricked by their rulers. Nor was the time favourable to patience. The idealism of the romantic revival, the excitement of victory could not

[1] Thus Hungary, the Polish provinces of Austria and Prussia, Pomerania, east and west Prussia, and Schleswig were excluded.

endure to postpone the hope of national unity.   The older
generation of cosmopolitan humanists like Goethe might
be remote from constitutional struggles, but nearly all the
youth and imagination of Germany were on the side of
nationalism.   The discontent was greatest among the middle
class, yet even the Prussian conservatives were dissatisfied
with a settlement which had consolidated Austrian territory
in the Tyrol and left Prussia without a sea-coast, without
the coveted eastern lands, without a good military frontier
in the west.   When Prussia compared her gains with her
sacrifices she might well feel discontented with the maintenance of Austrian hegemony in Germany.   There was no
real foundation for Metternich's expectation of a lasting
period of tranquillity within the confederation.

For a time no danger was to be feared from Prussian
aggression.   Her king was under Austrian influence ;
her army was jealous enough of Austrian success, but
more afraid of the liberalism of the volunteers who claimed
to have won the war.   Her government had in hand a
task which would take up all the energies of the state for
a generation.   Prussia had doubled her population by the
acquisition of land in the centre and west of Germany.
Her new territories included the subjects of a hundred
different sovereignties of the old empire.   Negotiations
over the delimitation of her frontiers took ten years.   There
could be no question of granting a representative constitution, whatever Metternich might fear and the liberals
might hope.   In 1823 it was only possible to set up eight
provincial assemblies ; nothing more could come within the
bounds of practical achievement until the new subjects
of the Prussian state had learnt more about their mutual
interests, and the economic and administrative problems
had been settled.   Economic needs came first.   In the old
provinces alone there had been sixty-seven different tariff
systems ; therefore some common rule was the most urgent
necessity of the larger state.   Out of this simple need, and
not through any deep political motive, arose the Zollverein,
or customs union.   Once this union had been achieved
for Prussian territory, geography set Metternich a problem
which he had not anticipated.   Prussia now controlled the

roads and the waterways which were the main trade routes from north to south Germany. Neither Prussia nor her smaller neighbours were slow to see the importance of this position. The new Prussian tariff came into force in 1819, and covered an area inhabited by some ten or eleven million Germans. Fifteen years later the Zollverein included a population of twenty-three millions. Five millions more were added in the next eight years. Metternich was not long blind to the danger to Austrian trade, and to the strength of an economic weapon which might be used for political ends. He used every means, from smuggling (through Anhalt) to the formation of rival unions, to neutralise the effect of the Zollverein. He tried to bring Prussian tariff cases within the sphere of the confederate jurisdiction ; but Prussia replied by securing the recognition of the independent right of the German sovereigns to abrogate any part of their sovereignty, that is to say, the right to join the Prussian Zollverein. The plan of rival unions broke down. Fortunately for Prussia, there were two rivals : a southern and a middle German union. The latter was the more dangerous, since it included Hanover, Bremen, Frankfurt, Leipzig, and Dresden. The Prussian government therefore offered good terms to the southern union, whose constituent states had more to fear from Austrian economic competition. With the entry of Bavaria, Saxony, Würtemberg, and the Thuringian duchies into the Prussian system, the danger was past. The appearance of the name " Deutscher Zollverein " in 1833 showed the hollowness of Metternich's rash generalisations about race and separatism. The building of railways—an easier task in north Germany than in the mountainous districts of Austria—made the northern economic position more secure. Thus by means which did not fall within the compass of Metternich's eighteenth-century ideas Prussia had begun to build up a power in Germany to which the old talk of " land-hunger " did not apply.

Even more serious for the plan of " immobility " were the political consequences of industrialism and increasing wealth. Inevitably the " balance " between the middle class and the other classes in the German states would turn in favour of those whom Metternich most feared. Here again the danger was not immediate. The industrial revolution was late in coming, and late in its development in Germany. In 1850 the population of the thirteen largest German towns only exceeded by a quarter the population of Paris. Between 1815 and 1852 the percentage of the Prussian population which could be classed as " rural " had only fallen from 73·5 to 71·5 per cent. Agriculture was as backward as industry. Berlin kept its three great fields until 1819, Wiesbaden until 1845. Only in the eastern provinces was there much production for export. Here the great landowners grew corn for the Danzig market ; while in the west the peasants scarcely thought of more than local needs.[1]

Metternich put little store by the talk of liberals of the years about 1815 when they spoke only the language of the romantic revival ; nor did he find it difficult to lay his hand upon the centres of this talk, the universities and the press. The German, indeed the European press, of the early nineteenth century might cause embarrassment to statesmen. There was a multitude of local journals, with their circulation limited by the elementary fact that news travelled faster than newspapers. The great news agencies did not exist ; the smaller papers could not afford to spend much money upon correspondents ; their revenue from advertisements was small, and they were forced to content their readers with comments of a political kind written by journalists without much talent for a public without much instruction.

The irresponsibility of the press might cause annoyance and anxiety, but the execution of repressive measures was not difficult. The universities were a problem of another order. Care for knowledge had long been one of the sources of German strength. German scholarship had developed new sciences while France was living upon a proud tradition or was disorganised by political conflict. The university of Berlin was founded at a time of national

---

[1] The best English account of economic conditions in Germany during the early nineteenth century is in Clapham, *The Economic Development of France and Germany, 1815 to 1914.*

humiliation, and was a most splendid answer to the Napoleonic rule of force. The buildings of the university were set up in the neighbourhood of the royal palace and the military headquarters. The effects of this re-cognition of knowledge as one of the chief instruments of government increased with the years ; Bismarck had a legion of competent subordinates where Metternich was almost single-handed.[1] Here also the consequences of a far-sighted policy were not visible at once. For a time the close connexion between university and state might seem to make control of public opinion an easy task. The older German universities, like those of England, had kept their independent constitutions, and were able to use their academic liberties in a less responsible way. Most of them were set in the narrow life of the smaller German states. Their teaching staff was drawn mainly from the middle class which had as yet little familiarity with problems of government as distinct from the routine of administration. The students exchanged the narrow repression of school life for the exaggerated freedom of the universities, and knew little of that English training in the exercise of authority which at least gives men a liking for moderation in judgment. In a time before the development of organised sport there was nothing to relieve the tension or the monotony of life in the provincial university towns, nothing to take the mind off politics. The romantic enthusiasm of the age led of itself to an exalted belief in the future. Idealism and the simplest of ordinary economic motives worked together. The little principalities, the undeveloped con-ditions of the national life, offered to the ablest students or professors few chances of a great career. How different were the prospects of the middle class in the constitutional states of France and Great Britain.

Therefore from the time of the war of liberation, and the disillusionment which followed the congress of Vienna, the universities became centres of discontent ; a negative and unorganised discontent, which was none the less

[1] A month before the outbreak of the revolution of 1848 Metternich complained of the shortage of men capable of filling important admini-strative posts. (*Mémoires*, vii. 581.)

dangerous because it lacked the elements of political experience. The more serious and active professors and students attempted to organise a public opinion by the foundation of societies. A beginning was made in 1815 at Jena, whence the Burschenschaft, or German students' association, spread to nearly all the protestant universities of Germany. The government of the association was federal and democratic ; its aim was typical of the romantic age : the moral improvement of student life, and the political rebirth, not only of Germany, but of Christendom.[1]

Upon these elements Metternich fixed his attention. Unless they could be suppressed there was no hope of keeping a new generation free from the taint of liberalism and revolution. The societies could only be suppressed if their members went to extremes. Metternich's opportunity came with the assassination of Kotzebue in 1819. The assassin was a theological student. The act was not only criminal but foolish. Kotzebue was a person of no importance or influence ; but many students and not a few professors gave unguarded approval or acquiescence. The murder had followed an important and provocative demonstration of students who were keeping the three-hundredth anniversary of the reformation, and, by a useful coincidence, the fifth anniversary of the battle of Leipzig. This demonstration, known to history as the Wartburg festival, had taken place in the territories of the grand duke of Saxe-Weimar. The rulers of the Saxon duchies had shown themselves friends to constitutionalism, and had taken advantage of the clause in the pact of confederation which allowed the German princes to bestow constitutions upon their subjects.[2] Metternich took the chance which the extremists had put in his way. He was able to use the indignation of the moderate public, and the fears of

[1] The gymnastic societies started by Jahn in 1811 had also developed political tendencies of an exaggerated " Teutonic " and liberal character.

[2] Article 13 of the constituent act of the Germanic confederation determined that " eine landesständische Verfassung wird bestehen " in all the German states. Metternich had suggested the less definite term " soll bestehen." It need hardly be said that by " landesständische Verfassungen " Metternich did not mean popular assemblies based upon the recognition of popular sovereignty.

the Prussian government, to bring about a stricter censorship of the press and supervision of the universities, and
a modification of the awkward clause about constitutions.
The well-known Carlsbad decrees of 1819 were forced
through the federal council at Frankfurt, and followed by a
series of conferences in Vienna. In the interest of sound
political doctrine a watch was to be put upon the universities;
the student societies were dissolved ; a press law empowered
the governments to control all publications of less than
twenty pages. A central committee was formed to exercise
general supervision over political agitation. Article 13
of the constitution was modified by a declaration that
complete sovereign power must remain with the princes ;
there could be no recognition of popular sovereignty, no
freedom of debate in questions of public safety ; in other
words, no criticism of the Carlsbad decrees.

These measures kept Germany quiet for a generation.
Metternich hoped that at last, with God's help, he had
struck down the revolution, as he had defeated the conqueror
of the world. He seemed at Carlsbad to live again the
great days of his life. He had followed his " principles "
to their conclusion, and had carried into effect his ideas
of public right. On the opening day of the Vienna
conferences he remembered a saying of Talleyrand :
" L'Autriche est la chambre des pairs de l'Europe ; aussi
longtemps qu'elle ne sera pas dissoute, elle contiendra les
Communes." [1]

Had he done anything to strengthen Austria, or to devise
a policy in real accord with the facts of the present as well
as the facts of the past ? Was his forecast of the future based
upon a reasoned calculation of probabilities ? Metternich
hoped that he had made an end of the attempt to poison
the minds of the coming generation. Not only were his
measures of repression likely to be effective, but they
would be reinforced by the very weariness of the students
themselves. [2] No longer was there any need to fear that the
universities were educating a nation of revolutionaries.
Could there be a greater refusal to consider the slow-moving
processes of economic change ? Metternich had con-

[1] *Mémoires*, iii. 313.   [2] *Ibid.*, iii. 262,

centrated upon disturbances which had their causes in the past, and ignored the transformation of society which was taking place under his eyes. He spoke of Austria as " possessing an imposing body of moral and material forces which could be put at the disposal of the Germanic confederation."   In 1830, when Germany believed that she might again have to face an attack from France, the weakness of Austria was shown to the world. In a review of the possible contingents which the states of the confederation could provide against the common enemy, Prussia was able to offer nearly a quarter of a million men, while Austria could only spare a hundred and seventy thousand. Austrian finances were being strained beyond their power of expansion even to maintain the armed force necessary for the protection of Austrian interests ; there was no possibility of outbidding the Prussian claim to protect Germany. By 1833 the political consequences of the Zollverein were manifest enough for Metternich to draw up a report to the emperor. He did not disguise the unpleasantness of the position.[1]   The equality of rights within the confederation was giving place to a new relationship : there were now a patron and clients, a protector and states under protection.   " Within the great Confederation there is being formed a smaller Confederation, a *status in statu* in every sense of the term. . . . Little by little, under the influence of Prussia and through the necessary formation of common interests, those states which make up the (smaller) union will form a more or less compact body, and in all questions which come before the Diet—not merely in questions of a commercial nature—will act and vote in common and according to pre-arranged principles." [2] The ultimate consequences would be the extrusion of Austria from Germany.   " Prussia will make use of all the resources of her political activity ; she will employ the satisfaction of material interests to weaken the influence of Austria over the courts devoted to her system . . . to make Austria appear a foreign country. . . . If this aim seems distant enough to-day, when the sentiments of these courts are still uncertain, and the foundations of the (Prussian)

[1] *Mémoires*, v. 517-36. June 1833.   [2] *Ibid.*, v. 525.

system are not thoroughly established . . . an impartial observer, enlightened by the lessons of history and politics, cannot doubt that the links which bind Austria to the other states of the Germanic Confederation will gradually become loosened, and at last break entirely, thanks to this barrier . . . and to those clever machinations which tend to change a material into a moral and political separation." [1]

Seven years later the position had changed for the worse. After a journey through Germany and Bohemia Metternich wrote to Kübeck, the president of the chamber of finance, that if Austria could not alter her mode of action the consequences " would be of a gravity which it would be difficult to determine. . . . The creation of the Zollverein . . . has had the most unfortunate effects upon the material interests of Austria, and is bound to produce the most lamentable political consequences, if we cannot find a means of redressing the balance.. . . Without Austria, Germany is incapable of meeting external danger ; without the co-operation of the whole of Germany, Austria cannot find the means of developing her power, or of accentuating the attitude which is the foundation of her conservative influence, and the guarantee of the general peace. Austria is on the point of seeing herself in a certain measure excluded from the rest of Germany . . . and treated as a foreign country." Nor could Metternich conceal from himself the awkward fact that his policy of internal tranquillity, his fear of developing an independent and progressive middle class in Austria, had serious economic consequences. " While in the centre of the industrial movement in Germany, I observed the forces in operation, the direction which they were taking ; I felt clearly that we were in a position of inferiority because we had no commercial policy of our own, no policy which was definitely Austrian, and in harmony with the situation. I felt that our policy was passive in contrast to the incessant activity which I noticed elsewhere." [2]

[1] *Mémoires*, v. 528. The years did nothing to simplify Metternich's style of writing !
[2] *Mémoires*, vi. 561-9. October 20, 1841. This memorandum to Kübeck is an important statement of Metternich's views on Austrian commercial policy. It was followed by a ministerial council the con-

The remedy was, as usual, inadequate and superficial. Metternich wanted Austria to build a railway connecting south Germany with the Adriatic and the Mediterranean, and competing with the alternative route through Bâle. The deeper cause of Austrian stagnation was beyond remedy, or beyond the remedies of Metternich. Even the practical suggestion that Trieste might become the strongest competitor of the Italian ports was itself a condemnation of the other side of Metternich's policy : the maintenance of Austrian predominance in Italy.

clusions of which are given in a footnote to *Mémoires*, vi. 569. In another memorandum, dated December 10, 1841, Metternich set out his ideas upon the commercial policy to be followed with regard to Italy. (*Ibid.*, pp. 570-5.)

VI

METTERNICH AND THE ITALIAN QUESTION

In Italy, as in Germany, Metternich's reasoned plans for Austrian predominance were countered by a less ordered view of European society. Neither German nor Italian nationalists thought of Europe in terms of a common country ; neither German nor Italian patriots could accept as paramount the claims and the interests of European stability. Years later, when the nationalist movements had been stripped of most of their idealism, Bismarck could still write of Europe as a " notion géographique," [1] much as Metternich had spoken of Italy as a " geographical expression." Death has taken a rich harvest from this nationalism which has wasted the resources of a common European culture ; out of the record of the last hundred years it may be that a little wisdom has been learned. In the early days of nationalist excitement, before the victims of the last European war were born, there was an optimism, and almost a religious hope, that in the development of national strength lay the greatest guarantee of general progress and of European peace. Whatever his shortcomings, Metternich never thought that the future of civilisation depended upon an accentuation of its divisions. He was therefore bound to face the demands of nationalism in Italy, as in Germany, with a counter-theory of his own.

His method of approach claimed, as always, to be historical. Nations had a right to independence if their character and their environment made this independence an historical necessity. On neither ground could the Italians put forward a valid claim. The Italians were not born for action, and their political loyalties were local.[2] No

---

[1] *Die Grosse Politik*, ii. 87. (Marginal note of Bismarck to a despatch from Gortchakoff.)
[2] *Mémoires*, iii. 255.

Italian would lend his money to a city of which he could not see the church tower. Only a strong government, which the Italians could not themselves provide, would save Italy from falling into provincial anarchy. The Italians were, as Napoleon had discovered, incapable of working liberal institutions and deserved to be given a sham constitution. Nor could there be any geographical reason for uniting the country under one national sovereignty. Italy was made up of four different areas, each with peculiar features of its own : Lombardy-Venetia, Piedmont, the central duchies and the states of the church, and the kingdom of the two Sicilies. The only possible form of union would be a federation of republics, and this type of government was in itself unstable.[1] As late as 1846 Metternich spoke of the " unity and indivisibility of Italy " as " no more than a dream." [2]

Such a view of Italian conditions was superficial. It ignored the effect of those unexpected and far-reaching material changes among which Metternich was himself to include the invention of railways. Yet Italy never had been united since the Roman empire ; the Roman unity, when it had been a living reality and not a dead weight upon Europe, had been the unity not of a nation but of a number of cities. Men as different as Ranke and Cobden and Lamartine shared Metternich's opinion that the Italians were incapable of creating and directing a unified state. Even more striking was the conversion of Niebuhr to the same belief after he had lived in Rome. " Kein Italiener erhebt sich zum Nationalgefühl." If the Italians could never bring about any firm and valuable unity by their own efforts, the country would be disputed among its stronger neighbours. Spain was now out of the reckoning. French control of north Italy would be a danger of the first order for Austria. The strengthening of the kingdom of Piedmont as a barrier against French invasion was not enough. Austria must control the plain of Lombardy, the fortresses of the quadrilateral, and the Alpine passes to which these fortresses were the key. It was in

[1] *Mémoires.*, vii. 407, 416, and 388-478 *passim*.
[2] *Ibid.*, vii. 388.

the Italian interest that Austria should save the little states from anarchy or French despotism. It was in the interest of Austrian security that Austrian troops should hold, and Austrian governors rule, the Lombard plain and the Adriatic seaboard, and that the control of the foreign and domestic policy of the other states of the peninsula should be in Austrian hands. Treaty settlements recognised these mutual needs. Any attempt to upset the settlements must therefore be the work of conscious revolutionaries, or the malevolence of those who sought the embarrassment of Austria. Thus the interference of Austria in Italian affairs was justified by the logic of facts. History and geography created the need for Habsburg predominance ; the European mission of Austria could not otherwise be fulfilled. The rise of constitutionalism in Italy and the expulsion of the Habsburg influence would be followed by the collapse of " international right " as the principle which determined the affairs of central Europe. There would no longer be any barrier against the military despotism of France ; the age of war and revolution would return, without the man who made order out of chaos. There could hardly be another Napoleon.

. . . . . .

In 1815 Austrian hegemony had been restored in an Italy which had suffered less and gained more than any other country from the revolution and Napoleon. Her institutions had been remodelled. She had new codes of law, new methods of trial, new systems of taxation, religious toleration of a kind, a new experience of the art of war. Above all, she had been given a national cohesion such as the Italians had not known since the end of the Roman empire. The petty kings had been removed ; the question of the temporal power of the popes had been settled in the only way in which a settlement was possible before certain " doors in heaven " were closed. The papal states were secularised, the pope and cardinals removed to a new centre of the catholic religion. At the very last Murat might have been a king after the Italian heart, and Italy might have kept the French reforms without the tyranny of the French conscription and the French tax-gatherers. Even so, the Austrians came back with much in their favour. If Francis and his minister had to ignore the forces of the future, the forces of the past were mainly on their side. Every class in Italy wanted peace and economic relief ; the call for a contingent of eighty thousand men for the Russian campaign had been sufficient proof that no relief could be expected from Napoleon. The Habsburgs returned to Lombardy as legitimate sovereigns. Venetia had lost even the ghost of independence ; in any case the republic had been destroyed by the French. There could not be any question of its restoration. Little political resistance or intelligence was to be expected from a society whose naïf obscenity and pointless frivolity had been well represented by Casanova. The Austrians lowered the taxes and subsidised the opera and the carnival. They were safe until a new generation should become more worthy of the history of their city. The title of the " Regno Lombardo-Veneto," and the establishment of two governments, seemed to promise a recognition of the different traditions and needs of each half of the kingdom. The promise of a vice-king, and the hope that the next emperor would be crowned with the iron crown of Lombardy, seemed a guarantee against a return to a policy of " amalgamation " with the Germanic elements of the empire. The governments were to be aided centrally and locally by congregations who should ascertain the wishes of the inhabitants and advise the bureaucracy. Napoleon's concordat and most of his civil code were maintained. The peasants were supported against the landlords ; religious liberty was promised to protestants and Jews. The Austrians set up, or allowed Italians to set up, a system of elementary education as good as any in Europe.

This government might have reconciled the inhabitants to their inclusion within the Austrian empire at least for a generation. But the emperor insisted upon treating north Italy as a country which must be assimilated to the rest of the empire. He would not let himself be called king of Italy, lest he should hurt the feelings of the other kings of the peninsula ; moreover he disliked the revolutionary associations of the title. No viceroy was appointed until

1818. No care was taken to develop even the Lombard feeling of separation from the rest of Italy ; the local authorities were not given control of their own local government ; the civil service was directed by inefficient and overworked officials at Vienna ; all the most important and the majority of the lesser posts were given to Germans or Slavs. The congregations had little opportunity to occupy themselves in useful work. They drew up a petition in 1825 with demands for legal and fiscal reform and the exclusion of non-Italians from the civil service. No answer came from Vienna. The next petition, presented from Lombardy thirteen years later, asked for an increase in the numbers of the emperor's Italian bodyguard !

Thus there was nothing of what Metternich himself, in speaking of England, was to call " lightning-conductors." The dismissal of nearly all the civil servants and officers of the French period created a whole class of discontented men. The pedantry of the alien bureaucrats, honest and dishonest alike ; the arrogance and brutality of the officers ; the silliness of a censorship which would not allow Italians to read Machiavelli, Rabelais, Bentham, or Hallam ; the wrongheadedness which taught Austrian and not Italian history—all these annoyances, hindrances, and slights, trifling or serious, put the middle class out of humour with the government. Add to this the closing of the " career open to talent " which the French had offered and an Italian state might offer again, the high taxation, and an economic policy which was not primarily based upon a consideration of Italian needs. Where except among the timid, the ignorant, or the bought, could the Austrians expect support ? Even if Italy had been without a history, even if the idea of nationality and of popular government had not been spread abroad by other and prior causes, even if the independent state of Piedmont had not been the neighbour of the Lombards, the sense of a common grievance would have been enough to draw the Italians together for at least as long a time as was necessary to get rid of Austria. What resources had Metternich for meeting the danger ?

The absurdity of the position was aggravated by the

support given by Austria to the dismal rulers of the rest of Italy. Lombardy and Venetia were at least as well governed as they had ever been. Outside the territory under Austrian rule good government scarcely existed. Victor Emmanuel of Piedmont had brought back the shadow as well as much of the substance of the old régime. He re-established feudal dues, restored the judicial immunities of the clergy, and the minor privileges of the nobility. He prescribed the court dress of his youth, ignored seniority in the civil service and the army which did not belong to the years before his expulsion, and dismissed all clerks who wrote the letter " R " in the French fashion ! He would not allow the French road over Mont Cenis to be used for lawful traffic (with the result that it became a smugglers' highway), and only kept the new French bridge over the Po at Turin because it was the most convenient way from one palace to another. Yet the interests of this pitiful man were as much anti-Austrian as those of the liberals ; he was soon forced to make administrative concessions. Sooner or later his dynasty would have to choose between war with Austria and political death.

In the south of Italy the kingdom of the two Sicilies had been the scene of one of the more fantastic experiments of an English Whig. Lord William Bentinck, who commanded the English garrison in Sicily in 1812, had paid a gentleman's tribute to the beauty of his country's constitution by assisting the Sicilians to set up a parliament of two houses, with the English division of powers and, in a country where only one person in fifteen hundred could read,[1] the support of a free press. The constitution disappeared with the revival of the Bourbon fortunes, and the Tory government in England found good reason of state for allowing King Ferdinand to break his word. On his return to full authority Ferdinand bestowed upon the Sicilians a constitution of a different type which kept in his hands the right of initiating legislation, and reserved all the more important posts for Neapolitans. On the mainland Ferdinand was less hampered. He need do no more than

[1] The city of Palermo spent ten times as much upon its foundlings as upon education.

conciliate the debased populace of the "great, sunlit, wicked streets" of Naples, and keep up a good show of benevolence to impress the English visitors who wintered in Naples before the discovery of the French riviera. With these reservations his government was all that his subjects deserved. He had neither budget nor civil list ; Canosa, his chief minister, thought that the first servant of the crown should be the executioner, and that the king, if he wished, could walk upon the necks of his people !

The smaller duchies were in the hands of rulers scarcely more fitted for power. Few women have played a more ignominious part on a great stage than Marie Louise. She was married to Napoleon for her country's good. She neither loved nor hated him, but obeyed him in his prosperity and deserted him in his exile. Her son was the king of Rome. A Margaret of Anjou, or even a Marie Antoinette, would have fought to the death for him. She merely let him die in Austria. When she heard of the fall of Napoleon after Waterloo, her main concern was the pleasure of the messenger in the beauty of her ankles. Even before Waterloo the Austrian government gave her a dashing one-eyed cavalry officer for a lover, and thereby controlled the administration of her duchy of Parma. Modena was given over to Francis IV., of the houses of Borgia and Este. In spite of his own large fortune and the exhaustion of his small territory, he increased the taxes for the support of an entirely unnecessary army. The grand duke of Tuscany was almost enlightened in comparison with his brother sovereigns. He believed that a prosperous state was less likely to rebel, and took care that prosperity was combined with ignorance.

At the Vienna congress nearly all the states of the church were restored to the government of a corrupt and feckless pashadom. The provinces were sacrificed to Rome, and Rome was sacrificed to the supposed interests of the church. In return the charity and organisation of the church maintained more beggars and small functionaries than even Rome had known.[1] Consalvi, the one statesman

---

[1] It was estimated that three-quarters of the population lived upon alms, and that of the remainder three-quarters were employed at small salaries in the Vatican and the ecclesiastical bureaux.

in a hundred years of papal history, tried to reform papal administration, but could do nothing against the dead weight of clerical vested interest. When Consalvi tried to attack a nest of brigands in Sonnino (the birthplace of the ineffable Antonelli) the wives and children of the inhabitants implored the pope not to destroy their means of livelihood. Of such high prestige was the prerogative of mercy that for a time they succeeded. Even the noblest of Christian virtues was used fitfully against good government.

.   .   .   .   .   .

In such an Italy there was no chance of redressing the grievances of the bourgeoisie, no promise of better times until the poor creatures upon the thrones were sent away. There was no free press, no right of public meeting or even of discussion in any of the states. Therefore discontent was driven into secret societies. Of these the best known was the organisation of the Carbonari. From the kingdom of the two Sicilies, where the society had been founded in the Muratist interest against the Bourbons, the Carbonarist movement spread northwards. In Naples it was little more than an instrument for the furtherance of private vengeance. As it travelled north, it became more respectable. Nowhere did it attain to singleness of purpose or unity of composition. There was little positive force behind its ramifications. Too much time was given to fantastic ritual and wild talk. Dark distinctions were made between sins against members of the society and against " pagans " ; these distinctions applied to adultery and outrages against women. The local differences in the peninsula were, as Metternich had foreseen, too strong to allow of combination for one Italian purpose. In Sicily the islanders wanted the expulsion of the Neapolitans. On the mainland the Neapolitans wanted a constitution. In Rome and the Marches there was a demand for government by laymen. Romagna wanted incorporation with Tuscany ; Piedmont a liberal government under the Savoyard dynasty. A few conspirators had already thought of an Italian league under Piedmontese hegemony. Outside Italy a number of émigrés, after the fashion of their kind, preached violence in the hope of immediate success. Finally there was no real secrecy. Conditions of admission to the societies were so vague and easy that any spy or secret agent might join.

If there was little chance of immediate success, there was every chance of immediate rebellion. Rebellion would embarrass Austrian finances and give the French an occasion for interference, and would discredit Austria and the " principle of legitimacy " as the guarantees of social order. Failure in one, in two, in many little rebellions would show the Italians that the surrender of their separatist traditions was required in the common interest of the national cause. In other words, the failure of the secret societies and their conspiracies would make men see the need for the united action suggested by Mazzini, and the failure of Mazzini to secure the idealist aims of his own society of Young Italy would at last leave the way clear for the common-sense realism of Cavour.

What did Metternich think of these " facts " ? How did he propose to deal with them ?

In 1817 Metternich's eyesight had been particularly troublesome ; his doctors advised him to take a holiday in Italy. He used this opportunity to observe for himself what was happening. He drew up a report of his journey for the emperor's consideration, and gave not only his own views but the information supplied by an agent.[1] This agent, one Tito Manzi, a former Muratist minister, had been sent at Metternich's suggestion to Florence, Modena, Parma, and Rome. His investigations in the winter of 1816-1817 brought him to the obvious conclusion that there was discontent throughout Italy. He divided the embarrassments of the country into two categories : general and particular. The general distress was due in the first place to natural causes ; for three years in succession nature had treated the country " en marâtre." A second series of causes was the dislocation of trade and order during the long period of war. The particular troubles of the different states were dealt with in detail. The report began with the kingdom of the two Sicilies. Manzi re-

---

[1] For this report see *Mémoires*, iii. 76-96.

gretted that Austria had not been ready to support the Sicilian demand for separation. Metternich disagreed with this view ; his arguments reveal the weakness of the Austrian position. Austria could never have allowed the Sicilians to keep their constitution " lest the large constitutional party in the [Neapolitan] kingdom should be moved by the [Sicilian] example to enforce the grant of representative government." Here the matter ended. Metternich had the poorest opinion of King Ferdinand, and expressed himself strongly about his inferiority after the rebellion of 1820 ; yet the logic of the situation bound him to the support of this creature and his ministers. For a time he believed, or affected to believe, that the Neapolitan government was actually carrying out a policy of progress and amelioration. He wrote to his wife from Naples in 1819 : " One must see this people to get an idea of what they are like " (he is speaking of the processions at the time of the miracle of St. Januarius), " and indeed they are a hundred times more decent and more civilised than they were twenty years ago. The government has accomplished much, and is still doing a great deal of good every day." [1] He was even more confident in a letter to Gentz : " In the region of Naples in particular the population is positively content with the line taken by the government." [2]

The report comes to earth when it deals with Rome. Metternich had no illusions about the rule of the clergy in the states of the church. He appreciated the work of Consalvi. Consalvi had introduced into the papal states a form of government capable, while he was himself in office, of keeping the more dangerous reactionaries in check. He had created a small and efficient army, and done much to put down brigandage ; but he was not rigorous enough in the suppression of administrative abuses to make it at all certain that his work would survive him. In the Legations, and particularly in the city of Bologna, there was a party in favour of annexation to Austria. This would be no remedy for the discontent. Here again was the difficulty. Austria could not grant the popular and liberal government for which the Bolognese were asking. From the

[1] *Mémoires*, iii. 205.   [2] *Ibid.*, iii. 254.

day upon which Bologna belonged to Austria the city would become the centre of the party of opposition to the Austrian government in Italy. "The restlessness which to-day is clamouring for annexation to Austria would turn against us as soon as Bologna was in our possession." Metternich saw the weakness of the position, and foretold that Consalvi's reforms would not survive their author. Yet he made no attempt to meet the future ; no suggestion that the Austrian government should use its authority to secure the election of a reforming pope. When Metternich's hours of opportunity had nearly run their course a reforming pope was elected ; his election seemed to Metternich the greatest of dangers.

Manzi thought that Tuscany was not well governed, and that its population was discontented. Metternich agreed with him, but did not attempt to penetrate beyond the defects of the administration ; a better fiscal policy would mean lower taxes, and lower taxes would mean content. The troubles of Parma and Modena were treated with the same superficiality. In Modena there was no need to seek for any deeper cause of trouble than the attitude of the reigning sovereign to the former functionaries of the kingdom of Italy. These men had lost their chances of a great future, their influence, their large salaries, and everything which flattered and nourished human ambition. The grand duke had begun to see his mistake ; discontent would soon pass away. The duchy of Parma was suffering from too high taxation ; the expenses of the court and the army were too heavy for the revenues.

No serious danger was to be expected from discontent within the kingdom of Piedmont. The Genoese disliked their incorporation into a kingdom. The whole population of Piedmont felt the weight of taxation imposed in the interest of an unnecessarily large army ; but there was no likelihood of revolution. The most serious problem from the Austrian point of view was the policy of the Piedmontese government. The ambitions of the court of Turin could only be realised at the expense of Austria. Great Britain would not allow any disturbance of the balance of power in north Italy, and British influence could be used to counteract the

intrigues of Russia. Metternich does not seem to have
realised that sooner or later these ambitions of the Piedmontese dynasty would lead to an alliance with the revolution, and that the sympathy of English governments and
of the English people would turn against Austria and in
favour of constitutional liberty.

There remained the Lombardo-Venetian kingdom.
Metternich made no secret of the disaffection in these
provinces of the empire. He allowed for the good side of
Austrian rule. There was equality before the law ; the
upper class and the clergy were kept in their place ; property
was respected, whatever might be its revolutionary origin.
In all these things comparison with the rest of Italy was
entirely to the credit of Austria. But here the favourable
judgment ended. " Your Majesty is probably not unaware
of the principal causes of discontent : the slowness of the
administration ; the belief that the government intends
wholly to ' Germanise ' the Italian provinces ; the composition of the tribunals ; the regular nomination of
German magistrates to judicial posts (a continual source
of irritation to the Italians) ; and the indefinite prolonga-
tion of the dispute between the Court of Vienna and the
Holy See." All these causes of disaffection could be
removed. The emperor might quicken the routine of
administration, nominate Italians to high places in the
government and the magistrature, and give the provinces
a proof that there was no intention of " Germanising " them.
These concessions to the " public opinion and self-esteem
of the nation " (in his unguarded moments Metternich
did not always speak of Italy as a " geographical expression " !) " would have a great effect, and win over the clergy
and the press." Metternich realised that the inclusion of
Lombardy-Venetia within the Austrian tariff system had
raised the price of French and English goods to the Italian
consumer. The remedy was a closer commercial union
between north Italy and Austria and Bohemia.

It is hard to think that Metternich was really speaking
his whole mind when he told the emperor that these and
similar concessions—such as the permission to young
Italians from Lombardy and Venetia to study the Italian

language in Tuscany—would make an end of all measurable discontent, and that the Italians would come to regard Austria as " the only government which is able to guarantee to them the maintenance of public order."

Yet Metternich remained convinced that the movement for a united Italy would never get beyond the secret societies. Of these he was not afraid. They had no leaders of ability, no central organisation, no money, and no consistent plans. They were never united among themselves, and could never keep their plans from the knowledge of spies. The only danger was that other powers might make use of the societies as an embarrassment to Austria. In the first years after the Vienna congress neither France nor England would go far in the support of revolutionary elements. Russia seemed to be making mischief; but the Russian secret agents were unable to do more than agitate the secret societies ; they could have little effect upon the population at large.

.   .   .   .

The years brought no change in Metternich's view of the Italian problem. The Italians were unfitted for unity, and unable to unite. " L'Italien crie beaucoup, mais il n'agit pas." [1] . . . " En Italie on se déteste de province à province, de ville à ville, de famille à famille, d'individu à individu. Si le désordre éclatait à Florence, l'habitant de Pise ou de Pistoie se déclarerait pour le parti contraire, parce qu'il hait Florence." [2] . . . and so forth, with more repetition.

Revolution broke out sooner than Metternich had expected. In Naples, where a few months earlier the British minister had written to his government that " the quiet and prosperous state of these kingdoms affords but few subjects worthy of being brought to Your Lordship's notice," [3] the king was forced to promise the widest of concessions ; in Piedmont a military plot appeared to have the support of the heir to the throne ; in Lombardy Silvio Pellico,

---

[1] *Mémoires*, iii. 255.   [2] *Ibid.*
[3] A'Court, March 1820. Quoted in Webster, *The Foreign Policy of Castlereagh*, p. 260. The Neapolitan rebellion was the occasion of Shelley's Odes to Naples and Liberty.

one of the greatest Italian writers of the time, and Count
Confalonieri, one of the greatest names among the Milanese
aristocracy, were discovered to be the leaders of a conspiracy.   Once the risk of international complications
had been removed, the suppression of these movements
was not difficult.   Ferdinand of Naples was put on his feet
again, though Metternich felt a certain annoyance at the
king's indifference to his responsibilities.   Of the Piedmontese conspiracy Metternich wrote almost in jest : " Après
tout, les révolutions sont un peu usées ; aussi cette mode
passera-t-elle comme celle de défendre la vertu de la
reine Caroline d'Angleterre." (Metternich was writing in
1820.)   " Je ne dis pas qu'il n'y aura plus de révolutions,
mais elles seront sans consistance ; elles ressemblent aux
œillades des vieilles coquettes, elles seront accueillies
avec sympathie par les amateurs, mais elles ne passioneront
réellement que des jeunes gens et des échappés des Petites
Maisons." [1]   Metternich might well feel contempt for
those patriots " qui s'engagent à dénoncer leurs complices, si l'on veut leur assurer une prime. Quiconque
veut avoir de ces héros à dix louis d'or la pièce n'a qu'à
s'adresser à moi ; j'en ai à revendre. . . . Et c'est devant
un patriotisme de ce genre, devant de telles vertus civiques
que je courberais la tête." [2]

Yet not all these prisoners could be bought for ten louis a-
piece.   Between 1820 and 1830 Metternich was moody and
depressed about the inaction of the Austrian government.
He could not prevent the incredible callousness and
pedantry [3] of the subordinate officials in Italy.   But he
might have remembered that among those who were
atoning in Austrian or Bohemian fortresses for their part
in the Milanese conspiracy was a master of the language of patriotic denunciation.   Metternich made some
effort to persuade the emperor to behave with humanity
towards the conspirators under sentence at Laibach,
but took no interest in the fate of those kept in the
Spielberg.   No preoccupation with foreign affairs, no

---

[1] *Mémoires*, iii. 463.   [2] *Ibid.*, iii. 463-4.
[3] Such as, for example, sending an account for a rope to a mother
whose son had been hanged.

fear of offending the decrepit emperor, can excuse this neglect to see that the political prisoners of Austria were treated in a manner worthy of a civilised power.   On grounds of policy alone he ought to have brought the weight of his authority to bear upon the insolence and cruelty of the prison governors.   When Silvio Pellico's book *I Mei Prigione* appeared in 1832 it was forgotten that the author had been found guilty of high treason ; that the Austrian government had not put any of its prisoners to death, and that even the ringleaders had been released from life sentences.

During the last twenty years of Metternich's ministry there was no change in his general principles ; no better understanding of the force—and in these early days it must be called the moral force—behind the nationalist movement.   The revolutions which followed the fall of the Bourbons in France seemed dangerous only in their possible international consequences.   If Louis Philippe chose to encourage liberalism in Italy, Austria could have no hope of keeping her possessions : here again was a confession that Metternich's policy was beyond the resources of the Habsburg empire.   But the revolutionaries played into Metternich's hands by allowing the Bonapartes to take part in their movement.   A warning was sent to Paris.   The Bonapartes had appealed to Austria in terms which were not likely to encourage French intervention on behalf of Italian revolutionaries.   Joseph Bonaparte had written to Metternich in October 1830 that " Napoleon II. could alone prevent the usurpation of the duke of Orleans. . . . Napoleon, as emperor of the French, would be bound by gratitude, affection, and political interest to Austria." [1] This letter, and others in the same strain, served Metternich's purpose.   Once again the danger to Austrian predominance was staved off by dexterity and a fortunate combination of circumstances.   Yet the weakness of Austria had been shown in Italy at a time when Prussia had been able to assert her claim to provide the greater part of an army for the protection of Germany.   Nor were Italian pretensions in the least abated by another failure.

[1] *Mémoires,* v. 160.

Metternich was now nearly sixty. If he had not seen the heroic and creative aspect of the Italian movement in his younger and more receptive years, he was not likely to understand the ideas of men forty years younger than himself. He had been content with mild protests against Austrian mistakes of policy and administration when he was at the height of his power and his influence over the Emperor Francis. He was unlikely to take a stronger line of action when Europe was slipping out of his control and new rivals were disputing his authority under an incapable emperor.

There is no need to follow the details of Metternich's treatment of Italian questions between 1831 and 1848. He persisted in regarding Italian discontent as the work of secret societies. For a moment he believed that there was an improvement in the general attitude of the population towards the Austrians. The reception given to the Emperor Ferdinand by the people of Milan might be set against the effect of Silvio Pellico's book. In any case Metternich thought of an increase of disaffection merely in quantitative terms. He would not see that a movement which had begun as a protest against local misgovernment or the closing of a career for bourgeois talent might in its course discover for itself a new programme and new leaders, and win the fire almost of a new religion.[1] It is true that Mazzini, with his idealist republican hopes, was almost as out of date after 1840 as Metternich himself ; but where is the mind which claimed to be " tout à terre, tout historique " ? The election of a liberal pope was an unexpected calamity for a statesman who was not even prepared for the inevitable. Therefore in the last two years of office Metternich could only protest with increasing verbosity against a sequence of events which he could foresee but was unable to control.

[1] Kübeck noted in his diary the words of a Frenchman who had travelled in the Austrian provinces of Italy in 1825, 1827, and 1828. Italy was " le véritable paradis terrestre ; où l'homme avec sa compagne a la liberté de jouir de tout, hors une seule chose, des fruits de l'arbre de la connaissance. L'Autriche ne demande à l'esprit humain que de se faire eunuqe ; cela fait, elle lui accorde toute licence." (Kübeck, *Tagebücher*, 1. 2. 388-9.)

VII

CONCLUSION

It is impossible to doubt that Metternich had attempted a policy which was beyond the resources of the Austrian empire. Austria could not hope to maintain a paramount influence in Italy and Germany, and to bring under her domination the material and spiritual life of the people of the north sea coast and the inhabitants of Sicily. Metternich had underrated the difficulties of his policy when he accepted the view that he was the keystone of an arch ; scarcely a stone in his baroque construction was sound.

Moreover, for the fulfilment of her immense obligations Austria had not only to stay the growth of the nationalist movement, disregard the most reasonable political demands of the age, and divert to her own interest the economic forces which were working against her ; she was bound to assume that the other great states of Europe would share her views and further her purposes. This assumption was unlikely to be realised.

The European policy of Metternich had taken form at a moment of general weariness after a long war ; this policy was no less than an attempt to " federalise " Europe, as Germany had been " federalised " ; to apply to the whole continent the conditions which were necessary for the continued existence of Austria. The attempt was made in the interest of European peace when the greatest dangers to peace came from the possibilities of French aggression. The particular grouping of the powers in view of the danger from France had no guarantee of permanence. There had been difficulty enough at Vienna to prevent a break in the alliance ; the eastern question had been untouched at the congress, because its complications would divide those forces which had been united with such painful effort. The partitioning of Poland was nearly as fatal to the success

of the Vienna congress as it had been to the alliance of
Prussia and Austria in the first years of the revolutionary
wars. For the moment differences between the political
temper, the governmental traditions, and the deep-seated
ambitions of the powers of the grand alliance had been
set aside. These differences would reassert themselves ;
the personal union and understanding between the leading
statesmen upon one great issue—the overthrow of Napoleon
—could not be lasting ; the danger from revolutionary
France would diminish with the years. The passing of
time actually changed the relative strength of the powers.
Prussia grew stronger in men and resources. Between
1815 and 1848 England underwent an internal revolution,
the importance of which was guessed, but never sufficiently
considered, by Metternich. Those English historians who
have written the diplomatic history of the years between
Waterloo and the first reform act have shown how events
were weakening the bonds of the alliance even before
the death of Castlereagh.[1] The commercial interests of
England, the refusal of a colonial power to be entangled in
European questions, English dislike of absolute government
and sympathy for nations who seemed to be following the
example set by English precedents, could hardly be kept
in check by Castlereagh. Castlereagh's successors had not
worked with Metternich in the critical years before and
after the fall of Napoleon. They would not give up their
popularity in England, or put English interests at the disposal of Metternich to maintain the position of Austria in
Italy or Germany, and to preserve the Austrian scheme of
things. Metternich might call Canning a " baleful meteor "
and compare his destructive activity with that of Napoleon
during the Hundred Days ; but Canning was to have in
Palmerston a successor with even less care for the delicate
balance of European forces. Nor could Metternich keep
the eastern question from clouding the European sky and
dividing Russia from Austria and England. Greek
merchants of the Ægean Islands, Greek peasants of the
Morea, Albanian adventurers like Ali Pasha or Mehemet

---

[1] C. K. Webster, *The Foreign Policy of Castlereagh, 1815-1822.* H. W. V.
Temperley, *The Foreign Policy of Canning, 1822-1827.*

Ali, could not be suppressed as though they were professors at a German university. Long before the revolutions of 1830, as every text-book knows, the old justification for Metternich's policy had gone. He was maintaining at ruinous cost for Austria a position in Europe which no longer corresponded to the relations of the great powers. His theory of Europe was out of date nearly two decades before his fall.

His only apology was that circumstances had compelled him to develop this policy. Unless he were successful, ruin would come to the house of Habsburg, and to the European interest which the Habsburgs served. He could not change this policy without hastening the calamity. He could not resign without making his resignation the signal for a new policy. A new policy would be directed by men without his experience and, in the last resort, without that despair of ultimate success which was the only safeguard against immediate failure.

The later years of Metternich's career, before his fall in 1848, show every sign of this clear-sighted despair. Most statesmen of long life have to meet in old age the consequences of the mistakes of their youth. To some changed circumstances give an occasion for repairing or, at worst, concealing, their errors of judgment. Metternich had no chance to gather up these wasted arrows. Like Guizot, he was forced to be content with a noble disdain of failure. Like Guizot, he believed in a future whose shape he could not outline ; a certain instinct, through all his obvious shortcomings, made him sure that the coming generations would do justice to his aims. His care for European peace, his refusal to take the loud-spoken claims of nationalists at their own valuation, or to think in terms other than those of the well-being of many millions of men of different nationality and place and language, may redeem much of his narrowness and some of his mistakes.

Good intention, intelligence, and persistent loyalty to a cause do not transform ability into statesmanship ; nor can the name of statesman and the title of greatness be given to one who could only see difficulty and danger in the thoughts and plans of betterment cherished by a whole generation of civilised men. Even a sense of what might be achieved cannot avail without that magnificence of execution which takes men in their good hours, and from these good hours builds up the future. Rousseau believed that the legislator was of the nature of God, and that his appearance was a miracle. There is nothing of the miraculous about Metternich.

II
GUIZOT

I

INTRODUCTION

GUIZOT has left as a memorial of his life eight volumes of memoirs,[1] and another five volumes of public speeches.[2] The speeches were for the occasion ; much of their interest has vanished into the darkness which happily overtakes the detail of parliamentary debates and election addresses. The memoirs were put together from ten to thirteen years after the fall of Louis Philippe, and more than a generation after the earliest of the events they describe. The affairs of a moment, the lesser rivalries had fallen into their true proportions. Guizot could write more coldly of his own failure because the republicans who had brought about the fall of the monarchy of July had themselves failed upon a more terrible scale. " Aujourd'hui tous les partis, je pourrais dire, tous les hommes qui ont pris part à la révolution de février, sont, comme moi, des vaincus." [3] Universal suffrage, which Guizot's opponents had proclaimed to be the gage of freedom, had established the empire of a more charlatan Napoleon ; this empire had again brought order without liberty.

It was in the nature of the man that his memoirs should be universal history rather than biography ; that he should write almost without passion, and without personal reference. He appears as a statesman acting upon certain principles, in certain circumstances. He discusses the

---

[1] *Mémoires pour servir à l'histoire de mon temps.* 8 vols. 1858-1861.

[2] *Histoire Parlementaire de France. Complément des Mémoires.* 5 vols. The *Mémoires* and the *Histoire Parlementaire* (with its long introductory essay : *Trois générations : 1789 ; 1814 ; 1848*) contain the substance of most of Guizot's political pamphlets. Some of those pamphlets were republished by Guizot in 1869 under the title, *Mélanges politiques et historiques.*

[3] viii. 521. [The *Mémoires* are cited in those notes simply by reference to the volume and pages concerned.]

principles ; he describes the circumstances ; he relates the acts. Other men appear, and are judged in the same light of general principles. There is no humour, no irony. A cold magnificence, a splendid disdain set a barrier between Guizot and the men whom he governed. They and their posterity have a right to know his conduct of the great business of state, the immediate or distant ends he tried to serve ; all else is his own.

Yet the setting of his life is of peculiar interest.[1] His father ; a protestant bourgeois of Nîmes, marked out in his time for a fine career, but put to death by the Jacobins in 1794, when his elder son was only seven years old. His mother ; strong in body and mind, long-lived and imperious, tempered by misfortune to a high sense of duty, with a love of teaching, and a full share of the intellectual curiosity of the eighteenth century. His first wife ;[2] a woman of character and great gifts of mind, fourteen years older than her husband, and to the last caring for him and understanding him to the fulfilment of self-sacrifice.[3] There is one reference, grave and noble, to the deep happiness of this first marriage. Years later, he speaks of the death of his eldest son. Beyond this there is almost nothing that is not political. More is said about the Holland House circle in London than about Guizot's own friends in Paris. After 1840 he was in the habit of visiting Mme de Lieven —now a woman approaching sixty—twice or three times a day. With her he discussed all the business of the chamber ; at her house he met the great European diplomatic families whose doors were in general closed to the bourgeois of July. Yet there is only one casual reference to her in the memoirs.[4]

[1] There is a good account of Guizot's life by his daughter Mme de Witt : *M. Guizot dans sa famille et avec ses amis*. (4th edition. Paris, 1880.) Mme de Witt also published a volume of Guizot's letters : *Lettres de M. Guizot à sa famille et à ses amis*. (Paris, 1884.)

[2] Mlle Pauline de Meulan. In March 1807 Guizot heard by chance that Mlle de Meulan and her widowed sister (neither of whom had he ever seen) were in serious financial difficulties. He at once sent articles in Mlle de Meulan's name to various journals. See *Guizot dans sa famille*, pp. 36-44.

[3] See *ibid.*, pp. 96-8.

[4] Still less was he likely to mention (for example) that one of the causes of the success of his dinners at the London embassy was his good fortune in inheriting Talleyrand's cook !

Even of his historical and literary work Guizot speaks only in connexion with greater impersonal things. He never mentions that as a young man he (like Moltke) translated Gibbon ; that he published translations of Shakespeare.

His memoirs were to be a contribution to the history of his time. As such they are among those pieces of historical writing which will remain for the world. Guizot told the Austrian ambassador in Paris why he had chosen such a title. "Thucydides and Machiavelli wrote and published contemporary history. Why should not I do the same?" The ambassador's comment was "Comme c'est Guizot." [1] In reviewing the first two volumes Renan said that the style of M. Guizot was " le vrai style des grandes affaires." [2] Whether it is in the summary of political events, or in the recording of a judgment, or the expression of hope or foreboding, there is the same grand manner ; a certain Roman massiveness and antique order. Guizot shared with Metternich among contemporary statesmen a proud belief in the ultimate, the cosmic rightness of his first principles. Experience justified them : " l'expérience, qui est le suffrage des siècles." [3] Metternich, the lesser character, had vanity as well as confidence. When Metternich gave as the explanation of the revolution of 1848 in Austria, " c'est que j'ai gouverné l'Europe quelquefois, l'Autriche jamais," Guizot thought him conceited and superficial. When Metternich, half seriously, claimed that " l'erreur n'a jamais approché de mon esprit," Guizot answered that he had himself been more fortunate in that he had more than once found out his mistakes.

The answer was wide of the mark, for Guizot's greatest mistakes were those which he never found out. Nor was he inclined to doubt his own rightness. In 1857 he

[1] Hübner, *Neuf ans de souvenirs d'un ambassadeur*, ii. 85. Guizot, in his letters, speaks of Cromwell and Washington as two men whom he had known (through writing about them) " comme si j'avais passé ma vie avec eux." (*Lettres de M. Guizot*, p. 278.)

[2] *Revue des deux mondes*, July 1859. Sainte-Beuve has given an admirable description of Guizot's style : " Son style, aux beaux endroits, a des reflets de cuivre, et comme d'acier, mais des reflets sous un ciel gris, jamais au soleil." (*Causeries du lundi*, i. 322.)

[3] *Hist. Parl.*, i. 221.

H

could read again "avec une satisfaction presque sans mélange" a book he had written in 1821.[1]

But the difference between the two men was that Guizot had made his most splendid claims in the face of a violent parliamentary opposition. It was after the wildest scene in the French chamber, after the most savage attacks and interruptions, and at the close of a speech which had lasted two hours, that he told his enemies : "et quant aux injures, aux calomnies, aux colères extérieures, on peut les multiplier, les entasser tant qu'on vaudra, on ne les élèvera jamais au-dessus de mon dédain."[2] Thus might have spoken a great orator in Rome. Twenty years later Guizot found pleasure in the memory of this Tacitean ending. It is indeed worth the boredom of a thousand debates. But it was no final answer to those who had used his past history to disprove his present infallibility. Yet he was no less confident, only more charitable, when he began his account of the last few months of the July monarchy by the claim that he was still firmly attached to the beliefs which had then governed his conduct, "mais peu surpris que les hommes d'un esprit éminent et d'un cœur honnête aient obéi à des convictions différentes."

This constancy of hope was in itself noble. Cynicism might have been pardoned to any Frenchman whose active life had been set under the empire, the restoration, and the monarchy of July, and who contemplated in his retirement the collapse of the second republic and the public life of the second empire. Yet Guizot was able to speak of the "sot orgueil" of those who disbelieved in the rule of moral ideas. He was sure that these ideas were beginning to govern the intercourse of nations.[3] He could speak of the justice, the happiness, the security of his own time as

---

[1] *Des moyens de Gouvernement et d'Opposition dans l'état actuel de la France.*

[2] *Hist. Parl.*, iv. 238 (and, as is often the case with Guizot's quotations from his speeches, with slightly different wording in *Mémoires*, viii. 71). This speech was made on January 26, 1844. It was not merely a sudden expression of anger. Fourteen years earlier Guizot had told the deputies that the rule of liberty meant "liberty for the false as well as for the true," and that "dans le régime où nous vivons . . . les corps politiques, comme les individus, ont besoin de se munir d'une large provision de facilité, et quelquefois même de dédain." (*Hist. Parl.*, i. 167.)

[3] ii. 77.

beyond the dreams of earlier societies.[1] This progress was
gradual, and was more apparent by comparison with the
past than by observation of the present. There might
seem to be no improvement in the political life or the international relations of states. Guizot knew that reasons of
morality and practical sense could do little enough towards
keeping the passions of men within the limits of right. He
knew (and pointed to the utopian socialists as an example)
how easily men of high intelligence could be deluded by
the slightest element of truth into accepting the most monstrous errors.[2] But he could write in 1850, at the end of
his active life, " la vie, selon moi, vaut bien ce qu'elle
coûte " ; in all who thought otherwise there was either
egoism or weakness.[3]

This clear-sighted serenity gave a completeness to Guizot's
political career. Whatever the immediate results, he was
working for a day which must come. There was no haste,
no enclosure within the success or failure of a few years, no
narrow personal ambition. " Impatience irritates and
displeases me. I have need to believe that I am doing
what I wish to do ; I am willing to accept necessity in
order to escape even the appearance of constraint." [4]
Exaggeration meant falsehood ; impatience meant disorder ; " I hate vagueness of statement, and decisions taken
in haste." On the other hand : " I have a full confidence
in facts, when they are considered on a wide enough scale,
and come up for judgment after passing the test of time." [5]

Like Metternich, Guizot had that sense of the future
which is a sure sign of political greatness. " J'ai horreur
de l'oubli, de ce qui passe vite : rien ne me plaît tant
que ce qui porte un air de durée et de longue mémoire." [6]
For the future he wrote the history of his political life.
" Most men and most things are doomed to forgetfulness,
however great a stir they may have made in their day." [7]
He knew that the history of the day before yesterday had
little interest for those who had taken no part in it : he was
content to wait for the turn of the wheel. " Many years,
perhaps even centuries, must pass before the history of a

---

[1] v. 401.   [2] ii. 205-6.   [3] *Lettres*, p. 304.   [4] v. 177.
[5] *Hist. Parl.*, i. 182.   [6] v. 134.   [7] vi. 244.

recent age again takes hold upon men's thoughts and interests. It is with a view to this distant return that the actors and spectators of the immediate past can and should speak of their own time." [1]

For external display Guizot cared as much and as little as most men of his power and ability. When in 1846 the queen of Spain and Louis Philippe offered him dukedoms he wrote to the French ambassador at Madrid : " I am neither a Puritan nor a democrat. I have no contempt for titles, or indeed for any of the external signs of greatness. No contempt for them, yet no desire for them. If we had a house of hereditary peers, if I could leave my titles and my honours to support my descendants in their mediocrity of talent or of fortune, then perhaps I might act differently." [2] (It is amusing to compare Guizot's pride in his name with Mme de Lieven's remark : " Me voyez-vous annoncée Madame Guizot . . . ! ")

This cool and far-sighted balance of forces is again characteristic of the man. He can admit that personal motives may have weighed too strongly in his attack on Molé in 1839. " Even for the most honourable of men, the life of politics is no affair of saintliness. There are certain necessities, certain dark passages, which a man is bound to accept because they are bound to affect him. . . . No one, if he is an honest critic of his own political life, can be sure that his actions, at one crisis or another, have been entirely free from self-tenderness. A man who cannot bear lightly the weight of these imperfections proper to a political career would be wiser to keep within the sphere of private life and abstract speculation." [3]

Yet this proud man expected more from himself than from others. Any one who hoped to play an enduring and creative part in the political life of his country must be resigned to the destined imperfection of men and things. The good hours of men are so short. " Le cœur humain est naturellement généreux et sympathique. C'est dommage que ses beaux élans soient si courts." [4]   In one

---

[1] viii. 516.   [2] viii. 78.   [3] iv. 287.

[4] vii. 19.   Cf. iv. 297 : " Les hommes sont gouvernés par leurs préjugés et leurs instincts beaucoup plus que par leurs intentions réelles et réflechies."

of the few references (curiously few for an historian) to
French statesmen of an age earlier than the eighteenth
century Guizot remembered the disgust of Michel de
l'Hôpital at the conditions of his political life. " Pourtant
il est resté dans la mêlée : il a persisté dans la lutte, à son
grand honneur comme au grand profit de son pays." [1]
Michel de l'Hôpital had placed his name among the greatest
in French history, and established in France the bases of
religious liberty and civil order. Public life was a severe
and persistent struggle in which a man risked his fame and
self-respect and fortune ; victory was always contested ;
success, even the greatest and most obvious success, brought
no lightening of the burden. Every day the labour and the
battle must be begun again as though nothing had yet been
accomplished.[2] " Dieu n'a pas voulu faire aux meilleurs
serviteurs des princes et des peuples un sort plus facile ni
plus doux." [3] Guizot always assumed success, nor was he
vindictive after failure. " I brought to my public life a
temper which was always optimistic, ready and even
obstinate in my hope of success." [4] He preferred to point
out the good side of his political opponents. Even of
Palmerston he records in his memoirs : " Je fais grand
cas de son esprit. J'ai confiance dans sa parole, sa manière
de traiter, quoiqu'un peu étroite et taquine, me convient :
elle est nette, prompte, ferme "—and this in spite of
Palmerston's love of argument, and of enclosing himself
within his own scheme of thought and working out the
consequences to the end.[5]

[1] viii. 26. [2] vii. 350. [3] viii. 26.
[4] vi. 7. In his study of Washington Guizot speaks of " cette espérance
pleine d'inquiétude et de travail, la seule que permette aux esprits
élevés l'imperfection si profonde des affaires humaines, mais qui suffit à
soutenir leur courage." (*Étude historique sur Washington*, liii.)
[5] vi. 131. This judgment on Palmerston was passed in 1841, after
the diplomatic isolation of France over the eastern question. In another
passage of his *Mémoires*, Guizot wrote that Palmerston had no hatred of
France and bore no ill-will to French interests. He was English, and
worked for the advantage of England. His own reputation and the
political good name of his country suffered from the " égoïsme patrio-
tique " which took too little account of the moral aspect of international
politics. Moreover, Palmerston concentrated too much upon the question of the moment. He did not possess that largeness of imagination
which could give to particular interests their place and importance in
the general scheme of national policy. (iv. 90-1.)

II

GUIZOT AND THE MONARCHY OF THE RESTORATION (1814-1830)

GUIZOT came to Paris in 1805 as an austere protestant determined to keep himself free from the contagion of the times.[1] His education had been in Geneva, where, according to the best principles of Rousseau, he had been taught a carpenter's trade, as well as the elements of literature. In Paris various chances—his mother's friends, his own knowledge of German—brought him within the small circle of society which still cultivated the liberal philosophy of the eighteenth century, and refused to recognise the empire. The influence of Royer-Collard,[2] with his scornful rejection of this easy and self-confident philosophy, soon neutralised for Guizot the superficial brilliance of the salons. Mme Guizot had wished her son to be a barrister ; Guizot himself hoped to make his name by writing. He soon became less hostile to the administrative side of the Napoleonic empire, and was even ready to join the civil service, though he would have nothing to do with the political side of the government. He was not given the post for which he applied, but was offered in 1812 the chair of modern history at the Sorbonne. He had made a certain reputation for himself by his writing ; yet it is a sign of the

[1] There is an excellent account of Guizot's political and literary career between 1814 and 1830 in C. Pouthas, *Guizot pendant la Restauration : préparation de l'homme d'état (1814-1830)*. (Paris, 1923.)

[2] Guizot outgrew the influence of Royer-Collard. Their friendship had begun to grow cold even before the revolution of July. " Il me regarde," said Royer-Collard, " comme une pièce dans son jeu d'échecs ; c'est ce que je ne veux pas souffrir." Barante attributed this " superiority " of Guizot to his belief in the greatness of his future ; " cette conviction changeait son ton et ses manières." (Barante, *Souvenirs*, ii. 375.) After Royer-Collard's death Guizot wrote of him : " Il m'a ouvert des perspectives et appris des vérités que sans lui je n'aurais peut-être jamais connues." (*Guizot dans sa famille*, p. 49.)

118

rudimentary state of historical teaching in France that a chair of such importance should have been given to a young man of little technical equipment. Guizot refused to make the usual complimentary reference to the emperor in his inaugural lecture ; Royer-Collard had also refused, and regarded the refusal as an act of independence, not a gesture of revolt.[1]

It is significant that, nearly fifty years later, Guizot passed one of his most splendid judgments upon Napoleon. " It was after I had actually taken part in the government of men that I learned to be just towards the Emperor Napoleon." [2] To Guizot Napoleon was always the man of genius who had put an end to the anarchy in which France had been left by the revolution. " Napoleon reconstituted in France an order of society. . . . He recalled, and set in the highest place, those elements which deserved such precedence. His own life was not very moral ; yet he cared for men who were honourable, and whose lives were regular and of good repute. He was not made for the subtler things of life ; he could be careless and over-familiar, or sudden and brutal ; but he liked elegance of conduct, nobility of manners, and refinement of form. He thought—and he was right in thinking—that a certain external display, a certain elevation of custom and taste, are natural to an old civilisation, and one of the elements of its greatness. This self-made man had a personality lofty, free, and unprejudiced enough to set store by things which had a long life behind them. . . . Napoleon accomplished an even greater work ; this work, upon which all else depended, was his own peculiar and personal achievement. He restored authority in France when authority was misunderstood, trodden to the ground, insulted, degraded ; when authority had been made either hateful or ridiculous—sometimes both hateful and ridiculous—by the revolution. In the small group of men of his order throughout history none like Napoleon possessed as of

---

[1] Fontanès, the Grand Master of the University, did not take the refusal very seriously : " Que les protestants sont entêtés. Je m'en tirerai comme je pourrai." (*Guizot dans sa famille*, p. 48.)
[2] i. 4.

right and exercised with such boldness the instinct and the gift of authority." [1]

During the Hundred Days Napoleon was as great in power and intellect as ever he had been ; but his cause was no longer the cause of honest Frenchmen. The Hundred Days were indeed a great evil ; " they rekindled that old quarrel which the empire had smothered and the charter was designed to extinguish, the quarrel of the old and the new France, of the ' emigration ' and the ' revolution.' " [2]

With or without this interlude, this act of an immense egoism, planned and carried out upon an heroic scale,[3] the task of the Bourbons was terribly difficult. Before the first abdication of Napoleon the people of France had seemed to Guizot " a nation of perplexed spectators, who had entirely lost the habit of interfering in their own destiny." [4]

In a journey from Paris to Nîmes in March 1814 Guizot noticed the agitation and the inaction, the poverty of town and country, the troubled contradiction of opinion : on the one hand, a longing for peace ; on the other hand, a hatred of the invader. Napoleon himself seemed the cause of so much suffering, and yet the only defender of France. The rich and poor were divided. The comfortable and educated classes foresaw the fall of Napoleon and looked for a more quiet rule. The common people only left their apathy for bursts of revolutionary excitement ; " le régime impériale l'avait discipliné sans le réformer." [5]

Here was an omen for the future government. For the people were now the political masters of France. Throughout the changes of twenty-five years the idea of national sovereignty had remained firm. Even Napoleon had held plebiscites in 1800, in 1802, in 1804. In his first pamphlet of opposition to the government of Richelieu Guizot described the political situation in terms which forty years later still expressed his views : [6] " French history has been for thirteen

---

[1] *Hist. Parl.*, i., Introd., pp. xxxvi-xxxviii.
[2] i. 109-10.   [3] *Hist. Parl.*, Introd., p. lx.
[4] i. 24-5.   [5] i. 26.
[6] *Du Gouvernement de la France depuis la Restauration et du Ministère actuel.* The summary in the *Mémoires* differs slightly from the original text of the pamphlet. Although Guizot took care to explain that he was not attempting any " filiation historique," his use of the terms " Francs et

hundred years a struggle between two peoples, conquerors and conquered." The decisive battle in this struggle was the revolution. Its result was beyond doubt. The once conquered majority were now the conquerors. They held France in their possession. Their victory was recognised by the charter, and proclaimed as of right. " By this single act the king made himself the leader of the new conquerors." [1] What kings were they who had to rule a new France? Even before the first restoration Alexander of Russia had written of the Bourbons : " If you knew them, you would be convinced that the burden of such a crown is not for men such as they are." After the Hundred Days both Alexander and Talleyrand would have preferred the duke of Orleans. Louis xviii. and his brother seemed too old to learn ; their past was against them ; they had lived too long in exile. Guizot called Louis xviii. " a moderate of the old régime, and a free thinker of the eighteenth century. The intelligence of Louis xviii. was full of egoism and scepticism, but serious and genuine." [2] . . . He had indeed given up the extreme views of his first days as an émigré, but he was lazy, ungenerous,[3] too careful of etiquette,[4] unlikely to inspire affection. During the first restoration he had re-

---

Gaulois, seigneurs et paysans, nobles et roturiers " laid him open to attack. In any case the theory of the two races was not new. It is found in Boulainvilliers, État de la France (1727) and Essai sur la noblesse de France (1732), and in Sieyès' pamphlet on the Tiers État (re-edited in 1820). Thierry and Mignet accepted the theory. See Pouthas, op. cit., p. 273, and Halphen, L'Histoire en France depuis cent ans. A novel development of the same theory appears in O. Seeck, Geschichte des Untergangs der antiken Welt (vol. i. bk. 2), where Seeck tries to show that Semitic and Levantine migration had profoundly affected the character of the population of Gaul before the barbarian invasions.

[1] i. 256-300.   [2] i. 276.

[3] Molé and his colleagues remarked upon the king's callousness at the court-martial of a colonel who had allowed a soldier of the guard to be beaten to death by his comrades for shouting " Vive l'empereur " when he was drunk. (Molé, Mémoires, iii. 288.)

[4] There is a well-known story that when Louis xviii. fell down in front of the palace guard-house he would not allow himself to be put on his feet again until the captain of the guard had appeared to perform the act of picking him up. When his favourite minister Decazes asked to be made a gentleman of the chamber, the king answered : " The cookery books tell you that to make jugged hare you must first take a hare. To make a gentleman of the chamber you must first take a gentleman."

fused to pay Napoleon's pension ; after 1815 he allowed
Napoleon's son to be kept as a Habsburg prince in Vienna.
Charles x., who succeeded his brother in 1824, was a better
man, but without any sense of political realities. Pozzo di
Borgo spoke of his " imperturbable incorrigibility." Guizot
thought that he was wise, when he was wise, only by
accident. Occasionally indeed Charles x. understood the
danger of his position : " Il n'y a que M. de la Fayette et
moi qui n'ayons pas changé depuis 1789 ; " [1] but these
flashes of insight never came when they were most needed.

The men to whom these kings entrusted their government were unfitted for the work of reconciling the old with
the new France. Talleyrand was the ablest diplomat in
Europe. To the end of his life, when he read to an astonished
Institute a lecture upon the value of theological studies in
the formation of remarkable men,[2] Talleyrand showed his
perfect knowledge of the art of living. But he was a man
of drawing-rooms and of quick intrigue, no leader of men,
and without moral authority.[3] Chateaubriand was under-
valued by the royalists as a friend and as an enemy, partly
because his estimate of himself was ludicrously high. " He
could march with the rarest minds and the most splendid
talents, but he had deluded himself into thinking that he
was also the equal of the greatest masters in the art of
government, and was struck at the heart when he was not
taken for the rival of Napoleon as well as of Milton." [4]

---

[1] i. 372.   [2] iv. 255.

[3] i. 37. Two judgments upon Talleyrand sum up his character and
the limits of his political talents. His character : " Tenez, Monsieur,
vous n'êtes que de la m . . . dans un bas de soie." (Attributed to
Napoleon. See Sainte-Beuve, *Nouveaux lundis*, xii. 30.) The sphere of
his abilities : " Un courtisan consommé . . . propre aux grandes affaires
du gouvernement absolu, mais à qui le grand air et le grand jour de la
liberté ne convenaient point ; il s'y sentait dépaysé et n'y savait pas
agir." (Guizot, i. 38.) One sentence has described for ever Talleyrand
and Fouché passing through an ante-room on their way to make their
peace with Louis XVIII. : " . . . entre silencieusement le vice appuyé
sur le bras de crime, M. de Talleyrand marchant soutenu par M.
Fouché ; l'infernale vision passe lentement devant moi. . . ." (Chateaubriand, *Mémoires d'outre-tombe*, iv. 25.) Molé has given an equally
devastating account of a morning levée at the house of Talleyrand.
(Molé, *Mémoires*, i. 287-9.)

[4] i. 88. Chateaubriand carried his romanticism literally to the grave.
He chose for himself a tomb on a rocky island off St. Malo. The tomb
is now within full view of three watering-places.

This temperamental poseur might restore a sentimental religion ; but he could bring little wisdom to the working of a newly devised constitution.

The duc de Richelieu was a man of a different stamp. Without charlatanism of mind, with none of the prejudices and exaggerations of an émigré, he had learned how to govern men ; but he had learned government in Russia, as the agent and the personal friend of an absolute monarch. He had no prejudice against free institutions, nor had he any understanding of them ; in the last analysis, he was not anxious to hold political power.[1] Within a few years Richelieu had modified the terms of the treaty of Paris, removed the foreign armies from France, lessened the war indemnity. His royalism was beyond question ; but the royalists twice caused his fall. If Richelieu, with his great name, great authority, and great services to France, and with the support of a king who prided himself on being the most enlightened member of his family, could not stand against the narrow fanaticism and silly nervousness of the extreme right, lesser men like Decazes and Villèle could not hope to be more successful with Louis XVIII. or his brother.

Decazes was a royal favourite who was not above opening letters in the post to amuse the king with scandal about his ministers.[2] Villèle, in power from 1821 to 1828, might say that he was born for the end of a revolution ; but as Guizot wrote, he was not at the end of a revolution.[3] He was clever, moderate, adroit in disciplining a party, yet not strong enough in imagination or in character to meet a great crisis. His absence from France during the titanic years of the revolution had saved his life, but had not fitted him for the government of the French people.[4] Guizot

[1] i. 212.

[2] Guizot saw the folly of Decazes' attempt to reconcile by little concessions men who were divided upon questions of principle : " le tort de M. Decazes, c'est de vouloir toujours de petits remèdes aux grands maux : il croit que tout peut se guérir avec de la tisane." (Broglie, *Souvenirs*, ii. 99.)

[3] i. 281.

[4] Villèle was a junior officer in the navy at the outbreak of the revolution. His ship was ordered to the French colonies in the Indian Ocean in 1791 ; Villèle only came back to France (with a wife and a fortune won in the colonies) in 1807.

has described Villèle's successor, Martignac, as a man of charm who would have made a good minister under an established constitutional monarchy, but no man for a storm. He was more epicurean than ambitious, and did not care enough about success to have much chance of achieving it.[1] Polignac, under whose ministry came the catastrophe, was an amiable fool, who thought he had received a special revelation from the Blessed Virgin.

These were the men who in their turn had to work a system new to themselves and new to the French people. Their own supporters did not believe in constitutional government. The one great institution on their side, the Catholic Church, could hardly accept the principle of popular sovereignty. Little confidence was inspired by churchmen when an archbishop of Paris could speak of Jesus Christ as " l'héritier légitime du trône de Judée," nor could the church recover for a generation from the breaking of her order and the destruction of her seminaries during the years of revolution. In any case, the support of the church was of little use against those who disbelieved in any sort of revealed religion. The bourgeoisie had not yet learned to follow the noblesse in a religious conservatism based upon political expediency.

The men who came to the chamber were without experience of free parliamentary life ; in Guizot's words, they lacked the " spirit of government." [2] Long-established traditions of centralisation imposed upon successive ministers a burden of administrative detail at a time when they needed leisure to concert a policy and educate a party. Moderate men all over France supported the moderate royalists. Yet a centre party was little positive help to a government struggling with two extremes ; it was too ready to acquiesce now with the left, now with the right, without making an effort to develop ideas of its own. The wildness of an irresponsible press and the excesses of the revolutionary party outside the chamber did not favour the chances of conciliation. The assassination of the duc de Berri wrecked the ministry of Decazes at a moment when a more liberal policy might have been possible.

[1] i. 331. [2] i. 114.

The fall of the monarchy was a thing foredoomed unless a new king should appear with sympathy for the achievements of the revolution ; unless a minister should combine a love of order with a love of liberty, a power of leadership with a care for new ideas ; unless a party should grow up in France to support a wise king and a government directed towards something more than the satisfaction of a class. No such king, no such ministers, no such party dominated the state. Therefore in 1830, on a trivial occasion, and without real resistance, the Bourbons were overthrown, and the security of the social order was threatened.

What was Guizot's attitude towards this procession of ministers ill-fitted for their task ? Under the first restoration he held the post of secrétaire général de l'intérieur. In this minor office he set himself at once to undertake a work of the highest importance ; the composition of a general report on the condition of France. The Hundred Days began before he was master even of the routine of his department. Guizot was sent back to the university. He took the formal oath of submission to the government of Napoleon, but refused the special oath laid upon those who had served the government of Louis XVIII. He can scarcely be said to have kept the letter of the general oath when he accepted the mission of representing the moderate royalists at the court of the king in exile. After the excesses of the ultra-royalists in 1814, the choice of a protestant of Nîmes was in itself the declaration of a programme. In fact, Guizot was sent by the moderate party to warn the king against the mistake of putting himself in the hands of the émigrés. The chances of a Napoleonic victory seemed small enough when Guizot set out for Ghent ; yet there was some risk in a mission which might have meant exile from France and financial ruin. Guizot was not too well received at Ghent. He felt a certain nervousness ; in his few months of public life he had held no conversation with Louis XVIII. He wrote to his wife : " Qu'on est sot la première fois qu'on se trouve en tête à tête avec un roi." The interview was over before he had recovered his self-possession. Years after, when he was writing his memoirs,

Guizot, now familiar with the conversation of princes, had forgotten this nervousness. He called to mind a long discussion, and imagined that he had suggested the removal of Blacas, who enjoyed the king's full confidence ! [1]

After the second restoration Guizot was made secretary-general to Pasquier, the minister of justice. Pasquier held two ministries, and left Guizot with more work and greater responsibility than would normally have fallen to a secretary. Guizot held minor posts until 1820,[2] always hoping that the king would break with the extreme royalists, always supporting a moderate policy, and moving slowly towards the opposition. He cleared his own mind, and developed his own views, by writing pamphlets and articles. He tried to think out a sure basis for political society ; his temperament found this basis in the idea of duty rather than in the idea of right. " Que la société repose sur l'idée de devoir et tend même constamment à ne reposer que sur cette idée." [3] He began to understand that the rivalry of the higher classes in French society was ruining the attempt to establish a free government. Neither the nobility, who could not forget what they had lost, nor the bourgeoisie, who could not forget what they had won, would remember that in any great and lasting society there must be at once " an upward movement and a breaking down of barriers, and a certain hierarchy of conditions and ranks." [4] These two natural facts of the social order demanded neither an " impertinent" nobility nor a jealous bourgeoisie, but the united action of the two. The immediate threat to the liberties of Frenchmen came from the nobility. For three centuries the nobility of birth had been cut off from a sense of political reality because it had ceased to direct the country. Its members were now trying to rule the king and the French nation.[5]

---

[1] i. 83-9.

[2] He resigned the secretariat within a few months, on the retirement of Pasquier, but remained a maître des requêtes au conseil d'état. In 1819 he was given by Decazes the direction of commercial and departmental affairs under the ministry of the interior.

[3] Notes for a pamphlet, *Du gouvernement représentatif et de l'état actuel de la France* (1816). See Pouthas, *op. cit.*, pp. 141-2.

[4] i. 295. [5] i. 114.

Guizot is most interesting when he is trying to interpret the revolution. He saw that his countrymen were at a difficult stage in their history, and that they could hardly comprehend a series of events which were out of range of the present, and yet did not belong entirely to the past. He was quick to understand that Mme de Staël's *Considérations sur les principaux événements* was the starting point for a new criticism and a new interpretation of the revolution. Guizot refused to see the revolution *en bloc* ; he distinguished between the philosophical ideas behind the events and the Jacobinism which was only a resurrection of the practice of *raison d'état*. The revolution as such was finished, and belonged to the past. The restoration of the monarchy was not merely a bargain and a compromise ; it was a new phase in the history of France. Yet if the revolution had completed its destructive work " en tant que fondatrice elle commence." [1] Nor indeed had the effects of revolutionary disturbance passed out of sight. " Revolutions take almost as many years to reach their term as they take in their preparation." Liberty is conquered before it is enjoyed.[2]

To this view of the revolution Guizot remained firm throughout his life. In the remarkable summary of French history which, under the title " Trois générations," is the preface to his five volumes of speeches, he wrote that the men of 1789 made two profound mistakes of moral judgment. They believed that man was naturally good, and that evil had its origin not in human nature but in bad social and political organisation. They believed in man's omnipotence. These errors of moral judgment led them into political mistakes ; mistakes which Guizot formulated in the words : " no one is bound to obey laws to which he has not given his consent ; all legitimate authority resides in the principle of numerical decision ; all men are equal." [3] His final judgment was that revolutions were always " profoundly imperfect and impure," because they shared in the " impureté naturelle " of all great historical events. This

---

[1] Quoted (from a review of Guizot's in the *Archives Philosophiques*, iii. No. 12) in Pouthas, *op. cit.*, p. 182.
[2] *Hist. Parl.*, i. 7-8.   [3] *Ibid.*, i., Introd., pp. xviii-xxiii.

mixture of good and evil, wisdom and folly, nobility and shame, was common to all the works and actions of men. At the last Guizot would apply to revolution Pascal's judgment upon mankind : " s'il se vante, je l'abaisse : s'il s'abaisse, je le vante." [1]

It was to be expected that, with these views, Guizot would be repelled by the narrow views of the royalist government, and would join the constitutional opposition. The opposition took form almost of itself. " They came together as the inhabitants of the same quarter might congregate from every side and, without knowing one another, might combine to put out a great fire." [2] From among the moderate royalists there emerged in the summer of 1817 the so-called " doctrinaires." The name first appeared in a newspaper of April 1816.[3] The leaders of the group were Royer-Collard,[4] Broglie, and Guizot. They announced their support of the Bourbons and the charter. Their importance was that they stood midway between those who attacked the facts of the revolution and those who defended the philosophical principles upon which it was based. They accepted the new France. Guizot said of himself : " je suis de ceux que l'élan de 1789 a élevés et qui ne consentiront point à descendre." [5] But the achievements of the revolution were as right and lasting as the revolutionary principles were false and transitory. " The ' doctrinaires ' had at heart both the intellectual good name and the good order of society ; the ideas which they brought forward were intended to regenerate as well as to close the revolution." [6] They defended the monarchy ; they did not defend divine right ; they did not defend absolutism.

Forty years later Guizot still maintained that the " doctrinaires " were right in their ideas, though he was able to see their faults as a party, or rather as a group. They were too much of a coterie, too heedless of outside opinion ; too

---

[1] *Hist. Parl.*, Introd., pp. xxiii and xxxi.   [2] i. 116.

[3] See Duvergier de Hauranne, *Histoire du gouvernement parlementaire en France*, iii. 534. A good account of the development of the views of the " doctrinaires " is given in Pouthas, *op. cit.*, chap. vi. See also Michel, *L'Idée de l'État*, Bk. 3, chap. 2.

[4] For the political career of Royer-Collard see Barante, *La Vie politique de Royer-Collard*. 2 vols.

[5] i. 27.   [6] i. 156-9 and 199-201.

pugnacious, more ready to criticise others than to win supporters. They had not sufficient feeling for the difficulties of the art of government, for the importance of leadership. They underrated the work of reconciling general ideas with conflicting interests and particular situations. Among the "doctrinaires" Guizot was least open to the charge of neglecting the work of propaganda. His method of approach to contemporary political questions can be seen in his speech in favour of a censorship of newspapers.[1] He argued that the French people were highly sensitive to the influence of the press for three reasons : the events of the immediate past ; the peculiar circumstances of French society ; the nature of French institutions. Under the first heading Guizot meant to include the reverberations of the revolutionary age. " It is a work a thousand times shorter and easier to restore the cities of a country devastated by a tremendous earthquake than to re-establish a society the moral foundations of which have been shaken." One of the results of the revolution had been to give to France not only a new government but an entirely new society, a society which seemed to have no parallel in history. This change was caused by the application of the principle of equality ; its effect was to leave in France nothing but the government on the one hand, and on the other a mass of individuals. Hence, with the disappearance of all intermediate bodies and all lesser allegiances, there was developed a greater " susceptibilité sociale " ; [2] the population was affected by a kind of " moral dispersion." Furthermore, the revolution had changed the social position of very many Frenchmen. But the intellectual and moral improvement of men does not keep pace with improvements in their material conditions ; " la Révolution n'a pas réparti les lumières avec autant de rapidité et d'égalité que les fortunes." These new men might well be good judges of their particular interests, but they lacked the broadness of view, the independence and calm-

---

[1] *Hist. Parl.*, i. 1-13. Guizot made this speech in 1819. As he was under forty, he could not be a member of the chamber, but appeared before it and took part in its debate as a conseiller d'état and commissionnaire du roi.

[2] This was also the view of Tocqueville. See below, p. 205.

ness of mind which would preserve them from undue responsiveness to the suggestions of others.

Finally there was the peculiar character of the French government. The administration in France was more closely connected with the government than could be the case in a country differently constituted. Elsewhere (for example, in England) the administration was controlled locally by authorities who were almost independent. Attacks upon the government would therefore be directed against the centre of authority—" aux actes généraux des pouvoirs supérieurs." But in France the government was vulnerable at every point in the administration ; there was an incessant local war against the minor agents of the executive, a war which touched the whole of legally ordained authority. Hence the need to protect the government against this continual confusion of local abuses with general principles ; a need which was all the greater because the ordinary man took more notice of local abuses than of the general principles of policy.

This very speech, for all its cleverness and subtlety, was more dogmatic than convincing. Guizot was disliked for his tone of intellectual superiority, and the harshness of his manner towards the subordinate officials of his department. Therefore it was with a certain relief that the government removed him and his friends from the conseil d'état after the assassination of the duc de Berri had ruined the chances of a policy of well-poised intellectual conciliation.

Guizot was now free to devote himself to the duties of his professorship, which had sat lightly on him for a good many years. As he was neither a rich man nor content to live merely on the scale which a professorial salary allowed, he had also to earn money by journalism. He was lent a house at Meulan by Mme Condorcet. Here he settled for the summer of 1820 to write pamphlets, and—occasionally—to shoot sparrows. ("J'ai trouvé un fusil avec lequel je fais quelque dégât parmi eux.") The first pamphlet appeared in October 1820.[1] It was a savage attack upon the government of Richelieu and the ultra-royalists. Molé thought that Guizot showed a lack of moderation which

[1] *Du Gouvernement de la France depuis la Restauration et du Ministère actuel.*

went beyond the bounds of good taste and even of gratitude to Richelieu under whom he had served. Naturally the party of the extreme right were angry. Bonald [1] compared the arguments of Guizot with the answers made by the assassin of the duc de Berri at his trial. When other pamphlets followed,[2] the critics began to ask what kind of history this professor was teaching his pupils.

Guizot thought that his position as a professor of history gave him the chance of enlightening his countrymen upon their political situation. By explaining the historical background he would suggest to his audience the premises necessary for drawing certain conclusions about the present. He aimed, not at erudition, but at the creation of a public opinion which should be based upon a knowledge of the great lines of French history. This view of the duties of a state professor had its dangers. Guizot had refused to allow to Napoleon the right which he now claimed for himself. If a government had no right to interfere with academic liberty within the field of academic studies, a professor of history had no right to extend his historical studies to criticism of the government. It was scarcely logical of Guizot to permit criticism of authority without also tolerating support of authority. Moreover, if a government could find support in the lecture-rooms of a state university, there would be a temptation to open these lecture-rooms to professors whose loyalty to those in power was greater than their scholarship, and to close them to critics who might be dangerous.

But it would be superficial to condemn Guizot's view merely because it is out of keeping with modern ideas of " scientific " history ; nor would it be fair to judge Guizot's own lectures by the lengths to which propaganda was carried by Michelet [3] under the government of July, or by

---

[1] Bonald's theocratic views may be illustrated by the argument which he used in defence of the death penalty for crimes of sacrilege. In cases of this kind the culprit had offended God ; he should therefore be sent before his natural Judge !

[2] In October 1821 : *Des moyens du Gouvernement et d'Opposition dans l'état actuel de la France.*

[3] Guizot passed severe judgments upon Michelet's historical work. He would not allow his daughter to read Michelet's *Histoire de la république romaine.* " Ce n'est pas bon pour elle. Aucun ouvrage de M. Michelet

the liberal historian Mably, who saw in Charlemagne a " friend of the people," and the foundation of representative government in the May assemblies of the Franks.[1] The writing of history is of its nature something more than the collection of historical material. It is idle to pretend that the foreground of the present can be forgotten. The great historians have had a sense of the value of civil society which has impelled them to pass judgments as well as to narrate what has happened ; the very selection of their material from the mass of data implies these judgments. Nor should an historian forget that history is written in order that it may be read.[2] The reader will make his own judgment, and draw inferences which do not apply only to past times. The tradition set by the masters of history, Thucydides and Tacitus, has dominated the minds of all those historians who have looked deeply into the springs of human action ; this tradition must continue to affect all to whom the long memory of times past is more than an empty catalogue of fact.

Guizot himself understood the danger of degrading academic privilege into an instrument of political opposition. For this reason he distinguished between the two means of influence at his disposal : his public lectures and the press.[3] He would not bring into his lectures any reference to the actual circumstances and the political controversies of the moment ; he would keep within the sphere of general ideas and the facts of history. He took for his subject in 1820-1821 : " L'histoire des anciennes institutions politiques de l'Europe chrétienne, et les origines du gouvernement réprésentatif dans les divers états où il a été tenté " ; a wide enough field for a professor who had given very

ne convient à des enfants, même très avancés ; et pas plus comme instruction que comme impression morale. Ce sont des livres d'une science douteuse et d'un jugement mal réglé, quoiqu' honnête." (*Guizot dans sa famille*, p. 207.)

[1] To their credit it must be remembered that a better historical standard had already been set by the Benedictine order, and by the Academy of Inscriptions.

[2] When Thierry, converted by reading the chronicles, turned from propaganda to history, he ceased to interest his readers, and the journal for which he wrote soon ceased to take his articles !

[3] i. 312-13.

little time to his duties ! Within the limits of this subject, and using only the arm of knowledge, he would pursue a twofold aim. " I wanted to attack the theories of the revolutionary party, and to restore an interest and a respect for the past history of France " : [1] " L'histoire, c'est la nation." [2] French society had just come through a violent struggle with the old régime, " notre berceau séculaire." It was necessary to explain to a younger generation the true meaning of this struggle, and the folly of denying altogether the present value of the past.

Guizot's method was to make pointed allusions, or to intercalate general discussions in his historical narrative. Thus the study of pre-conquest institutions in England was followed by three lectures on the principles, the forms, and the guarantees of representative government ! There are passages in the lectures where Guizot has allowed his judgment to be distorted by a care not to give his political opponents useful illustrations from history. In his second course on French history he tried to show that feudal society was wholly oppressive, and had left behind it a memory of hatred and terror. Had he found any good thing in feudalism he might have been giving support to the thesis of Montlosier that the nobles were the French nation ! Guizot's attempt to prove the inevitableness of historical development, and to demonstrate that representative government must result from the recognition of social equality, brought him very near to a defence of historical materialism.[3] He formulated the view that legislation can only " register " the social conditions of the time. His purpose was to make clear the foolishness of the ultra-royalists in attempting to bring back the old régime by legislation ; but the theory was to lead further than Guizot contemplated.

In the choice and treatment of his subject-matter Guizot was scarcely faithful to his belief that historical science must be kept apart from political propaganda. He had spoken of his lectures as an attempt to " multiply ' doctrinaires ' under the very fire of the enemy."[4] He could not have been

---

[1] i. 312-13.   [2] i. 28.   [3] See Pouthas, *op. cit.*, pp. 310-12.
[4] Letter to Charles de Rémusat, 1820. (Quoted in Pouthas, *op. cit.*, pp. 300 and 304.)

surprised when the clerical Grand Master of the University suspended his course of lectures in the autumn of 1822—at the moment when Guizot admitted that he was beginning to convince his audience. It was some consolation that at the same time Cousin was silenced, and the École Normale closed. In the short moderate interlude of the Martignac ministry, before Charles x. destroyed his throne and the hope of his successors, Guizot was allowed to resume his lectures. He was more careful not to enter upon political discussion, but again, in the years between 1828 and 1830, tried to make his lectures a means of political education. In his new course he analysed the different elements in French society from Gallo-Roman times, " not only to satisfy the scientific or philosophical curiosity of the public, but with a twofold practical aim. I wanted to show that the efforts of our age to set up a rule of guarantees and of public liberties were not in any way new or strange." Such efforts, now successful, now unfortunate, often discontinuous, were to be seen throughout French history ; the men of 1789 were right to resume a work which had been abandoned for a time, but wrong to think that they were beginning something entirely new.[1]

The years between 1821 and 1828 gave Guizot leisure to read, and saved him from the worst faults of the propagandist. He began to make a serious study of English history ; the publication of two collections of memoirs,[2] hastily edited indeed, to earn money from a public which had developed a taste for the curious in autobiography,[3] taught him the complexity of history, and the impossibility of reducing the life of many centuries to a few general ideas. The later lectures, published as the *Histoire de la civilisation en Europe et en France*, show a great advance in technical accomplishment and a greater freedom from political bias. They also mark a change in Guizot himself.

[1] i. 336.
[2] *Collection des Mémoires rélatifs à l'histoire de France, depuis la fondation de la monarchie jusqu'au treizième siècle* (30 vols.) and *Collection des Mémoires relatifs à la révolution d'Angleterre* (25 vols.). The idea of these collections was suggested to Guizot by his wife.
[3] See Halphen, *L'Histoire en France depuis cent ans*, pp. 45-7, for an account of the widespread interest in memoirs, and the numerous forgeries produced to exploit the taste of the public.

The dogmatic determinism of the earlier lectures gave place to a stronger moral judgment and a recognition of the importance of men and of the actions of men.

In these years Guizot advanced further in the elaboration of a doctrine of progress. He had already made a serious attack upon the principle of sovereignty as set forth by the supporters of the sovereign people. He was not wholly unsympathetic to the theocratic view that the very idea of popular sovereignty was a blasphemy against God. In an unpublished fragment on political philosophy [1] Guizot said that men were wrong in looking for the principle of sovereignty where sovereignty did not even exist. " Any kind of sovereignty attributed to men, to one man, many men, or all men, is a lie and an iniquity." Reason alone is sovereign. Any attempt to find an objective, unalterable sovereign legitimate of itself, and always commanding obedience, must end in the establishment of a tyranny. " Man has attempted to set up sovereignty on earth, as he has tried to set up divinity. . . . He has been no more successful in fixing, irrevocably, and without limit, his obedience, than in localising his faith."

So far Guizot had but borrowed the sovereign reason of the idealogues. Yet reason was not to him, as to them, only that utilitarian good sense which defined good and bad according to human interest or desire. Nor was Guizot thinking of the autonomous reason laboriously expounded by Kant. Reason was the recognition of a rule ; the rule was the will of God. Here Guizot spoke as a Christian. Government was the instrument of reason ; therefore government and sovereignty could not be the same. Government exists where society exists ; society exists where men have recognised the need for a rule, the need for reason, and therefore the need for some power to watch over the observation of the rule. This power is government. Government is not the rule of force, nor the result of contract, but the consequence of the recognition that man must obey the will of God.

Up to this point the writers of the theocratic school, Bonald, de Maistre, and Lamennais in his earlier work, would have agreed with Guizot. The distinctively pro-

[1] See Pouthas, *op. cit.*, pp. 313-21.

testant turn of Guizot's thought comes out in his answer
to the question : how does man come to hear and to interpret the voice of reason ? The catholic writers said
that man was dependent upon the divine revelation given
to the church ; Guizot held that understanding came
through the painful effort of many men over long periods
of time. Here Guizot came back to the theory of progress
which was the characteristic discovery of the eighteenth-
century philosophers. Without the eighteenth-century belief
in the essential goodness of man, and therefore without
any hope of immediate perfectibility, Guizot yet put his
trust in the long processes of time. There is something
very much like a theory of natural selection in his view
that time alone can give a legitimacy which has a moral
value. " C'est aussi une majorité que celle qui se
compte par générations." This work of time is a work
of combat ; out of opposing forces comes the truth.
Political life, like the life of man, is " laborieuse et
éprouvée."

This political philosophy was held by Guizot throughout his life. It is not original. It would be interesting
to know how much Guizot was influenced by Lamennais,
or by Lamennais' master, Malebranche. The importance
of the philosophy lies in the tenacity with which Guizot
held it, and the consequences which he drew from it for
his political practice. These consequences were that liberty
was needed for the discovery of reason, of the will of God ;
that political power must depend upon the capacity for
recognising reason. " C'est la capacité qui confère le
droit. . . . La capacité n'est autre chose que la faculté
d'agir selon la raison." With equal clearness it followed
that the parliamentary system of government—"le gouvernement représentatif "—was the best means for the discovery
and exercise of capacity.[1]

Guizot did not mean that liberty had always been iden-
tified with parliamentary government, though in his enthusiasm he came very near to this assumption. Liberty had
taken different forms. In antiquity it was confined to

---

[1] See below, pp. 152 and 217-225. It must be remembered that
" capacité " was a technical term.

certain classes among the inhabitants of a state. During the course of history the conception of liberty had become deeper ; successive generations had added to its content ; its demands were more comprehensive, its determining conditions more complicated. Compare the simple political conditions of the Greek city state, based upon slavery, with the modern necessity for the free action of representative assemblies, a free press, freedom of contract, freedom of religion, civil equality, and judicial independence. Consider, again, the difference in history and circumstance between republican America and monarchical England, between England and Belgium, between America and Switzerland.

If free government implies a variety of forms, it does not mean confusion. One condition above all is essential. In every time and place, in every sort of circumstance, the exercise of power must be accompanied by responsibility of the governors to the governed. Here again, under the complexity of modern conditions, representative institutions are the best guarantee of free government.

By this road Guizot reached the monarchy of July and the policy of the *juste milieu*. He could reasonably claim for them both a metaphysical priority.

.   .   .   .   .   .

In the first years of the government of Villèle the Bourbons seemed at last to be well established. The extreme left of the opposition was discredited by the revolutionary plots of the secret societies ; the extreme right was being checked in its extravagance by the formation of a moderate party. French credit was steadily rising in the international money market.[1]

The monarchy was not popular enough to stand the strain put upon it by Charles x. French interference in Spain in the royalist and Bourbon interest brought a temporary excitement ; the Bourbons had succeeded where Napoleon had failed. Yet there was little glory in an invasion sup-

[1] It is curious that the government could not at first float loans through the French bankers, since these were nearly all liberal, and disbelieved in the stability of the monarchy. The loans were floated through the Hopes of Amsterdam, the Barings of London, and the cosmopolitan Rothschilds.

ported by ignorant peasants and priests.[1] After his restoration to a throne which he had disgraced—even if he were judged by the standard of the *epigoni* of Louis xiv.—Ferdinand of Spain began a violent reaction ; his chief agents were the members of the happily named " society of the exterminating angel " ; his opinions were a far cry from the constitutional monarchy of the charter.

Within France stable government was necessary for the prosperity of the country, and the economic measures upon which prosperity depended ; but stable government could now be secured without the Bourbons. The great towns were liberal without being revolutionary. The younger generation felt no personal attachment to a dull and out-of-date royal family. The church had indeed committed itself to the support of the royal house. Missions for the revival of religion were accompanied by acts of reparation for revolutionary violence to Louis xvi. and his family. Wayside crosses were set up entwined with the royal fleur-de-lys. The reaction which everywhere followed these missions did much to increase the sales of the works of Voltaire and Rousseau ; the symbolical union of king and church was only ridiculous. " Je vois," said a sceptic, " que Dieu est mort il y a mille dix-huit ans sur un gibet pour la famille des Bourbons." The government was kept in power because the electors were afraid of revolution and the young men were not on the electoral roll. The acts of authority were tactless in execution even when they were wise in conception. A proposal to close the question of the confiscated lands by a reasonable indemnity to the émigrés was brought forward at the same time as a measure cashiering a number of Napoleon's generals. Even the conservative upper house, largely made up of cynical old gentlemen who had " arrived " under the empire and deserted Napoleon to keep their titles, rejected a severe press law and a law applying the rule of primogeniture to the inheritance of land. The city of Paris was illuminated after the rejection of the press law ; it

---

[1] The government and the duc d'Angoulême as commander-in-chief were blamed for connivance at the clumsy attempt of the banker Ouvrard to make a fortune from the campaign.

was said that no illumination could be bright enough to enlighten the ministers.

The last ministry of Charles x., presided over by the ineffable Polignac,[1] contained La Bourdonnaye, who had been responsible for the White Terror after the restoration, and Bourmont, who had deserted Napoleon before Waterloo. Polignac made a fantastic attempt to win the Rhine frontier by altering the boundaries of most of the states of Europe. The Turks were to be sent back to Asia ; the king of Holland was to take the sultan's place at Constantinople. Belgium was to be given to France, Holland to the king of Saxony, Saxony to Prussia, and the Dutch colonies to England ![2] This diversion failed ; an expedition to Algeria alarmed England, without whose consent operations would have been impossible. There remained the hazard of a *coup d'état*. Charles x. issued five ordinances, on the strength of his right to take exceptional measures at a time of public crisis. Two of the ordinances conflicted with the charter. One of the two affected the property qualification for the franchise, and excluded the rich bourgeoisie ; the other, by establishing a preventive censorship affecting every paper under twenty pages, threw a number of Parisian printers out of work. There was no lack of hands to print the Orleanist proclamations ! The editor of the *Moniteur*, remembering the days of the Terror, was frightened when he was given the ordinances for publication ; but the king and the dauphin thought they had prepared a fine surprise for the undersecretary for war. " Champigny sera bien étonné demain en lisant le *Moniteur*." The king then went to Rambouillet to hunt, after the fashion of his family during revolutions.

The ordinances were published on July 26, 1830. On July 28 the tricolour was taken as the badge of armed revolution. On July 29 the revolutionaries were in possession of Paris.

---

[1] Pasquier (*Mémoires*, vi. 262) speaks of the king's belief in the genuineness of Polignac's visions.

[2] A second plan gave Rumelia to the tsar and Belgium to France. Both plans were at once vetoed by Prussia.

III

GUIZOT AND THE MONARCHY OF JULY
(1830-1840)

THE revolution of July gave a sudden reality to Guizot's fears and hopes. Again French society had approached a calamity. " In our country and in our time republican tendencies must always lead in the direction of anarchy." [1] It was the terrible novelty of political conditions in Europe, and above all in France—that insurrection could lead as never before to swift social dissolution. " Herein lies one of the gravest of the many evils which have affected our nation and our age. As soon as any part of the social structure is affected by trouble of a serious kind, the whole building is in danger of collapse. There is a sort of infection of ruin which spreads with a fearful rapidity. Public agitation on a large scale, extreme misuse of power are phenomena with which the world has long been familiar ; more than once nations have had to struggle not only legally, but physically, to maintain or recover their rights. . . . Resistance, even insurrection have had a term and a limit set to them by the state of society or by the conscience and the good sense of men ; the whole future of the social order has not been at stake on each occasion of disturbance. But to-day, and in our society, every important political conflict is made a question of life and death ; peoples and parties, in their outbursts of blind passion, rush at once to the furthest extremities. Resistance straightway becomes insurrection, and insurrection becomes revolution. Every storm develops into a deluge." [2]

After the fall of Charles x., Royer-Collard had said of himself : " Moi aussi, je suis des victorieux, triste parmi les victorieux." [3] On the other hand, when the crisis of the July days had been passed, there was a hope that the revolu-

[1] i. 216.   [2] ii. 4.   [3] *Hist. Parl.*, i., Introd., p. cv.

tion of 1830 would accomplish for France all that the revolution of 1688 seemed to have done for England.   Representative government, with due guarantees, would be given
a chance of success.   The new king could be under no
delusion about his position ; his character seemed to promise
that he would never attempt a restoration of absolutism.
His subjects, though they would not allow this term to be
used, had been well frightened.   The French people wanted
a strong government to stand between them and anarchy.
" France has no intention of putting herself into a state of
permanent revolution." [1]   After the fall of Charles x. the
national instinct had compelled the country to keep the
necessary changes within the narrowest possible limits.[2]

Here was the opportunity of the " doctrinaires."   Now
was the time to secure the work of the revolution and to
abandon the principle of revolution in itself.   From this
moment to the fall of Louis Philippe Guizot was one of the
political leaders of France.   Between 1830 and 1840 he
was three times a minister ; for eight months, during a
most important crisis in the eastern question, he was
ambassador in London.   From 1840 to 1848 he was
master of the French cabinet.[3]   In 1848 his work in defence
of parliamentary government seemed to be overthrown in
a few hours.   Elsewhere the policy of fallen ministers was
taken up again after the storm had passed.   In France a
republic, and after a republic an imitation of the Napoleonic
empire, took the place of the monarchy of July and the
policy of the *juste milieu*.   When the greater calamities of
the Franco-Prussian war and the commune brought back
the bourgeoisie to power no third trial was given to
constitutional monarchy.

This complete rejection of Guizot's plan for the government of his country was not due only to chance : to the
accidents of persons, the character of Louis Philippe, the
disunion of the monarchical parties after 1848 and again
after 1870.   Nor was it due to particular questions : the

---

[1] *Hist. Parl.*, i. 101.   [2] *Ibid.*, i. 139.
[3] Soult was for a time the titular president of the council.   Guizot
held the office of minister of foreign affairs, and became president of
the council upon Soult's retirement in 1844.

extension of the suffrage, or the choice of a flag. Guizot
had not persuaded his countrymen because he had not
understood their temper. This man who loved liberty so
intensely, so austerely, and to English eyes so wisely, who
cared for the long history of human effort to win liberty,
who was tolerant of weakness, hopeful of success, and never
embittered by failure, lived in a world of wide ideas and
intellectual charity beyond the reach of ordinary men.

There was one road by which he might have come to
understand the thoughts and desires of working men in
France. He might have seen that the social question was
more important to the mass of Frenchmen than all the
political differences of the possessing classes. Guizot was
not blind to the harshness of life in the industrial towns.
At least in his own dealings he had a high standard of
economic justice. He took a leading part in the direction
of protestant charities. He was the first minister to set up
a far-reaching scheme of primary education in France.
He was careful to bring home to teachers in elementary
schools the importance of their work. He hoped that a
more educated nation would find its own way through
political stability to economic betterment. But he knew
too much of the cold political economy of his time, and was
too much of a " doctrinaire " in every sense of the term, to
see that economic needs must be satisfied before any educational policy could bring the right results. The school
teachers, to whom he wrote with a certain distant nobility,[1]
would have told him that you cannot impress a reasonable
satisfaction with the social order upon a class of hungry
children. The fantastic socialism of the years before 1848
was more unpractical than the political philosophy of Guizot ;
its vague conclusions repelled his clear thinking mind. He
judged them by the disorder of which they seemed to be
the cause ; he knew that disorder was the enemy of liberty ;
he did not ask how far disorder was the result of material
conditions in which liberty was only the unchecked
opportunity of the strong to exploit the weak.

When he spoke of the triumph of the middle class, and

---

[1] He invited the teachers to send him a personal acknowledgment of
his official circular.

the attempt of the revolutionaries to push the social revolution one stage further, he described their criticisms of the existing order in terms which show how little he was able to understand them. " They have invented some kind of distinction between the workers and the idlers. . . . Consider a father of a family who is administering his fortune, who is developing his property, who is taking care to educate his children. . . . This, gentlemen, is the type of idler. An idler. Why ? Because he does not work with his hands, or because he does not . . . what shall I say ? . . . write books . . . or newspaper articles. Here you have the new theory of political economy which they have devised against the middle class. These are the absurd and barbarous arguments which they use to threaten us with a new social revolution." [1]

The collapse of the bourgeois republic of 1848 taught Guizot no lesson. In his memoirs he continued to discuss the folly of the socialist remedies, never the terrible realities of the social disease. When he asked why parliamentary government had not established itself in France he gave a purely political answer.[2] Parliamentary government depended on parties. Parties in France between 1814 and 1848 were too much disorganised. The party of order was divided against itself. The second republic had the support of men of great ability, and in its time Europe was at peace.[3] But although some might think that a republic was inevitable in France because " a republic is the government which divides Frenchmen least," the republic had in fact been a cause of division. Some Frenchmen were frightened ; others were over-excited. The republican party had made the mistake of considering itself exclusively the party of a class ; there were other classes in French society. Democracy might represent " the spirit of growth and progress, but it lacked the spirit of conservation and foresight." The republicans had promised too much.

[1] *Hist. Parl.*, ii. 225.
[2] See particularly the Introduction to the *Histoire Parlementaire*, vol. i., and below, p. 227.
[3] This is scarcely true. There was no general European war in 1848-1849. But Europe from Calabria to Schleswig-Holstein, and from the Rhine to the Vistula, was certainly not " at peace."

" They have opened up infinite prospects before the democracy which they have made sovereign ; they have scattered
lavish promises of satisfaction and happiness : promises
which no government, republican or non-republican, could
fulfil ; prospects in flagrant contradiction with the natural
law and the natural course of the world." . . . " The
natural course of the world." . . . The industrial revolution
in the eighteen-forties !

Owing to his inability to read the economic and social
needs of the time Guizot was deserted by the young and
the generous.[1] For this reason the monarchy which he had
served with magnificence and devotion fell without a regret ;
for this reason, in the inevitable injustice of general verdicts,
the good work of Guizot and Louis Philippe was forgotten,
and in a victory of nimble-witted adventurers over men of
long view and tempered greatness the monarchy of July
was superseded by the empire of Napoleon III.

. . . .

It is interesting to watch the relentlessness with which the
consequences of Guizot's mistake worked themselves out in
the history of the monarchy of July. His courage never
doubted the force of those difficulties which he was able
to foresee. The form of the government was a constitutional monarchy. What was the position of the monarch ?
Guizot's mind was made up at once, and finally. He insisted that the French people had no alternative to Louis
Philippe. France was monarchical ; in monarchy alone
had she any hope of salvation. This inevitableness was
understood " by that electricity of good sense which lays
hold of great agglomerations of men." But you cannot
take the first comer and make him a king. Kings are made
either, as Napoleon made himself, by their own swords or
by taking a crown for which they have been born. " They
are kings because they come of a royal line . . . or because
they are of the ' stuff of which kings are made.' " Louis
Philippe became king because his name had been bound
up with the national cause for many years ; he was a royal

[1] See below, p. 222, for the development of Guizot's view that the
chamber of deputies elected on a restricted franchise was representative
of the whole of France.

prince, and at the same time thoroughly French, " a French constitutionalist, a French liberal, a Frenchman of our revolution of 1789." [1]

Nor had Guizot any doubt about the constitutional position of the monarch. Throughout the reign the opposition was ready to repeat the maxim that the king reigned but did not govern. Guizot thought that this commonplace expressed neither the constitutional powers of the king nor the realities of the political situation. " The particular business of royalty is to represent in the government the principle of action and the principle of stability ; the crown is the executive power, the power that is always in being." [2]

Therefore the personality of the monarch could not be without importance. In 1846 Guizot told the deputies (so sure was he of the rightness of his view that he repeated a part of the speech twice in his memoirs) : " the throne is not a chair across which a bar has been put lest any one should use it ; it is not there merely to prevent usurpation. Upon this throne is set a person of intelligence and free will, with ideas of his own, feelings, desires, wishes of his own. The duty of this royal personage is to govern only in harmony with the other great authorities of state instituted according to the charter ; to govern with their approval, their allegiance, their support. The duty of the counsellors of the crown is to win the support of the crown for the ideas, the measures, and the policy for which they are sure of support in the chambers. This is what is meant by constitutional government. But to say that the inviolability of the monarch means the nullity of the monarch is strangely to forget the dignity and the moral liberty of a human being, even though this human being is set upon a throne and surrounded by counsellors who are responsible for his acts." [3]

Moreover, it is impossible in practice that a king should count for nothing in his government. The ministers of the crown must always discuss with the king, as they discuss

[1] *Hist. Parl.*, ii. 189-90.   [2] *Ibid.*, iii. 683.
[3] viii. 84-5, and ii. 184.   In *Hist. Parl.*, v. 227-8, the speech is given in full with slight variations from the text in the *Mémoires*. The speech was not made without frequent interruption.

with the chamber, the details of their proposals. In every discussion of this kind the man whose co-operation is essential must exercise an influence in proportion to his ability, his character, and the degree to which he is favoured by circumstance. The facts of history show that wherever constitutional monarchy has existed, the personality of the monarch has never been a matter of indifference. Guizot refers to the relations between Chatham and George II., Pitt and George III., Grey and William IV.

What was Guizot's judgment upon Louis Philippe? Did he think that this particular constitutional monarch understood his duties, and loyally accepted the limitation put upon his power ? In a temperate judgment upon the king (made after the death of Louis Philippe) Guizot showed a certain disapproval of two qualities which did much harm to the government : the king's talkativeness,[1] and his vivacious desire to get the praise for the good work done by his ministers ; and on the other hand, his pessimism. Louis Philippe over-emphasised questions of little import-ance, and thereby gave an impression of continual inter-ference. He was too petulant in the exposition of his own views.[2] Guizot wished that he would make more use of the royal weapons of silence and indifference, and check the superabundant flow of his ideas and impressions.[3] In the ministerial crises of March 1839 the king is described as " un peu moqueur dans ses conversations trop abon-dantes." [4] Guizot once warned him to distrust his first judgments, whether they led him to hope or to fear, because they were generally too strong. " Your Majesty has need to consider a question twice in order to take a right view of it, and to give it its due place." [5]

There is little doubt that Guizot regarded the king's impetuousness as one of the causes of the fall of the monarchy. For the moments of alarm were more frequent than the moments of satisfaction or hope in the mind of this sur-

---

[1] Tocqueville said that the king always improvised and always monopolised conversation. (*Souvenirs*, 9.)
[2] v. 13.
[3] viii. 94.
[4] iv. 300.
[5] ii. 173.

vivor of so many governments. The king had seen the strength of the revolution, and had always sympathised with its principles and distrusted its practice. To the end this grand seigneur believed in the philanthropic ideas of the eighteenth century. For good or for evil, and on the whole for good, the revolution seemed irresistible ; at best the monarchy could only gain time.[1] For this reason the king gave up his cause for lost when in February 1848 the bourgeois wavered in their support ; for this reason he went quickly into exile murmuring, " comme Charles x., comme Charles x."

Louis Philippe knew the great difficulty of his position. " A liberal government in the face of absolutist traditions and the spirit of the revolution is hard enough to realise ; we want liberal conservatives, and there are not enough of them. You are the last of the Romans." [2] Or at another time in one of his black moods he said to Guizot : "Quelle confusion! Quel gâchis! Dans quel triste temps nous avons été destinés à vivre." [3] Yet Guizot always acknowledged the king's loyalty to his ministers, and not least to those whom he disliked or feared. No words could be clearer than Guizot's denial that the king interfered too much in the affairs of state. He might believe that he could carry on a wiser policy by himself ; he might not make any effort to keep a particular minister or a particular government in power ; fidelity to constitutional principles did not mean that the king was bound to make particular efforts to secure the execution of a policy which he believed to be weak or mistaken. The charge that he was disloyal to the principle of ministerial responsibility, where it did not arise from the king's exuberance of conversation, came from the malevolence of his enemies.

Other judgments upon Louis Philippe are less favourable. His interest in popularity was a little undignified. A noble presence might have redeemed it, but the king's appearance was not royal in the traditional sense ; the pear-shaped figure and the " large sentimental umbrella " were seized upon by caricaturists. Towards their outrageous attacks the king showed a real sensitiveness, tem-

[1] ii. 48-9.   [2] viii. 91.   [3] Ibid.

pered by a sense of humour.[1] He felt that the attacks were directed not only against himself, but against the position of the monarchy. " During the whole of my reign I have been the victim of what Voltaire called ' le mensonge imprimé.' " [2] He had some reason for thinking that no monarchy could last long in France ; " le respect n'y existe plus." His position could not altogether command respect. He had perjured himself in the eyes of the legitimists ; he was thought a traitor to the house of France. He was fifty-seven when he came to the throne ; he had passed the age when ordinary men can begin anything new. He was chosen almost by accident. Thiers, whose clever proclamations helped to bring the Orleans family to the throne, had never spoken to Louis Philippe before July 27, 1830. From the beginning it was uncertain whether the French people wanted him to continue or to close the revolution. This uneasiness about his position, this uncertainty about what was expected of him, determined the policy of his reign. He had no positive mandate. The modifications of the charter were designed to prevent a repetition of the mischief of Charles x. The limit of the franchise was extended ; catholicism ceased to be the religion of state, though it was the religion of the royal family, and though the terms of the concordat still regulated the relations between the government and the church ; kingship by divine right disappeared without equivocation when the new king was elected to a vacant throne, with the title, not of Philippe vii.,[3] king of France, but of Louis Philippe, king of the French, by the will of the people as well as by the grace of God.

Yet what did these changes mean ? Was the king free to choose between the party of movement and the party of resistance, between the left and the right wing of the liberals ? Did the restoration of the tricolour mean the

[1] He once helped a small boy to finish a caricature of himself on the wall of his own country house. The fruit originally chosen to represent him was the apple. (" Domine, salvum fac Ludovicum ' Philippe-pomme.' ")

[2] In 1844 Guizot himself spoke of the " inépuisable puissance de mensonge " of the press. (*Lettres*, p. 227.)

[3] The English government had assumed that he would take the title of Philip vii.

revival of a militant foreign policy? On the point of
foreign policy Louis Philippe at once made up his mind.
He knew more of Europe than any of those who had put him
on the throne ; he knew that his position depended above
all upon the goodwill of the European governing class, of
" those who made peace and war." Upon their recognition, and upon their readiness to provide royal wives for
the Orleanist princes, depended the fate of the dynasty.
It would have been unnatural for this king of the noblest
royal line in Europe not to care for the future of his family.[1]
Hence the king soon accepted as his work the safeguarding
of the foreign policy of France. As long as the bourgeois
were on his side he had no doubt about the security of his
position in France. He stood between the middle class
and the fear of revolution. Others might see to the particular functioning of the machinery of government. The
king thought foreign affairs his own province, and strained
his constitutional prerogative to get a free hand. He read
foreign newspapers, especially the *Times*, more than the
press of his own country ; the French journalists amply
repaid him for his neglect !

He was careful to keep within the letter of the constitution. Yet Guizot himself took part in the attack upon the
ministry of Molé in 1839, on the ostensible ground that by
too great self-effacement the ministers were endangering
the dynasty. Nor was Louis Philippe prudent in thinking
that the only public opinion he need consider in France
was that of the electors. Tocqueville saw the weakness
of the point of view which regarded everything as safe so
long as there was no interference with the regular working
of the machine. The king forgot " the society upon which
the ingenious mechanism of his government was based : he
was like a man who thought it impossible that his house could
have been set on fire, because he had the key in his pocket." [2]

---

[1] The legitimists tried to wreck the future of the dynasty by the
" blocus matrimonial " which aimed at cutting off the Orleans family
from all intermarriage with the great reigning or princely families.
At times Louis Philippe could speak the proud language of a king of
France. In 1846 he found evidence of his friendship to the Coburgs
" dans la part que j'ai prise à faciliter les nouvelles illustrations de leur
maison." (*Revue Rétrospective*, p. 19.)

[2] Tocqueville, *Souvenirs*, p. 12.

Louis Philippe took little interest in the social question of the nineteenth century, and scarcely formulated to himself its perilous issues. His ministers, particularly those of the last eight years of his reign, were not likely to remind him of its urgency. Therefore, as he had thought his power securely based upon the will of the bourgeoisie, so he had never insisted upon an economic policy which might have won for his house the loyalty of the poor. Even in the February days of 1848 he never made a spirited appeal to the people of France, or to the more generous instincts—for such existed—of the Paris mob. One gesture might have saved the throne. The death of Louis Philippe's eldest son in 1842 robbed the dynasty of its most popular member. The duc de Nemours, the second son of the royal house, was not liked by the liberals ; in 1848 the direct heir to the crown was a child.

The person of the monarch was then insufficient for the foundation of a strong constitutional monarchy. What other basis did Guizot have in mind ? The constitutional king was the embodiment of the constitutional idea. This idea had been expounded by Guizot before the revolution of 1830 ; its application under the new conditions was clear. Guizot had found the theme of the political development of the Christian peoples of Europe in the idea of liberty ; " la liberté politique, c'est-à-dire l'intervention et le contrôle efficace des peuples dans leur gouvernement." [1]

This political liberty must take shape, in modern societies, in the institutions of parliamentary government. Parliamentary government implied three things : in the first place, the power which is responsible must also be free. " Ce ne sont pas des agents qu'il me faut," said Casimir Périer, " ce sont des complices." [2] Secondly, there must be political parties. " Party depends upon a free association, based upon common interests, common ideas, common passions, or a combination of the three. Without associations of this kind, embodied in some permanent form, there is no responsibility ; a governing power cannot be responsible to a mass of opinion liable to sudden and violent changes." [3] Guizot defended the view that deputies were

[1] viii. 2.   [2] viii. 7.   [3] viii. 7-8.

more than delegates of their constituents, but made it clear that he was not attacking the system of party. " Representative government can only be made permanent and effective by the formation of great political parties, and great political parties are only possible when men are serious and loyal in their political engagements." [1]

As a third condition Guizot required that these associations, these parties, should not be formed during the excitement of a revolution. They must represent the permanent conditions of the free societies in which they are formed. " Le gouvernement constitutionnel, c'est la souveraineté sociale organisée." A society without this organisation is a society without anchorage, at the mercy of any revolution. "You cannot organise a revolution.[2] . . . A government is not made by theory . . . neither can it be the work of passion." [3]

The practical aim of Guizot, especially during his years of power from 1840 to 1848, was the establishment of " a cabinet of men holding similar ideas, agreeing together upon the internal and external policy of their government, strong enough to control a majority in the chambers in favour of their policy, and to establish a real and lasting agreement between the king and this majority." [4] The first duty of a statesman with these aims was to organise a government ; that is, to suppress revolution. Again and again Guizot comes back to this point. It is the theme of all his speeches in defence of the *juste milieu*, the mean between anarchy and privilege, with which his name, his party, and his government have become associated. In 1838 he told the deputies : " Our first preoccupation, and the great duty of our time, is to establish our government. Many of the best minds of our day are still in doubt whether

---

[1] *Hist. Parl.*, v. 294.

[2] vii. 26. It is curious that Guizot does not see the need for pushing his own argument one logical stage further. " Le gouvernement constitutionnel, c'est la souveraineté sociale organisée " ; but is this organisation political only ? Are there no other forms of liberty which cannot be left to chance and the anarchy of competition, but must be the material for social organisation ? Must not economic life be kept free from the interference of those passions which are the enemies of liberty ? See below, p. 221.

[3] *Hist. Parl.*, i. 144.   [4] viii. 9-10 and 97.

a regular and stable government can come out of the ideas of 1789 and the social conditions to which these ideas have given rise. We are called upon to settle this question by the most convincing of arguments, by experience." [1]

This foundation could not be the work of a day, the achievement of a constituent assembly or a congress. A government could only be founded by the soundness of its own actions, by the harmony and interplay of the permanent and regular powers out of which it was made. So would a government be built up, a little one day, a little more the next day ; the work would take twenty years, fifty years, a century.

In the interest of this gradual process of creation and establishment Guizot developed a strong argument favourable to an hereditary peerage. Here again it is possible to see the method of his political thinking. The idea of an hereditary peerage might seem incompatible with the principle of equality secured by the revolution. But what were the rights which all men shared equally ? " I think that they can be summed up in these two : the right to be protected by public authority against injustice committed by any one ; the right to dispose of one's own existence according to one's own will and interest, in so far as there is no interference with the rights of others. These rights are personal, universal, equal for all men. This is the meaning of equality in the civil order and in the moral order. Political rights are not personal ; he who exercises them takes decisions which do not only concern himself, but which concern society or a portion of society. . . . Hence political rights are not equal for all. . . . In every time and place conditions and guarantees have been attached to political rights as proof or presumption of the capacity necessary for their exercise in the interests of society, which is the sphere . . . of their operation. To speak of equality in connection with political rights is . . . to confuse individual and social existence, the civil and the political order, liberty and government." [2]

Inequality in the distribution of political rights is therefore

---

[1] *Hist. Parl.*, iii. 153.
[2] See below, p. 158, and above, p. 136.

inevitable : this fact would not of itself justify hereditary inequality, the inheritance of rights by sheer accident of birth.
But inherited inequality, rights transmitted through the
sole fact of birth, are among the foundations of civil society ;
the transmission of property is an inequality of this kind.

Can the same principle be applied to the political order ?
It already exists in the case of hereditary monarchy. It can
be justified of itself, as one of the facts of life. Among the
principles which govern society and the world, outside the
sphere of written constitutions and political organisations
created by the hand of man, " the most ,powerful . . . are
heredity and individual action or personality." Of these
two elements man is made up ; in the union of these two
lies the distinction between man and other living creatures.
" Heredity is one of the principles written in the charter of
the world." If either of these two elements is pushed to
an extreme, the result is either a system of caste or a life
isolated from the past and the future, the life of the
nomadic savages who have wandered for generations over
the American continent. The abolition of all authority
which was not based upon election would be a dichotomy
of this kind ; a denial of the facts of history, a refusal to
face the conditions of the present. Therefore there could
be no theoretical objection to an hereditary peerage.

Was there a practical need ? Here Guizot came down
from these flights of theory to the conditions of French
political life. Society was divided between two conflicting
interests : " the interest of possession, of conservation, of
the maintenance of the existing order, and the interest of
achievement or the desire of innovation. . . . This conflict
is between the government properly so-called, the executive power, as representing and championing the interest
of conservation, and on the other hand the democratic
element which represents the interest of conquest." These
two general interests are personified in men. The passions
of men therefore complicate the issue. The more liberty
there is in a country, the greater the expansion of the spirit
of achievement and innovation. Therefore there is a
greater need to strengthen the interest of conservation.
The best way to fortify the government is not to strengthen

its authority directly, but to reinforce this authority by means of a power which will be free from the passions of the men actually directing the executive.   This is the function of an hereditary peerage, a body " living regularly on a level with the government, and within its sphere, knowing its needs, penetrated with its spirit, with the same general interests as the government but without the personal passions which move the government in its struggle with the democratic element."

Did this mean the creation of an aristocracy?   An aristocracy already existed in France ; the revolution had not destroyed it.   This aristocracy would not come into conflict with a political democracy.   Modern democracy was neither political nor, like the antique democracies, essentially given over to the political life.   The abolition of slavery, the size of modern states, and the complication of modern civilisation made political democracy impossible. Modern democracy had its own interests and private affairs, and asked to be allowed to concern itself with these affairs in freedom and security ; it asked from its government all the guarantees of this liberty and security—no more and no less.   For this reason there was a need for an " essentially political class," a class belonging by birth, position, and education to public affairs.   This class must be controlled ; it must be recruited continually, as in England, from the democracy.   These conditions could only be satisfied by an hereditary peerage.[1]

With the same end in view Guizot was as bold in demanding financial support for the education of the clergy.   French society had to face the fanaticism of revolutionaries and counter-revolutionaries.   It might be said that religion also made fanatics.   Yet, for every fanatic, religion also made a hundred citizens obedient to the laws, respectful of everything which deserved respect, enemies of disorder, shameless extravagance, and cynicism.   Religion was therefore a principle in the highest degree social, the natural ally and necessary stay of any constituted government ; no such government could separate itself completely from religion without the gravest risk.   Furthermore, religion

[1] *Hist. Parl.*, i. 303-22.

developed a love of order and an honest disposition, and gave to a government a character of elevation and magnificence which, without religion, it might often lack. . . . It was of the utmost importance to the revolution of July that it should not break with everything in human nature and the world that had an element of greatness and sublimity. It was important that it should not allow everything to lose its value . . . otherwise it might well find its own value debased. Human beings cannot for long live without magnificence . . . any government which should pretend to found itself merely upon the material well-being of its subjects would be making a grave mistake. . . . [1]

The first condition of this work of re-establishing government in France was to get rid of the revolutionary element, and to purge the principles of 1789 of the poison of anarchy. These principles had been employed to destroy the old government and society. In the course of this work they had contracted a revolutionary taint.[2] Here was the difficulty of the party of " resistance " with which Guizot did not hesitate to identify himself. The social order of France, the order which Guizot wished to preserve, had been given its form by the revolution of 1789 ; the particular government which Guizot thought to be the best guarantee of the political liberties of the French people had been secured by another revolution, the revolution of July. It might well seem that the party of " resistance " was inconsistent, and that revolution had been legalised by its necessity and justified by its success. Guizot himself had praised the work of the men of the barricades in terms which hardly fitted his permanent distrust of revolution. In the minds of his fellow-countrymen insurrection had become something more than a proud tradition ; it was almost a regular form of political action. The philosophy of the revolution was linked with its effective social measures and its bravely won victories against the enemies of liberty. Could the philosophy which bore such splendid fruit be altogether false ?

For this reason Guizot came back again and again to the distinction between revolution and the establishment of

[1] *Hist. Parl.*, i. 380-92.   [2] *Ibid.*, iii. 153.

liberty. The deep-seated right of a people to overthrow a government which had shown itself hostile to liberty was even more than a right ; it was a necessity. Yet this right could not be exercised continually ; nor could it be the foundation of a free government.

In the last days of December 1830 Guizot made a direct attack upon the belief in an extra-legal, extra-constitutional power to which appeal might be made at any time, and for anything less than the ultimate need of society. "The spirit of revolution, the spirit of insurrection, is a spirit radically contrary to liberty. It is an exclusive power . . . in its very nature and in its pretensions there is an incorrigible principle of tyranny. Liberty has as its result the division of powers, and a mutual respect among the holders of power. . . . Insurrectional power is fitted for the accomplishment of revolutions, the forcible overthrow of established governments, the forcible domination of barbarian societies ; but you must not ask for liberty from the powers of rebellion ; they do not carry liberty in their being." [1] . . . "You cannot build a city by means of a bombardment." [2] Before this appeal to violence, before this sword of Damocles held over the head of every government, this mad belief of the revolutionary party that they could begin the world again every day, and make an entirely new government and society, Guizot himself showed no hesitation.

But the men of 1830 were for the most part timid and half-hearted in the face of their most urgent problem. They owed too much to the revolution to see the fulness of the danger threatened by the revolutionary spirit. They were inclined to come to terms with a theory, a party, a programme which must lead to anarchy.[3] They knew too little of European history to see the need for the legal organisation of power in any society. They were too much under the shadow of the great names and the great events of their fathers. "They had lived, and were still living,

---

[1] *Hist. Parl.*, i. 176-7.   [2] *Ibid.*, ii. 456.
[3] *Ibid.*, i. 266. "Among the friends of the revolution of July there are some who think it necessary to conciliate the (revolutionary) party, to keep its alliance . . . as long as possible . . . and for this reason to make concessions to it. You have to choose between a timidity which will give way to this party and a boldness which will attack it openly."

beneath the rule of the theories, the traditions, and the habitudes of the revolution. They were far from wishing to begin the revolution again, but they accepted it without hesitation and without criticism." [1] The events of the last forty years of French history troubled the imagination of the French people. They looked for sudden and gigantic results ; they expected their governments to move like the gods of Homer, and to cover the earth in one stride.[2] The revolution was "one of those acts which add to the stature of a nation, and make admirable historical figures ; but a revolution of this kind is for long a cause of blindness and vain-glory to the people who have achieved it." [3]

If the results of the revolution were only to be secured by the abandonment of the revolutionary spirit, if the maintenance and extension of political liberty depended upon the establishment of a strong and well-secured government, it was the duty of the party of "resistance" to concentrate upon political issues and to build up a majority in the chambers and among the electorate.

Here again the men of 1830 were unequal to their work. Had they looked beyond the chambers, beyond the bourgeois electors, they would have seen that, although the traditional way of expressing grievances was political, the real grievances were economic, or social in the modern sense of the term.   It was a good answer, but not a complete answer, to the revolutionary party to say that "the persistence of a free government guarantees to a nation far more liberty and progress than a revolution can ever bestow." [4]

Guizot was not insensible to the charge that he paid too much attention to the parliamentary struggle. He wrote in the last volume of his memoirs : "I was convinced and I remain convinced that the principles and the acts of 1789 brought to our civil society those reforms which were necessary to its well-being ; the social revolution has been accomplished ; the rights of civil liberty and of civil equality have been won ; but after this splendid achievement the conquest of political liberty has remained incomplete and precarious. . . . Political liberty is as necessary for the

[1] iv. 297.
[2] *Hist. Parl.*, ii. 239-40.
[3] *Ibid.*, ii. 454.
[4] vi. 377-8.

poor as for the rich, for the workmen as for the bourgeois.
Without political liberty our civil liberties have, neither
guarantee nor dignity. Therefore, when . . . I have
devoted myself primarily to the foundation of a free government, I have wished to serve, and believed that I was
serving, the first interest of the people." [1]

The very use of the term " social revolution " to describe
the achievements of 1789 ; the assurance that this revolution had at last reached its conclusion, divided Guizot
from the deepest political thought of his day. Nor did
events justify his own view that the maintenance of the
bourgeoisie in power would secure order, liberty, and content.
After 1840 the government had not often to deal with actual
disturbance of a political kind ; the executive power had at
last shown itself strong enough to make sporadic disturbances hopeless. Yet there was no more content ; the
political leaders, the parties which gained a majority in
the chamber, were never popular in the country.

Guizot, with his predisposition to reduce the whole
movement of his time to terms of political government,
thought that the main cause of this uneasiness was the
" mobilité des lois et des fantaisies politiques." [2]   The chief
of these phantasies was the right of all men to participate
in political power ; the right of all men to share in social
well-being (" le bien-être social ") ; the substitution of
democratic for monarchical unity and sovereignty ; the new
rivalry between the people and the bourgeois, taking the
place of the old rivalry between the bourgeoisie and the
noblesse ; the cult of humanity and positive science in
place of the worship of God. In the political field these
ideas were fought for indirectly under the demand for
universal suffrage. Therefore the government of Guizot
refused to make any concession to the demand for the most
moderate extension of the franchise. [3]   For this mistake and
all that lay behind it their power fell into the dust.

The story of this misconception is worth telling in more
detail ; it has something of the sardonic contrast between

---

[1] viii. 539-40.   He also added as an appendix to this volume a *résumé*
of the political and social measures passed between 1830 and 1848.   See
below, p. 201.

[2] vi. 377.   [3] See below, p. 216-17.

the noble conceptions of the human mind and the withered achievements of human action.

.   .   .   .   .   .

The reign of Louis Philippe began with the usual comedy of the day after a revolution. Before the hand-shakings, the reviews of the national guard, and the congratulations of the first three months were over, the established government of Louis Philippe had to satisfy or turn away a mass of place-hunters. Guizot, as minister of the interior, had to deal with the greater number of the tribe. They were the talk of Paris. A popular vaudeville opened with a chorus of place-hunters in the ante-room of one of the ministries :

> " Qu'on nous place
> et que justice se fasse,
> qu'on nous place
> tous en masse.
> que les placés
> soient chassés."

Guizot was forced to justify the first nine months of free government by publishing a list of functionaries dismissed ![1] The new men who had crowded into the vacant places were often an embarrassment. Within a week of taking office Guizot received a message from the king that two of his new sous-préfets had arrived at the Palais Royal—completely drunk ! The drunkenness of two sous-préfets was a lesser evil ; the great difficulty of the monarchy was to live down the days of its own origin. The governments of Europe suspected a power which was based upon revolution ; for revolution in France was traditionally linked not only with war but with victory. The settlement of 1815 was attacked by the conquerors of the barricades and the many refugees who came naturally to France after the failure of the revolutions in southern and central Europe.[2] The king might hope to regain in time the political con-

---

[1] Guizot had done a similar work in the time of the first restoration. (See Pouthas, *op. cit.*, pp. 54-8.) It is clear that in 1814 and in 1830 Guizot acted as a restraining influence in his department. In 1815 only a quarter of the functionaries were changed ; the most denuded field was that of the sub-prefectures.

[2] ii. 82.

fidence of the European governments, but he had lost for
ever the esteem of some of the monarchs.

The most urgent problem was the restoration of order.
A violent outbreak of disturbance, ending in the sack of
one of the most important churches of Paris (St. Germain
l'Auxerrois), made it clear that the government must be
directed by a stronger man than the weak and conceited
Laffitte. Another banker, but of a different stamp, took
his place. Casimir Périer had the imperiousness of character which was becoming to a veteran of the army of Italy
of 1798.[1] Périer had attacked Serre and Villèle under the
first restoration, and supported the ministry of Martignac.
Dislike of revolution had caused him in 1830 to move
towards the side of authority. He never allowed himself,
like Guizot, to praise the " disinterested heroism "[2] of the
men of the barricades. He told an enthusiastic observer
of the sovereign people acting in defence of its liberties
that he would prefer to see them all in their homes. He
despised the king for stooping to get the goodwill of the
mob, and left the first cabinet of the monarchy out of disgust at its weakness. He was marked out for power, but
refused to take office until he had been assured of the king's
support. " I do not intend to play the part of a Strafford,
and to throw myself in the breach for a Charles i. who
would at once give way and sign my death-warrant. No,
if Strafford has to mount the scaffold, Charles i. must follow
him ! "[3] When at last he agreed to take office he knew
that he was condemning himself to death. He was only
fifty-three, but a man of his type burns away his life. If
he entered the ministry, he foretold that he would leave it
feet foremost. Never man fought better against greater
odds. He had no theory of government ; but he had all
the hatred of a great man of action for revolutionary disorder. . . . " L'émeute . . . l'indignait sans le lasser."[4]
Against this disorder he fought with no sure hope of success.
He was not a great orator. In the chamber his personality
was more convincing than his words. With his colleagues

[1] Périer was born at Grenoble in 1777, and was the son of one of the
first directors of the bank of France.   [2] *Hist. Parl.*, i. 113.
[3] Quoted in Thureau-Dangin, *Histoire de la monarchie de juillet*, i. 403.
[4] ii. 211.

and his civil servants he was absolute. He told Marshal Soult that he would break him like glass if he played the traitor, and Soult believed him. Outside, in the street, he faced an angry mob with a fury more burning than their own. Well might Royer-Collard say over his tomb that he had " ces instincts merveilleux qui sont comme la partie divine de l'art de gouverner." [1]

Périer called himself " un homme de circonstance et de lutte." He knew that his work would end with the restoration of order, and that he was not the man to initiate a period of mild constitutional rule ; this would be the task of Guizot. Yet in his few months of power Périer had a definite policy for his country. The weakness of this policy was the weakness common to all the ministries of Louis Philippe. Périer, like his successors, attacked the social evils of France in their results and not in their causes. Périer had indeed more excuse than Guizot for failing to see that misery, and misery alone, was the cause of much of the disorder which he was determined to suppress. But this failure of insight meant a neglect of the only means of restoring and maintaining the confidence and loyalty of Frenchmen.

Périer is more to be excused than Guizot, because he was dealing with an immediate crisis, with present effects rather than remoter causes. He had found a particular situation, from which there was but one way of escape. To his countrymen and to Europe he was frank in explaining his aims, and he was always as good as his word. He remained a liberal in his care for publicity. He made it clear to the European governments that the new monarchy did not propose to be aggressive. In the Belgian question, where the revolutionary impulse might be most dangerous, and where provocation from the conservative powers unwilling to recognise the inevitableness and finality of the Belgian revolution might be an excitement to the revolutionary party in France, Périer was careful not to separate

---

[1] ii. 480. Guizot also prints a remarkable character-sketch of Périer by C. de Rémusat (ii. 482-4) : " Il avait la passion de vaincre et non de nuire, et il concevait difficilement, n'apercevait qu'avec surprise l'inimitié que lui suscitaient parfois ses dédains et ses succès."

French from English action.[1]   At the same time, if France was not to take advantage of militant insurrection, if the dynasty of Louis Philippe was not to be allowed to establish itself in Belgium for fear of English susceptibilities, other powers must not think that the French government was entirely preoccupied either with internal questions or with a care to convince Europe of its peaceful intentions. There would be no weakness in upholding the traditional interests of France within what might be called the legitimate sphere of these interests.

The interference of Austria in Italy touched French prestige, and, to some degree, French security.   The ill-planned insurrections which had broken out in the Romagna and the duchies of Parma and Modena had been suppressed by the aid of Austrian soldiers ; at a meeting held in Rome during the spring of 1831 the ministers of the powers had insisted upon an amnesty to the rebels in the papal states, and the promise of a few reforms—enough indeed to make Gregory xvi. call them " the ruin of his power."   It was hoped that the introduction of laymen into the judicial and administrative services and some measure of municipal and provincial self-government would make it possible for the pope to maintain the peace of his states without the presence of Austrian soldiers.   But trouble began again in 1832, and the Austrians came back.   Périer denied French complicity with the disorders, and at the same time refused to allow Austria to extend her sphere of influence in Italy. When the Austrians occupied Bologna, Périer ordered

---

[1] In 1830 the Belgian people revolted against the decision of the congress of Vienna which had joined the former Austrian Netherlands to the kingdom of Holland.   The intention of the congress had been to form a strong barrier against France.   It was hoped that the interests which the two constituent elements of the joint kingdom had in common would be more powerful than differences of tradition, religion, and language.   Partly owing to the Dutch monopoly of the more important posts in the administration, and the unwillingness of the Dutch government to regard the Belgians as of equal importance with the Dutch in a kingdom of the united Netherlands, the union had been a failure.   In 1830 the Belgian people wanted as king a son of Louis Philippe. A full account of the long-drawn-out negotiations over the Belgian question is given in Hall, *England and the Orleans Monarchy* (1912), chaps. 3 and 4.   See also R. Guyot, *La première entente cordiale* (1926), chap. 2, and *Cambridge History of British Foreign Policy*, vol. 2, chap. 3.

French troops to land at Ancona. Here, in the support of the English government, he reaped the fruits of his moderation over Belgium. It was no small tribute to him that the opposition in England began to complain about the " neo-Stuart " policy which was sacrificing the English alliance with Holland and allowing the French a free hand in Africa and Italy.

Périer's firmness on the Italian question [1] established a tradition which was maintained by Guizot, and only given up, against the interest of France, by Napoleon III. Italy, in Guizot's language, had no claims upon France ; French policy required no more and no less than the maintenance of a counter-weight to the influence of Austria in Italy.

It is interesting that neither Périer nor Guizot believed in the future of the nationalist and revolutionary movement in Italy. There was too much talk, too little achievement. Guizot told the chamber in September 1831 that every attempt to bring about the political unification of Italy and the reconstruction of a great Italian nation had ended in failure. Napoleon had pointed to the geographical configuration of Italy as the reason for this failure. " Pour moi," said Guizot, " cela m'a convaincu." In the ten or twelve years before 1831 the nationalist movement had not been supported with sufficient energy. " Neither the courage nor the devotion of the Italians has reached the level of the great work they have undertaken. They may be passionately occupied in their talk and in their literature with the reconstruction of Italy ; they have shown

---

[1] On the other hand, it has been argued that this move of Périer's was a mistake. If the French went to Italy to support the liberals, they would be driven into war with Austria. They did not want war, and could not wage war without allies. If they went to Ancona simply to keep order, they would be committed to the support of the reactionary government. Their demonstration against Austria would therefore end in co-operation with Austria in an anti-liberal policy. But Périer was bound to show that France intended to maintain her traditional influence in Italy. French influence was in fact exercised in favour of clemency to the rebels and of securing some promise of reform in the papal states. It is indeed difficult to see how the French could ultimately escape from the position in which Napoleon III. found himself without giving up their influence in Italian affairs. This abandonment of a long-standing policy might have been the wiser plan, but it was a plan which no French government could have adopted without great loss of prestige at home.

themselves too weak and immature for the execution of such a task." [1]

Périer's refusal to commit his country to perilous foreign adventures, and the care with which he steered a middle course when excitement ran high, made it necessary for him to secure a good exposition of his policy in the chamber. He could be sure of the support of Guizot. But Guizot was already more unpopular with the opposition than was Périer himself, nor had he yet learned skill in debate. He spoke, at his best, as an orator ; at his worst, as a professor expounding a theorem to a class of students. He was now in his forty-fourth year ; during his seventeen years of political life he had not learned that quickness and sympathy which alone would make him a strength to the government in the day to day business of the house.

More important to Périer from the parliamentary point of view were Thiers and Dupin. Dupin had a longer parliamentary history than Guizot, but there was nothing of the man of genius or the statesman about his narrow common sense. He could speak well in debate. Périer, who knew his value, would call to him in difficult moments : " parlez, parlez, Dupin " ; but a nation sensitive to the parade of fine phrases was unlikely to find inspiration in the views of an orator who said he disliked the barricades because they closed the shops !

Thiers was a much abler man, with a longer future in front of him ; he was only thirty-four, and had already established a claim on the dynasty by his clever proclamations during the July days.[2] No one could be sure which party he would support. He attached himself to the party of order when he might have joined the left. His motives

---

[1] *Hist. Parl.*, i. 281-2. See above, p. 90, for Metternich's views on the moral and geographical obstacles in the way of Italian unity : . . . *Eppur si muove !*

[2] Louis Adolphe Thiers was born at Marseilles in 1797. His maternal grandmother was of Greek origin. After studying law at Aix (where he began his friendship with Mignet), Thiers came to Paris (1821). He joined the staff of the *Constitutionnel*. The German bookseller Cotta, who was one of the proprietors of the paper, made Thiers financially independent by the gift of the greater part of his shares. Thiers' history of the revolution appeared between 1823 and 1827. In 1830 he was one of the founders of the *National*.

are not altogether clear. He was tired of journalism, and impelled by that intellectual curiosity which often leads men to desire power.   There was in him, as his history shows, a masterfulness, a love of action which made him turn more naturally to a man like Périer than to the vague and turbulent men of the left. During the short-lived ministries of Lafayette and Laffitte he found some scope for his abilities in a subordinate position under the minister of finance. Laffitte was idle enough to give him the chance of displaying his administrative powers. Périer, though he is said to have subsidised him, never trusted him to the full. Thiers had begun by a revolutionary style of speaking, but abandoned it for the simpler and more convincing manner of his later speeches. Talleyrand is said to have recommended the change ; Thiers himself was clever enough to see that he must take the colour of his political surroundings.

Thiers was as little preoccupied as Périer with a theory of monarchy or the progress of society. But Périer's opportunism was selfless ; Thiers wanted government to be in the hands of the parliamentary majority because he realised his own powers of domination in the chamber. Once the excitement of using these powers had taken hold of him, he could never go back willingly to the writing of history. "Écrire est peu de chose," he told Nassau Senior in 1852, "quand on a été habitué à agir. . . . Je donnerais dix bonnes histoires pour une bonne session ou pour une bonne campagne militaire. . . ." Life was only bearable when a man acted strongly, because then only did he forget himself.

With this support the government was able to maintain itself against disturbance at home and suspicion abroad. But Périer died of cholera in the spring of 1832, and his ill-matched followers could only keep together for a few months. In the autumn the king chose a milder successor to inaugurate a milder rule. The duc de Broglie formed a cabinet which lasted until February 1836, though Broglie resigned for a year (April 1834 to March 1835) on the question of the French debt of twenty-five million francs to the United States.

The duc de Broglie was one of those men of talent in

whom a proud self-sufficiency takes the place of a desire to create or to rule. Fortune had given him a position for which most men have to fight, and to which few attain. A noble name ; great possessions ; a wide culture ; a beautiful wife [1] (the daughter of Mme de Staël) ; wise and lasting friendships. There was something of the pride of the grand seigneur in his disdain of the liberals because they seemed to have " un certain esprit court, étroit, et routinier." But his very sensitiveness to human failings showed a weakness of character, and precluded him from the rough excitement of conflict and leadership. A critical barrenness overtook his intellectual life after his retirement from politics. He produced nothing worthy of his powers ; he was interested in ideas, never taken by storm. Even his memoirs were left incomplete, and did not touch the years of his government. Such a man was not fitted to succeed Casimir Périer. He was not sympathetic to the king ; he could not dominate Guizot and Thiers sufficiently to get the best from both of them ; he never exerted himself to win popularity for himself, his cabinet, or the monarchy.

His government began a new policy which might have borne great fruit if it had been defended with the power and vitality of Casimir Périer, and if it had been taken as the beginning of a new era. The *laissez-faire* tradition of French governments in social and economic questions was broken in two directions. Guizot, as minister of education, introduced a law of primary education which was, for the time, liberal and far-reaching.[2] The construction of railways forced the government to interfere with the rights of private property and to sanction expropriation on a large scale. But these acts were without sequence. The king was, as always, preoccupied with foreign policy, and wanted a free hand to secure a *rapprochement* with Austria and a Habsburg marriage—still the greatest success for a monarchy without a past. He found the coldness of Broglie irksome, and tried to separate Thiers from Guizot. Metternich had seen from a distance that the two could not

---

[1] She died in 1838.
[2] For the parliamentary history of the " Loi sur l'instruction primaire " see *Hist. Parl.*, ii. 1-93. The discussions in the chamber show Guizot's oratory at its best.

long remain together. They might both support the same
policy, but their motives were very different ; nor was
there room within the same party for two men of equal
talent and ambition.

Thiers was not yet sufficiently well established to leave
Guizot ; the opposition still attacked him as a *nouveau riche*
and a turncoat. For a time Louis Philippe had to submit
to what he called " Casimir Périer en trois personnes."
The fall of the government over the ridiculously small
question of the conversion of the *rentes* gave the king his
chance ; such is the fate of ministries led by men indifferent to power. At last Louis Philippe could break
with the policy of union with the liberal states ; at last
he could come to terms with the monarchies from whom
he hoped to win a wife for his eldest son.

Thiers was bound by mutual compact not to take office
without his colleagues. But he was flattered by no less
a person than Talleyrand. The flattery was a little crude.
" Monsieur, l'Europe vous attend." At the same time
Thiers was drawn into the circle of the great European
families. He became an intimate of the house of Mme
de Lieven. His enemies were more sarcastic than ever.
" On sait," wrote A. Carrel in the *National*, " que M.
Thiers est le très-humble serviteur des grands seigneurs
hongrois, prussiens, russes, anglais, qui veulent bien lui
pardonner d'être plébéien comme nous." Or again : " M.
Thiers croit aux grands seigneurs ; quand un lord daigne lui
écrire pour le mystifier, cela le flatte." [1] There was indeed
more than this. Thiers was no fool to be overwhelmed by
the patronage of men less able than himself, and Talleyrand had lived too long for his flattery to be taken literally.

Thiers had some hope of bringing about the Austrian
marriage which Louis Philippe wanted. Broglie himself
had begun to weaken in his support of a liberal foreign
policy. His first view had been that France and Austria
were antagonistic states owing to the character of their
governments and their peoples. It would be dangerous
to ignore these great differences and to hope for any real

[1] Quoted in Thureau-Dangin, *Histoire de la monarchie de juillet*, iii. 54.
(Thureau-Dangin's judgments on Thiers are always severe.)

collaboration between the two powers for a long time to come. But towards the end of his tenure of office he had thought of the possibility of detaching Austria from Prussia and Russia. Thiers shared with Louis Philippe a belief in the danger of joining one of two enemy camps in Europe (the time was not far from the beginning of the armed European peace), and hoped for a chance of grouping the powers round France as a centre.

The king was anxious to try this new policy, especially with a man who had no permanent majority in the chamber, and was therefore dependent upon royal favour.[1] He asked Broglie to relieve Thiers of his compact. Broglie warned Louis Philippe that in choosing Thiers he was choosing a man whom he could never safely give up ; for if he gave him up, he would be presenting a powerful recruit to the revolutionary opposition.

So Thiers became president of the council before Guizot, with whom indeed he exchanged letters of the utmost cordiality. " M. Thiers n'est pas parvenu : il est arrivé." [2]

Europe was never ready for M. Thiers. The Austrian marriage at once faded from the king's view. Metternich pointed out that the difference between the Orleans family and " the throne of August 7 " was not apparent to political assassins. France had no claim upon the devotion of Habsburg princesses. Thiers could not take defeat coldly. He tried to repay Austria by supporting the Spanish liberals with vigour.[3] But the satisfaction of the *amour-propre* of M. Thiers was not part of the policy of Louis Philippe, nor did it bring a dynastic marriage any nearer. In September Thiers resigned.

Thiers had been the king's man, and the king had virtually dismissed him. The king therefore had a certain freedom in the choice of a successor. He chose Molé,[4] a peer of distinction who had served the empire and the restoration.

---

[1] Guizot thought that the king's familiarity of manner towards Thiers was a sign that he did not respect him.

[2] Attributed to Talleyrand by Thureau-Dangin, *op. cit.*, ii. 436.

[3] See below, pp. 191-2.

[4] Molé's memoirs contain a curious account of a love affair in which the scene was Molé's office on Sunday mornings ! (Marquis de Noailles, *Le comte de Molé : sa vie ; ses mémoires*, vol. iii. chap. i.)

Molé had never been more than a person of talent and dignity : he now showed a reserve of power which astonished his friends, and still more his enemies.   He had no obvious political attachments, nor did he command a strong party in the chamber.   From the king's point of view these were good reasons for choosing him.   Molé found that the king's confidence did not give him much authority in his own cabinet, nor did it lessen the distrust of those who thought that Louis Philippe was overreaching his constitutional powers.   The ministry was forced to find an orator ; the orator could not come from the left. Thiers was for the time impossible.   There was only Guïzot. Guizot agreed to enter the cabinet as minister of education. The king was astonished to find Guizot willing to break his earlier agreement with Broglie.   But there seemed no likelihood that Broglie would come back into any government of Louis Philippe ; Guizot and Broglie were close friends ; there could be no question of treachery between them.

Yet the presence of Guizot in the cabinet was not a real addition of strength.   If the policy of the government was to be conservative, why not include all the conservatives, and why keep Guizot in a subordinate place ?   If there was to be an inclination towards the left, why include Guizot ? In any case, Guizot was too magnificent a person to be content with a subordinate place, or to regard Molé as anything but a man of straw.   Guizot assumed that the government would continue the tradition of the Broglie cabinet, of which Molé had not even been a member. Molé was jealous of Guizot, and hinted at his unpopularity.   Guizot was impatient of the leadership of Molé, and hinted that he was pusillanimous, that he refused to face the danger of revolution.   The resignation of Guizot came over a personal question which was less to the discredit of Molé than of Guizot himself.   Gasparin, the minister of the interior, was notably inefficient ; Molé decided to replace him by Guizot.   He went to see Guizot after Gasparin had made a particularly unfortunate mistake.   To his surprise Guizot began the conversation : " Gasparin must go ; I will take his office."   Gasparin stayed ! After another of his mistakes, Guizot asked directly for his place. Molé refused him, and Guizot resigned.

The ministry continued in power because no successors could be found. Until 1838 the rivalry between Thiers and Guizot weakened the opposition ; but it was in the nature of party government that the two would sooner or later unite to overthrow their common enemy.[1] Thiers had to wait for Guizot, and Guizot, with the splendid naïveté and confidence of the men of his time, was writing a remarkable series of articles upon the revival of religion in France.

Molé became nervously excited, and confessed that he could only sleep from three to five hours a night ; he spoke of his government as the Martignac ministry of the monarchy of July. By the end of the year 1838 Guizot was ready for Thiers, and made overtures to the left. Odilon Barrot was asked to help in the overthrow of a " gouvernement personnel ; il est temps d'en finir avec ses ministres favoris." Barrot and the left were ready enough to help one section of the conservatives to fight the other. The combined attack was made in a series of splendid debates in January 1839, during which Thiers spoke thirteen times and Guizot twelve times.[2] Molé appealed to the country, but the coalition came back with a majority.

They had not ventured even to outline a plan for the future. In the first of the January debates Guizot had said that in joining the coalition he did not propose to sacrifice any of his principles or his antecedents. " Avec l'opposition, je combats le ministère, mais en le combattant, je reste, je suis toujours, du juste milieu." [3] All that the coalition could do was to accuse their opponents of electoral corruption. The charge was a little ungracious when their own journals had published an " avis aux fonctionnaires " in which the civil servants were warned to think of the

[1] It is said that Guizot subsequently voted against Molé's candidature for the Academy, so deep was the gulf made between them. (Barante, *Souvenirs*, vi. 400.) Molé's own memoirs are filled with criticisms of Guizot's harshness and ambition.

[2] During the debates Guizot had occasionally been met with an answer as disdainful as his own attacks. He once concluded a speech with the words of Tacitus : " omnia serviliter pro dominatione." Molé replied : " Tacite n'a point dit cela des courtisans, mais des ambitieux,"

[3] *Hist. Parl.*, iii. 184.

future, and to remember that nearly all the possible successors to the government were in the opposition ! The future ministers would be careful to observe the conduct of the administration at the time of the elections. They would not forget what they saw. The functionaries could not act in favour of the government without breaking with its successors. " C'est donc à leur sagacité qu'il appartient de discerner de quel côté il leur convient d'agir !"[1] Well might Guizot say that no one should engage himself in politics unless he was able to bear the weight of " certain necessities " of public life !

It was not easy to find a successor to Molé. The left had not a majority of its own. Thiers and Guizot seemed the obvious combination. Guizot was no longer content with the ministry of education ; Thiers would not allow him to be president. Broglie tried to reconcile the two men ; but the crisis was only brought to an end after serious rioting in Paris. The king took advantage of the general anxiety by putting Soult in charge of a cabinet from which were excluded " les grands amours-propres." Such were the results of the only serious mistake which Guizot admits in his political career. The coalition had failed in its aim. Molé had been attacked because he had allowed the king too great an influence in the government, particularly in the determination of foreign policy. Soult was much less likely to control the king, and had no pretence of a policy or a mandate of his own. For this exchange the two ablest men in French political life had disturbed public confidence and public order at a time of quiet and prosperity. They had alarmed foreign governments by showing how near to the surface were the revolutionary passions of Frenchmen. Above all, they had weakened the position of constitutional monarchy in France ; they had attacked the king almost openly, while pretending to defend him, and had broken the party of government without putting anything in its place. Well might Tocqueville think that the coalition was responsible for much of the later moral anarchy and indifference of the French people.

[1] Quoted in Thureau-Dangin, *op. cit.*, iii. 347-8.

It is fair to say that Guizot recognised his mistake. He did penance, in his own superb way, by supporting Soult, and then retired to the country to study the life and letters of George Washington !

The ministry of Soult could only be an interlude. It fell after a half-year, when for a second time the chamber refused to give a large allowance to the king's second son ; the rich bourgeois could never bring themselves to pay for their king to live in the grand style !

Thiers took the place of Soult, and Guizot allowed himself to be sent as ambassador to London. Guizot had been appointed by Soult,[1] but Broglie advised him to serve under Thiers. His acceptance of Thiers would be a guarantee of the conservatism of the government ; he could resign if the ministry went towards the left. Moreover, the London embassy was unusually important because the fate of Mehemet Ali was now in the balance.

. . . . . .

This Albanian adventurer, whom Sir Sidney Smith had saved from drowning at Acre in 1799, had made so successful an imitation of the first Napoleon in Egypt that Jeremy Bentham had congratulated him on his enlightenment and the French people had been flattered into thinking that he was, if not invincible, at least difficult to suppress ; Mehemet Ali had been pasha of Egypt since 1805. He had spent the first eighteen years of his government in consolidating his power in Egypt and laying the foundations of a military empire. He had rebuilt Alexandria, sacrificed twenty thousand workmen in the construction of the Alexandria canal, introduced a new system of agriculture and new products—olives, sugar cane, cotton, mulberry trees—into Egypt. He had founded a school of medicine under a French president, and borrowed French officers to train his army and supervise the building of an arsenal and a fleet. On the surface all this looked very fine ; it would look finer to the French, who had forgotten their experience of eastern military adventurers. When Mehemet Ali reconquered the holy cities of Mecca and Medina for

[1] Barante was told by the duchesse de Talleyrand that Thiers himself had wanted this post. (Barante, *Souvenirs*, vi. 392.)

the sultan, occupied the middle Nile, and founded Khartum, his military power seemed real enough. He had caused embarrassment to the powers by sending his son and his fleet to put down the Greek rebels of the Peloponnese. As a reward the sultan gave him Crete. He asked for more, and would be content with nothing less than Syria. In 1831 he thought himself strong enough to take Syria for himself.[1] Mahmud II., the sultan who had put down the Janissaries and suppressed feudalism in Asia Minor, outlawed Mehemet and his son. Mehemet could pose as the orthodox avenger of a sultan whose impious reforms had offended true believers. He was master of the sea, and ran no risk of leaving his good fortune behind him at Acre. He marched through Syria, completely defeated the Turkish armies, and drove Mahmud II. to make an embarrassed and embarrassing appeal to the powers. At first Mahmud found little encouragement. France was occupied at home with the establishment of her new monarchy, and abroad with the difficult legacy of the Algerian adventure of Charles X.; nor was she displeased at the success of the armies of Mehemet : armies which had been trained by Frenchmen. Palmerston had more belief in French sympathy with Mehemet than in the genuineness of his reforms ; but England was also busy at home and abroad. The reform agitation and the Belgian question were for the moment more important than the fears of the sultan.

This situation was Russia's opportunity. A Russian fleet sailed to Constantinople ; a Russian expeditionary force landed in Asia Minor. At once the other powers were frightened. Mehemet Ali was forced to accept the concessions which the sultan was forced to offer him. Syria, Aleppo, and even Adana were surrendered. But Russia also wanted payment. Mahmud was lucky to escape with a promise to close the Dardanelles in time of war to all except Russian warships. The sultan was clever enough to know what his other friends would think of his promise. At once England and France protested, and

---

[1] He made the picturesque declaration that Abdullah, pasha of Acre, had insulted his beard which had grown white in the service of the sultan !

made it clear that they would not allow the sultan to enforce the condition to which he had agreed.   But except in regard to the pretensions of Russia, England and France were still divided.   England was anxious to reduce the power of Mehemet Ali, and to strengthen Turkey.   France saw in Mehemet a chance of regaining influence in the eastern Mediterranean.   In Guizot's words, " the national instinct . . . had shown the necessity for a *rapprochement* with the pasha of Egypt."[1]   For a few years the difference of view was of little practical importance.   But English diplomacy in the near east was well managed.   In 1838 Great Britain made a treaty with Turkey forbidding any commercial monopoly within the Turkish empire.   The lands of Mehemet Ali were technically within the Turkish empire; his power in Egypt rested upon these commercial monopolies. In the next year (1839) Great Britain annexed Aden.

Mehemet Ali could hardly see his dominion crumble away.   He was an old man.   The last service which he could do for his family would be to defeat the sultan again, and again to make some profit out of the disunion of the Christian powers.   For similar reasons the sultan decided to attack Mehemet Ali.   Mahmud II. was already suffering from a mortal disease.   He too wished for a settlement of the Syrian question before his death.   In spite of Palmerston's advice, he sent his armies across the Euphrates. They were heavily defeated.   Fortune was even kinder to Mehemet Ali.   Mahmud II. died ; his successor was a boy of sixteen.   The Turkish fleet deserted the new sultan, and set sail for Alexandria.[2]   What should prevent Mehemet from taking Constantinople ?

At this point Soult was in office.   An adventurer of boldness and imagination might perhaps have attempted to strike a bargain with Russia.   Russia might have been persuaded to recognise the French control of north Africa, or to allow France to regain territory on her eastern frontier. France in return might have agreed to the predominance of Russia at Constantinople if Mehemet Ali were left in

[1] *Hist. Parl.*, ii. 160.

[2] Hall, *op. cit.*, pp. 243-5, gives interesting evidence in favour of the view that this act of desertion was encouraged by the French admiral at the Dardanelles.   See also Guyot, *op. cit.*, p. 167.

Egypt and Syria. England would have been threatened
with French predominance along the coast of the Mediterranean from Tangier to the Cilician gates, and with a
Russian advance into Asia Minor and Afghanistan.

Happily for England, and for the peace of Europe, Soult
was not the man to think of so hazardous a course, while
Nicholas of Russia was anxious to break the understanding
between England and France. Nicholas' principles would
not allow him to make an alliance with the monarchy of
Louis Philippe. " Soult is a jewel," said Palmerston. On
July 27, 1839, an agreement of five powers, Great Britain,
France, Russia, Austria, and Prussia (for no one thought it safe
to be left out), determined that the question should be settled
in concert. The sultan was told to await the decision.

The jewel fell from its setting. Thiers replaced Soult :
Guizot came as French ambassador to London. Thiers
was anxious to do something grand enough to redeem his
failure of four years earlier. He made the mistake of
overrating the power of Mehemet Ali,[1] and the worse
mistake of thinking that Palmerston would allow himself
to be outwitted by a Frenchman and a Levantine on a
question vital to the interests of England. Thiers was
indeed bound by the agreement of July to take common
action with the powers. The only way out of this promise
to accept a common decision, that is a decision in which
England and Russia would consult their interests, was to
anticipate it by an agreement between the sultan and
Mehemet Ali. The two parties most directly concerned
had every motive for settling their own quarrel without
paying the inevitable price for the arbitration of the powers.

[1] It is curious that Palmerston's judgment upon the military weakness
of Mehemet Ali was based to some considerable extent upon the reports
of the Polish general Chrzanowski (who behaved with singular incompetence in Italy in 1849) and General Jochmus, a Hanoverian who had
served in the British legion in Spain. The British admiral commanding
the Mediterranean squadron, and Colonel Campbell, the British consul-
general at Alexandria, thought that it would be difficult to drive the
Egyptians from Syria. Von Moltke, who was present at the battle of
Nezib in which the Turkish armies were defeated, complained that his
advice was neglected in favour of the foolish suggestions of the
" mullahs." These religious personages ranked as lieutenant-generals ;
while Moltke was only a captain, and a foreign military adviser ! See
Hall, *op. cit.*, pp. 251-2.

If they could agree to divide Syria, England and Russia could scarcely refuse to sanction the partition. France, and M. Thiers, would have scored a neat success.[1] The conditions of this success depended in part upon the skill of the French minister in London. He must know the secrets of the cabinet, and must guess the force of the English opposition.

Guizot was not well fitted for work of this kind. He was new to England, and new to diplomacy. He had not sat long enough at the feet of Mme de Lieven. He was too much of an orator to make a good listener in conversations with Englishmen : he misjudged English silence ; " the English sometimes give the impression of concealing opinions which they do not hold " ! [2] He warned Thiers that Palmerston would not lightly see himself beaten, and that his position in the cabinet was strong enough to stand a good deal of opposition from his colleagues. But he did not find out until too late the completeness of the French defeat.

The sultan knew that he could not get as good terms from the protector of Mehemet Ali as from the other powers ; nor could the French save him from the anger of his Russian and English " friends " when they heard that he had not waited for their " advice." Mehemet Ali was not the " nouvel Alexandre " pictured by Thiers. A Christian revolt in the Lebanon embarrassed him, and gave Palmerston the opportunity of associating the defence of Christians with the support of Turkey ! To the satisfaction of Nicholas, Palmerston persuaded Austria and Prussia to act without France. The four powers sent word that Mehemet Ali could keep southern Syria for his own lifetime, and Egypt for his family, if he accepted the conditions within ten days. Guizot was only informed of the new agreement after it had been signed.

Thiers had to choose between war against a European coalition and an acknowledgment of French weakness and isolation. He was sanguine enough to hope that his new

---

[1] Thiers denied that he had taken any steps to bring about a separate agreement. He even wrote to Barante (ambassador at St. Petersburg) that France had been scrupulous enough to forbid her agents to make any such suggestion. (Barante, *Souvenirs*, vi. 483.) See Guyot, *op. cit.*, pp. 178-83, for details of Thiers' negotiations.   [2] v. 408.

Alexander would save him from humiliation.[1] He talked loudly : " l'expectative armée, et fortement armée, voilà notre politique." [2] He made a beginning of the fortification of Paris. This in itself was not an immediate threat of war ; the work would take several years to complete. For ten years past there had been talk of these fortifications. They had been delayed because the soldiers could not decide whether they wanted a series of isolated forts [3] or a ring of fortifications, and because the politicians of the left disliked any scheme, especially the scheme of detached forts, whereby the guns of authority might interfere with the progress of a revolution.

Thiers left nothing undone to increase his failure. The collapse came at once. Mehemet Ali made no resistance to the bombardment of Beyrouth. His power in Syria vanished. He accepted the terms offered him by the English commodore, Sir Charles Napier (who had exceeded his instructions), and was glad to be left with Egypt.

Palmerston was not in the least afraid of war. He knew that Louis Philippe, as ever, did not want to offend the great dynasties ; he knew the danger which war would bring to the monarchy. Guizot himself had written to Broglie that he was more afraid of the internal than of the external situation. The bourgeoisie feared revolution more than they disliked the diplomatic isolation of France.

The resignation of Thiers was again a necessity. By process of elimination there remained only Guizot.[4] From October 1840 to the fall of the monarchy Guizot directed the government of France.[5]

[1] See the letters of Thiers to Barante. (Barante, *Souvenirs*, vi. 461, and subsequent correspondence.)

[2] *Ibid.*, vi. 486. See also Guyot, *op. cit.*, pp. 190-211.

[3] This had been the plan favoured by Soult (vi. 29). Wellington summed up in these words his view of the importance of the fortifications of Paris : " Vos fortifications ont fermé cette ère des guerres d'invasion et de marche rapide sur les capitales que Napoléon avait ouverte. Elles ont presque fait pour vous ce que fait pour nous l'Océan. Si les souverains de l'Europe m'en croyaient, ils en feraient tous autant." (vi. 36.)

[4] An alliance between Guizot and Molé was impossible on personal grounds. Anyhow the king did not want it, " préférant ne pas mettre tous ses œufs dans un panier." (Decazes to Barante. Barante, *Souvenirs*, vi. 532.)   [5] See above, p. 141, note 3.

IV

THE MINISTRY OF GUIZOT (1840-1848)

GUIZOT had undertaken the government at a time of crisis. The crisis was more serious than he knew. Metternich thought that Thiers' attempt to imitate Napoleon had succeeded well enough to arouse national feeling in Germany.[1] Still more ominous for the future of Europe was the beginning of the use of the term " armed peace " to describe the state of European politics.

For the first nine months of his government Guizot did his best to bring back France into the concert of the powers, and to ease the strain of unreasoning patriotic excitement. The desire of Palmerston to expel Mehemet Ali from Egypt contrasted with the eagerness of the other powers to settle the eastern question : it was soon possible to leave Mehemet Ali in peace. In the summer of 1841 Guizot could turn to a more positive policy. The years that follow give the opportunity for passing judgment upon the mature statesmanship of Guizot, and upon the ability of a conservative and constitutional party to satisfy the real and imagined needs of the French people.

Guizot was now fifty-three years old. His health was strong enough to endure a great deal of physical and mental effort. Even after the strain of seven years and more of office he lived for another twenty-six years in the full use of his powers of mind and of expression. Towards the end of his ministry he had begun to feel the strain of his work. Yet some of his most splendid speeches were made in the months before the revolution, and the sustained intellectual achievement of his memoirs makes it impossible to think of him as in any way a spent force before or during the critical weeks of the winter of 1847-1848.

---

[1] Becker's patriotic song, " Sie sollen ihn nicht haben, den freien deutschen Rhein," appeared at this time in a Trier newspaper, and was copied by almost every journal in Germany.

For more than twenty years Guizot had explained to his countrymen his views on the government of France, and his conception of the art of managing men. The strength of the man was in his own will, his idea of an ordered liberty, his personal uprightness and charity, his pride and his courage : his weakness lay in his preoccupation with political ends, his blindness to the equally serious need for the organisation of the economic conditions of modern life if order and liberty were not to become but a name and an evil jest.

He had entered into power at a time of crisis in the foreign relations of France. He could not apply to foreign affairs those canons of *laissez-faire* which were so dangerous a rule of his domestic policy. It is significant that the conduct of foreign affairs became the chief interest of Guizot. The defence of his foreign policy takes up a greater part of his memoirs than any other subject during his years of office ; the general political interest of the speeches recorded in the *Histoire Parlementaire* gives place, as time goes on, almost wholly to discussion of the affairs of Spain, or the eastern question, or the occupation of Algeria.

It is true that Guizot, as foreign minister, was bound to be called upon to expound and defend the foreign policy of his government ; but Tocqueville, with his usual insight, gives another reason for this preoccupation. " In substituting interests for opinions, in disintegrating parties and making out of them a kind of political dust, in disgusting the country with itself, in taking the interest and magnificence out of its internal policy, you have of necessity driven it . . . in spite of itself towards foreign affairs." [1]

Guizot claimed that he applied his rule of liberty to the direction of foreign policy. As early as 1831 he had made a splendid defence of the foreign policy of Périer against those who wanted a revival of the propagandist ideals of

[1] Tocqueville made this speech in the chamber of deputies in 1843. (*Collected Works of A. de Tocqueville*, 2nd edition, ix. 397.) Another reason for the disproportionate importance of foreign affairs in the parliamentary debates was the desire of a number of politicians to overthrow the ministry but not to break with the parliamentary majority which approved of the internal policy of the ministers. Tocqueville's analysis of the situation applied with still greater force, and more sinister consequences, to the political life of the second empire.

the revolution : " cette fantaisie de soumettre l'Europe à l'unité, de la ranger à un seul système, sous la loi d'une seule idée." [1]   This was the idea of Louis xiv., of the Convention, of Bonaparte, of the Holy Alliance. It was always followed by a reaction, not of governments only, but of nations. Against this idea of domination Guizot set the contrary principle of " non-intervention."   " This is the principle which to-day represents the liberty of peoples in their mutual relations. The principle of non-intervention is identical with the principle of a nation's liberty. . . . There are a thousand ways of violating this principle. I do not find that any one of them is better than any other. . . . Intervention may be by means of diplomatic relations or by conspiracy, by congresses or by secret societies . . . in the name of the principle of legitimacy or in the name of the sovereignty of the people." [2]

With the principle of non-intervention went the right of nations to consider their own interests. " There is a certain degree of national egoism which is the law governing the policy of nations, and from which it is impossible to escape." [3]

Non-intervention and enlightened self-interest were the cardinal points by which Guizot would direct the policy of France. But this was the tradition set for England by Castlereagh, and still more clearly by Canning. If this tradition should guide the English government, what could be more to the advantage of France than an understanding with England ? The accession of the Tories to power made this co-operation with England practical and, as far as the leaders went, easy. Aberdeen and Guizot were in close sympathy ; the strained relations which had become almost a tradition in the case of Thiers and Palmerston disappeared before an *entente* which suited the needs of both parties. Guizot once reminded the French chamber that the question of the balance of power among the European nations had been a question of the Rhine, the Alps, and the Pyrenees ; only after many centuries had there been an extension of the limit to the Volga and the Vistula ; in the nineteenth century it was world-wide. " La question des forces relatives des États se pose partout,

[1] *Hist. Parl.*, i. 191.   [2] *Ibid.*, i. 192-3.   [3] *Ibid.*, i. 199.

dans le monde entier." [1] English interests marched with French interests in nearly every field ; but there was no question at issue between the two countries of such difficulty as the question of the eastern frontier of France. Once the affairs of Belgium had been settled, England had no reason to fear the dynasty of the man who had fought at Jemappes. On the other hand, with English support the monarchy of July was safe in Europe. " I knew the weakness of the cabinets of the continent in resisting the government of England, when that government had a real will of its own," [2] wrote Guizot in a discussion of the affairs of Greece.

The *maladresse* of the other powers made the *entente* with England more desirable. Austria counted for very little ; her embarrassment would be shown to the world in any great war. Italian publicists openly told their countrymen to wait for the chance which would come to them when Austria was preoccupied in the east.

Russia was not a possible ally either for France or for England. England was alarmed at Russian policy in the east ; France was scandalised by the Russian treatment of Poland, and ashamed at the powerlessness of French arms and diplomacy to interfere. The undignified caprice and boorish manners of Nicholas 1. had made an understanding with Louis Philippe incompatible with the dignity of France.[3]

The friendship of England would give France a free hand in north Africa, within the limits of Algeria, at the very moment when Guizot had decided to secure the French hold of Algeria by definite conquest.

After the marriage of his eldest son into a reigning German family Louis Philippe had no longer to consider the feelings of the continental dynasties. But his house gained in prestige when Queen Victoria came to France and allowed herself to be charmed by the affable respecta-

---

[1] *Hist. Parl.*, iv. 127.   [2] vii. 334.
[3] In October 1841 Nicholas gave the Russian ambassador in Paris indefinite leave of absence. Louis Philippe replied by giving Barante similar leave from St. Petersburg. (vi. 335-342 and 469-524.) (It was said that Nicholas conducted most of his important diplomatic business on horseback during the many reviews of his troops. Barante was a bad horseman !)

bility of the king. Guizot could say with pride that this visit was for him " ce que fut, pour Jeanne d'Arc, le sacre du roi à Reims." [1] Nor was the pleasure lessened by the news that the Emperor Nicholas was making a hurried and not altogether tactful journey to Windsor to see that no harm had been done.

Yet the *entente* was unpopular both in France and England. Guizot and Aberdeen were wise enough not to attempt too much. Guizot did not wish for an alliance which would divide Europe into two parties, and unite more closely the " despotic " powers of Russia, Austria, and Prussia.[2] He had learned from Broglie that the good understanding between the two countries must not be a drag upon the development of their respective interests. But the good work of Broglie in the earlier days of the monarchy had been roughly handled by Thiers and Palmerston. There remained in England, among the members of the cabinet as well as in the country, a distrust of France. Peel was particularly suspicious.[3]

On the other hand, Guizot himself was a little irritated by the characteristic " vice " of the English : " l'orgueil ambitieux, la préoccupation constante et passionnée de soi-même, le besoin ardent et exclusif de se faire partout sa part et sa place, la plus grande place possible, n'importe aux dépens de quoi et de qui " ; [4] a description of the fault which Englishmen have always observed in the French ! The ministers whom Palmerston had sent to different parts of the world survived his government and served his successors with the ardour which had marked them out for their appointment. Above all, there was the danger that Palmerston might come back to power. The fall of the Tories in 1846 appeared to Guizot almost a national calamity for France.

The alliance, or rather the *entente*, was equally suspect to the French people. Guizot complained of the unreasonableness of the chamber over the question of the " droit de visite." [5] The maintenance of a friendly understanding

---

[1] vi. 196. [2] *Hist. Parl.*, iii. 514.
[3] vi. 299. [4] vii. 309.
[5] In January 1844 Guizot made a long speech in the chamber of deputies on the subject of the *entente* and the advantages which it

was therefore no light task, in spite of Guizot's optimistic view that a free government, unlike a despotism, had not to divert its subjects from the loss of liberty by an exciting display of chauvinism.

Guizot's delight in long-sighted views led him to connect the detail of his foreign policy with general principles. He was not satisfied unless he could think that the tide of the time was with him ; that he was acting in accordance with the needs of modern civilisation as well as serving the particular needs of France.

In this respect it is curious to compare him with Palmerston. Nothing could be more different from the seriousness of Guizot's early career than the idle, dilettante arrogance of Palmerston's early years of office ; years in which so sharp an observer as Canning could see no more in him than a man " who nearly touched the top of mediocrity." In the one case there is a careful examination of the tendencies of European history ; in the other the gradual absorption of a gifted and high-spirited amateur in the excitement and interest of his work. Guizot thought that in the earlier centuries of history—centuries about which Palmerston never troubled himself at all—the foreign policy of states had been directed by " l'esprit de conquête, l'esprit de propagande, l'esprit de système." [1] The ambition of princes was satisfied with territorial expansion ; the fanaticism of religious or political reformers expressed itself and spread its faith by a forced conversion of the conquered ; statesmen attempted to organise the nations of Europe upon lines dictated, not by facts, but by elaborate inventions of their own fancy. Yet in spite of the evil caused by continual war, European civilisation had struck deeper and more spreading roots. The day of armed propaganda and preconceived system was not over ; passion still won victories over reason. But the very progress of civilisation weakened the force of the old motives which

brought to France. The opposition had proposed to exclude from the " projet d'adresse " a paragraph approving the results of collaboration with England in Spanish, eastern, and Greek affairs. (*Hist. Parl.*, iv. 171-94.) For the general attitude of Frenchmen towards England in the years 1841-1845 see Guyot, *op. cit.*, pp. 220-42.

[1] vi. 7-8.

had become out of harmony with the new conditions of the
world. The fantastic hopes of those who wished at once
to abolish war were at least on the side of the future ; the
collapse of the work of the greatest of conquerors was
sudden and complete enough to show that he had been
living in a world of the past. "A travers les chimères des
uns, les doutes et les moqueries des autres, les sociétés se
transforment." When the spirit of conquest and the spirit
of armed propaganda arise to renew their enterprises,
"scarcely have they taken a few steps before they come to a
halt ; they hesitate, as though embarrassed, as though dis-
trustful of themselves ; so little are they in harmony with
the real needs, the deep instincts of modern societies, with
the unbroken line of direction taken, in spite of resistance,
by the civilisation of our time." [1]

The conflict between old and new was most evident in
France. On the one hand, the ideas and needs of a high
and complicated civilisation demanded peace and a respect
for law ; on the other hand, the dramatic achievements of
conquest and propaganda in the near past had made the
idea of peace dull and uninteresting to an over-excited
people. "We are set in the midst of two conflicting
currents ; one of them is deep and regular, and draws us
towards the rightful end of our social organisation ; the
other is troubled and superficial, and drives us hither and
thither in a search for new adventures and uncharted
lands." [2]

It was the duty of Guizot's government to avoid the
temptation of novelty, and to keep within the limits of a
wise if unexciting rule of conduct in the detail of foreign
policy. The *entente* with England was an act of prudence ;
but even here these years gave at least three chances of
adventure, and, at the last, exhausted the store of mutual
confidence. It was typical of the new age that, apart
from continual differences over tariff questions and minor
conflicts of interest in Greece and Morocco, the three
problems which came up for settlement affected widely

[1] vi. 9. Here again Guizot, like so many other thinkers at the same
moment in different fields of inquiry, came near to a theory of natural
selection. See above, p. 136.
[2] vi. 10.

separated parts of the world : the equatorial coast of Africa, the Pacific Ocean, and Spain. In two of these questions each country appeared to the other so clearly in the wrong that the greatest tact was needed to quiet an angry public opinion ; in the third, personal rivalries played a greater part than was creditable to the statesmen of either country ; but in any case the two countries had, or seemed to have, interests which could hardly be reconciled.

The first question arose out of the methods used to suppress the African slave-trade. The only way to put down this trade effectively was to prevent slave-ships from leaving the African coast ; the only way to prevent slave-ships from leaving the coast was to give the warships of those nations whose fleets patrolled the coast the right to examine all ships under suspicion. An effective police measure would therefore need an international agreement. A number of agreements of this kind had been made between England and other powers, notably between England and France in 1831 and 1833. Palmerston had prepared a treaty whereby the cruisers of England, France, Prussia, Russia, and Austria were allowed a general right of search, or, in French diplomatic language, " le droit de visite." England and France were the only powers likely to exercise their right of search, since they alone kept a number of cruisers off the coast of Africa.

The reopening of the eastern question had delayed the signature of the treaty. In the last few months of Palmerston's government Guizot had refused to sign, mainly as a protest against Palmerston's outspoken and ill-informed criticism of the French treatment of the native population of Algeria. No such objection could be made after Peel and Aberdeen had come into office. Guizot agreed to sign with the other powers. So little did the leaders of the opposition in the French chamber question a practice which had been allowed for a decade, and which had behind it no attempt to assert the general maritime supremacy of England, that they did not propose to mention the treaty in the opening debates of the house. A deputy from Nantes insisted that the subject should be discussed. The shippers of Nantes disliked the right of search ostensibly on the grounds that it was misused by the English, who provided the greater number of cruisers. In fact, during the eleven years in which the right had been allowed only seventeen complaints had been made, and only five or six were found to have any foundation. Nor was the number of cruisers overwhelmingly in favour of England.[1] The real reason for the opposition was jealousy of English sea-power. It was even suggested that some of the objections were raised by men who had a sinister interest in the slave-trade. Once the protest had been made it was echoed throughout France. Guizot was in a difficult position. He knew the protest of the opposition to be unreal, unreasonable, and discreditable. He told the house that their consent to the ratification of the treaty was not a constitutional necessity. Yet the government was unable to take a strong line against a stronger popular prejudice. Guizot could not persuade the deputies that they had no reason suddenly to object to a procedure which had been allowed for more than ten years, and no right suddenly to refuse to ratify a promise made in concert with the four great powers of Europe. Tocqueville suggested that the destruction of the slave-markets would be a better means than the right of search for bringing the trade to an end ; but he too was uneasy at the consequences which might follow from the refusal of the deputies to stand by the treaty.[2]

Finally Guizot could only settle the question by the good offices of the English government. An Anglo-French·commission drew up a convention, signed in 1845, whereby the term "vérification du pavillon" was substituted for the unpopular "droit de visite." Each nation had the right to assure itself of the nationality of any ships which might come under suspicion, but the actual right of search was not reciprocal.[3]

[1] Since the first agreement had been made, the numbers of cruisers were : English, 124 ; French, 105. The French cruisers were in a majority off the coast of Madagascar and the Île Bourbon. (*Hist. Parl.*, iii. 527.)

[2] Tocqueville, *Collected Works*, ix. 400-2.

[3] See P. Faucille, *Traité de droit international public*, 8th edition (1922), tome i., première partie (" Paix "), paragraphs 402 and 403. Faucille quotes the view of a French authority that the anti-slavery movement in England arose after the English had found that their Indian conquests

The second question had about it a certain air of comedy. The actors were at first a queen of the South Sea islands ; an English dissenting minister ; and a French admiral. The queen and the missionary were in possession. The missionary, Mr George Pritchard, had lived, with Mrs. Pritchard, in the island of Tahiti since 1825.[1] He had persuaded Pomare, queen of Tahiti, to ask the most Christian defender of the faith, George IV., to give her the benefit of his protection. Pritchard was appointed English consul in the island, and for some years no danger disturbed this protestant peace. In 1836 two catholic missionaries came to Tahiti, but were not allowed to set up their dangerous work. After a second attempt and a second rejection the missionaries appealed to the nearest French officer. This officer, Captain Dupetit-Thouars, demanded an apology and an indemnity.[2] The indemnity was paid in 1838, and the queen, partly owing to the importunity of the Tahitian magnates, agreed to sign a treaty of friendship with France. As soon as the French were gone, Queen Pomare and Mr. Pritchard appealed to Queen Victoria. Queen Victoria was much touched ; but her government would not allow the annexation of the island. Three years later Mr. and Mrs. Pritchard left Tahiti on furlough. In 1842 the queen made a tour of the other islands under her crown. Dupetit-Thouars—now an admiral—reappeared with fresh com-

made it possible for them to maintain their commercial monopoly without slavery, and, by the abolition of slavery, to weaken their competitors ! He also thinks that England intended to use the right of search to assure for herself " une domination presque exclusive par mer." Although he gives a reference to Guizot's memoirs, and the debates in the chamber, he does not mention the statistics which Guizot used to clear the English of the charge made by those jealous of English seapower. He lays it down that the other European powers signed the Treaty of 1841 because they had no colonies in the regions where the slave-trade was carried on, and wished to save themselves the expense of examining ships which sailed under their flag !

[1] Pritchard was born in Birmingham in 1796. He worked for some time with his father (a journeyman brassfounder) and then became a local preacher. He left England for the South Seas in 1824. Both he and the French consul at Tahiti found time to engage in trade.

[2] Guizot himself said that the establishment of religious toleration in France was no argument against the maintenance of the " natural " right of France to protect the catholic religion throughout the world. " C'est son histoire, sa tradition, sa situation. Elle y est naturellement appelée." (Hist. Parl., iv. 125.)

plaints. He saw indeed only one solution for the misrule and intolerance of the Tahitian government. Islanders and settlers must put themselves under the protection of France. Some of the Tahitians agreed ; others felt that the French had been thrust upon them. In due time Mr. and Mrs. Pritchard returned to the island with presents from Queen Victoria to Queen Pomare—a set of Victorian drawing-room furniture and a carriage ! The French admiral now went further. In the interest of Tahitian peace, and in his anger that Queen Pomare had dared to substitute a crown of coco-leaves for stars in the flag which he had made for her, he annexed the island to France. Four months later, in the next year (1844), one of his subordinates arrested Pritchard, put him in an improvised and undignified gaol, and then deported him from the island. During his absence French sailors helped themselves to his livestock, with the result that he was " to his loss some four thousand pounds down."

Guizot was once more in a difficulty. Peel made an English speech in the house of commons ; but French opinion was well satisfied with the annexation. Thouars had exceeded his orders. His instructions made no mention of Tahiti ; he had been told to annex the Marquesas islands. These islands would form a healthy, distant, and cheap penal settlement ; " there was a good port for our shipping ; the tribes who inhabited the islands were few and could easily be won over or subdued." [1] Such are the beginnings of many great undertakings.

The French government could not disavow the annexation without appearing to give way to England ; nor was the nearness of the Society Islands to the Marquesas group without importance. French opinion was quickly aroused ; when Guizot told the chamber that English and protestant missionaries could be as devoted as French and catholic missionaries, he was interrupted by cries of " commerçants " from the representatives of the French people. Guizot himself insisted that the French could not be left behind in the mission of commerce and civilisation ; in the sonorous language of the parliamentary orator he declared :

[1] vii. 46-7.

" partout où la civilisation européenne et chrétienne se porte et se déploie, la France doit prendre sa place et déployer son génie propre." [1] (In 1846 the French government sent out to Tahiti " a large reinforcement, with a brigade of mountain guns " !)[2] " Ce qui lui est indispensable, c'est de posséder, dans tous les grands foyers d'activité commerciale et internationale, des stations maritimes sûres et fortes."

Tahiti was a relatively small island in comparison with the giant holding of England in the Pacific.[3] Guizot disavowed the annexation, but did not withdraw from the natives the benefit of French protection. There remained the losses of Mr. Pritchard. Fortunately Mr. Pritchard was ready to accept a money indemnity ; his catholic colleagues, or rivals, had set him an example of this new way of turning the other cheek ; his claims were not too high. Louis Philippe provided a thousand pounds out of his private fortune, and the honour of France was also saved. Queen Pomare kept her state in Tahiti to a great age ; Mr. Pritchard died at Hove in his eighty-seventh year ; in 1888 Tahiti was annexed to the French republic. It now sends deputies to the Palais Bourbon.

The projected advance of the French into Morocco, and the proposal for a customs union between France and Belgium, might have had serious consequences. But the French govern-

---

[1] vi. 275. The Tahitian point of view, expressed in the English of Mr. Pritchard, is less appreciative of the march of European culture. " The blessings of your religion which . . . you taught us to follow opened to us two new entrances into two new worlds, unknown heretofore to our poor people. . . . With the assistance of Jesus Christ and the pastoral care of the missionaries, we may hope to secure one of these worlds . . . the other into which civilisation leads us into [sic], begins to embitter our life, and will ultimately deprive us even of the dominion of the graves of our ancestors, if we are left to our own resources. . . . The commerce and industry which civilisation attracts to our islands puts [sic] us daily into relations with the white people, superior to us in mind and body, to whom our institutions appear foolish, and our government feeble." (Queen Pomare and Chiefs of Tahiti to Queen Victoria, Nov. 8, 1838. *British and Foreign State Papers*, vol. 27, pp. 1139-40.)

[2] Bulwer, *Palmerston*, iii. 322.

[3] New Zealand had been annexed by Great Britain in 1840 mainly to assert British priority of occupation before the arrival of a French company which was being formed to exploit the islands.

ment was unwilling to extend its responsibilities in Africa, and would not risk the loss of the consent of England to the development of French power in Algeria. The plan of a tariff union with Belgium was disliked by the French manufacturers, and did not outlive the fear that Belgium might be drawn into the German Zollverein.

The *entente* with England finally broke down over the question of the marriages of the queen of Spain and her sister, Doña Luisa Fernanda. Spain had given to European politics the name of liberal, but there was little of the spirit of liberalism in her own government. " Spanish politicians out of power either go to bed or conspire." Spanish politicians in power were too often of the type of General Narvaez, whom the British ambassador described as " possessing a fiercely expressive countenance " ; a man who said on his death-bed that he had no enemies to forgive because he had killed them all.

The causes of the decline of Spain are the property of every schoolboy. Nature and man and circumstance combined to produce an instability which made Spanish affairs in the nineteenth century the despair of lovers of order. " Spain," said Wellington, " is the only country where two and two do not make four." Not the least of her difficulties had been King Ferdinand VII. Six years after his restoration by the French, Ferdinand had married a fourth wife, Maria Christina of Naples. When in 1830 a daughter was born of the marriage, a Spanish succession question came into existence. Ferdinand had no other child. If his daughter were excluded from the throne, the heir would be his brother Don Carlos. Don Carlos was no less of an absolutist than Ferdinand, and more consistent and ferocious in his persecution of " liberals." Consequently the clerical and absolutist party supported him, while the liberals hoped for a liberal regency under the nominal rule of Ferdinand's daughter. The law upon the question was not at all certain. After the war of the Spanish succession at the beginning of the eighteenth century Philip V. had instituted something like a Salic law whereby females were excluded from the throne in favour of males in the direct or collateral lines. Philip's law was intended to prevent the union of the crowns of France and Spain. After two generations this danger had passed away. In 1789 Charles IV. annulled the law of Philip and restored the rights of women. Ferdinand reintroduced the law of Philip in September 1832, but withdrew it three months later. In the summer of 1833 the Cortes swore to recognise the succession of Ferdinand's daughter Isabella ; in the autumn of 1833 Ferdinand died ; the supporters of Don Carlos refused to accept Isabella, and began a civil war.

It happened that a similar chance of civil war had been provided in Portugal. King John VI. had died in 1826. His eldest son, Dom Pedro, the regent of Brazil (whither the royal family had fled from revolution in 1807), preferred the pleasures of South America to the excitements of the crown of Portugal. He left the throne to his daughter Maria, a child of seven years old, and appointed his own brother Miguel to be her guardian. Miguel came back from Vienna to Portugal to find himself the hero of his country, the man whom all wanted to be king. He took the kingship, and Maria went, earlier in years than most sovereigns, on the royal way of exile to England. Four years after Dom Miguel's usurpation Dom Pedro, expelled from Brazil, arrived with a fleet. For some time he could not get beyond Oporto. Miguel, who had to govern Portugal, was perforce an absolutist ; Pedro and Maria, who had to conquer it, were perforce liberals.

The civil war in Portugal could be settled more easily than the war in Spain because Portugal was within reach of the British fleet. Miguel was defeated on land and sea, and Maria set in his place. In 1836 she was married to a prince of the house of Saxe-Coburg.[1] In both countries therefore liberalism had secured a dynastic triumph. Palmerston was anxious to give the liberals the support of England, and thought he had reason to fear a French intrigue with the Carlists, although Louis Philippe protested against the sinister motives attributed to him by England.

[1] Although she was under seventeen, Maria was already a widow. Her first husband, Prince Augustus of Leuchtenberg, died shortly after his marriage. Palmerston believed that Louis Philippe had bribed the queen's aunt to persuade her niece to ask for one of the Orleanist princes.

The French government had insisted upon the inclusion of France in the agreement between England, Portugal, and Spain which finally brought about the fall of Dom Miguel. In August 1834 this agreement was extended to deal with Don Carlos. The French promised to prevent the transport of war material across the Pyrenees to the Carlists. Great Britain guaranteed to provide the Spanish government with arms and ammunition ; the regent of Portugal was to give as much help as possible in a general way. Yet Louis Philippe seemed in no hurry to put an end to the disturbed condition of Spain, and felt no enthusiasm for the liberal cause. The Carlists fought with some skill, and showed in the treatment of their prisoners a ferocity which belonged to earlier centuries. Many of these prisoners were British subjects who had been permitted to take service under the Spanish government by the suspension of the Foreign Enlistment Act. Louis Philippe would take no part in protesting against the barbarities of the Carlists, and refused to associate himself with a special mission sent to Don Carlos by Great Britain. At last, in spite of the lukewarmness of France, the Carlists were defeated. Don Carlos escaped into France ; by the end of 1839 the war was over.

Nevertheless a Spanish problem remained. In 1840 Queen Isabella was only ten years old ; but in a few years she would marry, or rather she would be married. Here was one of the occasions of peace or war, according to the wisdom of those who held the issues in their hands. There was no doubt that Louis Philippe wanted one of his sons to be the husband of the queen. Guizot recognised the seriousness of the question, though he would never admit that England had anything to fear from the increase of French influence in Spain, or any reason, in spite of the experience of the Carlist war, for doubting the good faith of Louis Philippe in Spanish affairs. He commented upon the " obstinately retrospective " policy of the English government with regard to Spain. He allowed that there were historical grounds for the suspicion of French designs ; he would not understand that a new element of danger had been introduced by the French occupation of Algeria, and that Gibraltar could now be threatened more directly by a Franco-Spanish combination.

In any case, there was no hope that Europe would allow the dynastic union of the crowns of France and Spain, however uneasily these crowns sat upon the heads of their wearers. The governments of England and of Spain would have preferred a Coburg ; the son of Prince Ferdinand, and cousin of Prince Albert, was ready to hand. This was the great age of the marriageable Coburgs. Baron Stockmar, their *deus ex machina*, was at the height of his powers and of his private influence.[1] The magic of his loyalty was almost turning sand into gold. But his law was not recognised in France. The French government insisted upon a Bourbon, though they were ready to accept a Bourbon of the second order, and from Naples. The Bourbons of the second order knew that, however insecure might be the throne of Naples, Madrid was even more unsafe for a Neapolitan prince. The Spaniards for their part could not forget that they had conquered Naples ; nor did they rate highly the qualities of the Neapolitan reigning house. As the sons of Don Carlos were impossible, there remained only two Spanish cousins of the queen. The elder of these two young men was noted for effeminacy ; the younger for wildness of living. The younger inclined towards the liberals, and the young queen seemed to incline towards him. The queen-mother had quarrelled beyond hope of reconciliation with the mother of the two princes.

In this unhappy atmosphere the governments of England and France tried to come to an agreement with one another, with the Spanish royal house, and with the men of " fiercely expressive countenance " who were the leaders of parties in Spain. Superficially some progress was made under the government of Aberdeen. Unfortunately neither France nor England had a clear idea of each other's conditions. Whether it was a certain uneasiness of conscience that made Guizot and Aberdeen doubt their right to dispose so lightly of the queen's happiness, or limit by conditions of their own the choice of the Spanish people ; whether it was that

---

[1] For Stockmar's connexion with the Spanish marriage question see *Memoirs of Baron Stockmar* (English translation), vol. ii. chap. 21.

fateful cloudiness which comes over the highest resolutions
of statesmen when there is mischief to be made by heaven ;
whether it was Guizot's hesitation to face the desire of his
constitutional king for a dynastic marriage, or Aberdeen's
hesitation to face the desire of the constitutional prince
consort to continue the good success of his family ; whatever the reasons, Guizot and Aberdeen each remained mis-
informed about the other's views.

As early as 1843 Guizot had told Aberdeen through the
French ambassador that France had a right to render exclusion for exclusion ; that there must not be a Coburg
husband ; that Louis Philippe would only accept a Bourbon.[1]
In September 1843 Guizot met Aberdeen during the visit
of Queen Victoria to Louis Philippe ; Guizot wrote immediately after this meeting to the French ambassador at
Vienna that, although no exclusion was formally pronounced,
neither France nor England would work in the interest of
the candidate disliked by the other. If this agreement
were not kept, each side would have full liberty of action.
" The appearance of the prince of Coburg would be the
resurrection of the duc d'Aumale." [2] Nevertheless the
French ambassador in London thought Aberdeen preoccupied with the wishes of Victoria and Albert, and
unwilling openly to oppose them.[3]

Guizot soon had another preoccupation. In November
1844 he mentioned for the first time the possibility of a
marriage between the duc de Montpensier, the youngest
of Louis Philippe's sons, and the queen's sister. This
marriage would only take place after the birth of an heir
to the queen had secured the succession.

In 1845 the royal families of England and France again
met at Eu. Once more Guizot told Aberdeen that French
policy could not allow a Coburg husband. Guizot thought
that Aberdeen had seen his point, and had agreed with
him.[4] But he had no positive word from Aberdeen :
" point de convention, ni engagement politique." [5] There
is no doubt that Aberdeen wanted a settlement pleasing

[1] viii. 135.   [2] *Hist Parl.*, v. 314.   [3] viii. 181.
[4] viii. 227.   " Il fut bien entendu et reconnu par lord Aberdeen et
moi . . ."
[5] *Hist. Parl.*, v. 318.

to France, and was ready to agree that the queen should marry one of her Spanish cousins, and that after the queen had had children (not " a child " ; no risks were to be taken about the succession) there might be a marriage between Montpensier and the Infanta Luisa. There is also no doubt that Aberdeen had little difficulty in convincing the Coburg at Windsor that, in spite of the single-heartedness of Stockmar, the interest of European peace did not always coincide with the advancement of the Coburg family. But Aberdeen felt that ultimately the question must be decided by the Spaniards, and that the " exclusions " were not of equal value. For while the Coburg marriage would not destroy the balance of power, a marriage with a royal prince of France might revive an international question of the first importance. He would not encourage a Coburg marriage ; it was unreasonable that he should be asked to prevent it. Aberdeen, whose word was above reproach, told Bulwer afterwards that " no such understanding [to prevent the marriage] was ever come to or even approached." [1]

Guizot thought that he had put the Coburg out of the list of suitors. But he was still uneasy. In November 1845 the family, father, mother, and son, paid a visit to Windsor on their way to the brother settled in Lisbon. The voyage, the stopping-place, and the destination were suspicious. In Spain the French ambassador noticed the sinister appearance of a certain Herr Buschentall [sic] at the British embassy. Aberdeen was asked the meaning of it all. He said plainly—and Guizot might have taken notice—that the Coburgs were not English, and that it was not his business to advise them. At the same time he went to Windsor to prevent any indiscretion. He came back to tell the French chargé d'affaires that Queen Victoria and the prince consort were entirely loyal, and were not taking any secret steps to bring about the marriage. He gave his word as a gentleman that Guizot need not be alarmed.

Many months before 1846 the question was distorted through those personal rivalries which are the ruin of

[1] Bulwer, *Palmerston*, iii. 270.

states. The French and English ambassadors at Madrid were on the worst of terms. The Englishman, Bulwer, said of the Frenchman, Bresson, that " he belonged by birth to the middle class, and was consequently vulgarly preoccupied with his position as ambassador " ! [1] Guizot said of Bulwer that he had little influence in Spain, and was a man of more address than authority. Above all, " il était, au fond, de l'école et de la clientèle de lord Palmerston ! " [2] Lord Normanby, who succeeded [3] Lord Cowley as British ambassador at Paris during the most important moment of the crisis, was not one of the greatest ornaments of the diplomatic service. When in the summer of 1846 Palmerston came back to the foreign office, the dignity of every Frenchman was almost wounded in advance, although Palmerston had taken care to come to Paris in April, and show himself favourable to the *entente*.

In the first six months of the year matters had become dangerously entangled. There were the Coburg intrigues ; there was the wish of the Spanish queen-mother to get a better match for her daughter than was offered by any of her Bourbon cousins ; there were the plots of Spanish ministers, and the mutual suspicion of the ambassadors. In March Guizot had sent a formal memorandum to Aberdeen. His reasoning was in a sense too good for his thesis ; [4] unfortunately the Coburg marriage was the best from every point of view except that of France. Aberdeen made no direct answer, but sent to Guizot a letter from Bulwer advising a Habsburg marriage, if a Coburg were impossible, and arguing strongly against all the Bourbon candidates. There was nothing secret about this letter.

[1] Bulwer, *Palmerston*, iii. 213. A *Quarterly Review* article in 1868 was shameless enough to tell the whole of the dreadful secret about Bresson : " his early years had been passed in a counting-house " ! But Guizot himself acknowledged that Bresson was " très préoccupé de lui-même et de sa fortune." (viii. 154.) When Bulwer sent Bresson a casual note, written on a torn and smudged sheet of paper, Bresson took " un papier du même format, dont j'ai déchiré le bord, sur lequel j'ai versé autant d'encre . . ." ! (viii. 160-1.)

[2] viii. 159.   [3] August 1846.

[4] The correspondence between Louis Philippe and Guizot at this critical time was published, together with other letters relevant to the negotiations, in the *Revue rétrospective : archives secrètes du dernier gouvernement* (1848). See especially pp. 179-87 and 194-9.

Bulwer himself had suggested that it might be shown to Guizot. None the less Aberdeen reprimanded him for " pro-Coburg " activity, and, to prove his own good faith, sent this letter also to Guizot.

The French ambassador for his part had gone beyond his instructions. If the marriage between Montpensier and the queen's sister was to be delayed until after the queen had children, it might never take place at all ; since rumour held that there could be no children of a marriage between the queen and the elder of her two Spanish cousins. But if only the condition of delay could be withdrawn, or circumvented, the children of Montpensier's marriage might in their time inherit the crown of Spain. The queen-mother of Spain was anxious that at least one foreign power should have a direct interest in the welfare of the Spanish royal house ; the French ambassador saw the chance of a victory for his country—and a defeat for Bulwer—if he could bring about the simultaneity of the two marriages. Louis Philippe was indignant at the suggestion : " je n'ai jamais trompé personne, et je ne commencerai pas aujourd'hui à laisser tromper qui que ce soit sous mon nom."

At this point Palmerston showed that splendid tactlessness which was the envy of ministers of less important states. Palmerston's mind worked simply and decisively. The English government had never promised to co-operate with France in excluding the Coburgs ; therefore it was absurd to leave the Coburg out of consideration. The elder of the Spanish Bourbon cousins, Don Francisco, was impossible " on account of his insignificance and the want of those qualities which the husband of the queen ought to possess." Between the younger cousin, Don Enrique, and the Coburg prince the English government was indifferent. The Coburg might be called a French candidate because he was more nearly related to the family of Louis Philippe than to the queen of England ; here Palmerston turned the tables upon Guizot. The Coburg prince was not a remarkable person in himself ; but he was better than the Spanish or Neapolitan Bourbons. " The English government would see with pleasure a good cross introduced into the Royal Family of Spain." Don Enrique was a liberal, and, if the Spanish liberals could be taught a little liberalism of feeling and behaviour, his marriage to the queen might give the country a stable government.

Without reference to the delicate half-understanding between Aberdeen and Guizot, and at the moment when the French government was proposing one of the Spanish dukes as the queen's husband, Palmerston sent the French a copy of his instructions to Bulwer. He had reduced the candidates to three ; the Coburg came first, and then the two Spanish dukes. There followed a lecture to the Spanish ministers upon their unconstitutional behaviour, and a hint that successors might be found for them. The first part of this despatch offended Louis Philippe. If Palmerston still insisted upon the reality of the Coburg candidature, then the French were released from any promise to delay Montpensier's marriage. Therefore the instructions sent to Bresson were modified.[1] The second part of the letter offended and frightened the Spanish politicians ; their pride was the more wounded in that no reasonable man could deny the truth of what Palmerston had said about them. Palmerston followed up his despatch by conversations with the chargé d'affaires in which he ignored Montpensier. Finally, after delaying a month to answer the French proposal,[2] Palmerston told Louis Philippe that the considered opinion of the English government was in favour of Don Enrique. The Coburg prince might be kept in reserve for the queen's sister. The French answer came in the form of an announcement of the betrothal of Don Francisco to the queen, and of Montpensier to Doña Luisa Fernanda ; the two marriages were to be celebrated at the same time.

Guizot had become a diplomat of the eighteenth-century style. Mme de Lieven had told him to be more *raide* with Palmerston. But he might have remembered his own judgment upon the danger of haste, and the need for thinking out the general effect of a particular line of conduct ;

---

[1] Guizot thought that the queen-mother must be given " une perspective claire du mariage Montpensier." (*Revue rétrospective*, p. 186.)

[2] A Coburg family council was one cause of the delay. The King of the Belgians came to England on their behalf to discuss the whole question. But Queen Victoria and Prince Albert kept loyally to their agreement. (*Memoirs of Duke Ernest II. of Saxe-Coburg-Gotha*, i. 177-99.)

he might have remembered his own belief in the importance of an understanding with England, and the efforts which he had made to secure and maintain the *entente* ; in a last analysis it must be said that he might have remembered his own honour. For the disdain was now on Palmerston's side. " I must say Guizot cuts a most pitiful figure in the whole transaction, but I suppose that all he cares for is carrying his point. . . . I should have thought, however, that he would have showed [*sic*] more regard to character." [1] So wrote Palmerston to Normanby in Paris ; so thought English opinion. Louis Philippe suffered as much in loss of esteem. His own ambassador told Clarendon that the king had only acted " en bon père de famille," to get the dowry of Doña Luisa Fernanda for his son ! Queen Victoria wrote, according to Palmerston,[2] a " tickler " to Louis Philippe in answer to his letter of explanation. Greville, who was no particular friend of Palmerston, came to the conclusion, after reading " for three and a half hours " all the papers shown to him at the French embassy, that " we have been jockeyed by France in a very shabby, uncandid, underhand way." [3]

Guizot had won an empty victory. In return for the loss of his good name and the friendship and confidence of England he had no substantial gain. If the queen of Spain should have children, the sons or daughters of Montpensier would not inherit the Spanish crown. If the queen were childless, the powers in general, and England in particular, would never allow the claim of a French prince or his heirs to the succession.

The absolutist governments of Austria and Russia could *not (?)* be more satisfied. The union of the two constitutional powers of western Europe was broken ; Russia, Austria, and Prussia were free to make an end of the republic of Cracow, and thereby to destroy the last remnant of Polish independence.[4] Guizot had protested in elevated

---

[1] Bulwer, *Palmerston*, iii. 306.   [2] *Ibid.*, iii. 299.

[3] *Greville Memoirs*, ii. iii. 6. The cartoons and letterpress of *Punch* reflected, to the point of vulgarity, the one-sided disgust of public opinion in England.

[4] See *Hist. Parl.*, v. 284-8 and 334-40 for the debate in the French chambers upon the incorporation of Cracow in the Austrian Empire.

language, but could do nothing.   He now found it necessary
to come to terms with Metternich.   Metternich, seeing his
opportunity, had flattered Guizot in terms which were
soothing to read after the sarcasms of Palmerston, and the
letter in which Queen Victoria had told Louis Philippe
that she would never again believe the word of a French
king.

French and Austrian interests had only a limited ground
in common.   Neither wanted revolution ; neither wanted
a united Germany, a united Italy, or a strongly democratic
Switzerland.   Beyond sharing these fears of what might be,
the statesmen of the two countries could not agree upon
common action.   In Italy their aims were openly divergent.
Guizot could not forswear the principles of constitutional
government ; Metternich could not tolerate them.   When
the two powers were faced by the feckless " enlightenment "
of Pius ix., they found themselves unable even to act
together against the danger of revolution.

Meanwhile Palmerston, " l'ennemi de ma maison," as
Louis Philippe now called him, could do his will.   He made
no secret of his support of the radicals in Switzerland, and
the constitutional parties in Italy.   He sent Lord Minto
on a special mission first to the Swiss and then to the Italians.
The connivance of England was enough to encourage the
Italians to make a beginning.   In January 1848 a rebellion
broke out in Sicily, where a generation earlier Lord William
Bentinck had set up, at the expense of the British taxpayer,
a constitution on the proper model of 1688.   Within two
months of the kindling of the fire both Guizot and Louis
Philippe were exiles in England.   Such was the end of a
foreign policy conceived after long reflection, justified in
magnificent language and deduction from first principles,
and devised to serve the general interest of civilisation.

V

THE PLACE OF GUIZOT IN EUROPEAN HISTORY

" A tous les pouvoirs, surtout à un pouvoir nouveau, il faut un peu de grandeur, dans leurs œuvres et sur leur drapeau. L'ordre et la protection régulière des intérêts privés, ce pain quotidien des peuples, ne leur suffisent pas longtemps ; c'est la condition nécessaire du gouvernement, ce n'est pas l'unique besoin de l'humanité." [1]

Such was the standard which Guizot had set before the government of the restoration. No man has better formulated the charge made against himself. For his own government after 1842 did not pass a single measure of social importance or interest. Even the timid efforts in the direction of economic reform were often defeated by the fear of offending those in possession. The sensible plan for the conversion of the *rentes* in 1847 was given up in the face of opposition from the *rentier* class of Paris ; the manufacturers successfully opposed the tariff proposals brought forward by the government.[2] The enterprise of Broglie's ministry was never continued ; practically nothing was done to lessen the rigours of the industrial revolution. Guizot was not blind to the faults of his party. He spoke of it in a letter written to Lenormant after 1848 as " without breadth of foundation, without loftiness of view, too cold and weak-hearted, caring sincerely for an ordered liberty, but refusing to grasp the principles of order, and the con-

[1] i. 208.
[2] Levasseur, *Histoire des classes ouvrières et de l'industrie en France de 1789 à 1870* (ii. 134), says of the government of July that its social legislation was " nothing for ten years " and then only four important measures " sur les brevets d'invention, sur les patentes, sur les prud'hommes ; sur le travail des enfants dans les manufactures." A few measures were in course of preparation at the time of the fall of the government. Guizot (see above, p. 158) gives a longer list : but the achievement was meagre enough in comparison with the need.

sequences of liberty ; overflowing with little jealousies and little fears, visited neither by greatness of hope nor greatness of desire, even shrinking from desire and hope lest its quiet should be troubled or endangered. . . . I dare not say more, lest I say too much." [1] Yet Guizot did not see, during his years of office, the mistake of trusting to those who supported him only out of self-interest. He was so much greater than his followers that he never realised his own isolation. He was almost alone in following principles, while they were almost unanimous in following success.

In a review of the first two volumes of Guizot's *Mémoires* [2] Renan described the type of man who had won his way to success in the troubled time of French history, the years of the revolutionary distress : " l'homme d'ordre, comme on l'appelle, prêt à tout subir, même ce qu'il déteste ; cet éternel Fouché, avec ses perfidies honnêtes, mentant par conscience, et n'importe qui a vaincu, toujours vainqueur." The interests of this sort of strong man " le portèrent à être toujours de l'avis du plus fort." The monarchy of July had been unwise enough to take the support of these men for the support of France. " Instead of representing rights, the government could only represent interests. Materialism in politics produces the same effects as materialism in moral conduct ; it can never inspire self-sacrifice, and as a consequence, loyalty. . . . The Gospel was right in saying : He who would save his life must lose it. Nothing can be founded upon self-interest ; self-interest is afraid of noble endeavour and heroic loyalties, and can establish no more than a rule of weakness and corruption, a rule which is at the mercy of any minority resolved upon its overthrow."

It is true that Guizot hated self-interest, and thought of society in terms of long duration, of magnificence, and of a freedom knowing its own law. But his own vivid historical imagination, his sentiment of continuity, blinded him—as Burke was blinded—to the realities before his eyes. His sense of the past and his instinct for the distant future were a perpetual fountain of contemplation to his mind ; he

---

[1] Quoted in Thureau-Dangin, *op. cit.*, vi. 49.
[2] In the *Revue des deux mondes*, July 2, 1859, p. 201.

saw the present as though irradiated by a rainbow from the driven water of history.

During the later years of the monarchy of July a mind as subtle as Guizot's, but without Renan's echoing regret for the closed windows of heaven, reflected upon the rule of the middle class. Tocqueville took care to study in Europe and in the larger letters of America the democracy which he disliked.[1] He came to the conclusion that the rule of mediocrity and ordinariness was destined to become world-wide.[2] The men of the middle class, to whom sovereignty had passed, and with whom it would rest for a season, were " active, industrious, often dishonest, limited in outlook, rash at times through vanity or egoism, fearful by temperament, moderate in everything, except in a liking for prosperity, and mediocre." [3] The rule of this class must be the transformation of government into private interest.

The monarchy of July illustrated this tendency. Towards the end of the reign of Louis Philippe the government of France " had the appearance of a business company, all the operations of which were undertaken in view of the profit which would accrue to the shareholders." [4] In spite of the wealth of talent in the chambers, the political world between 1830 and 1848 was made up of men of one class, men who were too much alike to form the material out of which different parties might be made. Hence the emptiness of the parliamentary debates, the powerlessness of the

[1] " Ce que je reproche à l'égalité, ce n'est pas d'entraîner les hommes à la poursuite des jouissances défendues ; c'est de les absorber entièrement dans la recherche des jouissances permises. Ainsi, il pourrait bien s'établir dans le monde une sorte de matérialisme honnête qui ne corromprait pas les âmes, mais qui les amollirait et finirait par détendre sans bruit tous leurs ressorts." (De la Démocratie en Amérique. Collected Works, iii. 215.)

[2] Tocqueville's remarkable analysis of the situation in France at the turn of the year 1847 is given in a draft of a manifesto drawn up by himself and his friends in October 1847, under the title " De la classe moyenne et du peuple," and in a speech made in the chamber on January 27, 1848. (Collected Works, ix. 514-35.) The contents of the manifesto and the speech are repeated in Tocqueville's Souvenirs.
It is of interest to compare the indictment of the middle class in England by Carlyle and, particularly, by Matthew Arnold.

[3] A. de Tocqueville, Souvenirs, p. 6.

[4] Ibid., p. 7.

political leaders, the heavy and stagnant atmosphere which seemed to surround the tribune and deaden the voices of the speakers. The talent of the orators was great ; the effect produced by their speeches was slight and ephemeral. Their words differed more than their ideas ; however much the parties in opposition might make their rivalries to stand out in high relief, they did not show clearly that, if they were in power, they would act differently from their opponents. Therefore the nation looked upon them not as political adversaries discussing the affairs of France but as children of a family occupied in settling their little domestic interests. " Elle s'endort en les écoutant, ou s'agite de ses propres pensées." [1] As early as 1839, when he first entered the chamber, Tocqueville found a coldness, an absence of generosity. " Rien n'y est jeune en un mot, même les plus jeunes." [2]

The indifference of the governing class to the widest issues of politics was the more serious, because there was still time for society and government in France to educate the democracy. This chance would pass. For this reason Tocqueville wrote under the impression of what he called " une sorte de terreur religieuse " [3] to arouse his countrymen to the danger of their situation. His outlook was pessimistic ; his remedies were not reassuring ; his hope was not brilliant. " We have destroyed an aristocratic society ; we have been content to sit among the ruins of the old building, and we seem willing to stay there for ever." [4] This " accidie " was the most deadly of modern sins. " Nothing now seems either forbidden or allowed, either honest or shameful, either true or false." [5] Yet there was still a cause where victory was better than defeat. The nations of Europe were moving towards a state where there was no alternative between democratic liberty, with all its faults, and the tyranny of the Caesars.[6] To fight against democracy was to fight against God Himself ; the world cannot but accommodate itself to the social state imposed

[1] Tocqueville, *De la classe moyenne et du peuple. Collected Works*, ix. 516.
[2] Tocqueville, *Correspondance. Collected Works*, v. 442.
[3] *De la Démocratie en Amérique*, i. 8 (and *Correspondance*, v. 428-9).
[4] *Ibid.*, i. 15.   [5] *Ibid.*, i. 18.   [6] *Ibid.*, ii. 257.

upon it by Providence.[1]   The wishes of a democracy were
changeful ; its agents were coarse ; its laws were imperfect.
Democracy lacked grandeur and poetry.   But every other
safeguard against the tyranny of one man had disappeared ;
great families, great corporations, all had been destroyed.
The development of the manners and institutions of democracy, the peaceable rule of the greatest number, was the
only means of securing any kind of freedom.   It was better
to be reduced to a level of uniformity by liberty than by the
most benevolent of tyrants.[2]

Guizot knew Tocqueville's anxiety, and shared his dislike of a society which had lost, or never found, elegance
and distinction.   But he would not understand the bearing
of this criticism upon the isolation of the middle class.   He
explained the differences between himself and Tocqueville as the result of a difference in the orientation of their
academic studies.   Guizot had followed the development
of the older European societies, and the various elements
of which they were composed.   In this long inquiry, " I
formed the habit," Guizot told the French Academy in
1861,[3] " of regarding diversity of composition as essential
to the existence of our great European societies.   I compared these constituent parts of the social order ; I examined
their rights and their relative importance ; I gave each
one its place and its function."   Tocqueville had made
democracy the main subject of his investigations ; he was
therefore led to give to the democratic element almost an
exclusive place in his political thought.   Guizot, on the
other hand, was bound always to attach great weight to
each of the orders in French society, and to do his best to
unite them under one banner.

In spite of Tocqueville's warning Guizot felt justified
in keeping his attention upon the chamber and the electors,
and in speaking of the comfortable middle class as " la
grande société saine et tranquille."   The critical minority
who troubled the peace of the nation and its leaders were

[1] *De la Démocratie en Amérique*, i. 8.   [2] *Ibid.*, iii. 258.
[3] Guizot, *Discours académiques* (1861), pp. 118-19.   The occasion was
Guizot's answer as Directeur of the Academy to the " Discours de
réception Lacordaire."   The speech is also printed in Tocqueville,
Collected Works, ix. 635-43.

no more than "la petite société maladive" ; no account need be taken of them in devising a policy of long view.[1]

Yet the development of a critical view of society in the years before the revolution of 1848 is of much greater interest to a later generation than the political rivalries which took up a disproportionate part of Guizot's thought and action.

It might seem that the bourgeois revolution of 1830 had little to do with any great artistic movement ; but this revolution, accidental as it seemed on its political side, was on a wide reading a victory for individualism against tradition. For in more than one sense the Bourbons of the elder line represented the tradition of the eighteenth century. The romantics who wanted to break away from this tradition, and to write for a public interested in the expression of personal emotion, were as much in need of freedom from priests and press-censors as were the bourgeoisie who hated absolute government and feared the restoration of the old monarchical order. For poets as well as for business men, small land-holders, and fathers of families with social ambition, the revolution meant the triumph of a cause.

The romantic movement in its search after individuality and colour of emotion, after "wonder" and "glamour," had led to a new interest in history, and applied to literature the vividness of painting. Historical writing became the best means of expression for those who could not create imaginative literature of the highest order. In history the "romantic" elements were ready to hand ; the events were personal and dramatic, touched with the sorrow of far-off things and the mystery of the remote in time.[2] The contrast between the past and the present, a contrast which any historian can use unfairly in an age hungry for romance, could be made to point a weapon against the dull and ineffective government, the unheroic interlude, of the monarchy of July. Thus Lamartine, anxious for "something to be done," wrote a history of the Girondins[3] as a tale of bold and generous action, and an attack upon a government which, by contrast with the fearlessness and movement of

---

[1] *Hist. Parl.*, iii. 562-3.   [2] See below, p. 242.
[3] From this point of view, Carlyle's *Past and Present* (1843) is an English parallel to the *Histoire des Girondins*.

the revolution, was made up of men "toujours immobiles, toujours tremblants." The study of personal emotion meant, especially in history, that great men and dignified actions were not alone worth consideration. Misery and distress, the common fortune of the common man, had as great a claim to memory and record as the capriciousness of kings.

From a closer attention to the suffering and the troubled lot of men in times past, from half-historical, half-romantic books such as Victor Hugo's *Notre Dame de Paris*,[1] arose the question : Whence all this misery ? The study of history made it possible to give some answer to this question. Out of the story of every phase and type of human action there developed an inquiry into the life and death, the movement and purpose, of human societies. With this material before them men of a questioning mind turned from the romantic search after the particular and the distant to the construction of general laws and of a philosophy of history. Their generalisations were made without an exact scrutiny of the material, and in many cases without the temper essential to a philosophical inquiry. Michelet [2] is the most striking example of an artist in words who believed himself to be more of an historian than a craftsman, and as much a philosopher as an historian. Guizot himself, although he blamed the superficiality of Michelet, had worked up a theory of human progress from a stock of knowledge too slight to bear the weight of his deductions.

The next step was to find in these general laws and in this philosophy of history the key to the understanding of the present, and the means whereby the future shape of society might be forecasted. It is true that the most far-reaching discoveries were yet to be made by the historical

---

[1] Published in 1831.

[2] For an account of Michelet's philosophy of history see G. Monod, *La Vie et la pensée de Jules Michelet* (2 vols. Paris, 1923). Monod explains the influence upon Michelet of Vico's *Scienza Nuova*.

Ranke's limitation of the historian to the duty of telling " what happened " is a reaction from the superficial history and philosophy of the school of Michelet and the German romantics. Ranke's own view is open to great philosophical objection, but was a necessary antidote to influences which put historical studies at the mercy of superficial generalisation, and allowed them to become the instrument of political or religious propaganda. See below, p. 293.

method : but the results already achieved with the aid of this new instrument were striking enough.[1]   Men became confident that by taking thought they could exercise a wider control over the form of their social organisation. The unexpected violence and unreasoned excesses of the period of revolution seemed to have discredited all belief in the capacity of man in society to order his fate in accordance with an enlightened good sense.   The restoration of this belief in the value of ordered thought was of the highest value to human dignity ; there was no other way of escape from the gloomiest views upon the future of European civilisation.   Out of this confidence arose a new mode of inquiry into the field of historical phenomena ; an inquiry in which economic facts and economic changes were given as great a weight as the manifestations of religion or the curiosities of politics.   The result of this new direction of interest was the literature of the social question.

Here we come to a new appearance in human history ; a dawn as bright as that which first opened undiscovered continents to view.   In the past many voices had denounced the covetousness of rich men, or pitied the hard case of poverty.   Yet no one had dared to think, and few had even wished to think, that disease and drudgery would ever be conjured away by human power.   The philosophy of classical antiquity had disdained the humble case of the greater number of human beings.   The Christian middle ages had seen in human tears the only guarantee of repentance, a lighter chastisement against a darker eternity.   The political thought of the seventeenth century had begun to escape from the tyranny of priests, but had scarcely applied its measure to economic conditions.   The political writings of the age of reason were directed against the despotism of rulers ; the philosophers who believed man to be born free under a clear heaven could hardly rebel against the tyranny of nature.   The economists of the eighteenth century concerned themselves mainly with the ordering of states and the wealth of nations.

[1] It must be remembered that the application of the historical method to the studies of geology and the textual criticism of the Bible had produced the most startling results even before the new method was applied to the study of the evolution of living organisms.

Yet in the generation before the French Revolution the physiocrats had pointed the way to the new methods of investigation, and laid the foundations upon which their successors could build a new house of life. With or without a passionate attack upon those who multiplied the pains of life or were callous to suffering, this age had turned to a colder study of the economic conditions which might admit of far-reaching improvement. A better knowledge of the social transformations of the past showed the possibility of change ; mastery of the forces of land and water gave a greater control over change. At first certain principles were taken as immutable.[1] The historical analysis did not reach beyond the immediate past. But it soon became realised that principles of action, like the principle of *laissez-faire* (if such can be called action), which were thought to be true of all human conditions, were only historically devised rules for dealing with particular situations.

The rule of non-interference was a necessary weapon against the multiplicity of regulation and illogicality of custom which hampered human freedom in the later eighteenth century ; other circumstances might demand other rules. In the intellectual excitement of discovering new rules for a rapidly changing society the more active minds were led to exaggerate both the rate of change and the power of human forethought to fix and control an unstable material. The lesson of the failure of the political enlightenment of the previous century was not fully learned ; cloud - cuckoo - land remained a familiar mark on the horizon.

Within this literature of the social question it is possible to see many stages between the romantic movement proper and the pseudo-scientific socialism of the eighteen-forties. On the one hand there is the religious exaltation of Lamennais. Here there is little that does not belong to the order of ideas of earlier religious reformers or prophets. Lamen-

---

[1] Dupont de Nemours, in a pamphlet of 1768, entitled *De l'origine et du progrès d'une science nouvelle*, had spoken with the confidence of his time of the physiocratic doctrine, " qui, d'après la Nature de l'homme expose les loix *nécessaires* d'un Gouvernement fait pour l'homme, et propre à l'homme de tous les climats et de tous les pays." (Ed. A. Dubois, Paris, 1910, p. 35.)

nais understood the pitilessness of an impersonal order of society. His own experience had led him to denounce, in the temper of a Hebrew prophet, the abominable rule of kings and priests.[1] Beyond an appeal to fellowship and pity there is no specific inquiry into the remedy for long-perpetuated misery ; no investigation into the impersonal causes which seemed to aggravate the offence. Nearer to tempered political action are the attacks of Lamartine upon the blind power of rich men without mercy. But Lamartine had not that crystalline mind which takes account of the slow development of institutions, nor did he show any of the confused political wisdom of the early socialists.

It is in the school of Saint-Simon that the most original and most remarkable thought is to be found. For all the vagueness of his theories and the futility of his life, Saint-Simon [2] was more practical than most men of his age in that he saw the general drift of society. He was the first philosopher to understand the immensity of the political consequences of the industrial revolution. This contemporary of Burke and of Napoleon saw that the old formulae of power were ceasing to apply to the conditions of civilised life ; that it was time to abandon the " songes menteurs " of antiquity ; that, if things were not to govern men, the work of statesmen and the conception of authority must be transformed from the old conception of " rule over men " into the new form of the " administration of things." But with this clear-sightedness into the fundamental order of the present and the future went only a disconnected and untried conception of the method and character of the necessary changes. The Saint-Simonians made a few brilliant suggestions of a practical kind, of which the most important was a plan for

[1] See especially the *Paroles d'un croyant*, and see below, p. 272.

[2] Saint-Simon (b. 1760) came of a younger branch of the ducal family of Saint-Simon. He took part in the war of the American Revolution. During the French Revolution he was imprisoned for a time, but managed to make a considerable fortune by speculating in land. He proposed to use this fortune in the execution of schemes such as the construction of a canal between the Atlantic and the Pacific. Towards the end of his life Saint-Simon fell into great poverty. His most important work, *Le Nouveau Christianisme*, was left unfinished at his death in 1825. The best summary of his doctrine was made by one of his followers, A. Bazard, *Exposition de la doctrine de Saint-Simon* (2 vols. 1829-30).

the mobilisation of credit by means of banks. They coined
a few phrases which still echo through the modern world :
the " exploitation of man by man " ; the " right to work."
It was unfortunate that they left the field open to charlatans
without their insight and often without their disinterested-
ness. It was particularly unfortunate for France that the
most influential of the young writers who borrowed their
ideas was almost the least fitted for the handling of men or
the steady development of a practical policy. Louis Blanc
was the son of a Corsican mother and a father who had
been a legitimist in politics but had become reconciled to
Napoleon. The Bourbons gave him a pension ; the pension
was stopped by the monarchy of July, and Louis Blanc had
to earn his living as a teacher and a journalist. Only in
1840 did he begin to secure the notoriety for which his
vanity and ambition were hungry. In this year he published a book with the title : *L'Organisation du travail*.[1] The
idea of the book was to suggest a remedy for the pheno-
menon of cyclical unemployment. The name and the
character of this disease of a newly industrialised society
were "undiscovered " by economists ; its miseries were
none the less real because they were wrongly diagnosed.
The facts obtained from the statistics of the health of the
French people supported Louis Blanc's thesis of the degradation of life caused by the uncertainty of employment and
the severity of " blind " competition. There was a steady
increase in the number of conscripts from urban areas who
were physically unfit for military service (a nineteenth-
century test of suitability for the good life). In these
same urban areas the number of crimes showed a similar
increase. Guizot might well think of the Marquesas islands
as a cheap, safe, and not unhealthy place where French
citizens could continue to enjoy the rights of man !
   Louis Blanc's remedies were superficial, and unlikely to
bring anything but chaos to a highly organised society.
The very simplicity of his ideas made them popular. Competition was to be destroyed by competition itself. National

---

[1] The *Organisation du travail* first appeared in the *Revue du progrès*.
An English edition, with an introduction by J. A. R. Marriott, was published in 1913.

co-operative workshops were to be opened by workmen who would be provided with capital by state loans. These workshops, owing to their superior productive powers and the substitution of a better motive for work than mere competition, would drive the capitalist out of his own markets. Therefore capitalism and its attendant evils would disappear !

None the less, for this guileless belief in a self-propelled and self-steered mechanical ship of safety, Louis Blanc gave expression to the general anxiety about the disorganised society of his time. Even political adventurers like Louis Napoleon found it necessary to venture across the border-land of the ground common to Lamennais and Saint-Simon. In 1844 Louis Napoleon, with his feeling for what the people wanted and his real sympathy with the poor and the dis-inherited, published a plan for the extinction of pauper-ism in France. The plan consisted merely of a few vague suggestions for the establishment of agricultural colonies.

.   .   .   .   .   .

All these men, who had left the literature of " glamour " for the literature of scientific inquiry, all the poor men of France who felt the distress of economic life, all except the bourgeois and the newly arrived rich men, despised a government of outworn parliamentarism, statesmen with a policy of fear, and a ruling class apparently indifferent to the real problems and the real suffering of the people. The president of the chamber once told the deputies : " We are sent here to make laws, not to give work to workmen." Little wonder that the socialists could see no hope for the regeneration of society upon the lines laid down by Guizot and his party.[1] The French people must be careful not to begin again the cycle of revolutions and wars in pursuit of deceptive political forms, or waste their energies in the establishment of some kind of republic. Fourier attacked the sacred revolutionary principle of equality : " l'égalité

---

[1] For an account of the earlier socialists and their influence in 1848 see, among other works, Levasseur, *op. cit.*, vol. i. bk. 3, chap. 7, " Les études sociales sous la Restauration " ; vol. ii. bk. 4, chap. 1, " Ques-tions politiques et questions sociales " : Gide et Rist, *Histoire des doctrines économiques* (English translation) : Quentin-Bouchart, *La Crise sociale de 1848.*

politique n'est qu'un leurre; il faut passer de l'égalité de droit à celle de fait " ; aristocracy was not founded upon a law, but was the consequence of a fact : the fact of private property.   Like most intellectual minorities, the Saint-Simonian school of socialists did not care for universal suffrage.   Victor Considérant thought that the French people were not, as electors, capable of giving the slightest mandate " en connaissance de cause."   Political right was no real benefit. " Le droit est la protection métaphysique et morte qui a remplacé, pour le peuple, la protection vivante qu'on le devait."   This doctrine of right, laid down in the charter with a pompous sterility, had only served to mask the injustice of the establishment of the rule of individualism.

The socialist attack upon the foundation of government might seem to be no practical danger.   All the leaders except Proudhon agreed in looking to the state to introduce their new society.   They were not hostile to religion ; they believed that their systems, based upon the idea of social justice, would reconcile all classes ; they discouraged violence ; they were " apostles, not prophets " ; they expected that reason would lead men to see the faults of a society which was historical and not logical in its order, the piecemeal work of time.   The very diversity of their utopias was enough to prevent a concerted plan ; they could not even come to an agreement upon the principle of social justice to be applied to the distribution of wealth.

Nevertheless these ideas, popularised by current imaginative literature, and a mass of imaginative work at second hand, in which the virtuous workman was the hero, became the reading of the proletariat.   Even so, their effect must not be exaggerated.   Not all the proletariat could read. Most men were more occupied in earning a living than in thinking about the justice or injustice of the social order. The actual numbers of the urban population of France engaged in large-scale industry in 1846 was scarcely more than a million (out of a total population of thirty-five and a half millions).   But the discontent was not limited to those who were actually miserable.   Dissatisfaction with the government had become fashionable.   Only a month before the days of February [1] in which the dynasty was overthrown Tocqueville had warned the chamber of that " instinct and sentiment of instability in the country which was often a precursor and sometimes a cause of revolution." [2] " Le désordre n'est pas dans les faits, mais il est entré profondément dans les esprits." [3]

If a new attack were to be made, Tocqueville thought that property would be the objective. Property had not been attacked in the earlier revolutions, because of the existence of other privileges which had indeed an origin in the system of property, but an origin which was concealed. As soon as the outworks of the social defence had fallen, the rights of property appeared as the last stronghold of a fallen world of aristocracy, an isolated privilege in a society wherein all institutions had been brought down to a common level. The impracticability of the socialist remedies was beside the mark. Those who were most influenced by the socialist writings were least able to judge them critically. The poorer class had lost the beliefs, but kept the prejudices of an earlier generation, and had admitted the doctrine of self-interest as the rule of its action without understanding the science of self-interest ; its egoism was as unenlightened as its loyalty.[4]

In the face of this movement of opinion which they did not in the least understand, the ministers of the bourgeoisie had also to meet a difficult economic situation. The enterprise of the country was causing a drain upon its capital. The development of railways increased this call upon the national resources. Commerce was falling behind industry

[1] In August 1847 Tocqueville had not thought that there was any need for excessive anxiety. In spite of the symptoms of instability in the state, society was firmly established, if only because there was no other foundation for it. (Tocqueville to Nassau Senior. *Collected Works*, vii. 231.)

[2] *Ibid.*, ix. 521.

[3] Tocqueville, *Souvenirs*, p. 15. (From *De la classe moyenne et du peuple*, ix. 516-19.)

[4] *De la démocratie en Amérique*, i. 14-15.
There was not in France, as there had been in England during the early days of the industrial revolution, a strong belief in another world wherein are redressed the wrongs of this life. No great religious movement existed to divert the enthusiasm of an orator or the passion of his audience.

in its rate of growth. New markets were not being exploited fast enough to carry away the multitude of goods produced for sale. The bad harvests of 1845 and 1846, the outbreak of the potato disease, and the great floods in the Loire valley (in 1846) called for large imports of foodstuffs. At the moment when French credit looked for the aid of foreign loans, Great Britain had to meet a similar industrial and economic crisis, and could give little help. The effects of this crisis were indeed less severe in France than in Great Britain, but there was much distress. Relief measures were so inadequate that in parts of the country food convoys had to be escorted by soldiers.

In the end the government of Louis Philippe was overthrown by violence. Until this decisive hour came, the opposition had to make their attacks in the chamber or among the electorate. The parliamentary opposition was as much divided as were the socialists outside the chamber. The legitimists indeed possessed a principle, but a principle which every Frenchman distrusted ; the Bonapartists had a name which every Frenchman knew. Their hour would come when the name was carried by a man. The republicans had no political leader of the first rank. Thureau-Dangin has described Ledru-Rollin, the most important politician of the left, as a big, melodramatic bourgeois, an imitator of Danton, " mais ne comprenant l'audace qu'en paroles."

Whatever his limitations, Guizot was unrivalled in a house where he had long been master. Thiers might attack him, but Thiers was himself a man of order, and felt as little as Guizot the need for a new idea and a new policy to save the house of Orleans.

In 1846 the opposition, having no other charge to make, accused the government of attempting to corrupt the electorate. Very few facts were proved, though a little later two of Guizot's own colleagues were attacked on the charge of personal corruption. Thiers' attitude towards these attacks showed the curious ingenuity of his mind. He acknowledged that a free government could not escape from the unpleasing work of flattering deputies and electors. He made an odd comparison between the corruption carried

through the body politic by the rule of liberalism and the
poisons distributed over the human body by the beneficent
process of the circulation of the blood. He refused to
blacken his own time and country by accepting the stories
of a widespread corruption. There was never more private
honesty, though at other times there might have been more
" elevation." Even so Thiers was afraid that the government was in danger of accepting the satisfaction of private
interest as inevitable. The conservative party as a whole
felt that it was time for its leaders to make a stand against
the place-hunters who had clung round it from the beginning. Barante warned Guizot against too much com-
plaisance to the " exigences des députés." [1]

Guizot's defence, which satisfied Tocqueville, was that
isolated cases of corruption were bound to occur ; free
institutions weakened the power of the government to prevent these cases ; therefore the work of a free government
must be judged as a whole. Guizot was too ready to take
his own apology as sufficient, and, like Chatham, to wrap
himself in his own stainless honour. The French people were
unlikely to be satisfied with Guizot's declaration that a
man's first duty in life was to submit to imperfection while
keeping himself free from its stain ! The non-voters, jealous
of the electoral class, exaggerated the abuses of authority,
and began to think that the representative system was " a
political machine designed to bring about the domination
of certain private interests and to settle all the salaried posts
in the hands of a certain number of families."

Owing to this belief the attack upon the government took
the shape of a demand for the reform of the electoral law.
The demand was popular. It was a convenient way of
uniting all parties without making more definite plans for
the future. A movement favourable to an increase in the
numbers of the electorate had been growing in force throughout the years of the monarchy. The franchise was limited
to men paying 200 francs in direct taxes. Between 1830
and 1846 the electoral roll had been increased from 99,000
to 224,000. The proposals of the moderate reformers would
have lowered the property qualification to include all who

[1] Barante, *Souvenirs*, vii. 229 and 240.

paid 100 francs in direct taxation. This would have meant an increase of 200,000 in the number of electors.

Why did Guizot refuse this moderate demand? If he had allowed this extension, he would have taken from the opposition the most popular element in their programme. There was no danger that the small bourgeois who were to be enfranchised would support a campaign against the monarchy or an attack upon property. Guizot himself, when minister of instruction, had described his scheme of public education as a means of educating the French people. In 1837 he had told the chamber that the limits of political capacity might be extended when, in course of time, the progress of enlightenment, the increase of wealth, and all those causes which transform the state of society had called a greater number of men and a greater number of classes to the exercise of political power. " It is the perfection of our government that political rights, limited by their very nature to those who are capable of using them, should be open to extension . . . as the capacity for their exercise is itself developed ; and it is at the same time the peculiar excellence of our government that it is always encouraging the exercise of these capacities, that it goes on its way sowing the seeds of political enlightenment in such a manner that at the very moment when it is assigning a limit to political rights it is also trying to extend this limit." [1]

Why should Guizot have been afraid of the voting power of those who owed to his own scheme of education the means of their political enlightenment? Why did he misjudge the elements of the political situation, and forget the warning which he had given to the monarchy of the restoration? "Des capacités méconnues n'en demeurent pas moins réelles et actives ; et il y a, à leur refuser le droit qui leur appartient, autant d'imprudence que d'injustice, un grand malaise pour la société, un grand péril pour le pouvoir." [2]

The answer lies partly in Guizot's temperament, partly in the history of his political life. He had fought so long and so difficult a struggle for the establishment of order and the destruction of anarchy that he had come to exaggerate

[1] Hist. Parl., iii. 105.
[2] Essay on Élections (1826). Printed in Discours académiques, 1861.

the strength of the revolutionary parties. He had fallen into the curious mistake of trying to establish the sovereignty of the people without the co-operation of the people. He saw the monarchy of July under the ideal form of the legislator of the *Contrat social* imposing upon society the rule of its own safety. The exclusion of prejudice, excitement, demagogy, violence was the first and essential work of his time ; therefore the measures which furthered this work were good in themselves. " Le principe de la capacité politique, introduit dans notre législation comme source des droits politiques, est peut-être la plus belle, la plus utile conquête que nous ayons faite depuis quinze ans." (Guizot was speaking in 1831.) " Le principe de la capacité politique a effectivement détrôné l'anarchie. Je prends donc acte de l'hommage qui a été rendu par tout le monde à ce principe." [1]

Hence the failure to look beyond the need for the political organisation of the liberties which had been achieved in the revolution of 1789 and reasserted in the revolution of 1830. Guizot would not see that in a great society the safeguarding of liberty is something more than the work of the few ; something more than the suppression of anarchy in the streets. Freedom is many-sided, and there were depths in the content of liberty which Guizot never sounded.

Enough has been said of Guizot's character to show that the particular form of political action to which he was accustomed was a form suited to his temperament. He was by nature a leader of men ; he had acted as a leader long before he had found any followers ! His view of government implied domination, self-sufficiency. " Le gouvernement sera toujours et partout la plus grand emploi des facultés humaines, par conséquent celui qui veut les âmes les plus hautes." [2] There is little room here for a saying deeper than any desire for power . . . *beati sunt humiles.*

It is not mere fancy to take some account of Guizot's protestantism. Like Bismarck, he failed to see that the close and continual co-operation of every element in society can alone lead to the attainment of the good life. He lacked the feeling for a commonwealth wherein inequality of condition

[1] *Hist. Parl.*, i. 214.   [2] Guizot, *Washington*, p. 154.

was no barrier to the positive contribution of all the citizens to a common cause. He never attained to the catholic conception of the church. As a Christian he knew the value of a high standard of personal conduct and charity ; his association with protestant organisations had been one of the most important elements of his inner life. Yet he was not free from that spiritual pride which saw liberty only in individual action, and religion only in the right development of personal holiness. He would not understand the solidarity of human life, the common responsibility of men for the common weaknesses of men ; the greater corporate responsibility of the strong for the failures of the weak.[1]

Hence he never understood the meaning of the agitation for electoral reform. He never saw it as a symbol ; as the expression of an obscurely felt need for common action ; as a means whereby men together might put an end to the exploitation of man by man. He ignored the hopes of common men ; he forgot that hope was more noble than disdain.

Once taken from its association with the deep instincts of mutual aid, the principle of universal suffrage, or any lesser extension of the franchise, could be discussed with an irrelevant penetration. In the early years of his political life Guizot had developed a broad, and yet an entirely insufficient view of the whole question. As mediæval thinkers had spoken of the *oratores*, *bellatores*, and *laboratores* who together made up the earthly city, so Guizot divided modern society into three categories. He included in his first category those who had no need to work for their living, but drew an income from land or capital. In the second

---

[1] A letter from Molé to Barante (August 28, 1847) attributed the weakness of the government to the over-development of individualism : " Avec tout notre étalage de légalité, au fond le gouvernement sans principe, indifférent et athée que nous avons, n'est que le gouvernement du plus fort." (Lamennais had said the same thing years before in his *Essai sur l'indifférence*.) " On récompense par l'argent ou des emplois ceux dont on est content ; on tâche d'atteindre par des lois ceux qui troublent ou qui résistent." The doctrinaires had tried to reconcile individualism with morality. " En le légitimant, en l'écrivant dans les lois, en le faisant accepter aux consciences les plus sévères, en subordonnant enfin le droit et l'intérêt de l'unité sociale au droit et à l'intérêt de chacun, ils ont rendu le gouvernement et, peut-être la société impossible." The effect of this individualism was to make the poor think themselves oppressed. (Barante, *Souvenirs*, vii. 226-7.)

category were those who exploited their land or capital, and thereby enriched themselves and provided subsistence for their dependents and workpeople. The rest of society fell into the third category of those who were without land or capital, or the means of borrowing capital, and whose work only provided for their own subsistence and the maintenance of their families.

It is unnecessary, in an age already wearied with the repetition of Marxian formulae, to point out the insufficiency of this analysis. There is more economic truth in any one of a hundred little handbooks. Nevertheless the conclusions which Guizot drew from this threefold division determined his views on the question of the franchise. The economic categories corresponded to a similar division in the moral order. In the first class were men whose leisure permitted them to devote themselves almost entirely to the culture of their intelligence. The second category of men were compelled by their business to acquire knowledge and ideas by means of which they could understand general notions, form some conception of the complexity and inter-relation of things, and recognise conclusions established by intelligence superior to their own. The men of the third category were prevented by their work from leaving the narrow circle of their individual interests, interests which were limited to the satisfaction of the daily needs of exist-ence. Political capacity, that is to say, the franchise, belonged only to the first two classes. Political intelligence and general intellectual capacity were not to be found among the class " qui ne travaille que pour vivre, et ne vit que pour travailler."

Guizot developed this thesis in an essay on *Élections* pub-lished in 1826. He gave his opinion almost in the same words nearly a quarter of a century later and after the fall of the monarchy of July.[1] He repeated his statement of 1849 in a pamphlet which he published in 1855.[2] He used the same argument in 1831, when he was defending the principle of an hereditary peerage,[3] and in 1846, when he

---

[1] *De la démocratie en France* (January 1849).
[2] *Nos mécomptes et nos espérances* (1855).
[3] See above, pp. 152-4, and also below, p. 224.

told Ledru-Rollin that inequality in the distribution of political rights was the inevitable condition of a great society, since it was a consequence of the inequalities of fact—material and intellectual—which must exist in such a society. There could only be an extension of political rights in proportion to the increase in the capacity of Frenchmen to use them.[1]

The day would never come when these rights could be extended to every one.[2] Universal suffrage might be of use in certain crises, as an accompaniment of great social changes, as the means of delivering a state from anarchy or establishing a new government. As a permanent instrument of government universal suffrage meant the death of liberty and order. Its principle was "routinière et fausse." It was based upon the theory of a war of classes.[3]

As Guizot had steadily refused to accept the need for any great social changes, or to see in the socialist attack on property anything more than seditious propaganda,[4] he was not likely to understand why the interests of the different classes in France might be regarded as hostile. The government had secured liberty and order. Each man could pursue his calling in peace, without fear of arbitrary government, arbitrary arrest, or the insolence of privilege. Guizot would not consider that the " calling " of some might be the exploitation of others. He shared to the full the orthodox view of the economists that it was not the business of government to interfere in the relations between labour and capital. " In the ordinary course of things " (Guizot does not define what might be " out of the ordinary course ") "these relations settle themselves. I am convinced that any attempt of government to interfere in the settlement is chimerical and disastrous." [5]

[1] *Hist. Parl.*, v. 214-15. See above, pp. 150-2, for Guizot's earlier defence of a constitutional monarchy with a representative assembly elected upon a restricted franchise.
[2] *Ibid.*, v. 383.
[3] *Ibid.*, iii. 555. This speech was delivered in 1842, a year before Marx came to Paris to study socialism, and five years before Marx and Engels made one of their greatest contributions to history in the communist manifesto.
[4] *Ibid.*, iii. 558.
[5] *Ibid.*, i. 327.

Therefore, with his liberty secured, there was no need for the common man to be interested in politics.   This again was a corollary from the view that the people of a modern democracy had neither the time nor the desire to take part in the public life of the state.   " La démocratie moderne . . . est laborieuse, occupée, essentiellement vouée à ses intérêts domestiques, aux besoins de sa vie privée. . . . Elle n'aspire pas à gouverner elle-même, elle veut intervenir dans le gouvernement autant qu'il est nécessaire pour qu'elle soit bien gouvernée, et qu'elle puisse, en toute sécurité, vaquer à la vie domestique, aux affaires privées." [1]   Here indeed we have something not unlike the view of the ineffable Monsignor Talbot that the duties of the laity were " to hunt, to shoot, to entertain " ! [2]   Government, like theology, must be left to the experts.

The democracy might well go about its private affairs, for there was no separation of interest between the different classes.   " What can be said at the present time to divide the electors assessed at two hundred francs from those assessed at a hundred and fifty francs ?   The elector of three hundred francs does not exclude the elector of two hundred, of a hundred ;   he represents him, he protects him, he safeguards his interests, for these interests are his own.   Never before in history has a similarity of interest accompanied the diversity of professions and the inequality of conditions." [3]   In the year 1842, when Guizot made this speech, the average wage of the workmen of France was one franc and seventy-eight centimes a day ;   women's wages were seventy-

[1] *Hist. Parl.*, i. 316.   [2] Purcell, *Life of Manning*, ii. 318.

[3] *Hist. Parl.*, iii. 556, and *Mémoires*, vi. 374.   It is interesting to compare with this argument—the argument by which Burke had justified the unreformed house of commons—Guizot's opinion upon the exclusion of women from politics :   " Les femmes sont vouées à la famille ;   leur destinée, c'est le développement individuel dans les affections de la vie domestique et les relations de la vie sociale.   Le pouvoir politique n'y entre pas naturellement.   De tout temps et en tout pays, sauf un petit nombre d'exceptions, ce principe a été adopté et pratiqué." (*Hist. Parl.*, iii. 686.)   There is not a word about the employment of women in factories !

Guizot held this view throughout his political career.   In the essay of 1826 on *Élections* he wrote that society had to deal with matters for the settlement of which women were sufficient neither in force nor in reason :   Providence had assigned women to a life of domesticity. (*Discours académiques*, p. 387.)

seven centimes a day ; children's wages were fifty centimes a day ! [1] Until 1841 nothing had been done to limit the hours of work of children in factories. Yet Guizot could maintain that " all the great conquests have been made ; all the great interests are satisfied ; our first, and almost our only duty is to enter into possession of these conquests, to secure for ourselves a free and complete enjoyment of them." [2]

In such a happy state of things, in the France of Guizot's imagination, the agitation for electoral reform could be no more than an appeal to human vanity, or a dishonest party move : " a parliamentary necessity not called into being by a social necessity." [3] The origin of the movement was false, artificial, an invention of newspapers and committees; it was not a demand of society in its widest aspect; it did not represent its needs, its interests.[4] This was Guizot's view in 1842. He repeated his thesis in 1847 ; he

---

[1] These figures are taken from the *Enquête du comité de travail de l'assemblée constituante sur le travail agricole et industriel* of 1848. Extracts from the report are given in Levasseur, *op. cit.*, ii. 300-34. Levasseur has computed this average on a purely arithmetical basis. He is fully aware of the difficulties and uncertainty of a calculation of this kind, and gives a detailed analysis of the statistics collected in the report (Levasseur, *op. cit.*, vol. ii. bk. 4, especially chapters vii. and ix.). The report did not include figures for Paris. Wages in Paris were higher than those in any other French city. Generally, wages in urban areas were higher than wages in agricultural areas. The level tended to be higher in the east than in the west of France. The report arranged its statistics according to cantons. The industrial departments usually had a higher rate of wage than the agricultural departments ; but this was not always the case ; the rate in the departments of Pas de Calais, Vosges, and Somme was below the average. Levasseur finds it hard to say whether there was any increase of money wages or in the purchasing power of money wages between 1830 and 1848. At the end of the period there was a greater consumption per head of the staple articles of food, and a greater sale of ordinary articles of household use. There would seem to have been a general rise in the standard of living in working-class families. But, on the whole, a working-class family lived upon the margin of subsistence, and had no means of meeting the recurrent crises of illness or unemployment. Women workers without help from the menfolk of their family were in a particularly bad position. These figures are enough to account for Barante's comment : " Les classes inférieures sont devenues peu patientes . . . une sorte de maladie sociale rend le gouvernement difficile." (Barante, *Souvenirs*, vii. 200.)

[2] *Hist. Parl.*, iii. 564.

[3] *Ibid.*, v. 381-2.

[4] *Ibid.*, iii. 557.

could still maintain that no real or important interests in France were in need of protection.[1]

Nor was it true to say that a property qualification excluded intelligence. The moral union of French society had been brought about because " intelligence, in every career, could find its place, could attain to fortune and power ; because intelligence was satisfied, and property was not attacked." [2] Guizot was not likely to remain on the defensive. He turned the tables on those who were asking for reform by pointing out that the electoral law of 1817 (which the monarchy of July had maintained in principle) was itself something more than a reform. This law had been a " real and salutary revolution in our ideas and our political institutions." Those who framed the law had been courageous enough to abandon the view that an electoral law should aim at giving the vote to the greatest number. They had definitely proclaimed the connexion of the franchise with political capacity, and had looked for political capacity at a point in society where it would be connected with property in land or in industry " . . . in those elevated and stable regions where is to be found a true understanding of the grand interests of the social order." [3] This assumption that intelligence must be connected with property was a further refinement of the doctrine of capacity. Excessive confidence in human intelligence, human self-sufficiency, and mental superiority was one of the diseases of the age, the cause of a great part of the evils and misfortunes of the time. Intelligence must at every moment

---

[1] *Hist. Parl.*, v. 381.

[2] *Ibid.*, iii. 558. If a workman did not thrive, the fault was his own ! Guizot wrote of the labouring class in 1849 : " Les uns, par intelligence et la bonne conduite, se créent un capital et entrent dans la voie de l'aisance et du progrès. Les autres, ou bornés, ou paresseux, ou déréglés, restent dans la condition étroite et précaire des existences fondées uniquement sur le salaire." (*De la démocratie en France*, p. 76.)

[3] In one of Guizot's letters to Broglie there is a recognition of the danger of the rule of a rich middle class. Guizot comments upon the forthcoming English elections : " La bourgeoisie riche y gagnera ; le talent pauvre y perdra. C'est la pente générale du temps. Tout n'en est pas bon et glorieux, et j'en suis plus convaincu que personne. Cependant le bon y domine, et de beaucoup. Quelques hautes futaies pousseront un jour dans ces terres qu'on laboure et engraisse si bien aujourd'hui." (Guizot, *Lettres*, p. 123-4.)

be cautioned, restrained, enlightened, guided by the social environment ; intelligence should be under the obligation to fulfil certain conditions, to satisfy certain tests, to give certain pledges of its uprightness and its fidelity to the principles of the social order.[1]

Could anything come nearer to proving the bitter thesis of those who accused Guizot of saying to poverty and distress, " Enrichissez-vous " ?

.   .   .   .   .   .

It is a pretty piece of irony that the political party which proposed an extension of the franchise, and, in particular, the small group who wished for universal suffrage, were as mistaken as Guizot himself in their estimate of the immediate political result of their victory. The wider the suffrage, the greater the security of the established order ; the majority of the voters were peasants, with no wish for disturbance and no thought for the reorganisation of society. It was significant that the legitimist Berryer grasped this simple fact. It was more significant for France that the nephew of the first Napoleon understood it, and ominously significant that it was soon to be understood by Bismarck in Germany.

But Guizot does not seem to have known much about the peasants near his country house, and his preoccupation with townsmen was in no small measure his ruin.

.   .   .   .   .   .

The detail of the revolution of 1848 does not belong properly to the history of Guizot. An accident transformed a riot into a revolution. A revolution without plan and without leaders was allowed to gather strength and to overthrow a monarchy which had met far more serious trouble in earlier days. The lack of imagination which dulled the reign of Louis Philippe, after the first great work of restoring order had been accomplished, prevented the king and his advisers from making the appeal to Frenchmen which would have saved the dynasty. The governing class showed neither firmness nor generosity. Louis Philippe himself awoke suddenly to find that the rich bourgeois were not the people of France ; but he had forgotten how

[1] *Hist. Parl.*, v. 384-6.

to speak the language of those who won the battle of Jemappes.

. . . . . .

After the fall of the monarchy Guizot was for a time an exile in London. He found that freedom from office was no hardship. There was more than mere physical relief. The richness of his inner life, the disdainful isolation of his mind from the political circumstances in which his external actions had been set, freed him from any distress at his own fall. " Hors de moi, toutes mes préoccupations sont fort tristes : en moi, non." Public life and success had meant a continual struggle against vulgar errors and low cupidity. He was glad to be free from this unprofitable business.[1]

He acknowledged that he had not measured the gravity of the evils against which he had fought. " In seventeen years we used up all the capital of good sense and political courage which the country had accumulated since 1789. In 1848 no further drafts on this capital could be honoured. Hence the bankruptcy of France and of ourselves. How long will it take to collect a new capital ? I cannot say." [2]

Guizot's view of the immediate future was not happy. In September 1849 he spoke of the government as transitional : " la France sait qu'elle est dans une auberge où elle ne doit pas rester, mais elle veut s'y reposer un peu." [3] The *coup d'état* made an end of the " petite république," and introduced the " petit empire." How long would this empire last ? Guizot saw that its difficulties would come with time. " You can put down a riot with soldiers ; you can make an election with peasants ; but soldiers and peasants cannot carry on your government. For this you need the help of the upper classes, the classes naturally fitted for government." But these classes were hostile to Louis Napoleon, or divided among themselves. " C'est le chaos, et le chaos stérile. Je n'ai pas cessé de croire à la lumière ;

---

[1] *Lettres*, p. 253. Guizot wrote of Washington's retirement from politics in terms which evidently referred to his own experience : " Le pouvoir est lourd à porter et l'humanité rude à servir contre ses passions et ses erreurs. Le succès même n'efface les impressions tristes que le combat a fait naître, et la fatigue contractée dans cette arène se prolonge au sein du repos." (*Washington*, liii.)

[2] *Lettres*, p. 255.   [3] *Ibid.*, p. 269.

elle se fera un jour sur ce chaos ; mais quand et par où viendra-t-elle ? Je n'en sais rien." [1]

Louis Napoleon had nothing of the good sense, the elevation, the foresight, the restraint which make a great ruler of men. "He is intoxicated by the 7,500,000 votes which have elected him, and by the 400,000 bayonets which surround him." [2] It was easy to foretell the second empire. Guizot looked beyond its proclamation, and feared an attempt to secure the Rhine as the frontier of France. For the faults of Napoleon III. would be the faults of his character. He was a mixture of rashness and patience, of fatalism and prudence. He wanted to enjoy his power ; he had nothing of the inexhaustible creativeness of the first Napoleon ; he was slow and indolent, too fond of his leisure and his amusements. He would do what he could to reassure Europe about his intentions, and would postpone as long as possible the moment when he must commit himself seriously to the realisation of his ultimate vision. Nevertheless this moment would come. A fatalist could not fight for ever against what he believed to be his destiny. In any case, Napoleon would have to occupy and amuse France. He might wish to practise the policy of Napoleon I. without war, the policy of Louis Philippe without parliamentary life. He would fail, and would have to return, as a conspirator if not as a conqueror, to the tradition of the empire. "Ne le voulut-il pas, c'est là son avenir, et je suis convaincu qu'il le veut." It is not often that the leader of a beaten cause can make so accurate a forecast on the very day of the triumph of the conqueror. [3]

Enough has been said of the faults of Guizot. It must be remembered that he never wished to be judged by the men for whom he worked ; that he never lost confidence in the ultimate victory of his ideas : "La liberté politique gagnera sa cause." He believed in his government because it had been true to its principle. "Il a pratiqué la politique de la résistance avec les seules armes de la liberté." If he had thought too much in terms of principle, and cared too little for men, his single-heartedness saved him in the end. "For

[1] *Lettres*, p. 328.   [2] *Ibid.*, p. 330.
[3] *Ibid.*, pp. 343-4. The date of the letter is December 2, 1852.

fifteen centuries Europe and France have been moving along the same road towards freedom and progress. This common civilisation is above all the fruit of the magnificent conception that every man, as a man, can claim his right to justice, to sympathy, and to liberty. This conception was given to the human heart by Jesus Christ ; from the mind of the individual it has struggled to make its way into the consciousness of society. . . . God does not cheat the human race. The nations are not for ever deceiving themselves in the course of their long destiny." [1]

Such an appeal to universal history might allow to Guizot the apology of the mediæval papacy. As the greatest of the popes were forced by the historical categories of their age into a ceaseless material war for a kingdom not of this world, and as they fell to destruction by the weapons they had taken up in their defence, so Guizot in his effort to found a modern state on the rock of liberty was driven by the conditions of his time, and the imperfection of his material, to tolerate a construction which would tumble into the ruin of the storm.

Courage and pride never failed Guizot. " J'ai besoin de croire que je veux ce que je fais." Sixteen months after the revolution of February, at the beginning of another outbreak in the streets of Paris, Ledru-Rollin, the leader of the left, had said of himself and of his party : "Je suis leur chef ; il faut bien que je les suive." Ledru-Rollin went into exile, and reappeared twenty years later, a pale shadow amidst the political conflicts of the third republic. Guizot never came back to the public life of his country. But happier than it deserves is the nation whose politicians are destroyed by their courage.

---

[1] *Hist. Parl.*, i., Introd., pp. cxl.-cxli.

III

THE CATHOLIC CHURCH IN THE NINETEENTH CENTURY

I

THE CATHOLIC CHURCH AND THE REVOLUTION

WHY was the Catholic Church in the nineteenth century predominantly on the side of political reaction ? Was any attempt of European importance made to dissociate religion from a dangerous and unwonted subservience to the current theories of the secular powers ? By whom were these attempts made, and under what circumstances ? Why did they fail ?

These are questions which involve a study of the relation between the Catholic Church and the states of Europe before, during, and after the French Revolution ; a history of liberal catholicism—for the protestant and orthodox churches had little positive influence in determining the issue ; and finally a study of several men—above all, of Lamennais and Pope Pius IX.

How did the princes and governments view the church in the years before the revolution ? When he began his account of the condition of Europe in 1789, Albert Sorel took as his theme the ominous prophecy made by Rousseau in 1772 : " I see all the states of Europe hurrying to their ruin." [1] In 1789 the catastrophe was nearer by seventeen years. The governments of Europe claimed to act according to the theory of enlightened despotism. Benevolent monarchs were assumed to direct a capable and upright bureaucracy in the spread of rational and humanitarian ideas. In fact, too many of the " enlightened monarchs " were mad without hope of recovery like the queen of Portugal, or mad intermittently like George III., or illiterate and half-civilised like Ferdinand IV. of Naples, or heavy and abnormally dull like Louis XVI. There were exceptions :

[1] A. Sorel, *L'Europe et la révolution française*, i. 93.

Joseph II., a man of unbalanced ability, without the sense of political realities and the feeling for history which had made and alone could justify the house of Habsburg ; Gustavus III. of Sweden, an old man whose heir was stark mad ; Catherine II. of Russia, a woman whose public policy was as immoral as her private conduct. Such were the princes of Europe.

What then of the " capable bureaucracies " and the " rational systems of government " ? In every country, not excepting England, most of the wealth and offices of the state were held at the disposition of a privileged few. In nearly every state of the continent, and to some extent in England, the chief burdens of taxation were set upon the poor and the middle class, while the annual expenditure of the governments too often exceeded the revenues. Every war added to a nation's debts. Every new source of wealth, every new device of credit, was turned at once into an instrument of war. In France and Germany the judicial system was absurdly out of date ; in England there was a savage penal code and a magistracy drawn mainly from one class. In Prussia the civil service and the army had lost the impulsion given to them by the great Frederick. The machinery of the Empire had almost come to a standstill. Russia was parasitic upon western civilisation. The dying institutions of Spain spread corruption over two worlds. Italy was dead save to the more contemptible vices. In France the ministers were too busy to undertake great reforms, or at all events to give the time necessary for the detailed consideration of change ; the upper class was too much in debt to give up its fiscal privileges, and too much preoccupied with a brilliant social life [1] to care for the loss of political responsibilities.

What was the position of the Christian Church in this society ? How far was it making any attempt to convince those in authority that the danger to Europe lay in the

---

[1] Talleyrand once said to Guizot : " Qui n'a pas vécu dans les années voisines de 1789 ne sait pas ce que c'est que le plaisir de vivre." (Guizot, *Mémoires*, i. 6.)

moral indifference of its leaders ? More than once the church had risked its temporal possessions in a struggle with moral evil in high places. In an even darker age churchmen had treasured, increased, and brought again to the world a lost inheritance of culture. The faithful of the church, whether catholic, orthodox, or protestant, believed, as their hope of salvation, that at a certain time and place a divine revelation had been made to men ; this revelation had declared humility, poverty, enthusiasm to be of higher value than riches, pride, and caution. Upon this revelation was based, in theory, the whole order ruled over by the most Christian kings, the most Catholic kings, and the defenders of the faith.

In fact, the Christian Church was divided. The orthodox church was under the secular tyranny of Russia and Turkey, and in some respects enjoyed more freedom under Turkish indifference than under Russian control. In neither country did it exercise any spiritual or moral influence upon the policy of state. The protestant churches were hardly less bound to temporal authority, and hardly counted for more in the moral education of the governing class. Dissent from the orthodox church wasted itself in an extravagant literalism, from which it was led into the most bizarre forms of ascetic practice. Protestant dissent was nobler, and more deeply influential, but its other-worldliness was of more effect in schooling the poor to endure their sufferings than in teaching the rich to know their responsibilities.

The Catholic Church might seem to have greater independence. It had a greater tradition ; its organisation contained all the machinery of holiness and all the precedents accumulated over centuries of defiance of the princes of this world. But the papacy had long been enmeshed in the nets of secular authority. The Vicar of Christ and the head of the catholic priesthood was also a temporal sovereign : in theory one of the enlightened despots ; in fact a ruler of a backward, ill-compact, and barren kingdom in Italy. Although they might keep the state of a world-monarchy, although they might still use the sonorous language of the bull *Unam sanctam*, the pope and his cardinals

were being thrust out of a world which had lost all fear of
the " kingdom of the fairies." Ranke has pointed out [1]
that of the five great powers in the world after the treaty of
Utrecht, one was orthodox and two were protestant ; the
political predominance of the three did not mean that protestant doctrine had overcome catholic doctrine, but the
ultimate consequences could scarcely be less than a victory
of this kind. For the papacy was unrepresented in England
and Russia, and did not know the diplomatic secrets of the
great courts of the north. The papal lands were less respected ; the affairs of Europe were managed by non-
catholics ; a protestant power controlled the sea. Latin
America had been colonised by catholics ; but half the
world was left for colonisation by protestants. Furthermore,
the catholic nations could see that the temporal gains of the
protestant powers had been the result of better organisation and discipline. Hence a desire to oust the church
from its control of wealth and education. This desire took
shape in an attack upon the Jesuits. The attack was made
in France, Spain, and Portugal ; its pretext was the unfair commercial competition of the society. The real
reason was that the Jesuits, almost alone among the catholic
orders, were definitely polemical, and were the strongest
supporters of the papacy in the national states. Pope
Clement xiv. (1769-1774), who had to meet the force of
this attack, was a man of peace and blameless life, dis-
trustful of the Jesuits, and even frightened for his safety
at their hands. He gave way before the storm and dissolved the order. His successor, Pius vi., was a handsome
nobleman of extravagant tastes, anxious to perpetuate his
name in works of architecture and engineering. But he
was only chosen after long delay, and on the understanding that he would make no claim to sovereignty over the
duchies of Parma and Piacenza, or the kingdom of the two
Sicilies. Thus the popes were content to drift with the
time, and to allow the catholic states to consolidate their
power at the expense of the church.

In this position the revolution found the papacy, and
thrust upon it changes which the popes had been too listless

[1] Ranke, *History of the Popes*, bk. viii. § 18.

or too frightened to attempt. The upshot was, curiously, to strengthen the central organisation of the church,[1] and, in a measure, to raise its moral prestige. In a measure only : for a church which had done little to condemn the moral evil of the age was unlikely to catch the fire of moral betterment. With the destruction of the vested interests and pride of place of the national churches, the material power of the papacy was further weakened ; the popes were driven to a helpless dependence upon the governments which succeeded the revolution, and which held the revolution in check throughout Europe. As the revolution in Italy attacked not only the outworks of the church, but the territorial basis of its temporal power, this dependence upon the conservative governments became more abject, more panic-stricken. The weakened, but intellectually more virile, churches in France and Germany could make little resistance to the central organisation of the hierarchy. To the papal court the conservative power in Europe, the stay of the church, was the house of Habsburg. When this power collapsed, the popes found themselves isolated from any direct political influence of the first order in Europe, and cut off by their own acts, definitions, and allegiances from the intellectual future of the rest of the Christian Church.

If the popes were fighting a losing battle in the eighteenth century against the secular powers and against the rich and privileged national hierarchies, the Gallicanism of the French church, the Febronianism [2] of the German ecclesiastical princes, why should they have found themselves in bitter opposition to the revolution which destroyed for ever the power of local resistance ? The answer does not lie in the

---

[1] See below, p. 240.

[2] In 1763 Johann Nicholas von Hontheim, a professor at the university of Trier, and for many years the chief ecclesiastical adviser of the electors of Trier, published under the pseudonym of Justinus Febronius a treatise, *De statu ecclesiae et legitima potestate Romani Pontificis*. This work was strongly anti-ultramontane in feeling, and made an appeal for the restoration of the rights of the episcopate against the usurpation of authority by the see of Rome. Naturally the book was condemned at Rome ; but its influence among the German clergy was, from the papal point of view, most serious. Febronius' recantation in 1778 was purely formal, and had no effect upon the popularity of his doctrine. See Nielsen, *History of the Papacy in the Nineteenth Century* (translated by A. J. Mason), vol. i. chap. v. and authorities therein quoted.

annexation of the papal lands of Avignon and the Venaissin.[1] The popes had lost other territories to secular greed. The enclaves within France were bound to disappear ; their loss was not a direct threat to the states of the church in Italy. Nor was the disendowment of the church likely of itself to cause a final break with the papacy. Most of the property which was taken from the church had long been put to secular employment by the monarchy ; the great landed wealth of the abbeys, bishoprics, and archbishoprics had been used by the crown for the reward of those younger sons of the nobility who had entered the church in order to profit by its inheritance. This wealth, and the kind of man which it attracted, did no good to the see of Rome, and only gave material support to Gallican theories of independence. The doctrine of national sovereignty was no more difficult to reconcile with the liberty of the spiritual power than the claims of absolute monarchy. The timidity which had surrendered to kings could equally well give way to any kind of secular authority.

The reason for the break with the new France came from the side of the revolution and not from the papacy. The constituent assembly took up an attitude towards the Christian Church which no pope, however time-serving, could dare to tolerate. The assembly brought forward a civil constitution of the clergy in which the principle of popular election was applied to ecclesiastical offices. Such a measure meant a complete break with the whole theory and practice of church government. Catholics believed that the form of this government was part of the divine revelation ; God who willed the end—the preservation of the church—had also willed the means to this end ; the papacy was a divine institution for the maintenance of the unchanging hierarchical plan throughout the changing circumstances of secular history. There was indeed a chance that the popes might for a time submit to an arrangement which papal theory could never recognise. With a certain accommodation on both sides the fictions which had surrounded the old method of royal appointment might have covered even the new system of election.

[1] These lands were annexed by the French nation in 1791.

But the assembly did not attempt an arrangement of this kind. They went to the other extreme, and insisted that every priest in France should take an oath to support the civil constitution of the clergy; the taking of this oath was the touchstone of loyalty to the whole revolutionary settlement of France.

Why should the assembly have added to the enemies of the new France? The revolutionary legislation was town-managed. The good bourgeois who came to Paris as representatives of the Tiers État held the views of well-to-do townsfolk; they were the provincial fringe of a reading public which was still under the spell of a false simplification of the world; their favourite books had about them something of the charming unreality of Marie Antoinette's dairy. Among the literary assumptions of writers who scarcely knew the ways of labouring men was the belief that the Catholic Church was already doomed, and doomed not only because of the abuses of its rich hierarchy, but because the practice of simple catholics was now old-fashioned, cumbrous, unnecessary, superstitious. Why trouble about a dying institution? The *ancien régime* had shown little enough care for the papacy; the grand bishops of the church had disdained the simple piety of the unenlightened people.[1] Why should the new enlightenment be more sparing? Add to this the bitterness of persecuted Jansenists [2] or protestants, and the indifference to the demands of canon law would be complete.

But why the insistence upon election? Here again the minds of provincial Frenchmen, affected by the social prestige of clever men in Paris, could hardly act otherwise. The principle of election was a practical safeguard against any return of court influence; but it had a subtler justification. The assembly was consciously archaistic; its members had escaped from the " gothic " middle ages only to fall into a more rigid obedience to an older world.[3] In architecture,

[1] Boisgelin, the bishop of Aix, a man of better life and higher standard of duty than most of the noble bishops, wrote to a friend that he was ashamed of the language which he was bound to use in his pastoral letters. See A. Lavaquery, *Le Cardinal de Boisgelin*, vol. i. chap. 5.

[2] *E.g.* Camus.

[3] The career of Baron Jean Baptiste Clootz, a Prussian of Dutch descent, is typical of this archaism. Clootz had settled in Paris even before the revolution. He abandoned his " gothic " title, and,

in clothing, in proper names, as well as in political theory, there was an attempt to go back to the tradition of the ancient city states. Election had been one of the safeguards of antique liberty, and was therefore a sacred principle. The purists looked into the history of the early church, and found that the early church had allowed the election of its officers by the faithful. But if, as a modern age knew, the heart of man was good, the faithful could be none other than the body of active citizens—the voters !—who were now divested of all mediæval superstition. What matter if they called themselves catholics, protestants, or Jews ?

The step taken by the constituent assembly was irrevocable. There was no chance of revoking any of the great measures of reform. Those who opposed any one measure were assumed by the people of Paris to be reactionaries in everything. If the assembly admitted itself wrong in any detail of its work, it was open to the charge of error on other points ; the royal veto would be justified. Therefore the opposition between the revolutionary government and the clergy, most of whom would have gained from a better distribution of ecclesiastical salaries, grew stronger, until at last a Danton felt bound to sanction the murders of September. After this outrage the revolution had stained itself with the blood of the martyrs. There could be no peace. French historians [1] have told often enough the miserable consequences of the reckless alienation of the steadiest and most law-abiding class of citizens ; of the panic-stricken ferocity with which the Catholic Church was for a time persecuted into silence, and for ever (if such a term can be used in this context) weakened in France. The story does not end with the well-calculated act of political strategy whereby Napoleon restored the priests and the church bells to the villages.

instead of his Christian name, called himself Anacharsis. He styled himself " the personal enemy of Jesus Christ," and wrote a book to prove the truth of Mahomedanism. He was ultimately guillotined during the Terror.

[1] Notably de la Gorce, *Histoire religieuse de la révolution française*. The effect of driving the better element of the clergy and laity into opposition can be seen most clearly in the provinces. There is an excellent account of this unnecessary confusion and bitterness in Rodolphe Reuss, *La Constitution civile du clergé et la crise religieuse en Alsace, 1790-1795*, (2 vols. Publications of the University of Strasbourg. Fasc. 7 and 8).

Napoleon won so many agents for the conscription of the peasants, so many repetitions of " Domine, salvum fac Napoleonem " ; but he did not favour the church out of a love of liberty, nor did he care for its reform. The Concordat was an instrument of policy. Napoleon had no interest in the reconciliation of catholics with republicans ; no wish for an educated and thoughtful clergy ; he would give no encouragement to a revival of the moral authority of the papacy. A single iron-bound sentence sets out his plan : " Sur les affaires publiques qui sont mes affaires, en matière politique, sociale et morale . . . personne, dans la génération présente ne pensera excepté moi, et dans la génération prochaine, tout le monde pensera d'après moi."

Therefore no peace was made between the political ideas of the revolution and the political traditions of the papacy, and all hope of a change of mind in the leaders of the church disappeared with the quarrel between Napoleon—the new Charlemagne !—and the pope over questions of territory and material power. In France two significant things had happened between 1789 and 1799. For a whole decade the youth of the country grew up without any religious instruction and learned only to associate the catholic priests with the counter-revolution. These were the men who were the active citizens of France during the years between the first and the third Napoleon. Furthermore, between 1789 and 1799 the greater number of the more zealous parish priests in France had been killed or banished. None came to take their place. There was a break in the tradition. When the ranks were filled again, the new men had neither the personal authority of the higher clergy who had been born into an upper class nor the habit of obedience to time-old law and custom. They had grown to manhood in an age when political experiment had succeeded experiment ; their education had been superficial ; their preparation for the priesthood had been hasty ; everything made them sensitive to the influence of unbalanced theories and uncritical modes of thought.

A less tempestuous but more sordid dislocation of catholic tradition had taken place in catholic Germany. Here the princes themselves had reaped a shameful harvest from the wealth of the church.[1] The catholic ruler of Bavaria, under the influence of his imported minister Montgelas, had not even spared the burial-place of his own family when he secularised the Bavarian monasteries. In France Napoleon had at least made some constructive arrangement with the papacy ; German catholics only saw the worst side of papal delay, Napoleonic caprice, and the greed of their own sovereigns.[2] But although little was done for the reconstruction of the order of the church, the papacy gained in power—whatever the total sum of catholic loss—from the expulsion of the tenants of " Priest Lane " and the collapse of the great Rhenish supporters of anti-papal theory. Moreover, Napoleon had insisted upon negotiating with the papacy over the heads of the French bishops and the German ecclesiastical princes. Pius VII. made little positive resistance, and was troubled no more than his immediate predecessors by the moral iniquity of secular powers ; but his passive dignity before the bullying of Napoleon gave him a prestige in Europe which had not fallen to the lot of any pope for more than a century. The centre of the Catholic Church had therefore asserted itself when the dangerous enemies within its own household had fallen. Unfortunately this increase of authority, such as it was, had been obtained at the very point where the church was intellectually most backward. The contribution of Italians to catholic thought in the eighteenth and nineteenth centuries was negligible.[3] The Roman see did not encourage scientific thinking ; the ablest of its prelates were employed in administration or diplomacy. Outside the papal states there was no opportunity for freedom and originality of mind ; scarcely even for erudition. No Italian

[1] Nor did the Bavarian royal commissioners spare the feelings of catholics. At one house they were said to have thrown away a monstrance containing the Host. See Brück, *Geschichte der katholischen Kirche in Deutschland im 19ten Jahrhundert*, i. 185, for an account of the treatment of monastic libraries.

[2] The bribing of Talleyrand by the catholic princes is one of the more humiliating spectacles in the unpleasing history of the lesser German rulers.

[3] The few distinguished names, such as Vico, among the Italian clergy cannot be called exceptions. Vico's thought is scarcely catholic in any of its remarkable manifestations.

university outside Rome had a proper faculty of theology. The bishops appointed to Neapolitan sees by the Bourbon kings were unlikely to be men of intellectual power. Typical of them was the bishop at the Vatican council who proposed the constant wearing of the long cassock because in this cassock Christ rose from the dead and ascended into heaven! The north Italian clergy were not more enlightened. Most of the Italian monasteries had lost their tradition of learning. Döllinger, in the next generation, complained bitterly that there were more books on religious questions published in Germany, England, or North America in one year than in Italy during half a century. Yet these Italians controlled the organisation of the Catholic Church throughout the nineteenth century without any sense of their intellectual backwardness. The pedantry of Gregory xvi., the uneducated shrewdness of Pius ix., were remote from the awakening of Europe. Even Leo xiii. did little more than carry into another age the literary culture of the eighteenth century. The men who made the popes were like them, and chose rulers of their own type. Italian cardinals presided over the administration of the curia, and had the ear of the pope. The few foreigners who played a major part on this " magnificent stage with poor actors " were unpleasing priests of the character of Monsignor Talbot.[1]

Thus the church was bound to this sterile and uncomprehending ignorance in the hour of its greatest intellectual opportunity since the counter-reformation. The disillusionment which had followed the collapse of the first revolutionary idealism and the failure of the philosophy of the eighteenth century had modified once again the attitude of European culture towards catholicism. The literary effects of the French Revolution have often been exaggerated. The romantic revival was as inevitable a change of fashion from the rationalism of the eighteenth century as the renaissance was a change from the formalism of the middle ages. In both cases the change was spread over a long period of time. In England the romantic movement began

[1] Mgr Talbot (a younger son of Lord Talbot de Malahide) was the channel through which the ideas of Manning reached the pope. Much of his correspondence with Manning is printed in Purcell's *Life of Manning*.

before 1789, and had little influence upon many branches of the art and literature of the country until long after the modes of the revolution had become old-fashioned and antique. In Germany the transition was more marked, and followed more closely the development of political events. Sainte-Beuve once said of Goethe, the most representative mind of the late eighteenth century, that he understood all the world except two kinds of men : the Christian and the hero. Living in a country with no great issues of state, with no occasion for a deep interest in the life of action, the Germans were thrown back upon self-culture, an indifference to political forms, a humane and rational universalism.[1]

The enormous happenings of the revolutionary and Napoleonic period broke through the guarded sensitiveness of the eighteenth century.[2]   After the Terror there was not much left of the theory of man as a rational creature corrupted only by bad government. It was impossible to find beauty or a sense of balance in the titanic changeableness of the last decade of Napoleon's career, still less in the shameful corruption of many and the continued exactions of all his agents. Hence the desire to find other forms of beauty ; the revival of a love of strangeness, an appeal to the remote in time, in place, in knowledge, in association.[3]   Now these different forms of glamour came most readily to the mind in the contemplation of the middle ages. This romantic contrast between past and present would be most marked to a generation in Germany whose oppressors had defied, overthrown, and mocked at everything mediæval (and, incidentally, removed many of the more galling discomforts and abuses of the mediæval order !). Turning with this intention to the middle ages, German writers would remember that in the great days of German history—days which were golden indeed in comparison with the rule of

[1] For the political side of this literary and cultural cosmopolitanism, and for the changes made by the romantic revival, see Goyau, *L'Allemagne religieuse*, vols. i. and ii., and Meinecke, *Weltbürgerthum und National-staat*.

[2] See above, pp. 206-10, for the effect of the movement upon the development in France of the literature of the social question.

[3] Such as in English : " In Xanadu did Khubla Khan . . . " ; or, a hundred years later : " O dark towers, fort of faery, steep as Jerusalem."

Frenchmen—the Catholic Church had been the first and the last institution to protest against the dismemberment of Germany. In this way there began a new school of thought favourable to catholicism upon æsthetic, political, and national grounds. There was little dogmatic background to this movement. It was founded upon a passing literary and artistic phase ; it was too much of a reaction to a given set of circumstances. It had nothing of the learning which gave strength to the earlier years of the Oxford movement, nothing of the political experience of the French liberal catholics half a century later. Above all, it was not guided, as other movements favourable to catholicism had been guided, by an enlightened papacy. Therefore, when the political setting changed, when the historical background was more fully explored, a new school arose, with a different view of the middle ages, and a different theory of the development of German history. For this new school nationalist theories took the place of universalism, as in practice the Hohenzollerns took the place of the Habsburgs. Protestantism was no longer an aberration, but a revival of the true German spirit after centuries of Italian adventure and moral bondage. Yet of all these things the popes knew nothing. To them the Habsburgs represented not a principle of European history, but the protectors of some thousand square miles of their Italian kingdom.

It is possible to see mirrored in one man the intellectual life of a generation in Germany to whom the revolution was the central event of the age. Joseph von Görres, a pamphleteer of genius, and " the man of most universal learning since Leibnitz," was born at Coblenz in 1776,[1] and died in Munich in 1848. The Germans of Coblenz were near enough to France to take the enthusiasm of the French reformers before it could reach the rest of Germany. Görres' literary career began with a book on universal peace and the ideal form of government. This was followed by a newspaper with the prophetic title of the *Rothes Blatt*, which preached war against tyrants and looked at first to France

---

[1] His mother came of an Italian family.

for aid in the ennoblement of humanity. Görres showed a curious sensitiveness to atmosphere by forecasting the end of the Holy Roman Empire at the hands of Napoleon eight years before Austerlitz.[1] But after 1799 he had given up his belief in France and the revolution ; his world citizenship now became something purely German. Two political missions to Paris taught him that the revolution had lost its general " weltbürgerliches Interesse," and that French " science " was " a bunch of flowers culled at random." To " science," or rather to all knowledge, Görres now turned with zeal undestroyed. In 1806 he became a professor at Heidelberg, and was attracted by the catholic art of the middle ages. It was characteristic of him, and of the superficiality of his " science," that he believed gothic architecture to be German in origin. By the time of Austerlitz and Jena Görres had come to think of the Germans as a chosen people. The Holy Roman Empire was the instrument of Providence ; the Thirty Years' war had been a divine chastisement ; the victories of Bonaparte were of the same order. But the fall of Germany could not be for ever. " The Germans are a caste of Brahmins ; they must be religious." Görres was still uncertain what should be their religion. After his rediscovery of the catholic middle ages he had found in the study of the religions of the east a way of escape from the rationalising of religion and the " reasonable " philosophy which had led to the revolution. He could not leave politics and pamphleteering. The support which he gave to Pius VII. against Napoleon was another step in the direction of catholicism. After 1815 Görres was again disillusioned. The congress of Vienna did nothing to restore the lost unity of Germany, or to undo the evils of the reformation and the treaty of Westphalia. More

[1] In December 1797, after the reoccupation of Mainz by the French, Görres drew up a curious obituary notice of the Holy Roman Empire : " Died at Ratisbon, on 30 December 1797 . . . aged 955 years, 5 months, 28 days . . . after complete exhaustion and apoplexy, in full consciousness and fortified by all the rites of the Church, the Holy Roman Empire." Then followed a life-history : " Born at Verdun, educated by court servants under the title of popes, canonised in youth . . . underwent a period of madness during the crusades . . . restored by a severe régime . . . attacked by violent hemorrhage during the Thirty Years' War . . ." etc.

pamphlets followed. " Chased by half the kings of Europe," Görres took refuge in Strasbourg. Here he continued his attack upon the restored German princes. " The people won the war ; the princes have betrayed them." His philosophy now became a curious syncretism. World history, which he had studied so rapidly, was the record of a struggle between the fallen nature of man and the power of the supernatural. Europe had developed upon wrong lines since the unfortunate transfer of power in the middle ages from priests to soldiers ; but the long expiation of the sins of the sixteenth and seventeenth centuries was nearing its end. Rome was to be the centre of a reformed religion. Two years later, in 1822, Görres could write that " the church is in no way subordinate to the state ; the state is an organ to serve the loftier ends of the church." After another two years Görres was speaking of his *History of Legend* as a defence of the Bible.[1] The next stage was the publication at Strasbourg of a catholic review which had been excluded from Mainz. Finally, in 1826, Görres accepted an invitation to a professorship in Munich. Louis I. of Bavaria was a king after Görres' heart : catholic, romantic, German after the supposed mediæval pattern. Here this turbulent and receptive scholar lived out his life. The year of his death marks the end of the long transition of thought he had portrayed so faithfully ; though it is worth remembering that through the influence of Görres upon Döllinger,[2] and Döllinger upon Acton, the Munich school of catholic historians has made itself felt in English historical writing. It is significant that this influence, though catholic in the best sense of catholic tradition, has been anti-papal. In itself this is evidence of the greatness of papal neglect.

Mere ignorance was one reason why the popes allowed their favourable hour to pass without any comprehension of its importance. The change from revolution to liberalism, from rationalism to historical idealism, passed unnoticed ; the curia was not even interested in the development of

---

[1] It is interesting that in its earlier stages the study of comparative religion turned to the interest of the church.

[2] See Goyau, *L'Allemagne religieuse*, vols. i. and ii. ; Vigener, *Drei Gestalten aus dem modernen Katholizismus: Möhler, Diepenbrock, Döllinger* (*Historische Zeitschrift*, Beiheft 7. 1926).

ideas. A practical effort, as well as an act of imaginative
sympathy, would have been necessary if the popes were to
get beyond a horizon limited by fear of the temporal consequences of the revolution. It was difficult for the Roman
see to think in terms unconnected with its territorial power.
The states of the church could hardly be abandoned by popes
who had grown to old age in the belief that the temporal
power was an indispensable guarantee of the independence
of the church. No machinery existed whereby this power
could be surrendered. Every pope took an oath to defend
it ; it was a property held in trust for the church universal,
for the good of catholics in all places of the world. On a
lower level, it was unlikely that the vested clerical interest
would ever elect a pope who would not make it his duty to
preserve so important a source of place and profit. The
clerical monopoly of office was a consequence of the temporal
power in fact as well as in the opinion of the clerics in possession. A government of laymen might commit the papacy
to a foreign policy which endangered the security of the
church. Yet the maintenance of the clerical monopoly was
more and more distasteful to the governed, incompatible
with the development of a competent civil service, and out
of keeping with the political theory of Europe. Under such
conditions there could be no question of government by
consent.

For this reason the popes were driven to keep on good
terms with the conservative governments of Europe, and in
particular with the Habsburgs ; for the Habsburgs alone
could be trusted not to give Italy to the revolution. The
support of the Habsburgs must be paid for by the disavowal
of liberalism in other countries. Isolated movements of
revolt in Ireland or Belgium might be permitted [1] where
they could not be prevented, but in the long run the leaders
of the church must condemn all that Metternich condemned. So the popes heaped anathemas upon a cause
which they never understood.

On the other hand, catholics outside Italy were more fitted
by position and education to understand the temper of their

[1] It must be remembered that rebellion in Belgium (before 1830) and
Ireland was directed primarily against a protestant ascendancy.

age. If they hated the revolution, it was because of its interference with liberty ; its absolutism ; its thoughtless abandonment of much of the inheritance of human culture ; its intolerance ; its false view of human nature. Liberty itself, the free exercise of the human mind, the changed basis of human authority in the temporal sphere, they regarded with no less reverence than the first revolutionaries who had attacked the temporal privileges of the church. Metternich, the Habsburgs, the Bourbons, and all the shabby paraphernalia of restored autocracy were no part of their scheme of things.

Herein lay the danger of the position. Suppose these two views to come into conflict. Sooner or later the autocratic governments, upon which the papacy depended for support against the inevitable rebellions of its Italian subjects, would ask the pope to suppress political liberalism among the catholics north of the Alps. Sooner or later the liberal-minded catholics, realising the dependence of the papacy upon the reactionary powers, would demand and work for the breakdown of this close political alliance, and would attempt to free the popes from a spiritual imprisonment within their temporal authority. When this conflict had been fixed upon a particular issue, a stubbornness on both sides, an unwillingness to understand the immensity of the issues and of the difficulties, would bring about a calamity for the church. There could be no doubt about the decision of the central catholic authority, especially since that authority had been unexpectedly strengthened against the dispersed opinion of the faithful. Once made, the decision would be made for ever ; the papacy can hardly escape from its own past. For a short time indeed Pius ix. weakly tried to avoid a sequence of effects which he both willed and did not will. But the force of events was too strong for him : the hour of reconciliation had passed ; Pius was compelled to make a final choice, with the scales heavily weighted against him by his predecessors and by his own character. He chose the road which led away from modern civilisation.

II

GREGORY XVI. AND LAMENNAIS

It happened that a man of erratic, unpolitical genius, a master of French style—the proper language of revolution —brought about the decisive moment in the determination of catholic choice, and settled the fate of Pius' timid concessions to liberalism some fifteen years before they were made. The career of Lamennais [1] is the counterpart of the career of Görres ; both reflect the movements of their time ; both were over-sensitive to their environment ; but the order of their development was curiously contrasted. The one began with the revolution and ended in a belief in catholic theocracy ; the other began with theocracy and ended as a revolutionary. Each made an act of faith in the future, and held with the enthusiasm of a convert the particular idea which had laid hold of his emotions at the moment. The influence of Lamennais was incomparably greater, because his life was set among issues as important as the whole future of religion, and because the changes of his thought brought him into closer relationship with a European movement from which the romantic catholicism of Görres became more and more isolated.

The years of the restoration, in which the problem of the relation between church and state was put clearly by Lamennais, were less barren of general ideas in France than in the rest of Europe. [2] While Germany was descending slowly from the general to the particular, from Goethe to Bismarck, the monarchy in France was given a problem of more universal interest and difficulty. The French kings had to combine the facts of constitutional monarchy with the theory of popular sovereignty. The house of Bourbon

---

[1] The best account of Lamennais is by C. Boutard, *Lamennais, sa vie et ses doctrines*. (Paris, 1913. 3 vols.)

[2] See above, pp. 121-4.

had no traditions of constitutional government ; the supporters of the elder line had little liking for a constitution
based upon the sovereignty of the people ; even Louis
Philippe found it easier to keep up the pose of a bourgeois
king than to practise the self-restraint of a sovereign bound
by ministerial responsibility. The French people had no
experience of parliamentary institutions in the English
sense of the term. They were like the Bourbons in that
" they had learned nothing and forgotten nothing." The
monarchy began its experiment under the most unfavourable conditions. Louis XVIII. was twice restored by the
enemies of the French nation in arms. Any confidence
which he might have regained from his first popularity as
the guarantor of peace was dispelled by the revival of the
revolutionary spirit during the Hundred Days. The country
was bankrupt, and had few civil servants who were both
loyal and competent.

In these ill-timed hours the king and his ministers saw
in the church a useful aid against Jacobinism. Louis XVIII.
had not discovered in exile the shallowness of the scepticism
which had been the fashion of his youth ; but he was ready
enough to use the loyalty of the church in the interest of
his house. Napoleon had set, or rather had continued,
the precedent that the state should dictate the terms of its
alliance. There could be no question of a " free church."
The government was generous enough in its marks of defer-
ence. Catholicism was described in the charter as the
religion of state ; divorce disappeared from the civil code ;
the " repos du dimanche " was made obligatory ; dioceses
were increased in number. The church was given a share
of the monopoly of education ; a share which was made
real enough when the lower classes of the seminaries [1] were
opened to children not intended for ecclesiastical orders.
But the secular control remained ; professors at theological
colleges [2] had to declare that they would teach the four
Gallican articles of 1682 ; bishops had to submit their
episcopal mandates to the censorship of the government.
When in 1822 Villèle appointed a priest—Mgr de Frayssi-
nous—to the Grand Mastership of the University, the new

[1] The " petits séminaires."   [2] The " grands séminaires."

master outlined his policy in the words : " celui qui aurait le malheur de vivre sans religion ou de ne pas être dévoué à la famille régnante devrait bien sentir qu'il lui manque quelque chose pour être instituteur de la jeunesse." Thus were the church and the Bourbons linked together.[1] When Charles x. succeeded Louis xviii. an elderly *dévot* took the place of an elderly sceptic. The opposition to the reigning house became more open. The answer of the government was to tighten its hold over the church, and at the same time to increase its regard for the outward observances of religion. A new law was enacted against sacrilege,[2] providing for the penalty of death in cases of extreme blasphemy against the Host ; though it was evident that the law could never be put into effect. But Charles x. was as Gallican as his brother ; his government actually passed a measure restricting the educational work of the religious orders, and in particular of the Jesuits. Yet the absurd antithesis created by the civil constitution of the clergy continued to influence the minds of French catholics. There was no thought of reconciliation between the church and the revolution. As the king became more unpopular, the royalism of the clergy became stronger. Lamennais wrote to a friend in 1830 : " Ce qu'il y a de plus déplorable, c'est les basses extravagances du clergé ; si la religion se perd en France, c'est lui, lui seul, qui l'aura perdue. Vous ne faites pas d'idée, même par les mandements de Messeigneurs, de l'idiotisme de la gent dévote." Yet Lamennais, who a few years later was to compare the kings of Europe to a crew of devils drinking blood out of skulls, had begun by thinking that the clergy and the house of Bourbon were the hope of civilisation.

Felicité Robert de Lamennais was born, like Chateaubriand, at St. Malo. He came of a seafaring family which had received the last patent of nobility given by Louis xvi. His mother was partly Irish. Her death in 1797 was an irreparable loss to a lovable and sensitive boy of sixteen.

---

[1] See p. 138 for the impression made upon non-catholics by this connexion between the house of Bourbon and the mysteries of religion.

[2] It is scarcely credible that a whole section of the clergy should have called this law atheist, because it protected all religions alike. See also p. 131, note 1, for Bonald's justification of the death penalty in these cases.

Lamennais' father sent him to be educated by an uncle at a country house, La Chesnaie, near St. Malo. The uncle found him at times an idle pupil, and as a punishment would shut him up in his library. Here, having nothing better to do, he began to read. The library was typical of the house of an eighteenth-century country gentleman ; Lamennais was able to read Plutarch, Tacitus, Plato, Cicero, Pascal, Voltaire, Montaigne, Rousseau. In 1796 the boy was apprenticed to his father's business. After four years his hatred of the shipping office and his depression were increased by an unsuccessful love affair ; he became profoundly convinced of the misery of human life, about which indeed he knew very little. (From this time he began seriously to devote himself to religion.) Under the influence of an elder brother with greater strength of character and less intelligence than himself, he set himself to ask whether his unquietness and distaste for the world meant a vocation for the priesthood. He gave up all part in the shipping business and retired to La Chesnaie. Here, in 1808, when he was only twenty-six, he collaborated with his brother in a first book : *Réflexions sur l'état de l'église en France pendant le XVIIIme siècle et sur sa situation actuelle.*[1] Lamennais pointed out the pitiful state of the church. The material and spiritual corruption of the upper classes had been the cause of the revolution ; the Napoleonic concordat had not brought about a real restoration of religion. In a phrase which resulted in the confiscation of the book by the imperial police, Lamennais accused Napoleon of wanting to keep the people in a condition of ignorance and servility, and hinted at his " secret dessein d'envahir l'autorité spirituelle." The French church must therefore undertake its own reform. The clergy must be reinforced in numbers, and develop a new corporate life by means of synods, conferences, retreats, and the foundation of religious communities. Catholics must write books as valuable as those which were being written by protestants—an order which might well have been given by Napoleon himself ! The laity must be organised in associations ; church services must be improved.

The book had little influence. The authors were un-

---

[1] *Collected Works* (1836-37 edition), vi. 1-119.

known men ; their measures of reform were the common stock of religious reformers from Julian the Apostate to the Tractarians. Six years later Lamennais made a greater stir by publishing a violent attack upon the Napoleonic university.[1] The attack began the dispute over the control of education which divided catholic from free-thinking Frenchmen during the nineteenth century. The vehemence of its language was prophetic of the future declarations of Lamennais against all constituted authority. " Of all the conceptions of Bonaparte, the most terrifying for a thinking man, the most profoundly anti-social, in a word, the conception most worthy of him, is that of his university.[2] . . . Because he is, by instinct, the enemy of civilisation . . . because he wishes to make of France a huge camp ready to take arms at the first signal and of Frenchmen a single body passively obedient to his caprice, and, as it were, animated by his own evil genius, he has resolved to give over the greater part of the nation to a brutalising savagery, while allowing a small minority to rise to a kind of instructed barbarism. . . . I am not attacking the university because it closes its doors to the children of the poor ; it thereby preserves them from its corruption ; the injustice against which I protest is the refusal to allow other schools to be opened for them. . . ." Lamennais described the military character of the system which Napoleon was to call his plan for the moral education of the French people. The results were such as might have been expected from its methods of narrow repression. Not only was the moral debasement of the pupils beyond description (here Lamennais was unfair in blaming Napoleon for the corruption of French society) but the very purpose of education was defeated. The more human interests were destroyed ; the iron rules of discipline, without a proper moral background, could not produce the results for which they were framed. " The work of the university is ruined above all by indiscipline, and this indiscipline is the fruit of irreligion and immorality. The university, with its military punishments, its prisons and its

[1] *De l'université impériale. Collected Works*, vi. 308-29.
[2] It must be remembered that the state monopoly of education was exercised through the centralised university of France.

cells, has still to find the means of suppressing a spirit of insubordination which is ever on the increase."

This attack was fairly well justified. It is probable that the empire of the first, or of a second, Bonaparte would have been undermined, as was the empire of the third Bonaparte, by the corruption of its own leaders and officials ; the strength of the master-mind must in time have weakened. But at the moment Napoleon was in possession. Lamennais had to leave France during the Hundred Days. On his return he was persuaded by his brother to become a priest. This step was the greatest mistake of his life ; the result of his two worst faults : impetuousness in action after long vacillation, and a submission to the influence of men of routine and narrow views. A year later came the first volume of a book which de Maistre likened to an earth-quake. The starting-point of the *Essai sur l'indifférence en matière de religion* was the assumption common to all the conservative thinkers of the age following the revolution : the belief, half-justified by the terrible happenings of their own generation, that society in Europe " s'avance rapide-ment vers un terme fatal." So thought Metternich when he said that the business of the statesmen at Vienna was not to rebuild society on a plan more in conformity with the divine will but to preserve it from the immediate dissolution with which it was threatened by its open and determined enemies. So thought de Maistre when he heaped argument upon argument, and distorted history to prove that in the chair of St. Peter was the only hope of a firm foundation for society. Lamennais saw a more serious danger than the open attacks of declared enemies. " Les bruits qui grondent dans son sein, les secousses qui l'ébranlent, ne sont pas le plus effrayant symptôme qu'elle offre à l'observateur : mais cette indifférence léthargique où nous la voyons tomber, ce profond assoupissement, qui l'en tirera ? " Man in Euro-pean society " had reached the last excess of intellectual degradation into which it was possible for him to fall ; ' cum in profundum venerit, contemnit.' " [1]

What was the reason for this fall ? " One of those men whose vision is wide because they have set themselves on a

---

[1] *Essai sur l'indifférence*, Introd., pp. i-iii. *Collected Works*, vol. i.

great height, seeing that already all the doctrines [of religion] had been attacked without success, foretold more than a century ago all that is happening under our eyes.   Bossuet declared : ' Je prévois que les libertins et les esprits forts pourront être décrédités, non par aucune horreur de leurs sentiments, mais parce qu'on tiendra tout dans l'indifférence, excepté les plaisirs et les affaires.' "[1]   With the indifference resulting from weakness of will Lamennais had no concern. " Nous n'avons en vue que les indifférences systématiques."[2] Of these there were three kinds.   Religion might be considered merely a necessity for the common people ;   a political institution, but nothing more.   Religion might be considered necessary for all men ;   but it might be dissociated from revelation.   Revealed religion might be accepted, but, with the exception of a few fundamental verities, the truths of its teaching might be denied.   All three views led to atheism, and the break-up of society. Lamennais concluded that there was hope of temporal salvation only in the sovereignty of the church over all temporal rulers.   By different routes Bonald and de Maistre had reached the same conclusion.   In each case a chain of reasoning, supported by evidence from history, led to certain startling and, it must be said, unpractical judgments.   The conditions under which these conclusions were reached deprived them of any philosophical finality ;   the good sense of ordinary men put a right value upon generalisations from the wide field of history made by writers whose training was essentially unhistorical,[3] and whose aim was only to justify their own reaction to the troubled years since 1789.

These men were too close to the revolution to understand its meaning.   They could see its destructiveness ;   they never explored the material cause of its excesses ;   therefore they built up an unreal world from their own fears and indignation.   De Maistre was more violent than Lamennais.

---

[1] *Essai sur l'indifférence*, Introd., p. xxv.   [2] *Ibid.*, i. 18.
[3] Lamennais, for example, uses the fantastic argument that the number of madmen increases in a country where the principle of authority has been weakened : " sous le règne d'Henri VIII. le nombre des fous augmenta prodigieusement en Angleterre, et depuis il a été toujours croissant " !   (*Ibid.*, ii., Preface, p. lviii.)

Émile Faguet has pointed out how difficult it is even to call de Maistre a Christian. His principle of authority is pagan; his infallible pope is an absolute Roman emperor;[1] his idea of sacrifice is nearer to the blood-bath of Mithraism than to an act of the divine compassion.

If Lamennais' work is taken not as an attack upon the long-drawn and terrible modes of human progress, but as an analysis of the dangers threatening the stability and even the existence of the states of Europe, there is much in the *Essai sur l'indifférence* which has not lost its meaning. The destructive criticism of the philosophy of the eighteenth century was unoriginal, but expressed in language which all could understand and which few could forget. Lamennais developed a counter-theory to the theory of the supremacy of the individual reason.[2] This counter-theory was based upon the recognition of certain ideas as common to the human race, and therefore providing the only basis of certainty; Lamennais borrowed his philosophy largely from Malebranche, whom he called " l'ange bon de la métaphysique "; but the political consequences which he drew from this doctrine of universal ideas were local, ill-judged, and temporary.

In his haste Lamennais believed that his principles led him to support the extreme royalists. To them indeed he came as a valuable recruit. His essay had put him in the front rank of the clergy of France. Judging him by their own standards, the politicians might think this academic priest an excellent tool in their hands. An incursion into political journalism in the interest of the house of Bourbon and the cause of high prerogative was bound to lead Lamennais to disaster. He thought in terms of a world order and included the Bourbons under a universal principle; Louis XVIII. and the returned émigrés took thought only that they should regain an inheritance, and not go on their travels again. Lamennais supported the royalists because the

---

[1] It is interesting to compare Napoleon's judgment on Alexander of Russia with that of de Maistre. The former called Alexander " un grec du bas-empire," the latter " une âme d'élite."

[2] The best short summary of his view of a " raison commune de l'espèce . . . une croyance universelle du genre humain " is given by Lamennais in the preface to vol. x. of his collected works.

liberalism which he and they opposed might lead to anarchy. He would have no compromise ; the politicians had to think of the electorate and were ready to take up a position, especially in church affairs, incompatible with their principles. Lamennais never believed in the divine right of kings. " Kings should know what they are " (this was not the language which a royalist would use to Louis XVIII. or to Charles X. ; but it was not unlike the style of the *Paroles d'un croyant*) : " they are the ministers of God for the accomplishment of His good will ; they hold His authority ; they have received it from Him, and cannot put it away. . . . A king, like a priest, is not a king for himself, but for the people whom he is called upon to lead. Authority never ceases to belong to God, and never becomes the property of those by whom it is exercised. . . . Louis XVI. died for the reason that he would only be an ordinary man, when he had been called to be a king." [1] " With a sovereignty which has its source in the sovereign himself, there is no alternative between slavery and anarchy." [2]

The royalists kept to their practice ; Lamennais kept to his theory. The two were bound to come into conflict when the government should appear to Lamennais to compromise the liberty of the church or the Christian character of the state. Within five years of the publication of the second part of the *Essai sur l'indifférence* Lamennais was preaching, with his usual whole-heartedness, complete detachment of the church from the royalist cause. At the same time he continued to ask for a complete submission to the authority of the pope. What if the pope should order submission to the house of Bourbon ?

In 1825 the new direction of Lamennais' mind was shown in a new book : *De la religion considérée dans ses rapports avec l'ordre politique et civile*. The chapter headings make clear his line of thought : " État de la société en France : que la religion, en France, est entièrement hors de la société politique et civile, et que par conséquent l'État est athée : que l'athéisme a passé de la société politique et civile dans la société domestique : que la religion en France n'est aux

---

[1] *Deuxièmes mélanges. Collected Works*, viii. 261.
[2] *Quelques réflexions sur notre état présent* (1823). *Collected Works*, viii. 315.

yeux de la loi qu'une chose qu'on administre." [1] The
book was full of absurd historical inaccuracies and exaggerations : none the less the situation of the church was described
clearly—too clearly for the liking of the bishops—and its
future under a society based upon popular sovereignty was
foretold in terms which were still more objectionable to
comfortable men.

Lamennais began by denying that France was really
governed by a monarchy. The levelling work of the revolution had reduced all Frenchmen in theory to a single category ; in theory, for in fact the " peu d'or de plus ou de
moins " made all the difference between men ; a difference which covered the whole distance separating sovereign
from subject. (Again there is a forecast of the future social
policy of Lamennais.) France was therefore an example
of a pure democracy. The chamber of peers and the
chamber of deputies formed one democratic assembly ; the
ministry was the executive of the democracy ; the king was
no more than " a venerable survival of the past ; the inscription from an ancient temple set up on the façade of an entirely new building." The character of such a government
was not pleasing to contemplate. A democracy had no
stability ; the whole social order became no more than " un
chemin de passage." For this reason mediocrity could
succeed in a democracy more easily than talent or genius,
since for the achievement of great things time and consistency were necessary ; but these two elements were most
wanting in a democratic state. Here Lamennais only outlined a theme which Guizot and Tocqueville were to
amplify and repeat in the next decade.[2] His reasoning took
him further. " The democratic state must be hostile to
religion, and particularly to Christianity ; for an authority which is supreme and unchanging in the sphere of
religion is incompatible with a political authority which is
continually changing." No Christian monarchy could be

[1] *Collected Works*, vol. vii. The headings of chapter vi. show Lamennais' uncompromising and dramatic modes of expression : " Point de
pape, point d'Église ; point d'Église, point de Christianisme ; point de
Christianisme, point de religion, au moins pour tout peuple qui fut
chrétien, et par conséquent point de société."
[2] See above, p. 203.

transformed into a democracy without a profound effect upon the religion of the citizens.

The picture of this atheist and democratic society is more gloomy than Tocqueville's forecast of the triumph of the obvious and the commonplace in thought and action. The development of the instruments of credit and the possibilities of financial speculation would bring about an incessant and fantastic activity. " Industry will use all its potentialities to maintain and strengthen this movement. Science will come to its aid. The arts and the skilled professions will bring their technique to perfection, and will invent new methods : men will extract from matter all that it can give them, all the pleasures that their senses can enjoy. Up to the very moment before this palace of folly and illusions vanishes into the gulf of universal ruin, human beings will boast about the progress of civilisation and the prosperity of society. Nevertheless reason will decay before men's eyes. The simplest truths will appear strange and remarkable, and will scarcely be endured." [1] Lamennais describes the degradation of the life of the ordinary citizen in the secularised state when men's hours are no longer lightened by the nobility of religion. As animals they will be born ; as animals they will beget their kind ; as animals they will die. " Un officier publique vient constater la mort. Il déclare qu'appelé en tel lieu il y a vu un cadavre ; on écrit sur un registre le nom du décédé ; deux fossoyeurs font le reste." [2] Such would be the France of the nineteenth century ; such would be the fate of the " royaume appelé très chrétien." In this society, under this government, the church could not but be attacked. " On mine avec art sa discipline, son gouvernement, sa hiérarchie. . . . Depuis l'athée jusqu'au janséniste, tous les sectaires se remuent. . . . Dans leurs rangs accourent les ambitieux, les intrigants, les faibles d'esprit, les faibles de conscience, les parleurs de Christianisme et de monarchie." [3]

Although the second half of the work has some splendid

---

[1] *De la religion considérée dans ses rapports avec l'ordre politique et civile. Collected Works*, vii. 28.
[2] *Ibid.*, p. 51.   [3] *Ibid.*, p. 101.

passages of declamation,[1] it lacks the conciseness of the first four chapters. The book ends with an appeal to the governments of Europe, and above all, the government of France, to cease from attacking the monarchical and infallible church, the one embodiment of the principle of authority which can save Europe.[2]

If Lamennais was disillusioned about the Bourbons, the ministers were disillusioned about the value of Lamennais as a pamphleteer in the royalist cause. The destruction of the book was ordered, and a fine of thirty francs was imposed upon the author. No better confirmation could be given him of the rightness of his thesis. He abandoned the Bourbons as hopeless, and tried to save the church from implication in their fall. " I believe they will have the fate of the Stuarts. But the first thought of the revolution will not be directed against them. . . . The destruction of catholicism is the aim, the only aim, of the revolution ; there is no other question in the world." If this were the case, how best could catholics meet the attack ?

This question was answered in another book : *Des progrès de la révolution et de la guerre contre l'église.*[3] Negatively, the catholic clergy could best serve their cause by complete abstention from political intrigue ; their most urgent duty was to isolate themselves entirely from a society which was in fact atheist. Terrible mischief was done by men like Mgr de Chaffey, bishop of Nîmes, who said plaintively

[1] Such as the attack upon the ministers : " La religion, c'est quelque chose ; mais leurs places, c'est tout. Dans l'embrasement de sa ville, Énée emportoit ses dieux : dans l'incendie de l'Europe, ils songent à leurs portefeuilles."

[2] M. Boutard (*op. cit.*, vol. i. pp. 329-31) has pointed out an interesting reference to Lamennais, made by Auguste Comte in No. 5 of the *Producteur.* Comte was as much alarmed as were the conservative writers about the danger to society from the dissolution of established ideas (" cette anarchie tient, en dernière analyse, à l'absence de tout système prépondérant "). Unless a new and positive system could be devised, society would break up in a riot of egoistic materialism (" cette licence que doit produire l'individualité non comprimée "). " Pour terminer radicalement ce désordre qui, s'il pouvait se prolonger, n'aurait d'autre issue que l'entière dissolution des rapports sociaux, la seule manière est de le détruire dans son principe, en ramenant par un procédé quelconque, le système intellectuel à l'unité."

[3] Vol. ix. in Lamennais' collected works.

of himself : "j'ai deux maîtresses, l'église gallicane et la maison de Bourbon ; je compte bien les garder jusqu'au tombeau." Positively, the catholics were to demand liberty. "We ask for the Catholic Church the liberty promised by the charter to all religions, the liberty enjoyed by the protestants and the Jews . . . liberty of conscience, liberty of the press, liberty for catholic schools. We are not asking too much, and twenty-five million catholics have the right to count for something, the right to refuse to be treated as a population of serfs . . . or outcasts. . . ." [1]

It is significant that Lamennais no longer includes liberals and revolutionaries in the same condemnation. "We do not confuse with these wretches [i.e. the revolutionaries] that large section of society which, in Europe and elsewhere, is fighting resolutely for what is known as the cause of liberalism. We must admit without hesitation that this movement is too general and too constant to be based entirely upon error and passion." Here Lamennais was following the logic of his own theory of the rightness of a view accepted generally by mankind. Once disengaged from its false theories and consequences, liberalism was the sentiment which must excite the members of a Christian society in the name of liberty. This liberalism was a sign of the inability of any Christian nation to suffer an authority merely human in its origin ; an authority with no other rule than its own pleasure. [2] Liberalism was pre-eminently social in so far as its aim was liberty. Yet no liberal movement could succeed if it were not able to free itself from the common faults of "dogmatic" liberalism ; these faults were a materialist view of the world, and a disbelief in any principle of sovereignty residing outside the judgment of the individual. Liberals made the mistake of looking for a guarantee of freedom not in the spiritual order where alone it could be found, but in the material forms of government. [3] Always and inevitably they would be disappointed. "The civil laws of society, which regulate only the external relations of men, presuppose laws anterior to themselves, laws which touch the inner life and regulate human thought

[1] *Des progrès de la révolution*, Preface, p. viii.
[2] *Ibid.*, pp. 22 and 60.   [3] *Ibid.*, p. 31.

and human affections, laws which must have their source
in an authority both sovereign and infallible, and are
thereby morally binding." [1] Until they recognised this
authority, until they looked for the spiritual foundation and
safeguard of liberty, liberals must be for ever destroying
their own work. This unending destruction must lead to
anarchy and the break-up of society.

On the other hand, the royalists, or rather the Gallicans,
in following the liberal idea of a complete separation of the
spiritual from the temporal order, left to authority no other
rule save its own will and desire, and, by this means, established for ever the tyranny of kings and the servitude of
peoples. [2] Here was another road to anarchy. The church
must therefore shake itself free from both these principles of
destruction, and must use its independence in the interest
of its divine mission. For this reason the clergy must not
commit themselves to any form of political attachment.
" Le christianisme ne réprouve aucune forme de gouvernement, il s'allie à tout genre de police." [3] The divine purpose
of this freedom was not to secure ease and tranquillity for
the clergy themselves, but to make possible the fulfilment
of the duties assigned by God to the church. The church
had saved society in the dark ages ; it could again prepare
the way for a better political order by bringing before men
the eternal bases of temporal well-being.

Lamennais came back to his earliest book when he complained that the clergy were unprepared for their most
important work. Theological studies had been interrupted
by the revolution ; the old methods of teaching had been
too narrow. The theology taught in most of the seminaries
was a stunted and degenerate scholasticism which repelled
the students and gave them not the least idea of the general
teaching of their religion. [4]

This was not the language of the bishops ; nor could it be
the language of the popes. Sudden attacks of this kind
isolated Lamennais among the clergy, and exposed him to
the discipline of those whom he offended or frightened.
Upon the issue of this conflict would depend the future of

[1] *Des progrès de la révolution*, p. 58.
[2] *Ibid.*, p. 61.   [3] *Ibid.*, p. 77.   [4] *Ibid.*, p. 192.

the relations between liberalism and the church. For by this time Lamennais was a power in France and even in Europe. Already the archbishop of Paris had spoken of him in a pastoral letter as presumptuous enough to shake the foundations of society by doctrines which spread distrust and hatred between sovereigns and subjects. Already Lamennais had begun to gather round him a school of young men with all his enthusiasm and little of his genius and simplicity. For a time events showed him to be a good prophet. The revolution of July treated the Bourbons exactly as he had foretold, and included the church in the unpopularity which was cast upon all institutions claiming divine right. The archbishop's palace was sacked by the Paris mob, and all the churches were closed. Seven months later the church of St. Germain l'Auxerrois was plundered by a mob indignant at the holding of a royalist service within its walls, and the archbishop's palace was again attacked. The country was flooded with scurrilous pamphlets against the clergy, and there were wild stories of clerical hoards of poisoned daggers. When Louis Philippe happened to use the word " Providence " in an address to the chamber, a newspaper which claimed to represent " moderate " opinion remarked that the government was tending towards mysticism !

This persecution convinced Lamennais that the catholics should unite in their demand for liberty. With this end in view he founded a newspaper, and gave it the title of *L'Avenir*. Union among catholics had proved possible and valuable in Ireland, where catholic emancipation had just been secured, and in Belgium, where liberty had been won from the protestant Dutch. Union among the catholics of France would strengthen their hands against a government which proclaimed its own " indifference " to religion. Lamennais soon forgot his own wise advice to the clergy to keep out of political controversy. He might excuse himself by the urgent need to protect the church from actual persecution. He might add that he could not discuss the best form of relationship between church and state in France without touching on the political situation. But his articles in *L'Avenir* were written in his usual passionate style, and raised up more enemies than friends.[1] The government of Louis Philippe, anxious to persuade the powers that the cycle of revolutions was closed in France, did not wish to be told that the July days were not merely a reaction from the aberrations of Charles x., but a new stage in a long series of revolutions. The French bishops could not listen without indignation to an unbeneficed priest who advocated the complete separation of church and state as an end, and complete disendowment as the means and indispensable condition of success.[2]

Lamennais annoyed the rich bankers and manufacturers by laying down the law on the social question, and disturbed the statesmen of other countries by the violence of his language about questions of international importance. A fiery article in *L'Avenir*[3] had commented upon the fall of Warsaw and the collapse of the Polish rebellion. The problem of poverty was called a matter of life and death for Europe ; nothing less than a total change in the industrial system would prevent a general revolt of the poor against the rich.[4] New economic experiments, such as agricultural colonies or an extension of the principle of association, demanded the co-operation of the clergy, and opened an immense field of work for the priesthood.

Lamennais was not content with preaching liberty in a newspaper ; he founded an " Agence générale pour la défense de la liberté religieuse." This body undertook every kind of work. It opened a school in defiance of the government regulations, with the dangerous programme : " La liberté se prend et ne se donne pas." The charter of its foundation was intended to attract catholics from all countries. Seventy thousand francs were collected for the relief of distress in Ireland ; the Polish sympathies of Charles de Montalembert,[5] who collaborated with Lamennais, were as

---

[1] Lamennais' most important contributions to *L'Avenir* are reprinted in vol. x. of his collected works.

[2] October 18, 1830. *Op. cit.*, pp. 155-9.

[3] September 17, 1831. *Op. cit.*, pp. 380-1 : " Que chacun garde ce qui est à soi : aux égorgeurs, le meurtre et l'infamie ; aux vrais enfants de la Pologne, une gloire pure et immortelle ; au czar et à ses alliés la malédiction de quiconque porte en soi un cœur d'homme."

[4] June 30, 1830. *Op. cit.*, pp. 338-50.

[5] Charles de Montalembert (b. 1810) was the son of a French gentleman who had emigrated during the revolution, fought under Condé,

well known as those of his master. Little wonder that
foreign governments were irritated at this novel form of
revolutionary propaganda. The French government, the
French bishops (of whom Lamennais had said that " there
were bishops in France, but no episcopate "), and the ministers of foreign powers had one certain means of silencing
this extraordinary priest. Lamennais had declared in the
plainest terms his submission to the pope. Then let the pope
suppress his newspaper, close down his association, and
make an end of his interference in politics.

For reasons as different as noble action differs from
intrigue Lamennais for his own part had decided to appeal
to the pope. This appeal was the ruin of liberal catholicism.
The bishops had closed round *L'Avenir* and the Agence
générale. The circulation to the one began to fall ; the sub-
scribers to the other began to decrease in number. There
were only two possibilities : either to suspend publication of
the journal and wait for its ideas to have their effect upon
the public, or to go to Rome and ask for the approbation
of the pope. The first course would have been the wiser ;
Lamennais had advocated it himself when he had asked
for the separation of the church from the state, and warned
the clergy against taking any part in politics. Lamennais'
views had been widely advertised ; time was on his side,
and moderate men would not blame him for delay. The
European situation was extremely difficult ; there had been
two papal elections within a year ; the beginning of a new
reign was not the time to ask for the confirmation of a
policy distrusted by the cardinal-electors. But delay needed
more patience than Lamennais possessed, and appeared too
much like surrender. The second course had a certain
dramatic boldness which commended itself to an impetuous

and married a Scottish wife. Montalembert first came into political
prominence through his attacks upon the state monopoly of education
in France. His liberalism at once brought him into contact with
Lamennais. More than twenty-five years after Lamennais' condemnation Montalembert attempted to revive the liberal catholic movement
in France, and to oppose in the *Correspondant* the ultramontane tendencies
represented by L. Veuillot and the *Univers*. His work was again cut
short by papal order. He died in March 1870. See R. P. Lecanuet,
Montalembert d'après son journal et sa correspondance. 3 vols. (Paris, 1895-
1902.)

man. Success would bring considerable human satisfaction in the discomfiture of the French bishops ; Lamennais refused to contemplate failure.

In February 1831 Gregory xvi. had succeeded Pius viii. in the government of the church. On the day of his coronation as pope he had heard the news of a serious insurrection in his states. Austrian troops were called in to restore order. In May 1831 England, France, Austria, Prussia, and Russia had impressed upon the pope the need for reforms in the administration of his kingdom. The pope knew well enough that Austria was half-hearted in her support of any movement for reform, and that, if he were subservient enough to the Austrian government, he could always rely upon Austrian help. No real reforms were introduced, and early in 1832 rebellion again broke out in the legations. The Austrian soldiers reappeared in force, and shortly after them came the French, suspicious as ever of Austrian advance in Italy.[1] The last stage of the temporal power had been reached ; for there could be no doubt that the rebels were aiming at the complete suppression of papal sovereignty. One of the revolutionary proclamations opened with the words : " the Roman hyena is in its death agony."

From Austria, Prussia, and Russia—three of the powers who had asked for reforms in the papal government—came demands that Lamennais should be severely reprimanded. To Austria the pope was forced to listen by pressing necessity. Metternich sent him a copy of an intercepted letter written by Lamennais. Lützow, the Austrian representative at the Vatican, was instructed to point out the personal ambition of Lamennais, and the dangerous, anti-social character of his teaching : " le détestable amalgame que La Mennais a fait de la politique avec la religion. . . . Le démon de l'orgueil s'est emparé de cet homme et quiconque est possédé par ce malin esprit est perdu." [2] Lützow was able to reply that the pope was grateful for the intercepted letter, and had put it away in his secret cabinet ; that he had spoken of " cet homme dangereux (qui) méritait bien d'être traduit devant le Tribunal du Saint Office." In March

---

[1] See above, p. 162.
[2] Vienna Staats-Archiv: Rome. (Metternich to Lützow, May 19, 1832.)

1832 Lützow had told Metternich that the pope would have Cardinal de Rohan with him when he interviewed Lamennais because he was afraid of " la vanité française et de gazettier." [1]

Nicholas of Russia had also claimed a careful hearing. The whole future of the Catholic Church in Russia had been compromised by the catholic priests who had taken part in the Polish rebellion of 1831. The Russian government, with the support of Austria, required a public disavowal of the rebels. This implied an abandonment of the Polish cause, and a toleration of the fearful reprisals taken by Russia. Lamennais believed that the tsar had offered to send troops to defend the papal states against yet another outbreak of rebellion. There is no need to assume so fantastic a bargain. The Austrians in the Romagna and the French at Ancona were well able to protect the miserable government of the papal states until a happier chance might allow them to divide the church lands between them. Gregory was thinking of the revolution within his own borders, but no less of the danger to the Greek uniates and scattered catholic communities within Russian territory.[2] More than one earlier Gregory would have died in agony rather than tell a people with the history of the Poles to trust a man with the history of Nicholas I. Not so Gregory XVI. The Poles were advised to have confidence in the kindness of their most powerful emperor, and were reminded of the Christian duty of submission to divinely appointed authority. Gregory went even further in his carefulness. The draft of the apostolic brief abandoning the Poles to the kindly generosity of Nicholas contained the text : "bonum certamen fidei certate " : "fight the good fight of faith." [3] Gregory thought the implication too dangerous, and erased the words with his own hand!

Of such poverty of spirit was the pope who was to decide the future of catholicism in so far as the fate of an institu-

---

[1] Vienna Staats-Archiv : Rome. (Lützow to Metternich, March 10, 1832.)

[2] The best account of the relations between the papacy and Russia during this period is to be found in Boudou, *Le Saint-Siège et la Russie : leurs relations diplomatiques au XIXe siècle.* Vol. i. *1814-1847.* (Paris, 1922.)

[3] 1 Tim. vi. 12. See Boudou, *op. cit.*, p. 186.

tion is in the hands of one man.   Gregory XVI. had become
a monk six years before the French Revolution.   Forty-five
years before his election to the papacy he had written a
thesis in favour of papal infallibility.   He was a man of
great erudition, though his learning was of the kind
described by Lamennais as entirely out of relation to the
real world.   In 1840 Gregory's friend Moroni—once a
barber's assistant—began the compilation of an enormous
*Dizionario di erudizione storico-ecclesiastica di San Pietro sino
ai nostri tempi.*   This work was to extend to a hundred and
twenty volumes.   Its character can be summed up in one
brief quotation ;   the Holy Office is described as " la
salutare e benigna instituzione del benmerito tribunale dell'
Inquisizione." [1]

Into this shabby Byzantinism, leaning for its support on
the moneys lent by the Rothschilds and the foredoomed
intrigues of Metternich, came a man with the simplicity
and unselfishness of St. Francis.   Lamennais' sadness of
mind and sensitiveness to outward impression made him
uneasy at the very appearance of Rome.   As he crossed the
Romagna he passed bands of political prisoners chained
together.   The city itself added to his depression.   The
churches of Rome seem scarcely Christian to those whose
religious experience is associated with the gothic churches
of the north.   His irritation at the delay in granting him
an audience, the coldness of his reception by nearly all the
high officers of the curia, the uneasiness of Montalembert,
and the almost open despair of Lacordaire [2] (Lamennais'
other companion), led to violent outbursts of anger in his
letters.   He could see in Rome nothing but " le mouvement
caché d'une multitude de petits intérêts qui rampent et se
croisent au sein des ténèbres, comme les vers au sein du

---

[1] Gregory ordered every commune in the papal state to subscribe to
the dictionary.

[2] Jean Baptiste Henri Lacordaire (b. 1802) came to Paris from Dijon
with the idea of becoming an advocate.   For some time he thought of
leaving his profession for the stage.   Lamennais' *Essai sur l'indifférence*
so much impressed him that he entered the seminary of St. Sulpice, and
was ordained in 1827.   He assisted Lamennais and Montalembert in
the editorship of *L'Avenir*.   After the condemnation of Lamennais,
Lacordaire gave his time mainly to preaching, and to the re-establish-
ment in France of the order of St. Dominic.

sépulcre." He felt the need of a free air, of faith, enthusiasm, love, " de tout ce qu'on cherche vainement au milieu
de toutes ces vieilles ruines sur lesquelles rampent, comme
d'immondes reptiles, dans l'ombre et dans le silence, les plus
viles passions humaines." Even Metternich, who never
hoped for much from his fellow-men, was shocked by the
corruption of Rome. To Lamennais the men who surrounded the pope were " ambitieux, avares, corrompus,
frénétiques imbéciles," whom God only tolerated " because
it was His plan to hasten the last destruction which should
precede the regeneration of society, and without which
regeneration would be impossible or incomplete."

These priests and their pope were anxiously engaged in
trying to save the papal kingdom from the government
which its inhabitants desired ; they had little time to bother
themselves with views already condemned by all the conservative statesmen of Europe. Lamennais was told that
the memorandum which he and his friends had submitted
to the pope would be examined at leisure. In the meantime they had better go home. But this meant to them that
judgment upon their cause would be passed by its declared
enemies, by the poor creatures whom God allowed to exist
as His unworthy agents of destruction. It was a matter of
life and death to Lamennais' cause that he should see the
pope. He insisted upon an interview. He had arrived
in Rome at the beginning of January 1832. His memorial
was presented early in February. He was allowed an
audience in the middle of March. The pope had taken
all precautions. The audience was to last only a quarter
of an hour. According to plan, Cardinal de Rohan
was to be present. Already the diplomats were assured
that nothing compromising would be said by the pope.
Metternich and " le Néron de la Pologne " would have
nothing to fear. As soon as the interview was over the
cardinal secretary of state wrote to assure the papal nuncio
at Vienna that Gregory had only seen Lamennais because
of the latter's insistence, and that there had been no talk of
politics between them.

Lamennais also had taken his precautions. Montalembert has described them in his journal. " Enfin arrive le

jour de notre audience si impatiemment désirée.   La bonne
Mme Ankwicz se met en prières dans une église pendant
qu'elle dure. . . ." [1]

The three suppliants were kept waiting for over an hour in
the ante-chambers of the Vatican.   At last the pope sent for
them.   Montalembert was moved more by the immensity of
the papal office than by the man himself.   " I should have
been put at my ease [Montalembert was a peer of France] by
the excessive simplicity, I might almost say by the lack of
dignity, of the pope.   His expression is pleasing, but has
nothing noble or spiritual about it.   He kept one of his
hands in his pockets.   For about a quarter of an hour he
talked to us with a great deal of kindness and affability about
M. Varin [the curé of Geneva], about Geneva, about the
brother of M. de Lamennais and his schools in Brittany,
about the piety of the French catholics.   He reminded us
of the saying of some cardinal that Frenchmen either go to
heaven or to hell, but not to purgatory.   He asked us
whether the French army was sincerely loyal to the present
government ; he praised the Association Lyonnaise for the
propagation of the Faith.   The Cardinal de Rohan gave
him a most complimentary account of my mother, and
asked for his benediction for her and for my brother.   The
pope himself then went to find a reproduction in silver of
the Moses of Michael Angelo.   He showed this reproduction to us, and gave us some gilded medals of his predecessor St. Gregory.   He blessed the rosaries which we presented to him, and sent us away most graciously.   But not
a single word of what he said to us had the slightest relation
to our mission or to the future of the church."

To this situation there could be only one end ; towards
this end events now moved.   Lacordaire went home ; he
was clear-headed enough to see what would happen.
Montalembert was less impersonal, and stayed in Italy with
his friend.   In the midst of his deep depression Lamennais
was bothered over money troubles and the consequences of
careless investment.   At the end of July, after the publication of the brief condemning the Polish insurrection, the two

[1] The account of the interview, taken from Montalembert's journal,
is given in Lecanuet, *op. cit.*, i. 286-7.

men left for France. They travelled through Munich. By
accident (according to his own account) Lacordaire happened to be in Munich.[1] He agreed with Lamennais and
Montalembert that a new review should be started. If they
had not gained the support for which they had made their
journey, at least they had not been condemned. On the
day before they left Munich they were entertained by the
Bavarian catholics who supported or encouraged their
liberalism ; catholics such as Schelling, Baader, and
Döllinger, men whose names were associated with a learning
five hundred years in advance of Gregory's dictionary of one
hundred and twenty volumes. After the dinner there was
music. During one of the songs Lamennais was called
outside. He found a messenger from the apostolic nuncio,
and was given a letter. He came back into the room,
and asked that the verses he had missed might be
repeated.

After some time he leant across to Lacordaire, and said :
" There is a papal encyclical against us. We must make
our submission." His hosts asked him to walk with them
to a little village on the outskirts of the town. All the time
he talked brilliantly, saying nothing of the letter in his
pocket. When at last he was alone with his two friends,
he read them the encyclical ; while he read it, his voice
trembled. At the end he said : " It is the condemnation
of liberty and Polish nationality." Then a pause : " God
has spoken ; nothing is left for me but to say ' fiat voluntas
tua,' and to serve with my prayers the two causes which,
by His Vicar on earth, He has forbidden me to serve with
my pen."

The encyclical left no room for doubt. It condemned the
suggestion that the church needed reform ; it denied that
liberty of conscience could be admitted by catholics as a
principle ; it refused to agree that liberty of the press

[1] The meeting was not altogether by chance. Lacordaire did not
wish to be in Paris at the time of Lamennais' homecoming. He feared
a rash step, and wanted neither to associate nor publicly to dissociate
himself from any action Lamennais might take. He decided to go to
Munich because it was a catholic centre, where, incidentally, the cost
of living was cheap. On his way to Munich he heard from Montalembert that Lamennais would be passing through the city. See
Boutard, *op. cit.*, ii. 328.

was a necessity for a modern state.[1] With the encyclical came a letter. The pope in his kindness had taken care not to mention by name the editors of *L'Avenir* and their newspaper. As though Lamennais cared more for his reputation than for the liberty of the church !

Surrender followed ; the publication of *L'Avenir* was suspended *sine die* ;[2] the Agence générale was dissolved. But Lamennais could not keep silent. He tried, as so many catholics have tried, to minimise the papal language of condemnation. Could it be that his methods and not his opinions were wrong ? The hopelessness of this attempt was soon clear. Lamennais published an apology for the Polish rebellion, and the pope publicly expressed a doubt about the genuineness of his submission. Finally, Gregory asked for a positive expression of obedience. After an effort to escape, Lamennais made a complete recantation in October 1833. The pope even had the folly to ask him to use his pen in defence of the encyclical *Mirari vos* !

But this man could not sell his conscience, nor could he escape from his temperament. His ideas could not be wrong. The church of God could not forswear liberty. If the pope denied the works of God, the pope could not be the minister of God. In such a case Lamennais would have been living in a dream. He must come back to reality from this image-worship. He must leave the church as he had left the royalist party. Another man might have retired into a proud silence, or attempted to understand by long study the net of circumstance from which the pope and his cardinals could scarcely free themselves. But Lamennais knew little of that wide imagination which sees in institutions the slow register of human progress, and looks

[1] The encyclical letter, known, according to custom, from its initial words " Mirari vos," was written in the harsh and ponderous Latin of the latter-day papal chancery. Liberty of conscience is described as " absurda illa . . . ac erronea sententia, seu potius deliramentum. . . ." Its origin is " ex . . . putidissimo indifferentismi fonte." Liberty of the press is called " deterrima illa, ac nunquam satis execranda et detestabilis libertas artis librariae ad scripta quaelibet edenda in vulgus." The faithful are reminded that the apostles burned books ! Union between church and state is regarded as a salutary concord, disturbed only by " impudentissimae libertatis amatoribus."

[2] The suspension during the absence of the editor from France had been described as temporary ; the prelude to a triumph.

beyond the men and chances of the moment. He saw things unhistorically ; his passionate love of justice set his mind on fire ; compromise, delay, and even charity were surrender to the evil powers. The pope might also have guided his action according to the same far-reaching tolerance of history. Was there not the passion of an earlier Gregory who "loved justice and hated iniquity"? Was there no impetuousness in the very tradition of the see of Peter ? Were there no papal precedents for a denunciation of the timid reasoning of kings ? There were indeed precedents even more illustrious, even more compelling. Nicholas of Russia had an army ; Herod and Pilate once had soldiers.

In the earlier disillusionments of a headstrong career Lamennais had never spared the men who had deceived him. The break with the whole visible order of the Christian Church would make a storm in his mind more thunderous than his angry abandonment of the house of Bourbon. This greatest injustice, this monstrous perversion, this utter degradation and enchaining of the instruments of God, would be proclaimed to the world in language worthy of the Miltonic catastrophe of Lucifer.

In agony of mind Lamennais came back to La Chesnaie, where he had first read Pascal and Voltaire and Tacitus. He had learned well from his masters of language. The *Paroles d'un croyant* were written in broken, oracular sequences of declamation, at once savage and compassionate. After years of belief, Lamennais was writing the condemnation of all his faith. The coldness and selfishness of kings and priests merited no balanced judgment and no measure of extenuation. There was no forgiveness for weak men entrapped by their past in the barren eminence of power. Only for the poor and humble of heart wronged beyond any hope of betterment was there any comprehending pity. The story of the Romanoffs, with their misery even yet half-told, might have touched Lamennais in other hours of his mind. But he had no thought that kings might themselves be tyrannised by the dead. He had found a new cause. He turned to the peoples with a terrible simplicity and a magnificence of hope. *Deposuit potentes de sede, et exaltavit humiles.*

Henceforth the life of Lamennais was lived outside the range of the church. A drowned man leaves no sign on the stillness of water after the struggle of his end. Yet this battle between mediæval Latin and the subtlety of modern French was fought for the future of liberal ideas in the church. The violence of Lamennais brought another of the timeworn formulae of condemnation : " Motu proprio, et ex certa scientia, deque Apostolicae potestatis plenitudine, memoratum librum . . . *Paroles d'un croyant* . . . propositiones respective falsas, calumniosas, temerarias, inducentes in anarchiam, contrarias Verbo Dei, impias, scandalosas, erroneas, jam ab Ecclesia, praesertim in Valdensibus, Wiclefitis, Hussitis, aliisque hujus generis haereticis damnatas continentem, reprobamus, ac pro reprobato et damnato in perpetuum haberi volumus et decernimus."

Twelve years after the condemnation of the *Paroles d'un croyant* the successor of Gregory XVI. attempted a reform of his government. But his hands were tied by the language of his predecessor, and the allegiances to which he was committed. No one believed that the reforms of Pius IX. were practicable ; few believed that he was sincere. For the papacy had been given its chance to make terms with modern civilisation ; the greatest of opportunities do not recur. The transition would have been difficult, perhaps impossible. Lamennais' action was ill-timed, and compromising by its exuberance of language, its violence and haste. Yet the curia had made only the clumsiest of attempts to distinguish between the man and his cause, his methods and his ideas. Gregory had never treated Lamennais with the consideration shown to the mighty of this world ; he had refused to admit that the church could learn anything from the moral and intellectual experiments of his own age ; he had denied the value of these experiments and said that the very thought of them was an outrage. It may be that in the nature of things he could have said nothing else without the gravest risk to his temporal power ; but he had made himself the instrument of proclaiming to the states of Europe the incompatibility between modern theories of political liberty and the teaching of the church, and had been willing to instruct catholics to look with horror upon what most men hold to be the indispensable conditions of a free society.

The consequences of the career and the condemnation of Lamennais were curiously far-reaching. Not only had Lamennais shown the contrast between the activity and receptiveness of mind of catholics north of the Alps and the unadaptiveness of the ultramontanes ; not only did he drive from the church an incalculable strength of liberal opinion, and make plain to the Italians what was to be expected from the Roman power ; his earlier propaganda had affected the character of French catholicism as much as any man except Napoleon had affected it in the nineteenth century. He could not undo his own work.

He had destroyed the vestiges of Gallicanism. His attack upon the misuse of ecclesiastical influence in the cause of royalist propaganda was unanswerable. Before he became a revolutionary he had impressed upon a generation of catholics the final hostility between the church and the revolution ; his own apostasy, his own condemnation by the papacy which he had set in the highest place of government, only completed the exposition of ultramontane theory. He had made popular among catholics the thesis of de Maistre that monarchical rule in the church was of the essence of Christianity, and that infallibility must be one of the attributes of the Vicar of God. Here was another proof that the popes were right in attacking the principles of the revolution ; here was another reason why there could be no compromise. Pius ix. inherited the legacy of infallibility, and the whole-hearted condemnation of nearly every mode of human progress since the middle ages ; Pius, after his fashion, followed the line of least resistance, and forged the last links in the chain which bound catholics to the most unenlightened periods of European history.

At the same time Lamennais had strengthened the ultramontane position by following the example of Napoleon, and appealing to the pope over the heads of the French bishops. He had recognised the dictatorship of the modern papacy. Finally, he had shown the value of journalistic propaganda in a religious cause. Fortune, wishing to complete the isolation of liberal catholic opinion in France, saw that a successor was found to carry on the tradition. *L'Univers* took the place of *L'Avenir,* and used all its weapons. Louis Veuillot,[1] sensitive and passionate as Lamennais, but without sympathy for the ideas of his age, attacked another generation of liberal catholics with no less vehemence than Lamennais had employed against the ultramontanes. Veuillot, " with French grammar on his side," worked for the pope ; he had no pupil worthy of himself ; none was needed, for the bastion between catholicism and modern progress had been built, and was blessed by the church as a wall of paradise.[2]

[1] Louis Veuillot (b. 1813) was the son of poor parents. He worked first in a lawyer's office and then became a journalist. He went to Rome in 1838, and came back a strong ultramontane. Henceforward his time and abilities were given to propaganda in the interest of extreme ultramontane views. Veuillot's attack upon liberal catholicism was supported by most of the French bishops (with notable exceptions, such as Dupanloup) and by the dominant party in the curia. Veuillot could write with great delicacy and gentleness ; but his methods in journalistic controversy led him far beyond the limits of charity and moderation. His mind was essentially uncritical, unhistorical, and unphilosophical. See E. Veuillot, *Louis Veuillot.* (Paris, 1901-4.)

[2] The development of the second phase of the liberal catholic movement in France is of less general interest. The second generation of liberal catholics were men of greater caution, but of less power. At the hands of Pius IX. they met with the fate which befell *L'Avenir* and the Agence générale ; but their cause was lost before they came to battle. The story of their defeat, tragic though it is in the history of religious thought, is but an episode. As the Oxford movement in England loses its universality after the secession of Newman, so the French liberal catholic movement becomes purely French in its interest after the excommunication of Lamennais.

French liberal catholic thought touches this essay again at two points : the publication of the Syllabus in 1864 and the promulgation of the dogma of papal infallibility in 1870. (See below, pp. 321-2 and 330.) The best histories of the liberal catholic movement in France are those of Leroy-Beaulieu, *Les Catholiques libéraux* (1885), and G. Weill, *Histoire du catholicisme libéral en France* (1909) ; Lecanuet, *op. cit.,* and Falloux, *Mémoires d'un royaliste,* are also of great interest.

III

PIUS IX. AND THE ROMAN REPUBLIC

THE Roman court had refused to learn the language of European thought. The possession of the worst governed and most backward and unfertile state west of the Balkans seemed of more avail to maintain the tradition of the gospels than the goodwill of generous-minded men. The papacy had made its choice. The consequences were not without their irony. A sudden attempt was made by Pius IX. to copy the externalities of liberal states ; the effort of the pope was not supported by the men whom Gregory XVI. had put into the high places of the church ; it was made without any clear plan, and at a time of great political disturbance. It failed. The discouragement of Pius IX. threw him back upon the Gregorian plan of fighting ideas by armed force. The French bayonets upon which the Vicar of Christ relied to protect the church were scarcely sufficient, and were not under his own command. He turned to a counter-programme of ideas ; but his ideas were as foreign as ever to the world of his time. He called in his own infallibility to redress the evils of the freedom of thought. Reckless use of anathema was followed by reckless insistence upon his own illumination. At the very moment of his victory he lost all for which he had been fighting. When the Vatican council proclaimed the complete success of the policy of centralisation of authority in the church, the Italian troops were preparing to march on Rome. The recognition of papal infallibility was made in the hour when the temporal power was lost. Yet for the sake of the temporal power the hopes of liberal Europe had been disavowed by the Catholic Church.

The Greeks would have seen divine irony in the contrast between the immensity of the issues and the littleness of the persons. Behind the magnificent tradition and antique language of the curia there was but the vanity of weak men misusing the words of the strong ; behind the splendid action of the Mass the fitful shifts of irresolute cunning ; these are the signs of the end.

.   .   .   .   .   .

A long story lies behind the liberal beginning of Pius IX. Unmoved by the Latin damnations of Gregory XVI., the middle class of Italy had learned from the undignified fate of the earlier revolutions to distrust haphazard agitation and secret societies.   A rebellion could never succeed unless the societies were linked together by a common aim and a common leader.   In the simplicity of his plan for unifying Italy by the united effort of Italians lay the power of Mazzini.   Mazzini had no originality of thought, no new ideas about government ;   the " first principles " upon which he based his action were held together more by the needs of his temperament than by their own logic.   In spite of his ideas upon God and duty his political morality some-times fell to the level of a *condottiere* ;   he was a townsman of townsmen in his neglect of the peasants ;   his liking for historical novels with a didactic purpose shows the lack of subtlety and humour common to most of the leaders of extreme nationalism.   He was obstinate and vain ;   but he had a generous sympathy for the beaten cause, an in-tensity of passion, and a feminine quickness of perception.[1] He had learned from Lamennais (here the papacy reaped its harvest) a vague social religion of humanity.   He trans-lated this faith into the language of the *Risorgimento* through the middle term of the providential mission of Italy.   The Italian nation would lead in the moral regeneration of the world.   The union of Italy was to be brought about by the help of the society of Young Italy.   Mazzini aimed at an Italian republic.   Monarchy was a bad form of government, since it offended against the principle of equality ; even con-stitutional monarchy left open the way for usurpation and the rise of an aristocracy between king and people.   Elec-tive monarchy was unpractical because it always led to

---

[1] It is interesting that Mazzini distrusted German philosophy because of its anti-social consequences, just as he distrusted socialism because of its materialistic outlook.   Socialism made man believe " che un popolo può regenerarse impinguando."

anarchy. Italy was republican by tradition ; her misfortunes began with monarchy. There was no Italian dynasty, as there was no Italian aristocracy. The republic must be unitary, not federal, in character. The great neighbours of Italy were united. A federal Italy would be weaker even than a federal Switzerland because of the strength of local feeling in the different parts of the country.

The society of " Young Italy " soon developed the failings of the earlier secret societies. Its leader was in exile ; [1] its headquarters were outside Italy. The exiles shared the optimism of all political émigrés ; the members of the society in Italy, with no central organisation to control them, fell into the old faults of impatience, submission to extremists, and extravagance of hope. The society wasted its moral force upon ill-timed and almost ludicrous insurrections ; Mazzini himself was saved from degenerating into the ordinary type of fanatic largely by the influence of the Carlyles and other English friends.

There was some hope in the later 1830's that the governments might themselves take steps towards liberalism if they were not frightened by revolutionaries. Northern Italy was prosperous ; the new Emperor Ferdinand had granted a political amnesty ; Charles Albert of Piedmont had introduced a new civil code. The papal states were free from foreign troops when the Austrians left Bologna and the French left Ancona. Even in Naples King Ferdinand II. won a certain popularity in his army by making 14 field-marshals (with St. Ignatius Loyola as a titular colleague), 6 lieutenant-generals, and 30 brigadiers ; a concession was made to revolutionary sentiment by allowing the common soldiers to wear moustachios.

Discontent reappeared with greater force in the 1840's, and new remedies were suggested for old evils. Mazzini had preached the study of history. In Italy an appreciation of mediæval history had already led a small group of men to think of the good work done by the papacy in civilising the Lombards ; a case might be made out for the past value

---

[1] Ruggiero (*History of European Liberalism in the Nineteenth Century*, p. 314) points out that Mazzini soon lost touch with the real problems of Italy, and thought in terms of European and not of Italian problems.

of the temporal power. A Piedmontese priest, exiled in the early thirties of the century, began to build upon this foundation. Vincenzo Gioberti, a disciple of one of the schools founded, or rather popularised, by Lamennais, published in 1843 a book extolling the supremacy of the Italians in all the arts of civilisation. The thesis was proved by examples and reasoning as flimsy as the historical arguments of de Maistre. The importance of the book was in its suggestion of a league of Italian princes under the leadership of the pope, who was the heir and the natural and pacific instrument of Latin greatness. Gioberti's scheme allowed for Piedmont as the temporal sword. " Da Roma e Torino unanimi pendono i fati d'Italia." [1] Here was a plan which was catholic, federal, monarchical. No wonder that it aroused the jealous anger of Mazzini.

Gioberti's book was followed almost at once by a more critical survey of the position. Cesare Balbo,[2] in *Le Speranze d'Italia*, set aside all the existing plans. Nothing was to be expected from the suggestion of a spontaneous rising of the princes. The princes were unenlightened, and dared not displease Austria. Nothing was to be expected from the conspiracies of secret societies. Conspiracies were only successful if made by the few against the few. They were useless against large states. The plan of a national insurrection was equally hopeless. Action of this kind was possible in a city or against one tyrant ; who could organise an insurrection of twenty-three millions of men ? Balbo's idea was that Italy should wait for the break-up of the Ottoman empire. The preoccupation of Austria on her eastern frontier would be the opportunity of the liberals of Italy and Germany. Balbo was less certain of the use to be made of the embarrassment of Austria. Although he hoped for a federation of the states of Italy, he saw the difficulties of the international papacy.[3]

---

[1] *Del Primato morale e civile degli Italiani.* (Brussels, 1843.)

[2] Balbo (b. 1789) had served in the Napoleonic administration. He came back to Piedmont after the restoration, but fell under suspicion during the revolution of 1821, although he disapproved of the outbreak. He was allowed to return, but, in spite of his efforts to obtain a post in the administration of Piedmont, he was never restored to favour.

[3] Gioberti and Balbo were not the first to publish books embodying their respective theses. Niccolo Tommaseo, another exile, had suggested

In the year 1844 a dramatic but hopeless attempt at rebellion was made by two naval officers. These two young men, the Bandiera brothers, had been trained in the Austrian naval academy at Venice. The Austrian government had allowed this academy to be staffed by Italians with liberal sympathies. Many Italians entered it to get a training in arms which they might use against Austria. The two brothers had long been disgusted at the employment of the fleet to capture Italian refugees. They decided to break their military oath and begin an insurrection in the Apennines. They expected a general rebellion to follow. Mazzini tried to dissuade them, but they would not listen to him. Their insurrection was a failure, and they met their death with magnificent courage. This example fired an outbreak of similar hopelessness at Rimini a year later. The leaders published a manifesto of remarkable moderation. They recognised the temporal sovereignty of the pope and the right of the censorship to punish attacks upon religion and the government, and asked for such reforms as the introduction of trial by jury and a civil code.[1]

A Piedmontese nobleman, who to the scandal of his family had become a painter, a novelist, and a liberal, happened to be in the Romagna when the disturbances began. Massimo d'Azeglio was a shallow, accomplished dilettante, with the ostentatious qualities admired by the crowd ; but much sound sense was mixed with his egoism. He tried to prevent the outbreak in the Romagna. After the inevitable defeat he wrote an account of the movement and its suppression. His book, *Gli ultimi casi di Romagna*, had a wide circulation, and was read by the future pope, Pius IX. D'Azeglio showed the folly of local insurrections, and the unlikelihood of getting foreign support ; on the other hand, he attacked the papal government and defended the claims of the reformers.

The interest taken in the suggestions of Gioberti, Balbo,

in his *Delle nuove Speranze d'Italia* (1836) that the reforming movement in Italy should be led by the pope. Mamiani, also an exile, had published a pamphlet in 1841 exhorting Italians to prepare for the opportunity which would come with the embarrassment of Austria.

[1] Mazzini complained of the " cowardice and stupidity " of this manifesto.

and d'Azeglio was strengthened by the growing care for the economic future of Italy. The development of a railway system required some form of united or federal action. The small states could neither finance a great trunk system nor agree upon its construction. The local customs barriers were out of date, and incompatible with the development of railways. The German states had shown the way of improvement in the Zollverein, and north German commercial interests offered a trade route into north Italy which would isolate Trieste and cut off Piedmont and possibly Lombardy from the Austrian commercial system. The Austrians had a rival scheme to capture the Mediterranean trade by means of a railway from Leghorn to Trieste (thus undermining the importance of Genoa), with another line through the Brenner to the Lombard plain. In 1846 Piedmont was already engaged in a tariff war with Austria. The king, Charles Albert, was weak, nervous, and uncertain ;[1] yet he could not belong to the house of Savoy without feeling that there was always something to be gained from the embarrassment of the great powers. He hoped at least for a little Swiss territory when the opportunity occurred ![2] Balbo and his followers made it clear that this opportunity was not far off ; Gioberti persuaded him that if he did not lead the movement for liberal reform, if he did not grant his subjects a constitution, the republicans would drive him and his family from the mainland of Italy.

At this critical time Pius IX. succeeded Gregory XVI. The new pope, Giovanni Mastai-Ferretti, had never known pre-revolutionary Europe. He was born in 1792 at Sinigaglia, near Ancona. His family were landowners of liberal sympathy, but orthodox enough in their views to expect for their children a pleasant career in the papal army or the administration. Giovanni Mastai was an epileptic ; the local peasantry believed that he had the evil eye ! He was refused a place in the Guardia Nobile, and for a time was

---

[1] There is a well-known saying that Charles Albert lived between his fears of " the daggers of the carbonari and the poisoned chocolate of the Jesuits." It was also said that the Austrians bribed the king's doctors to weaken his health, and that he lived chiefly on spinach and potatoes !

[2] Part of the canton of Vaud.

not allowed to take orders. He was not ordained priest until 1819. His health improved after a few years' teaching in a Roman school, and a voyage to Chile in 1823. In 1827 he was made archbishop of Spoleto. After the revolution of 1831 he was transferred to the bishopric of Imola. This transfer was said by many to be a sign of the pope's displeasure. The archbishop of Spoleto had fallen under suspicion of helping Louis Napoleon (disguised as his mother's servant) to escape from Ancona. On the other hand, the bishopric of Imola was a " vescovado cardinalizio " ; the occupant of the see generally became a cardinal. Gregory XVI. withheld this promotion until 1840.

At Imola Mastai lived an easy, pleasant life, and became known as an eloquent preacher after the fashion of modern Italian catholicism. The influence of liberal gentlemen in the neighbourhood, and the sight of open misgovernment in the papal states, made him think himself a liberal. His liberalism was never much more than the vague goodness of heart of a weak man ; nor was it free from that vanity and sense of his own superior knowledge and importance which became almost tragic at the time of the Vatican council. His intelligence never went north of the papal states ; he could not think himself out of his environment. He loved adulation and popularity. His emotional nature needed excitement and the continual stimulus of a crowd ; because it was without independence, consistency, or fire of its own. Pius thought of the political consequences of his actions as little as he foresaw the effects of his dogmatic extravagances. He was never cynical, because he never lived in a world of real things.

He became pope, as many men have reached high office, mainly because he had offended neither the party of movement nor the party of resistance. The Italian cardinals were anxious to make an election before the arrival of the Austrian archbishop of Milan, and the conclave only lasted from June 14 to June 16. Cardinal Mastai is said to have fainted with fear when he knew his fate ; the strongest conservative candidate fainted with anger as soon as he had left the hall of election.

Pius IX. began his pontificate by characteristic acts of

generosity and fecklessness. He reduced his domestic expenses for the benefit of private charity ; private charity had been for centuries the curse of the Roman people. He issued an amnesty to political offenders, and at the same time pensioned and rewarded the men who had suppressed the rebellion in the Romagna—including the president of a commission which had terrorised the country for three years. He set up an inquiry into the necessary reforms in the administration, and appointed as his secretary of state a man of eighty-nine ; an unusual age for beginning a new and difficult policy ! Early in 1847 the censorship was modified. In the spring a council of state was nominated ; in the early summer a ministry was announced.

Mazzini had foretold that after a month or two Pius would return to the ways of his predecessor. Mazzini always antedated the realisation of his hopes or fears ; but he was not far wrong. In the summer of 1847 Pius began to see that he had raised a storm. On the one hand, all the men whom Gregory had appointed, all the clerical place-hunters and corrupt officials, began to be alarmed. At Genoa the cardinal archbishop found it difficult to prevent his clergy from offering prayers for the conversion of the pope ; prayers for the same end were made in the edifying private devotions of the Neapolitan royal family. Placards appeared in Rome warning the faithful against the interloper Mastai who was endangering the religion of Christ. On the other hand, the unbalanced enthusiasm of his subjects began to disturb the pope. It was disquieting to be called " un gran carbonaro." It was unpleasant to receive an open letter from Mazzini. The Roman populace was organised by a picturesque ruffian of the old school ; one of the livery-stable keepers soon to be driven out of existence by modern progress.[1] In the beginning of 1848 this personage dared to jump into the pope's carriage, and wrap

[1] This man, Angelo Brunetti, generally known as Ciceruacchio, lived on the Piazza del Popolo, and was well known for his good tongue and his generosity. A swaggering walk, and clothes conspicuous even for the 1840's, completed the picture of the good Roman demagogue. A short velvet coat and waistcoat, Cromwellian boots, a large scarf of coloured silk round his waist, a flowing kerchief round his neck ; on his head a high-peaked, beribboned hat. Who could resist such charm ?

the pope himself in a huge banner with the words : " Holy Father, entrust yourself to the people." It was awkward to hear amidst the inspiriting cries of " Viva Pio Nono " the more compromising shouts of " A basso Metternich."

Here indeed was the greatest difficulty. The Austrian government, caring for facts and not for popularity, had warned Pius from the beginning to beware of what he was doing. Pius saw only too late the consequences of his liberalism in Italy. In Piedmont Charles Albert was no longer afraid of his clergy when the pope himself was liberal. He went as far as he could in annoying Austria. He opened negotiations for the transport of the Indian mail ; this plan meant a railway convention with Switzerland, and was a direct attack upon the Austrian carrying trade and the port of Trieste. Charles Albert allowed himself to say that, if God should permit a war for the freedom of Italy, he would lead the Italian armies. It would have been impolitic not to have said something of the kind.

If the king of Piedmont would not lead the movement against Austria, there were republicans ready to take his place. In Lombardy and Venetia popular feeling was dangerously high. Austrian centralisation, Austrian selfishness, and the arrogance of military rule had been given long enough measure of patience. Cobden found himself received in triumph in Venice not as the European advocate of free trade, but as the founder of the " Anti-Corn Law League " and the organiser of a movement to secure a political end by means of popular agitation. A "scientific" congress—no other congress would have been allowed—gravely discussed the potato disease, when every member knew that " potato " was a slang term for " Austrian." [1] A social boycott of the Austrians was begun by the upper classes in Milan, and spread through the Austrian provinces of northern Italy. The Venetians left the Piazza of St. Mark when an Austrian band began to play. On the first of January 1848 the Milanese refused to smoke the tobacco from the imperial factories. A free distribution of cigars was made to the soldiers, who puffed their smoke into

[1] *Patatucco* : a soldier's cloak ; hence a nickname for Austrian soldiers, and Austrians in general.

people's faces.   A riot broke out ; there were more martyrs
for the Italian cause.

In the first ten weeks of 1848 agitation was directed
throughout the greater part of Italy towards securing constitutions from the reigning sovereigns.   A successful rebellion in Sicily—after the suppression of an ill-managed
attempt in Calabria—frightened Ferdinand into granting
a constitution.   Piedmont and Tuscany followed.   Charles
Albert was more anxious than ever not to be anticipated
by the Genoese republicans.   Before the Austrians had
allowed him to come to the throne they had made him
swear never to grant a constitution.   When the pope himself
was about to give constitutional government to his subjects,
the Piedmontese clergy could absolve their king from his
awkward promise.

In the papal states, Pius was forced to announce an increase of the lay element in his ministry.   He warned the
Romans not to be moved by ignorant agitators who disturbed the Italian people " with the fear of a foreign war,
aided and prepared for by internal conspiracy or the male-
volent inertia of the governments."   His warning only
caused another demonstration.   Then came the news of
the fall of the French monarchy.   A republic in France
could not be unfavourable to liberalism in Italy.   On
March 10 a ministry was formed under the ill-omened presidency of Cardinal Antonelli ; after four days of continual
disturbance the pope made it his good pleasure to grant a
constitution.   The terms of this constitution were most complicated.[1]   It was difficult enough to combine the old
machinery of government of the church universal with
parliamentary institutions.   The upper house, or council
of state, was to be nominated by the pope.   The franchise
under which the deputies of the lower house were elected
was confined to catholics ; the deputies were not allowed
to discuss " politico-diplomatic " questions.   Laws brought
forward by the houses were to be submitted to the pope and
cardinals ; neither the council of state nor the house of
deputies was to sit during a pontifical interregnum.   The

_____

[1] This constitution is printed in *British and Foreign State Papers*, vol. 36,
pp. 879-88.

foreign relations of the church were no business of the lay-men who chanced to live in the papal states ; but what of the attitude of these laymen towards Austria and the question of Italian unity ?

How could the " Sovereign Pontiff " become a constitu-tional ruler ? Brougham in England might speak of the pope as a constitutional ruler partaking also of the divine nature. The first declaration of the papal ministers might include the words : " in accordance with his [the pope's] nature, his actions must always be good and can never be evil." Yet this was bad theology and bad constitutional law. The most infallible of popes is not impeccable. The king of England can do no wrong ; the reason is not that he is perfect, and can do all things well, but that his ministers take the blame and the responsibility for whatever he does as king. Who could be responsible for the actions of the Vicar of God on earth ?

There followed news even more alarming than the fall of Louis Philippe. Before the first half of March was out the revolution had appeared in Vienna and Budapest. As soon as the paralysis of the Austrian bureaucracy was known in northern Italy the people of Milan assumed that their time had come. The fall of Metternich was the embarrassment of Austria. The embarrassment of Austria was the long-desired opportunity of Italy. The Austrian troops would be needed north of the Alps ; in a short time the Italians would find no army to fight.

From the beginning the Italian liberals underrated the recuperative powers of the Austrian empire, and the courage of the Austrian military leaders.[1] Radetsky, the rough soldier in command of the troops in Italy, had been Austrian chief of staff at the battle of Leipzig. A man who had fought Napoleon in the battle of the nations was not likely to fear the army of any Italian state. Radetsky withdrew from Milan

---

[1] An excellent account of the Italian revolution of 1848-1849 in north Italy is given in the diary of Hübner, *Une année de ma vie*. Hübner had the good fortune to arrive in Milan, on a special mission from Vienna, immediately before the outbreak of the revolution. His description of the fighting in Milan, and the gradual change of spirit both on the Italian and the Austrian side, is a useful corrective to much of the literature of edification which has gathered round the history of the political development of Italy.

after five days of wild fighting between the citizens and his Croat and Bohemian soldiers. He took up a position in the strong quadrilateral of fortresses between Verona and Mantua to the south of the Brenner pass. Here he could wait to be attacked by the Piedmontese ; if he were recalled by urgent need to Vienna his line of retreat was secure.

A retreat to this fortified base was the more necessary because Venice had revolted ; under the daring leadership of Daniel Manin,[1] the rebels had captured the arsenal and its store of arms. Charles Albert, distraught between his fear of a French republican advance into Savoy, an Italian republican attack upon his dynasty, and the displeasure of the powers if he should turn revolutionary, sent an army into Lombardy, and issued his famous proclamation that Italy was " in grado di fare da sè." To his subjects his words meant that he had accepted the leadership of the revolution ; they might also be taken as a polite warning to the French. He told his generals not to advance too quickly ; he told the powers that he was keeping order in Lombardy. He was indeed doing his best to prevent the establishment of a Lombard republic.

The pope at once discovered the difficulty of limiting himself in his political capacity to actions which were of their nature " always good and never evil " ; his subjects discovered the difficulty of keeping clear of " politico-diplomatic " questions. Popular outcry forced the papal government to send a " corps of observation " to the north. Four regiments of Italians, two of Swiss mercenaries, and a number of volunteers left Rome on March 24. Their general was told to put himself under the orders of Charles Albert. On his own responsibility he invaded Venetia, and changed his army of observation into an army of crusaders. The pope, who was in tears when the troops left Rome with his blessing, disavowed the crusade but dared not recall the army. Yet the position was intolerable for the chief bishop of the German catholics. The papal nuncios in Vienna and Munich warned him that his action might bring about a

---

[1] Daniel Manin was born in the same year as Disraeli (1804) ; he was partly Jewish in descent, but also a relation of the last doge of Venice.   For an account of the revolt of Venice see G. M. Trevelyan, *Manin and the Venetian Revolution of 1848.*

schism. Either victory or defeat would have a dangerous repercussion within his own states. His troops were in the territory of a self-erected republic ; would they come back to endure a kingdom where churchmen must always have the last word ?

By the end of April he could delay no longer. He published an allocution in which he told the world that his soldiers had been sent to the north only to safeguard the integrity of the papal states. The first duty of a pope was to keep the peace of Christendom. War against Germany was "wholly abhorrent to him." He could never be " seduced by the hope of a more ample temporal dominion " to become the head of an Italian republic. It mattered little that he wrote at the same time to ask the emperor of Austria to give up Lombardy and Venetia. The allocution meant the collapse of the Giobertist idea of a federal Italy under the leadership of the pope. The effect was at once to weaken the papal army, and therefore to hasten the end of the Venetian republic. Some of the troops deserted for fear lest they might be shot as *francs-tireurs* ; those who remained were committed to war against the whole order of church and state in Italy.

In the kingdom of the two Sicilies the disavowal of liberalism by the pope (for the encyclical seemed no less than a disavowal) satisfied the doubts of the clergy. Dislike of fighting under Piedmontese command for the aggrandisement of Piedmont in northern Italy had cooled the ardour of the soldiers. The populace was weary of constitutions which did not bring riches without work.[1] No more than a fifth of the voters used their votes at the elections in April. In May the blood of St. Januarius only liquefied after strong remonstrance from the nationalist generals. As soon as the extreme liberals, encouraged by the presence of a French fleet in the bay of Naples, began to put up barricades, Ferdinand and Ferdinand's priests and generals saw their chance. Troops were sent out ; the revolution was over. The national guard was dismissed, and the expedi-

---

[1] Newman tells a story of a donkey driver who summed up his political hopes : " The English have a constitution : the English are rich."

tionary force recalled ; the two thousand who refused to come back had no more pay and no more supplies. In the north the Lombards, the Venetians, and the Piedmontese were quarrelling over the future organisation of north Italy even before they had beaten Radetsky. The provisional settlement in favour of annexation to Piedmont confirmed the fears of the pope, the French, and the Swiss ; the whole rebellion reawakened Austrian patriotism. The Italian troops fought well, but were badly led ; the peasants were unfriendly to the Piedmontese army. When Radetsky advanced from his square of fortresses the Italians were beaten near Custozza. Charles Albert retired into Piedmont and thought only of getting terms. He was willing to sacrifice the republicans of Venetia, but could not give up the Piedmontese constitution ; for it stood between him and the fall of his house.

The recovery of Austria brought no relief to the pope. The Romans, with some reason, held the papal allocution responsible for the military disgrace. After a fruitless attempt to secure a stable ministry under the leadership of a cardinal who was deaf and over seventy years old, the pope appointed Count Pellegrino Rossi minister of the interior. The choice of Rossi showed the extraordinary position of the papacy. Rossi was a friend of the protestant Guizot and had married a protestant wife. His books were on the Index. He was a naturalised French citizen and had begun his political career by supporting Murat. He had been sent to Rome by Guizot in 1845, and had given Pius ix. much sound advice and made many prophecies which had now come true. His ministry did not last long. He followed the plan of choosing reform and prosperity before adventure and constitutional experiment. He began to construct telegraph lines, and to negotiate contracts for the building of railways ; at the same time he arrested the most dangerous of the popular demagogues. He opened the whole of the civil service to laymen, and played with the idea of a league of Italian states. He made the league harmless by insisting upon the inclusion of monarchical Naples, and the exclusion of the Austrian provinces of Lombardy and Venetia. He would not agree to the hegemony of Piedmont, and sent troops to keep Garibaldi out of the papal states. Thus he annoyed every party in Rome. His foreign policy was anti-republican, anti-Piedmontese, and, by implication, in favour of the political arrangements against which the Italians had rebelled. His domestic policy alarmed the reactionaries, whom he openly despised, but was too moderate to please the mob.[1]

In November Rossi was murdered as he entered the parliament house.[2] The deputies crept home without a protest ; the Roman people went to serenade Rossi's widow. For very shame Pius could make no more concessions. Nor could he meet the storm. The Quirinal was bombarded ; the Swiss guards and the artillery were taken out of the pope's control. Nothing remained but to escape. The only interest of his flight is that Cardinal Antonelli drove him to Gaeta while the French ambassador was waiting with carriages to take him to Civita Vecchia and thence to Marseilles !

As soon as the pope had left Rome, the proclamation of a republic was the only course for the Roman people. Their logic was faultless ; but they had forgotten the loyalty of the catholic powers. In northern Europe the revolution was over before it had been carried to its historical conclusion in Rome. The army and the middle class in France had put the street fighting of the June days between them and the extreme left. In Prussia the king was in the hands of the conservatives, and the army was loyal. The Viennese had learned the mistake of giving up an empire from which they drew their means of living. The Hungarian movement for independence was being ruined by the intolerance of the Hungarians themselves ; the Slavs had no cause to

[1] For Rossi's mission in 1845-1846 see Guizot, *Mémoires*, vols. vii. chap. 43, and viii. chap. 46 ; and Farini, *Lo Stato Romano, 1815-1850*. (There is an English translation of Farini's work in four volumes, three of which were translated by Mr. Gladstone.)

[2] " Ciceruacchio " and his son were among those concerned in the assassination. The murderers used a stiletto, a weapon which is useless in an unpractised hand. De Cesare (*Roma e lo Stato del Papa del ritorno di Pio IX. al 20 Settembre*, i. 67) says that years afterwards he met one of the assassins. The man had survived a long term of imprisonment ; he was pock-marked and had a " sguardo sinistro." He kept a dirty little café, on the walls of which were oleographs of great political " delinquenti."

prefer the domination of Magyars to that of Germans. Russia had been untouched by the revolution. The future was therefore with the men of property who feared the break-up of the established order. The hour belonged to Louis Napoleon, to Schwarzenberg, to Nicholas, and to the " cartridge " prince of Prussia. A Roman republic ruled by Mazzini and the " pirate Garibaldi " was not in their plan for Europe.

The history of the Roman republic has been told by an Englishman in language worthy of its defenders.[1] It has the interest and nobility of a forlorn cause and a brave fight. Upon the life of the Catholic Church it had an effect as evil as the earlier break with the revolution. It isolated catholics from the noble idea of liberty for which the republicans died ; it gave to the church the predominance of Cardinal Antonelli for nearly thirty years. In Italy it helped to ruin the chances of Charles Albert at the moment when the Piedmontese democracy forced him to reopen the war against Austria. Monarchical Piedmont and republican Rome could not agree upon the conditions of a federal Italy ; nor could catholics support a movement which had reached its climax in an attack upon the pope.

After the second defeat of the Piedmontese at Novara, and the abdication of Charles Albert, the fate of the Roman republic was only a matter of time. The work was done by the French, and not by the Austrians. The Romans had looked to France for help ; but Louis Napoleon was now president of a republic for which few Frenchmen of influence really cared. In any case the president had plans which would lose him the republican support ; he was more concerned to have the goodwill of the catholic voters for the plebiscite which was to restore an undisguised Bonapartism.

In the beginning of July 1849 the keys of the city of Rome were sent to the pope at Gaeta. The pope replied with thanks and a copy of his allocution of April 29, 1848. Austria was already back in Lombardy ; Venice surrendered in August. The Sicilians had given themselves over to Ferdi-

[1] G. M. Trevelyan, *Garibaldi's Defence of the Roman Republic*. The French point of view is put clearly by de la Gorce, *Histoire de la seconde république française* (2 vols. Paris) ; and É. Bourgeois and É. Clement, *Rome et Napoléon III*. (Paris, 1907).

nand after the defeat of Piedmont.   It might appear that
liberalism had been completely defeated.   The republican
fire had burnt itself out in Rome.   The active republicans
were either killed or in exile.   The peasants, the priests,
and the shopkeepers were on the conservative side.   The
idea of a liberal papacy at the head of a liberal Italian
federation had vanished under the light of facts.   The sword
of Piedmont had been twice defeated.   Outside Italy no
help could reach the liberals.   England would not fight
Austria.   Russia lent troops to put down the revolution in
Hungary.   If France should become aggressively republican,
the king of Piedmont could never accept her alliance.   If
France should become imperial, England and Russia would
scarcely allow her to be warlike.   To men of little mind in
Rome the revolution was defeated when those who had
been willing to die for it had given their lives.   Pius ix.
turned to other fields for popularity and success.

IV

THE PAPACY AND CAVOUR

THE return of Pius IX. to the political negations of Gregory XVI. was as dangerous as the attempt to cover an absolute government with a show of liberalism. Outside Italy the French and German catholics were eager to convince the modern world that there was no fundamental opposition between the teaching of the Christian religion and the safeguards of liberty in a modern state.   The catholics in France turned mainly to political questions, and the defence of the traditional right of self-government allowed to the Gallican church.   In south Germany the attack upon papalism was more direct.   A new school of scientific historians undermined the theories of the ultramontane writers.   The wheel had now turned full circle, and the romantic, cosmopolitan vagueness of Görres and his age had been followed by a more careful study of church history and the development of doctrine.   There was a self-conscious national pride in German scholarship ; a brusqueness and aggression in the attitude of Germany towards the faded commonplaces of Italian theology.   The greatest of German ecclesiastical historians, Dr. Ignaz von Döllinger,[1] had taken up an attitude which could scarcely be called catholic in the pastoral sense of the term.   " For most people theology is a means to an end.   To me theology, or rather the science founded upon theology, was my end, and the choice of Orders a means."   These men were in daily contact with protestant thought and with the scepticism of the German universities.   As allies of the papacy their services might have been invaluable ; as enemies they were too formidable for the weapons of the Roman curia.

[1] For the life of Döllinger see Friedrich, *Döllinger* ; Acton's essay on Döllinger's historical work (*History of Freedom and other Essays*) ; and Vigener, *op. cit.*   For the development of historical studies in Germany see G. P. Gooch, *History and Historians in the 19th century.*

The time had gone by when a pope might go to a dangerous extreme in fostering a new learning. The nineteenth century had no Nicholas v., no Ignatius Loyola, no Bellarmine. The papalists could not meet the new learning on its own ground. They were driven to a dangerous insistence upon the plenitude of apostolic authority. If scholars north of the Alps attempted by argument to limit the extent of the papal prerogative, and to deny the right of the pope to take the place of the bishops or to dictate to the faithful, the way to meet them was to call the bishops of the church together and from them to secure the full approbation of papal infallibility. Hence the summoning of the Vatican council. But the issue at the council must be one of historical fact ; the question to the bishops, if a question were put, would take a historical form : has the infallibility of the pope received the consent of the church throughout the history of the church ? Unless this question could be answered by acclamation there must be a debate upon the development of papal power ; in a debate of this kind the opponents of papal prerogative would lay bare to the faithful the weakness of the ultramontane arguments. If the question were answered by acclamation, the outside world would have the spectacle of a decision taken by the Catholic Church upon a question of history without any reference to the facts of history, without even the thesis and antithesis beloved of scholastic theologians. In either case the estrangement of the intellectual world would be complete ; there would be an excuse for the attacks of the Italian nationalists upon a sovereignty thus exposed in its nakedness.

Of all these things Pius ix. took no account. Neither the pope nor his advisers considered the political consequences. The motive behind this acceptance of intellectual isolation in Europe was the supposed necessity for defending the temporal power. But the temporal power was being maintained by the troops of a government based upon principles which the popes condemned. The authority of Louis Napoleon as president of a French republic, the authority of the Emperor Napoleon iii., rested upon universal suffrage ; a principle of sovereignty which could never be applied to the kingdom of Pius ix. On the other hand, the tradition of a Bonaparte committed him to the principle of nationality. If Napoleon III. should be driven to choose between the Italian nationalists and the papal ultramontanes, force of circumstances might compel him to abandon the defence of the temporal power. Only Austria and the lesser Italian princes would remain faithful. It was scarcely likely that the Austrian government would put the interest of the temporal power before the more urgent needs of the Austrian empire. In any case the recovery of Austria was less real than it seemed. The ambitions of Russia in the near east, the jealousy and " land-hunger " of Prussia, the unsolved problems of German unity, and of Magyar and Slav national-ism, would bring Balbo's prophecies to fulfilment. Once again Austria's need would be Italy's opportunity ; a wiser leader than Charles Albert might see that the opportunity was not lost.

From their princes the Italians outside Piedmont could hope for nothing. The repression of the rebellions of 1848 had been brutal enough in the Austrian provinces of Lombardy and Venetia, where the civilians had vainly tried to check the cruelty of the generals. In the rest of Italy there was no thought of moderation. Ferdinand II. had earned the nick-name of " Bomba " from his bombardment of Messina ; he filled his prisons, which were as capacious as they were unclean, with political suspects and treated them with such brutality that Gladstone in 1851 called his government " the negation of God." [1] In Tuscany the grand duke wore the uniform of an Austrian general, and wanted to hold a service to commemorate the anniversary of the defeat of the Italian armies. The duke of Modena was a poor pedant ; the duke of Parma a mere blackguard, whose chief minister was an English groom. Three hundred of his subjects were whipped in the first five months of his reign.

The exception was Piedmont. Here a vulgar, flamboyant,

---

[1] W. E. Gladstone, *A Letter to Lord Aberdeen* (1851), p. 9. Ferdinand reprinted a catechism of 1832 which schoolmasters were bound under pain of dismissal to teach to their pupils. One question in this edify-ing work ran : " Are all who wear moustaches and a beard liberal philo-sophers?" (idem, *A Second Letter, etc.*, p. 15). Ferdinand's grandfather once seized hold of a nobleman's side-whiskers because he thought that the wearing of such appendages was a sign of Jacobin views.

and uneducated man [1] had succeeded his father, Charles Albert. Yet, for all his faults—and it was hard for one of the princelets of Europe to know how to behave like a gentleman—Victor Emmanuel had a feeling for his own honour, a quick sense of the possibilities of his own position, and a shrewd idea that he must be very careful if he wanted to stay on his throne. Above all, he was a brave fighter, and alone among the Italian rulers had a patriotic love for Italy. Liberal Europe was ready to pardon in liberal Piedmont tricks and deceits which would have seemed outrageous in a reactionary state. When the superstitious king was persuaded to make an attack upon the property of the Catholic Church, the British and Foreign Bible Society presented him with a copy of the protestant version of the Old and New Testaments ! [2]

The contest between the curia and the modern world, narrowed down to a fight between Rome and Piedmont over Italian territory, was fought between men unequally matched in wit and resolution. Behind Victor Emmanuel was Cavour. Behind Pius IX. was Antonelli. Cardinal Giacomo Antonelli came of a robber family of Sonnino. His face was the perfect type of a low political adventurer. In one of his most bitter passages of denunciation Gregorovius remarked upon the dominant jaw : " a jaw that is thousands of years old and belonged to the creatures of the mud who devoured, devoured, devoured." Cunning eyes and a pointed nose completed the edifying picture. This man had a certain taste for the magnificent. He collected jewels, wore fine clothes, grew roses and camelias, and lived in splendid apartments. He left a large fortune ; one of his illegitimate children went to law for a share in it after Antonelli's death. [3] He accumulated

---

[1] Victor Emmanuel was twenty-nine years old ; he had been given no instruction in politics during his father's reign. Charles Albert had scarcely concealed his preference for Victor Emmanuel's younger brother.

[2] Upon which de la Gorce comments : " Victor Emmanuel . . . s'émerveilla fort qu'il y eût tant de mérite d'être excommunié. . . ." (*Histoire du second empire*, ii. 315.)

[3] Papal apologists sometimes find satisfaction in remembering that Antonelli, though he was a prince of the church, was only in minor orders !

twenty-eight different decorations from sovereigns who found it easier to satisfy the personal needs of Antonelli than the requests of his master. He put his brothers into rich positions in the papal states. He excelled in the arts of makeshift, and was a good liar and a master of Levantine cleverness ; but he had no political ideas and no political foresight. The moral greatness of the church was outside the scope of his mind ; intellectual truth had no meaning for him. For a few years, while he and his family gathered the last harvest of the dominion of centuries, he kept the temporal power from dissolution ; but at the cost of its honour.

Antonelli had to deal with a man as clever as himself in little things, and as ready to lie and to intrigue. Yet with Cavour's sharp practice went a largeness of aim which redeemed it from the negative cheating of Antonelli. There is indeed a danger in justifying the unscrupulousness of Cavour by his success. He would have used this excuse, just as he approved of the English method of bribery to bring about the union with Ireland. Cavour held that public and private morality were different things.[1] It is easier to deny this distinction in a lecture hall than in a cabinet meeting. It is still easier to accept the distinction and to assume that reason of state is the only touchstone of public righteousness. Cavour took the line of least resistance, and reduced the difference to a matter of degree. His hard, superficial materialism did not expect too much from men or from movements. Yet in spite of all the trouble which extreme nationalism has brought to the world, few would doubt that the work of Cavour was for the good of Europe ; few would choose the cause of Antonelli.

Cavour belonged to a type which has gone out of fashion ; the type of successful, radical business man. He came of a noble and reactionary family ; but the march of the French armies through north Italy had left behind it many an echo for young men to hear. To his own relations Cavour seemed a changeling. " The poor boy is entirely absorbed in

---

[1] Cavour put the position very simply when he said to d'Azeglio : " If we were to do for ourselves what we are doing for Italy, we should be great rogues."

revolutions," said one of his aunts.   The custom and almost
the routine of his family sent him into the army ; his superior
officers noticed the absorption in revolutions, and sent him
to a distant fortress.   Before he was twenty-one Cavour had
resigned his commission.   He found the life of a soldier
as distasteful as the wayward Victor Emmanuel found the
etiquette of his father's court.   Cavour spent his time in
managing a farm, in reading, and in journeys to France and
England.   He was interested in large-scale agriculture and
the construction of railways ; he admired the commercial
policy of England, and the *juste milieu* of the government of Louis Philippe.   When Tocqueville's *De la démocratie
en Amérique* appeared in 1834, Cavour accepted it as the
prophecy of a coming time.   In England he met Cobden,
and liked Peel.   In Italy he was thought of as a hard-
headed anglomaniac [1] who hoarded corn to sell at high
prices in bad harvests.   No one liked him overmuch.   He
had to resign from a charity because the rich conservatives
would not subscribe to it while he was on the governing body.
On the other hand, liberals left the hall when he rose to
speak at a meeting of an agricultural society !   They did not
miss much ; Cavour was never an orator.[2]   In 1847 he
joined Balbo in founding a liberal paper, *Il Risorgimento* ;
but he was not trusted enough by the nationalists to be
given a place in the government of 1848.   By 1850 he had
become convinced of the failure of complete democracy, and
of the urgency for economic reform in Italy.   Here he came
into contact with Antonelli.   Economic reform in Piedmont
could mean nothing less than the confiscation of ecclesiastical property, and therefore a " revision " of the relation
between church and state.   The clergy were more numerous
and better endowed in Piedmont than in any other European country.   Belgium and Austria had one churchman
for every five or six hundred inhabitants ; Piedmont had
one for every two hundred and fourteen.   The ecclesiastical
revenues were estimated at nineteen million lire a year ;
so unequal was the distribution of this wealth that the

[1] He was nicknamed " Milord Camillo."
[2] It is a curious commentary upon the Italian nationalist movement
that Cavour spoke Italian with a French accent.

government had to give another million to the poorer clergy. The churchmen controlled education, and the prejudices of the uneducated. The clergy had their own courts, with the right of asylum. There were no laws of mortmain, no toleration of civil marriage. The archbishop of Turin would not agree to any change in a system which he found excellent ; the pope supported the archbishop. On the other hand, the government was almost bankrupt, and needed money for the army and navy, and the development of industry. Thus there were all the elements of a good quarrel.

The main attack was delayed for a few years. A bill was brought before the Piedmontese chamber in 1850 abolishing the ecclesiastical courts and their attendant privileges ; a mortmain law limited the right of the church to increase its property ; civil marriage was promised. The pope excommunicated every one who took part in passing these laws, and any one who should obey them. D'Azeglio, now chief minister of Piedmont, was tired of the hard and unpopular work of government and suffering from the effects of a wound received in the war. He looked about for a strong supporter, and chose Cavour. Victor Emmanuel, with his quick judgment of men, foretold that Cavour would soon dominate the cabinet. Cavour entered the government in October 1850 ; within a month he was minister of finance ; within fifteen months he was prime minister. He had seen the need for creating a centre party which should exclude the extremists of right and left. For this purpose he made overtures to the moderate men of the opposition. D'Azeglio did not look beyond the tactics of a good party leader, and gave him no help. When Cavour on his own account came to terms with the leader of the left centre, he was accused of disloyalty to his leader and forced to resign.

The ecclesiastical question had still to be settled. In the autumn of 1852 the king refused his consent to a law permitting civil marriage. " I must think of the heavenly side of things," said that debonair monarch. D'Azeglio could not continue in office ; there was only Cavour to take his place. Cavour at once began a forward policy. He made commercial treaties with France, England, Switzerland, Belgium, the German Zollverein, and even with Austria. He favoured the tunnelling of Mont Cenis ; a scheme which would benefit the commerce of Piedmont at the expense of Trieste and Venice.[1] He founded agricultural and co-operative banks in Piedmont, and spent money upon the army and the fortification of Alessandria. All these measures cost more than they brought back in immediate returns. Bad harvests and phylloxera in the vines added to the financial difficulties. Cavour again became unpopular, and an attempt was made to assassinate him. If constitutional government was to be maintained some relief must be found for the financial strain. It was reasonable enough to suggest the withdrawal of the subsidy paid to the lower clergy. Any move of this kind would be opposed by the church with the support of Rome. Therefore if the mildest of measures would meet with the same ecclesiastical thunder as a more thorough-going scheme of disendowment, the government might as well confiscate as much as possible. The clergy were already hostile to Cavour's union of the moderate parties. Any loss from the side of the right would be counter-balanced by the popularity of an anti-clerical policy with the left.

The government's proposal was extended to cover the dissolution of all religious corporations not directly engaged in teaching or looking after the sick. Their property was to be transferred to the state. A capital levy was set upon all other religious houses, the richer benefices, and the bishoprics. Out of the funds so obtained were to be paid the subsidy to the lower clergy and pensions to all those dispossessed of their maintenance.[2] The measure was nearly defeated. The king thought again of the heavenly side, and was terrified when his wife, his mother, and his brother died within a few months. The bishops offered to

[1] In 1848 Cavour had argued that annexation to France was not in the economic interest of Savoy, since the French would not wish to divert trade from Marseilles by means of a direct railway line from France to Italy.

[2] Victor Emmanuel had told Cavour that " if any one had to go to hell over the law, Cavour must be the man." It is curious that Cavour himself had provided against any such possibility by getting a promise of absolution " in articulo mortis."

pay the whole cost of the subsidy. As soon as Cavour re-signed, riots in Turin frightened the king into restoring him to office. A compromise left to the church a certain number of contemplative (or as their opponents called them " non-practical ") religious houses. Papal excommunications followed ; but the clergy were allowed to take the last portion of the subsidy !

For a time Cavour was preoccupied with the Crimean war, and an adventure into high politics.[1] The ecclesiastical question remained in suspense. Piedmontese aggression had become a danger to the papacy. How far would the church gain by submission to the conservative powers ? Would the support of France and Austria prevent Cavour from working for the restoration of Rome to the Italians, the logical conclusion of a liberal Italian policy ? Herein lay the nullity of the policy of Antonelli and Pius ; they could do nothing but wait upon events.

Events moved quickly. Although Cavour had no direct gain from the Crimean war he had won the goodwill of the English government by sending troops to counter-balance the military predominance of the French ; he had also won the admiration of Italy by exaggerating the part played by the Piedmontese soldiers.[2] His moderation at the peace conference, after a fiery speech from Clarendon on the subject of misrule in Italy,[3] only strengthened his claim that unless reform were thrust upon the Italian princes revolution was certain. Cavour had also been able to discover a possible ally in the event of war with Austria. Victor Emmanuel, on a polite visit to England

[1] The Piedmontese government came into the Crimean war in January 1855 at Cavour's suggestion. Their help was accepted mainly because the English were short of men and the French were short of ships, and both English and French were angry at the hesitation of Austria. The chief motive of the Piedmontese interference was a fear that an Anglo-French agreement would guarantee the Austrian position in Italy. Cavour also argued that Russian naval predominance in the Mediterranean would not be to the interest of Piedmont, and that by taking part in the war the Piedmontese would prove their military value and the stability of their country.
[2] 25 Italians were killed and 200 wounded at the battle of the Chernaya. The Piedmontese did not take part in any other fighting of importance. 2000 of the contingent of 15,000 men died of disease.
[3] Clarendon called the papal government a European scandal.

(where he was on his best behaviour in the circumspect atmosphere of Windsor),[1] took the chance of asking Clarendon whether he could manage for him " une petite extension de territoire." In spite of his strong words at the congress of Paris, Clarendon was not disposed to risk a European war for the sake of Piedmont.

It might seem that Napoleon III. would be as unlikely to encourage the creation of a greater Italy on the south-east border of France. But Napoleon had dreams of a Latin union of France, Spain, and Italy. The tradition of his family, his own vague theories of nationality and " great agglomerations," his belief in the reasonableness of the Italian liberal cause, worked together to put him in a frame of mind dangerously open to the clever persuasion of Cavour. Two other motives played their part. After the attempt of the Italian Orsini to assassinate him, the emperor was most anxious for a settlement of the Italian question. Orsini was no common political assassin. There was a danger that he might be followed by others. Napoleon had no need to prove his own courage, but he dared not risk the dynasty when his son was still a child. Finally there was the possibility that he might strike a bargain with Piedmont, and strengthen the French frontier at a danger point. One of the provisions of the Vienna settlement had been the enlargement of Piedmont as a barrier state against French aggression. Napoleon was bound to attack the Vienna settlement at every point where opportunity might offer. If, therefore, the victory of the Italian cause was only a question of time, it was altogether to the advantage of France to give help which might be paid for by the surrender of Nice and Savoy. A greater Piedmont could afford to give up its French-speaking lands ; the principle of nationality and the defence of France required the incorporation of Savoy. There were difficulties on both sides. Napoleon did not

[1] De la Gorce's comment upon the king's correctness is worth quoting : "' Il a vraiment l'air d'un gentleman,' écrivait Cavour, surpris autant que ravi." (De la Gorce, *op. cit.*, ii. 315.) (Greville's account is much less favourable. *Greville Memoirs*, Third Part, i. 303.) Cavour himself wrote of the court life of Windsor : " non è divertente." A minor reason for sending Victor Emmanuel on his journey to France and Italy was to get him away from the company of the daughter of a drum-major whom he had installed in a royal residence at Pollenzio !

want to see an extension of Piedmontese rule over the whole
of Italy. He must safeguard the temporal power, and get
the consent of the Piedmontese to an Italian federation
under the nominal presidency of the pope. This revival of
Gioberti's plan was not as foolish as it might appear.
Napoleon thought he might well put pressure upon the
papacy when the temporal power was being maintained
by a French garrison in the states of the church. Austria
would object ; but Austria, as Cavour had found, would
refuse to sanction any change at all. Napoleon might even
dream of conciliating Austria by giving her compensation
in the Balkans for the loss of the Italian provinces which
had become an embarrassment. On the other hand, if the
Italians were in his debt he might be able to restrain them
from going beyond a federal to a unitary Italian state. The
scheme was typical of Napoleon III. ; typical of his subtlety
of mind, his quickness and distance of view ; typical also
of his failure to understand that ingenuity alone can rarely
achieve great ends in great affairs. Napoleon thought
he knew the Italians, and imagined that he could control
Cavour. He could not know that Cavour would be dead
before the end of 1861.

There was a danger that Europe might take fright at
another Napoleonic campaign in Italy. The Austrians
might not be defeated before French public opinion had
come to the conclusion that the Italian cause was not worth
the loss of French lives. Prussia might take advantage of
the smooth talk about rectification of frontiers.

Cavour's own position was uncertain. Neither he nor
Napoleon dared to come into the open. Napoleon might
withdraw at the last moment ; Italian public opinion might
take ill the surrender of Savoy, the home of the dynasty of
Piedmont, or Nice, the birthplace of Garibaldi. Cavour
met Napoleon at Plombières ; [1] a meeting-place after the

[1] On his way home from this meeting Cavour passed the time by
reading Buckle's *History of Civilisation in Europe* ! The fact of the meeting
was known to Europe almost at once. The details were not published
until 1883. There is still no accurate account from the French side.
The whole intrigue can be followed in the first of four volumes issued
by the R. Commissione Editrice de' Carteggi Cavouriani : *Il Carteggio
Cavour-Nigra dal 1858 al 1861*, vol. i. *Plombières*.

style of an ex-conspirator who could not trust his own
foreign minister as Cavour could trust his king.[1]   A bargain
was arranged.   Napoleon would provide 200,000 French
soldiers to help in the expulsion of the Austrians.   Victor
Emmanuel would give up Nice and Savoy, and marry
his daughter, who was only sixteen years old, to Prince
Napoleon.[2]   After the Austrians had disappeared, a kingdom of northern Italy was to be formed for Victor Emmanuel
out of Piedmont, Lombardy, Venetia, the legations, and the
northern duchies.   Tuscany and Umbria were to be united
under the duchess of Parma ; [3]   Naples was to remain
as a kingdom in the south, possibly under a Murat.
The three divisions of Italy were to be joined in a federal
union under the pope.   The territory in the immediate
neighbourhood of Rome (the patrimonium Petri), and the
city itself, were to remain under the direct rule of the
papacy.

The plan nearly came to ground with a completeness
which would have been the end of Cavour's political career.[4]
In the autumn of 1858 Napoleon tried to secure Russian
neutrality by a promise to allow Russia to denounce the
Black sea clauses in the treaty of Paris.   On New Year's

[1] The French foreign minister was not told of the arrangements made
at the meeting until late in November.   The existence of a secret treaty
between Piedmont and France was denied by Napoleon in the *Moniteur*.

[2] Cavour did not want the marriage because he had already thought
of Leopold of Hohenzollern as a possible husband for the princess.
It is said that Prince Napoleon, who had the reputation of an elderly
libertine, used as a suitor the tactful argument that an earlier Clothilde
(this was the name of the princess) had been the means of converting
her husband to a catholic way of life !   When Cavour spoke of the
cession of Nice as contrary to the ' principle of nationalities ' for which
the war was being waged, " Napoléon caressa à plusieurs reprises sa
moustache."   (*Carteggio Cavour-Nigra*, 1. 106.)

[3] Cavour hoped that a woman would be more susceptible to Piedmontese influence.

[4] The pretext for a war was to be found, or rather invented, in
Carrara.   *Agents provocateurs* were to stir up a rebellion among the quarry
workers against the ineffable duke of Modena.   Piedmont was bound
to support the workers ;   Austria would be bound to support the duke.
The employment of Garibaldi was also contemplated.

A good account (from the Austrian point of view) of the development of Napoleon's plans is given in Hübner's *Neuf ans de souvenirs d'un
ambassadeur d'Autriche à Paris* (2 vols., 2nd edition, 1908).   Hübner
was sent as ambassador to Paris in 1851, and left at the outbreak of
the Franco-Austrian war.

day 1859 Napoleon said to the Austrian ambassador how much he regretted that the relations between himself and the emperor of Austria were not so good as they had been. At once the weakness of Napoleon's position was seen. Russia could not put any value on the French bribe until she knew the attitude of England. The catholics in France would resent the use of the French army to diminish the territories and compromise the political independence of the pope. The empress was under catholic influence, and the emperor had good cause to dread domestic scenes. The ministers were anxious about the state of the army, the suspicion of England, the hostility of Prussia, and the fall in the French *rentes*.[1]

Therefore, if the Austrians gave him a chance of drawing back, or at least of delay, Napoleon might be glad to take it. The Austrians themselves were not ready. The Semmering railway from Vienna to Italy was not finished. New guns for the fortresses of the quadrilateral were held up at the last completed section of the line.

At Napoleon's suggestion Russia proposed a meeting of the great powers. For Cavour delay or compromise meant ruin. The powers might think that the best way to deal with the troublesome aggressiveness of Piedmont would be to guarantee her position and give her the international status of Belgium or Switzerland. If the Piedmontese appeal for protection against Austrian attack were taken literally, there would be an end of the territorial ambitions of Victor Emmanuel![2] Hence Cavour did his utmost by argument and threats to prevent the summoning of a European congress. Happily for Cavour, Napoleon had most to lose if the whole story of the interview at Plombières were made public. Happily for Piedmont, Austria refused to come to any congress unless Piedmont should demobilise her army. Looking at the devastation of our own Europe, it is curious

[1] It was at this time that Rothschild reversed the famous epigram of Napoleon III. before the proclamation of the empire : " L'empire, c'est la paix." Rothschild's view was : " Bas de paix, bas d'empire " !

[2] Cavour, at Prince Napoleon's suggestion, went to Paris to counteract the influence of England and of the French ministers (!) on Napoleon III. He told Cowley that if the powers insisted upon Piedmontese disarmament, the future of Piedmont would be compromised : " Son existence politique est annullée."

to see how little Austrian diplomacy learned from its mistakes. Even so, Napoleon was anxious that there should be a general disarmament. But Austria, hoping to teach the Piedmontese a lesson, increased her armies, and sent an ultimatum to Victor Emmanuel.[1]

The war was miserable enough. A military historian might blame the Austrians for not advancing at once upon Turin, or find interest in the spectacle of modern armies fighting on a world-old battlefield under the new conditions of railway transport. The two most important battles, Magenta and Solferino, were more costly than decisive. Twelve thousand Frenchmen were killed or wounded at Solferino ; yet the quadrilateral was uncaptured, and typhus was breaking out in the army.[2] Napoleon III. had not won Napoleonic victories. He was stricken by the sight of the slaughter for which he was responsible ; he was browbeaten by the empress and the clericals, and alarmed at the progress of his own disease. He could not trust his minister of war to send him enough artillery or supplies. The peasants in Lombardy showed no excitement in his cause. Above all, Prussia was mobilising troops on the Rhine. The acquisition of Savoy and Nice might be balanced by the loss of Alsace and Lorraine. Russia was alarmed lest further Austrian defeats should lead to a Hungarian rising, which might be the prelude to an outbreak in Poland. Cavour would not or could not keep his word that there should be no revolutionary disturbance elsewhere in Italy. In the grand-duchy of Tuscany Ricasoli made no secret of his Piedmontese sympathies ; Bologna offered itself to Victor Emmanuel ; riots in Perugia were only put down by the Swiss mercenaries of the pope. There was a danger that the kingdom of upper Italy would be too large for French

---

[1] The Austrian government did not want the expense of a long mobilisation ; but Piedmont was even less able to bear the heavy charge of a large army. The Austrians did not see that the Piedmontese government had been living on capital, and that an army much too great for the capacities of the state could not be maintained for ever on the confiscated property of the church. The main fear of the Austrians was that they would be forced by a congress either to give up Lombardy, and possibly Venetia as well, or to grant reforms which would at once be asked for in other parts of the empire.

[2] The doctors had orders to call the disease by another name.

convenience. Again without weighing the consequences
Napoleon came to terms with Austria ; the Italians were
neither consulted nor forewarned. The Austrians knew Napoleon's embarrassment, and refused to give up Venetia ; but
surrender of Venetia was a part of the bargain with Cavour.

All this time the Roman curia had done nothing, save
indeed to countenance the brutality[1] of the Swiss at Perugia.
The pope took no part in determining the settlement with
Austria, nor could he be of any help to Napoleon. Emperor
and pope had to watch the annexation of Tuscany and the
Romagna to Piedmont. It might well seem that they were
watching the beginning of the end of the temporal power.[2]
The north Italians would hardly show much gratitude to
Napoleon ;[3] but they paid their debt. Savoy and Nice
were handed over to the French after the shabby plebiscites
which accompany transactions of this kind. The city of
Rome was still protected by French troops, and Napoleon
had still to think of the French catholic voters. If Cavour
had escaped from his control, Napoleon might hope at least
to persuade the pope to make concessions to his remaining
subjects. Pius spared neither Napoleon nor Piedmont.
Lamoricière, a personal enemy of Napoleon, and one of the
exiles of the *coup d'état* of 1851, was chosen to reorganise the
papal army : a tiny force which could never hope to defeat
the Piedmontese if the French soldiers were withdrawn
from Rome. To the north Italians the pope said that the
revolution was acting like a mad dog, and that he would be
prepared to meet force with force.

Within the papal states the government had destroyed
nearly every trace of the liberal mood of Pius ix. The only
layman in the ministry was the minister of war ; in 1860 his
place was taken by a Belgian priest who had served in the

[1] It is not unlikely that the anti-papal accounts of the suppression of
the riots exaggerated the brutality.

[2] On December 23, 1860, the canons of St. Peter's, fearing a liberal
demonstration in the basilica, thought it safer not to sing the sentence :
" O Emmanuel, rex et legifer noster, exspectatio gentium et Salvator
earum, veni ad salvandum nos."

[3] They showed the most outrageous ingratitude. Portraits of Orsini
took the place of portraits of Napoleon iii. in the shops. While
Napoleon was in Turin, a performance by a Mlle Orsini at the opera
was applauded with the words " Viva Orsini."

French army. The pope broke his promise that members of local and provincial councils should be elected. Priests were given all the vacant posts in the administration, the magistracy, and the schools. The finances became more ruinously confused, while Antonelli, his brothers, and his friends made large fortunes out of a dishonest handling of the corn trade.

In the meantime Pius IX. turned to less worldly matters. While Cavour was taking the goods of the church, Pius had in mind a signal act of devotion to the Blessed Virgin. He would define the Immaculate Conception as an article of faith. It was true that St. Thomas Aquinas, and for nearly six centuries the Dominicans, had opposed the thesis of the Immaculate Conception. It was true that long ago the documentary evidence (brought forward in its favour by Spanish Jesuits) had been exposed as a forgery. Innocent XI. in 1682 had described them as " figmenta " likely to corrupt the catholic faith ! But a Roman theologian [1] in 1847 produced the remarkable view that neither the words of the Bible nor the open tradition of the church were necessary for the validity of a dogma. The tradition might be secret and implicit, and come to the light of day only in a later age. This view absolved the pope from any necessity of proof. He consulted a number of bishops. The archbishop of Paris asked what was the reason for the definition of the doctrine. " Unde vero haec definiendi voluptas ? " On the other hand, the archbishop of Trani found that the modern world would be delighted at this recognition of the Blessed Virgin as the complement of the Trinity and the co-redemptress of the world : " necnon Trinitatis complementum . . . insuperque coredemptricis nomen et gloriam promeruerit." In the circle within which the popes had enclosed themselves Trani was more likely to be right than Paris. The pope decided in favour of the promulgation. The doctrine was proclaimed to the church in December 1854. Never before had a dogma been thrust upon the church by the initiative of the pope, and defined by his sole authority. Pius had come to believe that his authority was sufficient, and that an intellectual world,

[1] See Nielsen, *op. cit.*, ii. 188-98, and authorities there quoted.

looking for guidance in the confusion of the time, would be ready to accept his infallible authority.

The next step was to convince the world that he was indeed infallible. From this time forward was decided the calling of the Vatican council. As the temporal power seemed more ineluctably condemned to go down before the revolution, so the pope became more certain that the proclamation of his infallibility would be the means of salvation for the distress of the age.

Thus was the church bound to intellectual conservatism as closely as it was bound to the allegiance of any conservative power or any adventurer who wore the dress of conservatism. There was no escape from the temporal bondage as long as the temporal power should last. Gregory first, and Pius after him, took care that this bondage should also be a bondage of the mind. To Gregory the refusal to meet a new learning came in part from urgent political need. To Pius obscurantism became an end in itself.[1]

The promulgation of the dogma of the Immaculate Conception was announced to his troops by Ferdinand of Naples in the orders of the day ; a salute of guns was fired in honour of the new truth. But Providence had a time of trial in store for the pious house of Bomba. This ineffable king went to his own place in the spring of 1859. His successor, Francis II., had scarcely time to show his incapacity when a rebellion broke out in Naples and Sicily. The rebellion was organised from a distance by Mazzini, and, like all Mazzini's rebellions, broke out too soon. It was suppressed with ease in Naples ; but the danger lay in Sicily. Garibaldi had promised to go to Sicily, if the Sicilians showed that they were in earnest. Francis II., and Cavour, and Napoleon III. might well wonder whether he would keep his promise.

Garibaldi was no lover of priests, diplomatists, or kings. He had run away, or rather sailed away, from home at the age of fifteen to escape from the clerical schoolmasters to whom, with an unconscious irony, his family had

[1] An enormous and jejune fresco commemorated the promulgation of the doctrine in the palace of the Vatican which had been decorated by Michael Angelo and Raphael.

entrusted his education.[1] He came back to help his father in his small coasting trade, and ran away again after his complicity in Mazzini's unsuccessful invasion of Savoy in 1834. He was then twenty-seven years old. He spent ten of the next fourteen years fighting in the revolutionary wars of South America.[2] In 1848 he came back to Europe, with experience enough of guerilla warfare. He fought in the siege of Rome, and in a wonderful retreat escaped over the mountains to the Adriatic. He went to New York, took work as a candlemaker, became a sea-captain, and after saving enough money, bought (for £360) the northern half of the island of Caprera. Here he took to farming ; from here he observed events.

Garibaldi had a stupid directness about him which was disconcerting to the finesse of politicians. He saw in Cavour the man who had sold Nice—Garibaldi's birthplace—to France. He never thought of the awkward position of Napoleon III. if the rest of the scheme for an Italian federation should be destroyed. He did not trouble himself overmuch about the difficulties of Victor Emmanuel if a republican force should drive the house of Bourbon from Sicily and the Italian mainland. He did not even consider that the regular army of Naples was nearly one hundred thousand strong, and that the fortresses were in good condition. He started with a thousand men to conquer the kingdom. Within two months he had taken from Francis II. the whole of Sicily. What government was to be set up in place of the Bourbons ? Garibaldi was in no hurry to decide. Sicily might well get on for a time without a regular government. Garibaldi busied himself with a number of important humanitarian reforms, such as the

---

[1] He and some other boys had taken a boat with provisions and fishing tackle. They had reached Monaco when they were overtaken by another boat and brought home again. An abbé had noticed the sailing of their boat. Garibaldi commented on this recapture in his *Memorie Autobiografiche* (pt. i. chap. 2) : " Un abate avea svelato la nostra fuga. Vedete che combinazione ; un abate, l'embrione d'un prete, contribua forse a salvarmi ; ed io son tanto ingrato da perseguire quei poveri prete. Comunque, un prete è un impostore, ed io mi devo al santo culto del vero."

[2] The fighting was real enough. One of his battles lasted three days. At another time Garibaldi's limbs were dislocated by torture.

better treatment of foundlings.   Crispi, one of his followers, took on the work of organising an administration.   Clouds of little black-coated men descended upon a host of little jobs.   To whom were kingdom, foundlings, and administration to belong ?   Neither Crispi nor Garibaldi would agree to hand over their conquest to Victor Emmanuel.   Crispi had thoughts of popular sovereignty ; Garibaldi was afraid that Cavour would not allow him to cross over to the mainland.   Cavour might well feel anxious about the movements of this simple and most undiplomatic hero.   If he were defeated by the Neapolitan army, the government of northern Italy would be accused of deserting him : if he were successful, what was to happen to Naples ?   Garibaldi was capable of advancing upon Rome.   Here he would meet the French.

Cavour tried to anticipate him by starting a revolution in Naples in the interest of Piedmont ; but for once the Neapolitans would not rebel.   Garibaldi would not be stopped ; in August 1860 he landed on the Italian side of the straits of Messina, and overran half the kingdom within a week.   Already, after the fall of Palermo, Francis II. had appealed to England and France, granted a constitution, and telegraphed five times in one day for the papal blessing.[1] He now offered to lend Garibaldi fifty thousand men to fight Lamoricière and the Austrians.   His own generals discouraged him from leading his troops against the invaders, and in September this descendant of Louis XIV. left his capital almost unnoticed.

Cavour could only organise a rebellion in Umbria and the Marches, and send Piedmontese troops to put it down. The result would be another plebiscite.   The pope would lose more territory, and the Piedmontese would be in direct touch with the kingdom of Naples.   The plan was as dangerous as it was dishonest.[2]   If Napoleon III. were hostile to it, the Piedmontese could do nothing, and Cavour would have to resign.   Even if Napoleon did not interfere, Austria might take the chance of invading Piedmont while the

[1] The last three blessings were sent by Antonelli on his own authority !
[2] In 1860 d'Azeglio wrote that Cavour was no longer believed by any one.   (Treitschke, *Historische und politische Aufsätze*, 8th edition, ii. 355.)

Piedmontese army was occupied in the south upon work which was scandalising Europe. Napoleon III. might come to the rescue of the Italians, but his help could not reach them before the Piedmontese would have been heavily defeated. In any case the powers might refuse to allow any further extension of the kingdom of Italy. But Europe was tired of the misrule of the Neapolitan Bourbons, and the fecklessness and obstinacy of the papacy. Napoleon, a conspirator to the last, seems to have told Cavour to act quickly; he then left France for Algeria.[1] Austria was unwilling to take further risks in Italy at a time when the position in Germany was serious.[2] Cavour's insurrection was not well received in Umbria ; but there was more enthusiasm in the Marches, and the pretext served its purpose.[3] An ultimatum was sent to the pope asking for the dismissal of the foreign troops in his service. The behaviour of these mercenaries was causing unrest in his states. Victor Emmanuel would not allow Italians to be massacred by hired foreigners.

There was no time to wait for the pope's answer. On September 7 Garibaldi entered Naples in triumph. The miracle of St. Januarius was performed under his observation ! On September 18, thirteen thousand men of the Piedmontese regular army defeated five thousand of the papal troops at Castelfidardo. Lamoricière had trained his small army well ; but the Italians had no heart for the cause ; only the foreign troops, and particularly the Irish, fought with resolution. Twelve days later Ancona was taken. Cavour was still in difficulties. England alone of the powers gave him any positive support. The English kept their views on Italy apart from their Irish policy ; but their support was more the result of fear of Napoleon III., and, above all, of the Italian sympathies of Sir James Hudson, than of any direc-

---

[1] Cavour wrote to Nigra on August 29, 1860 : " L'Empereur a tout approuvé. Il paraît même que l'idée de voir Lamoricière se faire . . . lui a souri beaucoup. . . . Dieu aidant, l'Italie sera faite avant trois mois." (*Carteggio Cavour-Nigra*, vol. 4, p. 186.)

[2] The reopening of the Schleswig-Holstein question was imminent.

[3] Cavour was playing a most intricate series of intrigues. He had allowed the king to encourage Garibaldi's invasion of the papal states ; probably because he wished to prevent Mazzini from invading them from Genoa.

tion from the government.[1] Napoleon III. had to withdraw
his minister from Turin or lose the catholic vote in France.
Furthermore, Francis II. still had an army in the field ;
Garibaldi was still anxious to attack Rome, and there was
a limit to Austrian patience.

Cavour had nine months more to live. In this short time
he was able to extricate his countrymen from a most awkward
situation, and to give the papacy a last opportunity of
escaping with honour from the absurd position of sacrificing body and mind to the temporal power.

The Neapolitan question was soon settled. Garibaldi beat
the Neapolitan army, but could not take Capua or Gaeta
without heavy artillery. An advance upon Rome was therefore out of the question. For the moment Garibaldi was
preoccupied with the number of beggars in Naples, and the
cruelty of Neapolitan cabdrivers to their horses. He made
no difficulty about handing over his conquests to Victor
Emmanuel, and agreed to allow a plebiscite in the two
Sicilies. Garibaldi could understand a soldier, and did for
Victor Emmanuel what he would never have done for
Cavour ; herein lay one of the greatest services of the house
of Savoy to Italy. The plebiscite was not different from
other decisions of the people under similar conditions. Only
a few hundred in Sicily wished or ventured to vote against
annexation. There was greater opposition on the mainland,
and a certain pressure was put upon the voters. " I admired
the civic courage of two or three people who dared to say
' No,' " [2] wrote an observer of the poll. In the city of

[1] Sir James Hudson was British minister at Turin from 1851 to 1863.
Lord Malmesbury described him in 1859 as " more Italian than the
Italians themselves." Upon Hudson's retirement in 1863 the *Times*
reprinted (August 25, 1863) an article from the *Saturday Review* in which
he was described as " a rock of strength at the only Court where we
have any real struggle with the French . . . he encouraged Cavour
in all the efforts by which Piedmont held itself out as the leader of a
new Italy. . . ." The obvious parallel between Hudson and Stratford
de Redcliffe was recognised in a guarded way by the writer of the article.
" He [Hudson] never aspired to be a great Eltchi. . . ." But it is
interesting to notice that within ten years most important issues of
British policy with regard to Italy and Turkey were largely decided by
the action of the British ministers at Turin and Constantinople. Hudson's
successor was " a model of honest, gentlemanly mediocrity "—and a
relation of Lord John Russell !

[2] Persano's Diary : quoted in de la Gorce, *op. cit.*, iii. 441.

Naples only 31 out of 106,000 voters showed this " civic courage." A few days later another plebiscite in Umbria and the Marches rounded off the Piedmontese work of " keeping order." [1]

The kingdom of Italy now included nearly all the Italian peninsula ; but it had no capital city. Turin was impossible ; the local jealousies of the south would not have allowed such an exhibition of Piedmontese predominance. The Piedmontese would not consider Naples ; neither Piedmontese nor Neapolitans would be willing to accept Milan or Florence. Rome, and Rome alone, would satisfy the whole nation. [2]

Hence the necessity for a settlement of the Roman question ; hence the chance for the pope to make a splendid gesture of renunciation which would regain for him the respect of Italy and of Europe, and take him out of the middle ages into the modern world. The effect would have overflowed the sphere of the temporal power. An act of this kind would have freed the papacy from more than one tradition, and might have opened the way to more than one reconciliation. [3] There had been popes strong enough to make this gesture ; there had been cardinals who had advised the popes to make greater sacrifices. Pius was not of the order of the great founders of the papal state, and Antonelli had to consider the fortunes of his family.

Cavour's plan has become famous in the words " Libera chiesa in libero stato." He wanted the papacy to surrender its temporal power to the government of Victor Emmanuel, although the pope might keep a right of suzerainty. In return for allowing the Italians to take Rome for their capital, the church would be allowed to elect her own bishops without interference, hold her own synods, exercise her own ecclesiastical discipline, and manage her own

---

[1] Cavour wrote in 1861 that it was more difficult to establish harmony between north and south in Italy than to fight the pope or Austria.

[2] Apart from political reasons, Venice would have been dangerously accessible to Austrian attack. The military argument was also used against Turin.

[3] The refusal of Pius IX. to accept the plan of a free church in a free state is almost contemporary with the publication of Darwin's *Origin of Species* (1859).

seminaries. The confiscated church property could not be restored, but a subsidy would be given to the clergy by the state. The pope would no longer have to trust to foreign bayonets for protection, for he would have the support of the whole Italian nation.

Cavour announced his plan in the Italian parliament in October 1860. In the next four months he sent his proposals to Rome. Certain secret arrangements were added to the open clauses of the despatch ; Antonelli was to receive a " compensation " of three million lire, and his brothers were to be kept in their lucrative positions. All contracts between the Antonelli family and the Roman state were to be recognised by the kingdom of Italy !

There seemed a fair chance of success. Liberal catholics outside Italy were outspoken in their desire to see the settlement of the question which was poisoning the moral and intellectual life of the church. Döllinger, in his public lectures, discussed the loss of the temporal power in terms which made the papal nuncio leave the lecture hall.

At the moment when an agreement appeared possible negotiations were broken off. The papacy would not soil its hands with an immoral bargain. " Non patteggieremo mai cogli spogliatori," said Antonelli. The family contracts were not yet disturbed.

Many reasons have been given for the breakdown of Cavour's plan. Antonelli seems to have hoped that Spain would take the initiative in proposing joint intervention by the catholic powers. The presence of Francis II. in Rome, the extension of the north Italian " anti-clerical " measures to the kingdom of Naples, and the premature disclosure of the negotiations were factors working against Cavour. But it is easy to see why a liberal solution of the Roman question must have been rejected by the high conservatives. The catholic theory of society, as expounded by recent popes and their Jesuit advisers, had no place for the separation of church and state. Separation might be tolerated here and there, and for a time ; once it was accepted as a principle, and applied to the papacy and the kingdom of Italy, it must hold at all times, and in all places. To this difficulty were added the usual arguments of timid men. Who could trust these Piedmontese ? For how long would the subsidy be paid ?   These arguments were all the more foolish because no one could doubt that if a friendly settlement were made impossible Cavour would use trickery or force.   As soon as he knew of the pope's refusal, Cavour began to negotiate with Napoleon.   Let the French troops leave Rome.   The Italian government would guarantee the papal territory, or all that was left of it, against attack.   The idea behind this proposal, an idea which the convention of September 1864 brought into the foreground, was, that if a revolution should break out in Rome, Victor Emmanuel would have to accept the invitation of the Roman people, as Napoleon had been compelled by his principles to accept the result of the plebiscite in Nice and Savoy !

V

THE END OF THE TEMPORAL POWER

CAVOUR was dead before the spring of 1861 had turned to high summer. He left no successor. Henceforward the papal government had to fight men of lesser build, of no less ruthlessness, and of no more scruple. The Italian people and the Italian statesmen had lost the idealism of the earlier stage of the nationalist movement. Victor Emmanuel was becoming more vulgar and more unconstitutional ; Garibaldi was as vain as the pope himself ; Mazzini was at times little better than a professional conspirator. The politicians had been brought up in a school of revolutionary excitement, and had seen victories won more easily by intrigue than by force. The tradition of the country had no Chatham, no Burke to inspire its citizens ; but there was always Machiavelli.

It was hard to find enough honest men trained in affairs to supply the need of a kingdom which was creating a civil service and an army, and entering at the same time upon a period of great economic change. The functionaries, especially those from the south, had the tradition of the idleness and corruption of the old régime. The international situation was unfavourable to a peaceful development of the resources of the country. The American civil war had brought about a serious famine of raw material in the cotton industry, and was disturbing the whole course of European trade. Austria was drifting into war with Prussia. The Emperor Napoleon was ill, uncertain of his future, and ready to take up any adventure which promised success.

The pope had destroyed the possibility of a catholic party which might have exercised a moderating influence upon the self-conscious nationalism of Italy. Ricasoli alone among the successors of Cavour possessed the elements of greatness ; he was a better catholic than Cavour, and a better man

than Victor Emmanuel ; but what could be done with
Pius and Antonelli ? In 1861 d'Azeglio had published a
plea that Italy should have not one but many capitals, and
that the seat of government should be fixed at Florence.
Yet the politicians dared not resist the popular cry " Roma
capitale " ; nor could they face the possibility of leaving
Rome to be a centre of intrigue, a new Coblenz for all the
enemies of a new government. Antonelli played into the
hands of the anti-clericals by encouraging brigandage on
the borders of the papal states. If lawlessness were tolerated in Rome, how could the Italian government keep
order in Naples ?

Napoleon tried to make the Italians see that Italy should
" se faire oublier " for a time. Victor Emmanuel agreed,
and dismissed Ricasoli soon after he had reopened the
question of a free church in a free state. Ricasoli's successor, Ratazzi, was a stronger radical, and hoped to use
Garibaldi and Mazzini to stir up trouble on the southern
frontier of Austria. But Garibaldi would not be the tool
of any politician. He embarrassed the government by
encouraging an insurrection in the Italian Tyrol ; in August
1862, after his expulsion from the Tyrol, he led a foolish
attack upon Rome with the watchword " Roma o morte."
At once the Roman question reappeared in its worst form.
Napoleon telegraphed that Garibaldi was making it impossible for him to take his troops from Rome. The Italian
government was forced to stop Garibaldi, and the hero was
wounded. He was imprisoned for a time, only to be set
free as soon as popular excitement in Italy, and liberal
opinion in Europe, justified the grant of a pardon.

An incident of this kind could be used to show to the
world how urgent was the need for a settlement of the
Roman problem. The Italian government claimed that
it had done its best to suppress agitation. No government
could oppose for ever the reasonable wishes of a whole
nation. Napoleon might wish that he also could interpret
" the reasonable wishes of a whole nation " ; but there was
no middle way whereby he could satisfy the French liberals
and the French catholics. He changed his foreign minister.
The new minister, Drouyn de Lhuys, believed in the main-

tenance of the temporal power as the best means of preventing Italian unity. His predecessor, Thouvenel,[1] had proposed an understanding with the government of Turin. So much for the catholics ; could the liberals also be propitiated ? Napoleon allowed himself to be approached " confidentially." He made it clear that all he wanted was to get his troops away from Rome. He could do no more with Pius. The pope and Antonelli had a valid spiritual reason for distrusting the emperor. Several years earlier, Mgr Talbot, the confidant of the pope and of Cardinal Manning, had told Odo Russell that he knew from a trustworthy source of the emperor's league with the devil ; in fact, Napoleon frequently took the advice of his ally on political questions !

The Italians followed the suggestion made to them " confidentially " by Napoleon. The tension between Austria and Prussia over Schleswig-Holstein made it likely that Italy would get Venetia before Rome. Therefore she could afford to give Napoleon the few years of interval for which he asked. Anyhow it was important that the French troops should have left Rome before the death of Pius, and Pius was thought to be near to his end. These are the reasons for the convention of September 15, 1864. Under its terms the French were to leave Rome within two years ; the Italian army was to protect the territory still in the possession of the pope and allow the organisation of a papal army sufficient to maintain order within this territory ; the capital of Italy was to be moved for good and all from Turin to Florence. The convention was impudent enough. Napoleon in his earlier days would never have made so clumsy or undignified a surrender. The only aggressor feared by the pope was the Italian government. This government doubted its power to restrain popular enthusiasm any longer ; yet the Italian troops were to protect the papacy !

Mazzini might speak of the " ungodly renunciation," but Napoleon did not believe that the convention would be kept.

[1] Thouvenel's correspondence, published by his son, contains the most striking instances of Napoleon's vacillation and double-dealing. See L. Thouvenel, *Le Secret de l'empereur*, especially vol. ii. ; and *Pages de l'histoire du second empire*.

It was pointed out in the Italian parliament that there was no idea of abandoning the cause of " Roma capitale," but that the Italians would not take their capital by force of arms. The interpretation given by the French foreign minister to those discussions left no room for doubt. " Le cas d'une révolution qui viendrait à éclater spontanément à Rome n'est point prévu par la convention." [1] What did this mean ? Papal sovereignty existed upon the same terms as any other sovereignty ; that is, upon the consent of the governed. This might be the theory of Bonapartism, and of governments nearer to the rule of liberty ; it was not the theory of the Catholic Church. Even so, the convention was most unpopular. There were two riots almost at once in Turin. Acton wrote during a visit to Italy in 1865 of the unpopularity of the ministry, the bankruptcy of the new state, and the general uncertainty about the future.

The convention was the result of the curial policy of negation. Yet the pope still refused to listen to reason or moderation. He published his answer on the tenth anniversary of the proclamation of the dogma of the Immaculate Conception. The answer took the form of an encyclical letter (known from its initial words, *Quanta cura*) and a catalogue of modern errors. The catalogue, or syllabus, had its own history. As early as 1849 the future Pope Leo XIII., then bishop of Perugia, had proposed to the Umbrian bishops that they should ask Pius to make a collection of the worst errors of the time concerning the church and the temporal questions of the source of authority and the right of property. In 1854 a committee of theologians was asked to draw up such a list of modern errors. They worked with the slowness characteristic of commissions of this kind ; nor was it easy to cope with the multitude of the errors ! A catalogue of errors drawn up in 1860 by a French bishop (a former follower of Lamennais !) so much pleased the pope that he formed another commission to examine and supplement the list.

From this time the question of publication came into the

---

[1] Drouyn de Lhuys to Baron de Malaret, French ambassador at Turin, October 30, 1864. The whole despatch is printed in the French official publication, *Les Origines diplomatiques de la guerre de 1870-1871* iv. 324-7.

foreground.   The moderate French bishops favoured delay ;
for a time their advice was taken.   But the events of 1864
were too much for the pope's moderation.   The September
convention was clearly the first step towards an Italian
occupation of Rome ;   Pius was not constrained any longer
to spare the feelings of the French bishops.   This catalogue
of mistakes seemed an instrument given into his hands by
Providence at a time of crisis.   He was frightened by the
dangerous doctrines put forward in 1863 at a liberal catholic
congress at Malines.   Montalembert had been bold enough
to read two papers in favour of a free church in a free state.
To the pope this phrase of Cavour meant no more and no
less than the surrender of the temporal power for which great
sacrifices had been made.   He was as ready to denounce
this second generation of liberal catholics as Gregory xvi.
had been ready to silence Lamennais in 1831.   It did not
occur to Pius that Lamennais had not been silenced.   The
editor of *L'Avenir* was speaking through the mouth of
Montalembert.   Montalembert was indeed the link between
the two liberal movements in the church ;   the man was
incorrigible in his heretical love for the freedom of conscience.

The encyclical *Quanta cura* and the syllabus of errors
were an ultimatum to the world ;   a last protest—to be
reinforced five years later by the insistence upon the infallibility of their author—against any compromise with modern
ideas ;   a final throw to keep that rule over a few square
miles of land which seemed of more importance than the
peace of mind of thousands of catholics.   There was no sort
of moderation.   Socialism, communism, and Bible Societies
were grouped together as plagues.   The ideas upon which
the best minds of modern Europe were attempting to build
up a new society were " monstrosa opinionum portenta " ;
liberty of conscience and liberty of the press were dangerous
errors ;   the pope could excommunicate any one who
attacked the property of the church.   Against the devastating effect of these false opinions the pope asked for the
help of the Immaculate Virgin ;   Pius had long expected a
miracle.

The encyclical summed up the ignorance of the papal
court for a century and more.   The separation of the church

x

from the state was a damnable error ; so was the belief that
the papacy might well do without the temporal power ;
so was the belief that the pope could and should come to
terms with " progress, liberty, and the new civilisation." [1]

To liberal catholics the syllabus was the ruin of their
hopes. Outside the morbid atmosphere of the curia no man
could take this miserable catalogue with any seriousness ;
within the curia the words were scarcely understood. The
pope knew nothing of the way of life he was condemning.
He only saw the encroachment of Italian soldiers upon his
diminished kingdom. In France liberal-minded bishops—
notably Dupanloup of Orleans—tried to minimise the
violence of the Roman anathemas. The pope's words had
been taken out of their context ; he was only dealing with
general principles ; the church would always tolerate these
monstrous errors, and would adapt its theory to the practice
of the day. Yet the pope gave only a guarded approval to
Dupanloup's interpretation. Those who took the syllabus
literally were not condemned ; among them were the
pope's own friends. The French government repudiated
the most offensive clauses ; but the devil's ally was thought
of as outside the church. [2]

From this time the fall of Rome was a question almost of
months. The inglorious adventure whereby Italy won
Venetia after defeat on land and sea delayed the final attack.
But the financial difficulties of the kingdom made even the
catholic Ricasoli—now again in power—turn to the property
of the church. Seventeen hundred million lire were in the
scale ; the relations between the church and the Italian
government could not be worse ; why not get what benefit
there was to be gained from this persistent enmity ? [3]

[1] The Latin terms are : [" Errores, qui ad liberalismum hodiernum
referuntur] . . . Romanus pontifex potest ac debet cum progressu,
cum liberalismo, et cum recenti civilitate sese reconciliare et componere."
[2] It was in connexion with the controversy over the interpretation of
the syllabus that Newman made the distinction between " the pure and
serene atmosphere " at the summit of the rock of St. Peter and the
" malaria " of imprudence in Rome itself. (W. Ward, *W. G. Ward and
the Catholic Revival*, p. 249.)
[3] Ricasoli wanted to combine the art of confiscation with another
attempt to revive the idea of a free church in a free state, and to allow
the bishops themselves to arrange the sale of property and to pay over

A second and more sordid confiscation was followed by another raid upon Rome by Garibaldi. The French government remembered the confession of Victor Emmanuel that he could not hold back the zeal of his subjects a second time. The Italians asked permission to send troops to prevent another outbreak ; but there was a limit to Napoleon's patience, and to the patience of the catholic electors in France. Almost against his judgment, and certainly against his inclination, Napoleon sent the French troops back to Rome.[1] They stayed until they were wanted to fight the Prussians ; their presence was one of the reasons—though Napoleon's own failure to win victories was the main reason —why the Italians gave no help to the French in 1870.[2]

When Napoleon's hour had come, and the troops were recalled to fulfil his and their destiny, the party of the left in the Italian chamber declared that they would leave Florence and declare a republic in Milan and Naples if Victor Emmanuel would not allow a march on Rome. The fall of the empire in France forced the hand of the monarchy

600,000,000 lire to the state and the communes. The chamber would not agree. Ricasoli resigned ; Ratazzi again took his place, and complete confiscation followed, though the Italian state guaranteed to pay the salaries of the clergy. The government was therefore applying to the kingdom of Italy the measure which Cavour had carried out in Piedmont. The king does not seem to have been so much concerned about " the heavenly side of things."

[1] The orders and counter-orders given to the fleet of transports show Napoleon's vacillation at its worst. (See de la Gorce, *op. cit.*, v. 295-6.) The French troops defeated Garibaldi at Mentana. After the " victory " the commander, wanting to reassure the soldiers about the effectiveness of the new rifles, telegraphed, " Les chassepots ont fait merveille." The telegram was published, and Italian opinion imagined that the campaign against Garibaldi had been undertaken merely to test the French armaments ! At a meeting of protest at Leghorn (in August 1870) against an alliance with France one of the charges against Napoleon was the use of the " chassepots " against Italians.

[2] The French government was asked by Victor Emmanuel to withdraw the troops. The foreign minister, Gramont, who believed in a French victory over the Prussians, answered : " La France ne veut pas défendre son honneur sur le Rhin et le sacrifier sur le Tibre." The empress is said to have used even stronger words : " Plutôt les Prussiens à Paris que les Italiens à Rome." Victor Emmanuel felt under a certain obligation to Napoleon. He sympathised with monarchs whose thrones were not well established, and did not want to see a republic in France. The Prussian government was prudent enough to announce that it would not object to an Italian occupation of Rome.

in Italy. There were limits to the chivalry of Victor Emmanuel. After a last attempt to bring the pope to listen to a compromise—when he was expecting a miracle—the armies of Italy entered the city. The dominion of a thousand years, the oldest temporal sovereignty in Europe, had fallen.

The Italians had done their best to destroy the most characteristic of Italian possessions ; their one inheritance from a world-wide empire which was still of world importance. As for the popes, they had lost that for which they had thought it worth while to barter the goodwill of Europe.[1] It is almost incredible that Pius seemed to himself to have won an even greater triumph in the definition of his infallibility by the Vatican council.

[1] Guizot, in a letter (of December 1864) commenting upon the Syllabus, wrote : " C'est la bêtise de la routine. . . . Rome a perdu bien autre chose que son vieil empire : elle a perdu son vieil esprit " (Guizot, *Lettres*, p. 396).

VI

THE VATICAN COUNCIL

THE history of the Vatican council is the epilogue to the history of the isolation of the papacy and the last renunciation of the intellectual standards of the world outside its gates. Two days before the publication of the encyclical *Quanta cura* the pope had mentioned in utmost secrecy to one of the congregations [1] that he had long been thinking about calling an œcumenical council.[2] Nineteen of the twenty-one cardinals of the Congregation of Rites agreed that a council was desirable ; none was convinced of its necessity ; only two opposed its convocation. In the course of the year 1865 the pope consulted a number of bishops (including Manning), and the nuncios appointed to the European capitals. In 1867, during the celebration of the

[1] The congregations are the committees among which the routine business of the church is divided.

[2] The archives of the council are preserved in the Vatican. The speeches made at the general congregations have been published in five folio volumes (Vatican Press, 1875-1884). Apart from these and other collections of documents, the most important history of the Vatican council (written from the curial point of view) is Granderath and Kirch, *Geschichte des Vatikanischen Konzils* (3 vols. Freiburg, 1903-1906). This book has been translated into French with great care and accuracy. The first volume deals with the antecedents of the council, and contains a full list of authorities and a bibliography. Friedrich, *Geschichte des Vatikanischen Konzils* (3 vols.), is a large work, useful for the history of the ultramontane intrigues, but polemical in spirit and execution. Mourret, *Le Concile du Vatican*, gives a short account, written mainly from French sources, and favourable (though more liberal than G. and K.) to the ultramontane school. Acton's essay on the Vatican council (printed in *The History of Freedom, and Other Essays*) is by far the best account in English. Acton was in Rome for the most important months of the council. His diary was sent to Döllinger, through reliable channels, and formed the basis of Döllinger's commentary upon the proceedings of the council in the *Augsburger Allgemeine Zeitung*. This commentary was subsequently published under the title of *Römische Briefe aus dem Konzil*. Döllinger had other, and less reliable, sources of information, and his comments, written from day to day, at a time of passionate excitement, must be treated with caution.

eighteen-hundredth anniversary of the martyrdom of the apostles Peter and Paul, the pope announced to the assembled bishops that a council would be held.[1]

What was the council to discuss ? Pius wished for a recognition of his infallibility ; the school of Jesuit theologians in Rome were ready to support him. But the most careful preparations were necessary. It was known that the leaders of liberal opinion among the bishops north of the Alps welcomed the council—if they welcomed it at all— only because it would give an occasion for the episcopate to assert itself against the ignorant tyranny of the curia. The pope and the papalists had therefore to take care not to lose control of the procedure of the council, and the subjects of its deliberations.

Twenty years earlier Pius had drifted into a disastrous experiment from no other motive than a vague desire to do good in a popular and easy manner. His facile optimism had failed to foresee the thousand little difficulties in the way of any great undertaking. In the twenty years of makeshift and failure which lay between the attempt to liberalise the papal government and the summoning of the Vatican council the pope had never learned the difference between a good intention and a good action ; he had not understood what it meant to count the cost, to see the consequences of his acts. He never troubled himself about the opinions of the laity. His clerical advisers assured him that catholic opinion could only be his opinion, and recommended anathema as the right method of dealing with opponents.

From the outset there was no question of getting to the council a representative body of catholic thought ; of putting the case for and against the curial view of the needs of the times. The commissions set up for discussing the business of the council were formed out of the existing congregations afforced by representatives chosen from outside. The choice of the representatives was made in the interest of the ultramontane cause. In France and Germany the dominant school of catholic thought was out of sympathy

---

[1] It is not known for how long the pope had been considering the idea of a general council. Mourret (*op. cit.*, p. 3) suggests the influence of the Great Exhibition !

with Rome ; the most eminent representatives of these countries were therefore set aside in favour of lesser men who could be trusted to follow the suggestions of the Romans. In Germany the universities of Munich, Bonn, Tübingen, and Freiburg were ignored ; neither Döllinger nor Hefele,[1] the greatest of catholic historians, was invited. The pope made strange excuses. He wished to spare the scholars of the north the discomfort of an Italian summer ; they would be summoned later in the year. Antonelli pretended that Döllinger had been approached, and had answered that he did not wish for an invitation.[2] From England came two insignificant men. Manning and the Jesuits saw to it that Newman stayed at home.[3] Even with this careful discrimination the curia took no risks ; only thirty-five out of ninety-six members of the commissions were non-Romans.

Who were to be invited to the council ? Here the commissions came upon an unforeseen difficulty. Obviously all diocesan bishops must be invited. But what of titular bishops?[4] What was the duty of a bishop at an œcumenical council ? The difference of opinion between the Roman and the German schools was fundamental. According to the Roman view the bishops were not the administrators of a particular territory, but members of a college, the successors of the apostles in their corporate capacity. A general council was a meeting of bishops for a collective act. Every bishop must attend. As the pope is the head of the hierarchy of bishops, his consent was necessary for the validity of the decrees of a council. If God wills to preserve His church

[1] Hefele was invited at a later stage, owing to the insistence of Cardinal Schwarzenberg, archbishop of Prague.

[2] Döllinger denied that he had been approached. It is unlikely that the nuncio at Munich, who wished the council to condemn the Munich school of historians, would have wanted their leader to take part in the preparation of the agenda !

[3] Dupanloup later asked Newman to come as his chaplain ; but Newman was too great a man to appear in the train of a French bishop. On the other hand, Mgr Talbot was a member of the Congregazione direttice, which supervised the work of all the commissioners.

[4] Titular bishops, i.e. bishops who took their titles from ancient sees in eastern Christendom. The Christians belonging to the dioceses from which these titles were taken had disappeared many centuries earlier, or owed their allegiance to bishops of the eastern church. (In 1914 there were no less than five patriarchs of Antioch !)

from any touch of error, then the decisions of the church upon the highest questions must be divinely inspired, and infallible ; the necessity for papal consent to the decrees implied that infallibility must rest in the final " yes " or " no " of the pope. Upon this view the papal case would be decided in advance. According to the German view, the Christian people are the final authority in the church. From the whole company of the faithful is derived the defining power of a council. If God wills to give His church infallibility, this infallibility resides in the sum of the opinions of Christian men ; "securus judicat orbis terrarum." Therefore only those bishops who governed a diocese had a right to come to a general council. The bishops came to testify to the views of the faithful. Titular bishops could not testify to any views save their own ; they did not represent the catholics dispersed throughout Christendom. As a matter of course, the Roman view prevailed, and the curialists secured a majority on the council, since the titular bishops were for the most part under the direct control of the Roman congregations. Döllinger called them " papal boarders."

Any doubt about the programme of the ultramontane party disappeared in February 1869 when the Jesuit newspaper in Rome, *La civiltà cattolica*, published an article outlining the " wishes " of the French catholics.[1] The writer divided the French into " catholics " and " liberal catholics."

---

[1] Granderath (*op. cit.*, i. 184-6) gives the most authentic account of the publication of this article. The story was told him by the editor of the *Civiltà* (P. Candella), and was corroborated by documents. The editor had asked for Antonelli's help in getting a series of articles upon the views about the council held by catholics in different countries. Antonelli approved of the plan, and asked the nuncios to choose correspondents who should send fortnightly reports to Rome. The papal nuncio in Paris chose four French priests. These men sent two reports on January 12 to Antonelli, who forwarded them to the *Civiltà* without giving their source. The editor published an Italian translation of the articles in the current number of his paper.

It was clear, therefore, that the *Civiltà* was ready to publish letters claiming to give an account of French opinion on the mere authority of Antonelli, and that Antonelli was ready to take the partisan views of certain French clergy as " representative " of the views of the catholics of France. As the pope was accustomed to read the *Civiltà* in proof before its publication, the alarm of the anti-papalists was more justified than they knew.

The " catholics," who were said to be in a majority, wanted the council to define—by acclamation—the doctrines implied in the syllabus. The bishops were to listen and applaud while the positive truths were read out to them. Papal infallibility would be acclaimed. Some " catholics " would like a dogmatic definition of the Assumption of the Blessed Virgin. Whence came this astonishing programme if it were not the plan of the Roman party ? The acclamation of papal infallibility ; the solemn confirmation of all those papal theories which conflicted with the public law and the daily life of Frenchmen, and indeed of most Europeans ; the addition of another dogma to an overburdened creed ; such were Pius' remedies for the evils of his age !

The dean of the faculty of theology in Paris, Mgr Maret, wrote a temperate refutation of the thesis of papal infallibility, and circulated his book among the bishops. A copy was sent to the pope. The pope thought the gift an insult. Maret insisted upon the right of the bishops to express their views ; one of his opponents accused him of writing in French rather than in Latin in order that his book could be read by the laity ! Such was the Roman attitude towards the opinion of the whole company of the faithful.

The German scholars were less tactful. The truculence of self-conscious nationalism appeared in the attacks of Döllinger. In a series of articles published in the *Augsburger Allgemeine Zeitung* an anonymous writer—whom every one took to be Döllinger—said that if the papal view of infallibility were accepted, the words " definiens subscripsi " by which the bishops testified to the conciliar decrees would only be blasphemous. Since the eleventh century the church had been afflicted with the outrageous pretensions of the popes ; the papacy had been a tumour weakening and disfiguring the life of the church.

The German bishops dared not use such language. They sent a moderate address to the pope deprecating the opportuneness of any definition of infallibility and even doubting the need for the convocation of a general council. Their letter was never registered in the papal archives. There is, however, a covering letter in the archives, with a marginal note in the handwriting of Antonelli : " Rimessa la lettera a Sua Santità." [1] A hostile authority says that the address was torn up by the pope.

The French liberal catholics took up a more subtle line of defence. An article,[2] which was believed to be the joint work of Dupanloup, Montalembert, and Falloux, reassured catholic opinion by assuming that the programme of the *Civiltà* was " unofficial." As the commissions of preparation were bound to secrecy there could be no question of announcing plans for the council. It was impossible that an œcumenical council should renounce its rights in favour of an absolute papal monarchy. . ; . In any case, leaving aside the safeguard of the divine guidance of the bishops, no one would venture to face the practical consequences of a definition of infallibility.

The protestants did not understand the full intention of the council, and were more sympathetic than the pope had reason to expect. In the third quarter of the nineteenth century the leaders of protestantism were themselves alarmed at the disintegration of Christian belief. Guizot, now very near to the end of his long life, described the convocation of the council as an act of wisdom " d'où sortira peut-être le salut du monde." In England the leaders of the high church party hoped that the council would discuss the question of the reunion of the churches.[3] The liberal catholics might fear the consequences of an anticlimax ; they knew enough to discount protestant hopes.

The attitude of the schismatic Christians of the eastern churches was more picturesque though less helpful. Letters of invitation (the easterners were true bishops for all their schism) were carefully bound in red morocco with the styles and titles of the patriarchs in letters of gold. Unfortunately the content of the invitation was published in advance in the *Giornale d'Italia*. In these circumstances the reception of the letter was scarcely possible. The form of rejection

---

[1] According to Granderath (*op. cit.*, i. 238). Acton (*op. cit.*, p. 518) says that Antonelli denied the existence of the letter !

[2] In the *Correspondant*, October 10, 1869, and subsequently republished.

[3] A Scottish Presbyterian clergyman inquired from Manning upon what conditions protestants could take part in the council. He was told that they must follow the example set by the prodigal son ; if they came to Rome they would find theologians ready to convert them by argument.

differed according to the person.   The Greek patriarch of
Constantinople received the papal messenger, and, without
raising his eyes, asked him to put the letter down on a divan.
His Beatitude then delivered a set speech, concluding with
a prayer for charity.   After another speech the letter was
returned.   The Armenian patriarch in Constantinople promised to send the letter to his superior, the Catholicos at
Echmiadzin (near Erivan).   The Catholicos was under
Russian influence, and replied by relieving the patriarch of
his office !   The Coptic patriarch of Alexandria, whose predecessor was said to have been poisoned because of his catholic
sympathies, kept the papal representative waiting for a time.
The interval was occupied by a conversation between the
messenger and the patriarch's secretary (himself a bishop).
The secretary remarked how great was the cost of a long
journey to Rome.   The messenger at once reassured him that
the pope would pay all the expenses of the poorer bishops.

The most remarkable of the schismatics was the hereditary
patriarch of the Nestorians in Chaldæa.   This young man
of twenty-eight years lived in a fortress among the mountains
of central Kurdistan.   The premature disclosures of the
Giornale d'Italia had not echoed throughout his patriarchate ;
but when the papal delegate arrived with the official letter
he found that an act of grave discourtesy had been committed.   The Armenian patriarch of Constantinople had
sent a copy of the general invitation to the bishop of Mardin,
and asked him to forward it to the Nestorian patriarch.
The bishop had sent it to a priest ; the priest was also prevented from visiting in person the centre of Kurdistan, and
the letter was delivered by a simple muleteer !   The
patriarch graciously forgave the unpardonable affront, and
promised to reply by a letter in his own hand.   There is no
record of his answer in the papal registers ; though he told
the papal delegate of his difficulties.   He was dependent
upon the protection of England.   His people could not
forgo this protection ; the English on their side were
anxious to push the claims of protestantism, towards which
the patriarch felt no personal inclination.

While the nominal union of Christendom was thus cared
for by the pope, the governments of the catholic countries

were becoming alarmed at the extravagance of the papal plans for the council. The doctrine of papal infallibility had political consequences which the smaller governments in particular could not ignore. The Bavarian foreign minister, Hohenlohe-Schillingsfürst (a future chancellor of the German empire), proposed a conference in which the powers should agree upon a common policy. It was significant that the powers did not think there was any immediate danger. Europe had taken the measure of a papal court blind to its own isolation.

The procedure of the council was decided by the partisan principles and haphazard inefficiency which had been shown in the settlement of its preliminaries. It was necessary to safeguard the rights of the bishops to bring forward questions for discussion. It was equally important that the council should not waste its time in an aimless and desultory discussion of miscellaneous business. The pope agreed that a committee should receive, co-ordinate, and, if necessary, refuse subjects suggested by the bishops ; yet he would not allow the members of this commission to be chosen by the council itself.[1] The commission thus became a partisan body which could keep out of the council any subject disliked or feared by the predominant school of ultramontane thought. In any case the pope reserved to himself the final right of excluding any proposal from discussion. None of the bishops (with the exception of those on the commissions) knew what business was to be proposed ; therefore the liberty of action of the council was so much curtailed that the ecclesiastical validity of its proceedings might even be doubted.[2]

[1] The greatest number of proposals came from the bishops of the former kingdom of Naples ; most of these proposals affected church doctrine. The French bishops made suggestions for improving the education of the clergy, and for the reform of canon law. They wished to moderate the language of the Index, and make the college of cardinals more learned and less Italian. One petition, signed by a hundred bishops, suggested that the council should ask the Jews to embrace Christianity !

[2] The possibility of questioning the validity of the council owing to the curtailment of its liberties was always before the minds of the anti-infallibilist minority. The revised procedure of business (introduced on February 22) aggravated the position by allowing a majority in the council the right to close a discussion whenever they might think fit, and by declaring that amendments and particular clauses of decrees might be carried by a majority vote. Never before had an œcumenical

All speeches at the council were to be made in Latin ; special reporters were trained to take down the debates in shorthand ; it is an interesting sidelight upon the value of Latin as a universal language that a number of clergy of different nationalities had to be chosen to deal with the different pronunciations of Latin. The reporters, according to many critics, were unable to cope with their work ; no proper arrangements were made for the circulation of the speeches. This last failure was the more paralysing in that the council hall, the right arm of the cross of St. Peter's, was so large that no one could be heard except by his immediate neighbours. It is impossible to excuse the pope of negligence in this matter. Apart from the great height of the building, the dimensions of this transept, or rather such of it as was curtained off, were twenty-three by forty-seven metres ! Efforts were made to get the place of session changed. Five other halls were suggested ; the pope would agree to none of them. Only after some weeks did he allow the meeting-place to be divided by another curtain ; but this division could not overcome the difficulty of hearing Latin speeches which were soon lost in great echoes and reverberating sounds.[1] The long-drawn-out proceedings of the opening ceremony showed the lack of organising ability in the curia, and the lack of consideration for the comfort of the bishops. The procession into St. Peter's was timed to begin at 8.30 A.M. The final prayers ended at half-past three in the afternoon. The day was one of heavy and continuous rain, yet no arrangements were made to drive the bishops back to their homes. Three-quarters of them were men between fifty-six and ninety years old.

council come so near to the view that a dogmatic decision required not virtual unanimity but merely the consent of a majority of those entitled to vote. Acton (op. cit., p. 539) has pointed out that this regulation implied papal infallibility. " If the act of a majority of bishops in the Council, possibly not representing a majority in the Church, is infallible, it derives its infallibility from the pope." But the main question under consideration by the council was the infallibility of the pope !

[1] Even after these changes, which were not fully carried out until the end of February, Hefele, one of the ablest Latinists at the council, complained that he could only hear one out of every three speakers. One cardinal said that he had not understood a single word. Towards the end of the council a canvas was spread over the hall to deaden the effect of the great height of the building.

At the first session of the council it was found that no one had considered how long a time would be taken in counting the votes for the election of a small committee to deal with the excuses of the absent bishops. If the same procedure were to be gone through for all the minor elections there would be no end to the formal business.[1]

To the party of opposition from beyond the Alps these little annoyances were as nothing to the serious interference with the liberty of the debates and the choice of questions for discussion. The pope and the infallibilist party seem for a time to have kept their hope of carrying their definition by acclamation.[2] When the strength of the opposition made this impossible, indirect means had to be employed. Care was taken to pack the " deputations " in which the preliminary discussions were held. Not one of the opponents of infallibility was elected ; only one of the members of the deputation thought that the definition of infallibility was inopportune. The bishops were bound to secrecy ; meetings of bishops of the same nationality were not allowed. International meetings were of little use, for the bishops spoke different languages, and were strangers to one another.

The incompetence of the Roman dictators of the church was again shown when the first official schema, or draft decree, was distributed to the members of the council. For some time nothing at all had been circulated because the Roman commissions of preparation had taken too·long a time over their work. In its first form the schema met with unexpected resistance. It was entitled " De doctrina catholica," and contained a list of the errors of the time. These errors were condemned after the formal method of the schools, and with their traditional violence of language ("Monstra errorum . . . impia insipientia . . . cancer serpens . . ." and the like). Archbishop Conolly of Halifax proposed its complete rejection. The drafts of three other schemata, dealing with the college of cardinals, the bishops

[1] Acton had drawn up for the bishops of the anti-infallibilist party a memorandum giving an account of the methods of business in the parliament of Great Britain.

[2] The archbishop of Paris threatened that if an attempt of this kind were made a hundred bishops would leave Rome, " carrying away the council in the soles of their shoes." (Acton, *op. cit.*, p. 533.)

and clergy, ecclesiastical synods, and a general catechism were returned to the commissions for radical alteration. By February 22 no progress had been made ; a further interval was necessary while the commissions revised the schemata which had been sent back to them.

As time went on the pope became more excited and more anxious lest the council should disperse without proclaiming his infallibility. In the middle of January he took the occasion of a public audience to show his displeasure at those bishops who " lacked the temper of perfect faith." [1] He warned his hearers that he knew how to overcome the difficulties which were being raised. The character of the debates reflected the general disquiet. In February the archbishop of Paris was told that he had talked away his cardinal's hat [2] in a speech attacking the want of method in the council, and the waste of time spent in discussing one or two questions. On March 6 a supplement to the schema " De ecclesia " was distributed to the bishops. The schema, which had been circulated in the last week of January, was shown to coincide absolutely with the lectures of a Jesuit professor at the Collegio Romano. The supplement contained an assertion of papal infallibility. Before this draft was discussed a violent scene had taken place in the council.

Archbishop Strossmayer [3] was the best Latinist, and one of the most remarkable bishops of the church ; he was a figure of the great age of catholic history, and almost the prince bishop of his Croatian people. With all his eloquence and all his authority he had attacked in turn the acoustic properties of the hall, the prohibition against the printing and circulation of the bishops' speeches, and the omission from the schemata of the recognised formula of episcopal consent (*definientibus episcopis*). Strossmayer had dared to say that the rights of the bishops were the rights of God himself. After commenting upon the intolerable style in which the

---

[1] An anti-infallibilist pamphlet was described by the pope as " an attack upon him in his own house."

[2] The archbishop is said to have answered : " Je n'ai point de rhume de cerveau : je n'ai pas besoin de chapeau."

[3] Strossmayer (b. 1815) was of German descent. He was educated at Djakovo and Budapest. In 1849 he became bishop of Djakovo. He took part in the anti-Hungarian movement organised by Jellačić, and became one of the leaders of Croatian nationalism.

schemata were composed, Strossmayer turned to the out-worn formulae which ascribed the errors of the time to the false doctrines condemned at the council of Trent. He pointed out that most of the philosophical systems denounced in the draft under discussion were older than the council of Nicæa or as recent as the French encyclopaedists. It was absurd to connect them with protestantism or with the reformation. The mention of the names of Leibnitz and Guizot should suffice to show the folly of using violent terms against protestant thinkers as though they were atheists and revolutionaries. There were many protestants to whom might be applied the words of St. Augustine : " Errant, sed bona fide errant ; heretici sunt, sed illi nos hereticos tenent." [1] The scene which followed these words, words which most men of goodwill and religion would have made their own, was so violent that some of those present in other parts of St. Peter's thought that the Garibaldians had broken into the council ; others imagined that the pope had been declared infallible !

Less stormy hours were spent in discussing whether the purpose of God in creating the world was a question upon which absolute certainty was possible ; whether the divine revelation to man was an act of pure goodness or a divine obligation consequent upon the creation of man.

Still the infallibilists made no progress. Their original argument had been that the faithful demanded the defini-tion of the dogma. When they were driven from this position, they had recourse to an argument which carried even less conviction. They said that the agitation (which they had themselves created) had unsettled the minds of the clergy and laity ; therefore a pronouncement of some kind must be made. Furthermore, the doctrine of papal infallibility was clearly a part of the divine revelation ; therefore the first duty of the council was to proclaim the fact. This pronouncement must take the form of a declara-tion that papal infallibility was one of the dogmas of the Christian faith.

According to a report in the *Osservatore Romano* the pope

---

[1] " They are wrong, but in good faith ; they are heretics, but they look on us as such."

told an audience of papal vicars and oriental bishops that the treatment of Christ before Pilate was being renewed in the person of Christ's Vicar ; Caesar's friends were now the friends of revolution. Three weeks later Pius assured the bishop of Perpignan that only protestants and infidels denied his infallibility. In the actual debate on the clause of the schema in which infallibility was defined the weight of the speakers against the papalist view was in extraordinary contrast with their numbers. Even on the question of numbers the opposition complained that the three score bishops of the states of the church represented no more than seven hundred thousand catholics, while twelve million catholics of Germany were only represented by fourteen votes. At the third session of the council Italy was represented by 122 bishops, while there were only 175 bishops from the rest of Europe. Three hundred bishops were maintained at the papal expense.[1] One of the south Italians—there were more bishops from the former kingdom of the two Sicilies than from the whole of North America—remarked of the independence of the Germans : "They can take that line ; they are rich." Hefele, the historian of the councils, and (after Döllinger) the most learned man in Europe on the very points at issue, spoke not only against the opportuneness of the definition, but against the doctrine itself. Ketteler, almost the founder of the catholic social movement in Germany, attacked the form and the occasion of the definition, and warned the bishops against establishing absolutism in the church. Maret, the dean of the Sorbonne, and Strossmayer, representing a nation as well as a church, spoke against the doctrine. Darboy, the archbishop of Paris—the Paris of Renan and Pasteur—echoed in a temperate speech the words of Newman : " When has definition of doctrine *de fide* been a luxury of devotion and not a stern painful necessity ? "[2] American bishops followed a similar line of thought, and explained the almost insuperable difficulties which the definition would put in the way of the conversion of protestants.

[1] The cost of their maintenance was 25,000 scudi a day. Even in February the pope had complained : " per furia di farmi infallibile mi faranno fallire."

[2] The sentence occurs in a letter of January 28, 1870, written by Newman to Ullathorne, and reproduced in the *Standard* newspaper.

On the other side many of the speeches were of the order of the archbishop of Messina, who maintained that from the time of the apostles the Sicilians had always acknowledged papal infallibility. There had never been a time when the faithful of his own diocese had not defended to the utmost ("mordaciter") this truth of Christian doctrine. According to the archbishop the testimony of the Sicilians was of particular significance because the people of Messina had sent a deputation to Our Lady immediately after their conversion by St. Paul ! The only speech of serious importance was made by Manning. Manning spoke for nearly two hours. His arguments throw an interesting light upon his own temperament. He told the bishops that the greatest of his difficulties before joining the church had been to decide whether it did in fact possess infallible authority. The infallibility of the pope was questioned ; the infallibility of general councils was questioned ; how then did the Catholic Church differ from the protestant churches ? Manning said that the same difficulty perplexed the protestants who consulted him. He concluded that the definition of papal infallibility, so far from frightening protestants, would remove an obstacle in the way of their conversion. Such are the workings of minds which look for security before they look for truth.

In the first weeks of June the debates moved to their inevitable conclusion. The pope set aside all criticisms about the uncertainty of the tradition by answering a cardinal who had mentioned the doctrine of St. Thomas : "La tradizione sono Io. Vi faro far nuovamente la professione di fede." [1] The minority hoped for a time to prolong the debate until the summer heat should cause a prorogation of the council. But the pope said that if the definition could only ripen in the sun : "Eh bien, on grillera." [2] In any case Pius still believed that the Holy Ghost would enlighten his opponents. It is hard for a man whose own infallibility is being discussed to think himself wrong !

[1] Mourret gives the version in Dupanloup's journal : " Des témoins de la tradition ? Il n'y a qu'un. C'est moi." (Mourret, *op. cit.*, p. 299.)

[2] Nielsen (*op. cit.*, ii. 361) gives an even more callous remark : " Che crepino pure." (" Let them die.")

On July 11 the prince bishop of Brixen spoke for the commission which had considered the amendments proposed during the debates. The report of the commission fills thirty-four columns in the *Collectio Lacensis* ; it was wholly irrelevant in that no reference was made to the historical evidence brought forward by the minority. A deputation of bishops approached the pope. On their knees Ketteler and Darboy asked him to make a few concessions. The addition of such words as " innixus testimonio ecclesiarum " or " non exclusis episcopis " would make it possible for them to vote in favour of the definition. The pope was not unmoved ; he asked for the demand to be put into writing. As soon as the emotional effect of the appeal was over, the pope agreed with the opposite party in refusing the concessions for which the minority were asking. A last effort was made to persuade the pope not to confirm the vote of the council but to wait for a better time. The occasion was indeed inopportune. The Franco-Prussian war was about to begin. The recall of the French troops from Rome and the loss of French protection would mean the end of the temporal power. The pope would do nothing. The only protest made by the minority was to leave Rome before the final vote. The bolder course of voting " non-placet " and questioning the validity of a dogmatic definition obtained by a simple majority vote was abandoned because more than half of the minority refused to cause an open scandal. Two bishops alone remained to vote against the definition.

. . . . . .

While the votes were being taken, there burst over the city of Rome one of those ambiguous thunderstorms by which the indifference of nature is assumed to endorse or to condemn the enterprises of mankind. As an anticlimax, the rain of the afternoon and evening ruined the firework show which was to celebrate the first hours of the pope's triumphant absolutism, and which might have celebrated the last hours of his temporal kingdom. Two months later the Italian troops entered Rome.

A plan to reassemble the prorogued council at Malines was abandoned ; to this day it has never met again.

VII

LEO XIII. AND THE ROMAN QUESTION

THE rest of the years of Pius add nothing to the story. The pope still hoped for a miracle. He had never believed in the permanence of a kingdom based upon the fleeting errors of the revolution ; he would come to no settlement with those who had usurped his power. Victor Emmanuel and his ministers were the children of Satan [1] ; the editors of Italian newspapers came from the pits of hell. Yet the proclamation of his infallibility gave the pope no new weapon against those who thought that he had only made another great mistake. The distrust of Bismarck was a direct consequence. Bismarck was afraid lest France and Austria should strike a bargain with the papacy. The Vatican decrees gave the pope a chance to use spiritual power for political ends ; there was a danger that this power might be used against protestant supremacy in the new Germany. Bismarck underrated the latent force of religious institutions ; his personal and dark religion was blind to the value of a visible church. His attempt to bully the catholic hierarchy only weakened his position ; but the weakness was no gain to the church. Nor can the effects of the secession of Döllinger and the " old catholics " from the church be measured in quantitative terms.

The successor of Pius IX. was a man of a different stamp. Leo XIII. was the son of a fighting house, a fine scholar of the eighteenth-century type, a man who bided his time and kept his counsel. Throughout the debate on infallibility he had been silent. Pius and Antonelli had done their best to exclude him from the succession. Leo was in his

---

[1] On the other hand, in the last month of his life (and two years after the death of Antonelli), Pius IX. showed that he had forgotten neither his Italian citizenship nor his Christian charity. He sent his chaplain to bring the last sacraments to Victor Emmanuel on his death-bed.

sixty-ninth year when he became pope ; his health was weak ; he was uncertain whether he could bear the weight of the heavy papal coronation robes. Yet his flaming energy carried him through nearly a quarter of a century of ceaseless work. On his death-bed he began a long Latin poem about St. Ambrose ; in his last hours he complained of the good day's work he was losing. He hated to be thought old ; he would never keep his hands still enough to be painted ; he ordered a painter to take out the wrinkles from his portrait. Gambetta might well write of this man that he was dangerous because he seemed " propre à faire endormir les gens en face des dangers du cléricalisme."

This pope was more calculating, more supple, more tenacious of facts than Pius IX. ; but his Italian policy was directed towards the same end. Nor could it be otherwise. The thesis of Pius must now be the thesis of the papacy. Leo might be ready to recognise movements against the evils of an industrial society because he found many of the socialist theories written large and clear in the works of St. Thomas. He was sensible enough to dissociate himself from the folly of the legitimists in France. He was ready to accept existing governments outside the Italian peninsula, because he saw that by no other means could he restore the lost prestige and regain the lost possessions of the Holy See. He could not make the slightest concession of principle to the government which had fixed its capital in Rome. He must always consider the question of peace and war in Europe from the point of view of the temporal power. He must always support those who were politically hostile to Italy. When he found that Bismarck would only put the restoration of this temporal power in the most subordinate position in his policy, and, in fact, only thought of the Roman question as an incident in the calculation of forces in European affairs, Leo XIII. turned to the French republic. Italy was the ally of Austria and Germany. France was the rival of Italy in the Mediterranean and in Africa.[1]

As Leo was the superior of Pius in nobility of mind and power of thought, so his secretary of state, Cardinal Mariano

[1] See Crispolti and Aureli, *La politica di Leone XIII.*, and Ferrata, *Memoirs*, for an account of the critical years 1887-1889.

Rampolla del Tindaro, was a man of wider view and finer mind than Antonelli. Yet he was no more free than his master even to contemplate a new order in the church. The French alliance for which he sacrificed his chance of becoming Leo's successor was short-lived, and ended in disaster.

The folly of the men whom Pius had chosen, the bitterness of the French " religious " newspapers to which Pius had so often given his blessing, the intrigues and narrow-mindedness of the catholics who had taken literally the condemnation of modern political ideas, prevented a reconciliation between a church which was older than the very name of France, and a republic born of revolution.

Under the successor of Leo xiii. the church again forfeited its property to the French government ; the work of Napoleon i. was undone. Nor was there any real recovery of the old prestige of the papacy in Europe. For reasons of state Bismarck had allowed Leo xiii. to arbitrate in a petty dispute over territory in the Pacific ; [1] but in any serious question the popes of the twentieth century have been ignored. War has been made without them ; peace has been made without them ; nor have their criticisms of injustice done in war and peace affected the course of battle or negotiation.

The popes had defended a kingdom of this world, a dominion and a title resting upon documents long proved false and the use of a time long past. They had reached the height of unreason when they put forward for their anathemas, their denials, and their negations the authority of the Voice of God. Their pretensions, their methods, their alliances had darkened the hopes of generous men far from the organisation of the curia, yet near enough in temperament and loyalty to the impetuous surrender of the Prince of the Apostles. The successors of the Roman bishops who tamed the fury of the Lombards had lost the power of bringing into their antique order the men who

---

[1] The arbitration between Spain and the German empire over the question of the Caroline islands. Bismarck saw that he was paid in advance for his compliment. The pope promised to use his authority with the centre party in favour of the " septennate," i.e. the granting of credits for the army for seven years.

dreamed of a better time and thought more clearly upon the foundations of obedience and rule in civil society. Linked to the forces of the past and the unpitying complacency of the Neapolitan Bourbons or the house of Habsburg, the visible power of the church fell with these ignoble ruins. The denial of a new way of progress made the church powerless in a new world, powerless even for compassion in the evil days of Europe. In the interest of a vanished temporal authority the popes had sacrificed their claim to be heard. They might still embarrass statesmen ; they could not dominate Europe.

.   .   .   .   .

This story of the concentration of effort upon a limited end, and an end which seems strangely to contrast with the teaching of the Master of St. Peter, has attained its term. Nearly two generations after the Italian occupation of Rome, and the papal denunciation of the law of guarantees, a pope has declared the Roman question settled for ever. The settlement does little more than register the change in the European position of the church. At last a modern pope has accepted the despotism of fact. When Benedict xv. allowed his cardinal secretary of state to announce that the pope looked for a settlement of the Roman question not by foreign arms, but through the victory of a sense of justice among the Italian people, he admitted the isolation of the papacy. Once the admission was made, the Italian government could have no interest in prolonging a dispute which, in the words of an Italian statesman, was no less damaging to Italian political life because it was for the most part formal. The settlement was Italian and local. There was no question of restoring to the pope the kingdom which Pius ix. had lost. The territory which the Lateran Treaty of February 11, 1929, has given to the pope in full sovereignty is scarcely larger than the area delimited by the law of guarantees. But the shadow of kingship remains ; the shadow of a shadow of the Roman empire. The historical necessities have been covered under a solemn mantle of words. In fact, the Roman question has been solved by Pius xi. before it had become slightly absurd ; a " picturesque " anachronism, a subject of talk between guides and tourists.

The states of the church are gone ; the pope has surrendered for ever his claim to sovereignty expressed and embodied in terms of wide lands.   Even so, the surrender has not been made in the interest of liberalism.   The Italian statesman who made the settlement denied the need of any religious reform in Italy.   The pope who made the settlement spoke of the statesman as " Heaven-sent," and " free from the commitments of the liberal school."   Here is the last paradox of the history of the church in the nineteenth century ; a paradox which to some has seemed to contain the real meaning of Christianity, and to others a final interpretation of secular history.   " Men fight and lose the battle, and the thing that they fought for comes about in spite of their defeat, and when it comes turns out to be not what they meant, and other men have to fight for what they meant under another name." [1]

[1] William Morris, *Dream of John Ball.*

INDEX

Chich
23024